CW00765684

GOLD COAST DIARIES

GOLD COAST DIARIES

Chronicles of Political Officers in West Africa, 1900–1919

Thora Williamson

Edited by
Anthony Kirk-Greene

The Radcliffe Press
London · New York

Published in 2000 by The Radcliffe Press
Victoria House, Bloomsbury Square
London WC1B 4DZ
175 Fifth Avenue, New York NY 10010

In the United States and Canada
distributed by St Martin's Press
175 Fifth Avenue, New York NY 10010

ISBN 1-86064-451-1

A full CIP record for this book is available from the British Library
A full CIP record for this book is available from the Library of Congress

Library of Congress Catalog card: available

Typeset in Sabon by Oxford Publishing Services, Oxford
Printed and bound in Great Britain by MPG Books Ltd, Bodmin, Cornwall

Contents

Maps and Illustrations

Plates:

Acronyms and Abbreviations

ACC	Assistant Chief Commissioner
ADC	Assistant District Commissioner/aide-de-camp
ADO	Assistant District Officer
Ag	Acting
AGC	Ashanti Goldfields Corporation
ATO	Assistant Transport Officer
BCGA	British Cotton Growers' Association
CC	Chief Commissioner
CCA	Chief Commissioner, Ashanti
CD	seedy (ill)
CCNT	Chief Commissioner, Northern Territories
COP	Chief of Police
CSM	Company Sergeant Major
CWPA	Commissioner, Western Province [Ashanti]
DC	District Commissioner
DPO	District Political Officer
FW	Foreman of Works
GCR	Gold Coast Regiment
GNA	Ghana National Archives
HE	His Excellency the Governor
HH	His Honour the Chief Commissioner
HPMO	Head Provincial Medical Officer
HQ	Headquarters
MI	Mounted Infantry
MO	Medical Officer
MOH	Medical Officer of Health
NCO	Non-Commissioned Officer
NEP	North Eastern Province
NT	Northern Territories
NTC	Northern Territories' Constabulary

Acronyms and Abbreviations

NWP	North Western Province
OC	Officer Commanding
OCT	Officer Commanding Troops
O in C	Officer in Charge
PC	Provincial Commissioner
PE	Provincial Engineer
PMO	Provincial Medical Officer
PMG	Postmaster General
POW	prisoner of war
PS	Private Secretary
PWD	Public Works Department
RC	Roman Catholic
SCOA	Société Commercial de l'Ouest Africain
SE	Sanitary Engineer
SF	Sanitary Foreman
SI	Sanitary Inspector
SM	Station Magistrate
SMO	Senior Medical Officer
SOV	Supervisor of Villages
SP	Southern Province
SPG	Society for the Propagation of the Gospel
SSO	Senior Sanitary Officer
SSOR	Senior Superintendent of Roads/Railways
TC	Travelling Commissioner
TO	Transport Officer
VRPS	Volta River Preventive Service
WA	West Africa
WAFF	West African Frontier Force
WFPS	Western Frontier Preventive Service
WPPS	Western Province Preventive Service
YE	Your Excellency

Note on Orthography and Terminology

The common problem for historians of modern recensions of African orthographies is often compounded in these early twentieth-century texts. One difficulty is the difference between the Fante spelling of Twi and that preferred by the Asante and the Akyems. Another relates to topology in particular, for at the time when the diarists were writing the spelling of place names throughout the country was still in something of a hit-and-miss, frequently subjective, stage. Standardization of topography had not yet taken place, although a clear phonic harmony exists between the older form and the modern one, for example Coomassie/Kumasi, Seccondee/Sekondi, Akwapim/Akwapam.

A further difficulty has been the effect of the standardization of Twi on the forms of traditional titles. Basically, *oman* indicates both a town and a state. The suffix *–hene* means a king or chief. Thus *Juabenhene* means the chief of the Juaben people. In the plural use, 'o' becomes 'a', for example *oman/aman*. However, dialectical nuances mean that an Akan-speaking Akyemfo would write and say *omanhene* for the chief of a town or state, whereas an Akan speaker from Cape Coast would write and say *omanhin*.

For these reasons, following the example of Richard Rathbone in his *Nkrumah and the Chiefs* (2000: xi) and his advice on the particular diarists' problems here, we accept that not only would it be tedious to footnote modern place-name equivalents on every occasion, but also that in this case a glossary could well prove more confusing than the Ghanaian terminologies it seeks to explain. The following short list is therefore of Anglicisms current in the contemporary vocabulary. Those who wish to know more about Twi terms are referred to Ivor Wilks, *Asante in the Nineteenth Century* (1975: 725–

30) and, of course, J. G. Christaller's *Dictionary of the Asante and Fanti Language called Tshi* (1881, 2nd edn, 1933).

chop	food; to eat
dash	bribe; to give
dawa dawa	corn
fetish	inanimate object worshipped for its spiritual powers
harmattan	cold, dust-laden wind off the Sahara
juju	fetish (spirit, spell)
linguist	chief's official spokesman (*okyeame*)
palaver	discussion, talk/trouble
pito	locally brewed beer
scholar	schoolboy
swish	locally mixed 'cement'
tie tie	raffia creeper, whose strands can be twisted into rope
youngmen	the commoners, those holding no office of importance
zongo	stranger community's quarter

Currency value
sixpence (6*d.*) = 2.5p
one shilling (1/–) = 5p
five shillings (5/–) = 25p
one pound (£1) = 100p
Written as £3.13*s.* 8*d.*

Foreword

More than forty years have passed since the relatively brief period of European colonial rule in Africa moved towards its end. In the intervening years there have been few commentators and even fewer scholars who have found much merit in what is now fashionably called the 'colonial project'. A brief survey of the titles of books in print on the nineteenth and twentieth century history of Africa suggests that with few exceptions Europe's over-rule in Africa has been judged almost unequivocally to have been what Yeatman and Sellars would have regarded as a 'bad thing'. The responsibility for much of Africa's current tragedy is laid at the door of colonialism and its agents, a set of arguments which rather too conveniently tend towards a less than honest exculpation of contemporary politicians.

This has been a phase and almost certainly only a phase in what will go on to be an increasingly more rounded evaluation of this important part of world history. After all, historians continue to reappraise Roman rule in Brittania and Germania, Ottoman rule in the Balkans or Russian hegemony in its eastern empire. Late twenty-first-century historians of Africa will have more information to work with and better means of assembling it; even more importantly, when they turn again to colonial Africa they will have a growing degree of emotional distance from the events, processes and individuals they will study. This tool-kit will enable them to be more successful in escaping the decidedly unscholarly language of blame and justification than we, their intellectual ancestors, have been. And, above all, it will enable them to comprehend the essentially ironic nature of the processes they study. Their assessments will be better at demonstrating some of the iron laws of history – that good intentions frequently have wretched outcomes, that most policies' intentions are frequently derailed by ineptness or the unexpected and so forth.

Foreword by Richard Rathbone

One of the outcomes of the current understandings of the colonial period has been the depersonalization of the modern history of Africa. Africans have been the most obvious victims of this for they emerge from too much of the literature as either heroic resisters or craven collaborators. This tendency to create a Manichean universe over-privileges the political as opposed to other aspects of life. But, worse, it turns fully rounded, emotionally and intellectually complete people into cardboard cutout figures in otherwise complex landscapes.

Those whose careers were spent in that extended cluster of roles that comprised the colonial services have also been denied both character and history. As agents of colonialism they are usually assumed to have been at best insensitive, clumsy and unappreciative of the cultures within which they were privileged to work; at worst they aided and abetted the gross extension of heartless exploitation. Some certainly could be so described with some accuracy but more of them were more interesting than that. That seems to have been the *aperçu* that animated Thora Williamson's quest, a quest that resulted in this compilation. She saw, as too few scholars have seen, that an informed understanding of colonial officers, a significant aspect of a better understanding of colonialism, required a biographical approach rather than the use of stereotypes. As Anthony Kirk-Greene tells us in his scholarly introduction to this volume, a chance encounter with an obviously engaging veteran of the colonial service in the Gold Coast led on to a career in Oxford in which she helped in the acquisition of the raw materials for deeper and wider biographical enquiry. Most of that great collection consists of either the accidental or intentional retention of letters, diaries, photographs and other papers by colonial servants or their families. But she learnt that officers in the Gold Coast were also, somewhat unusually, required to write diaries.

Her appetite whetted, she went to Accra and in the National Archives on Castle Road was able to read and transliterate those diaries that survived. This was not entirely an exciting task. Not all of the diarists were good stylists, some had appalling handwriting and some of the typescript had faded to near invisibility. Much of what was recorded was, like that in innumerable diaries, mind-numbingly boring, repetitious and the result of an imposed task rather than inspiration. Anthony Kirk-Greene has done a major service to us all in editing out much of the 'Woke up, had breakfast, went to the District Office, had lunch' kind of material which is to be found in some of these diaries.

Thora Williamson's gift to all of us who are interested in the history of modern Africa is a many-tiered thing. First, she has made some of this exciting material more widely available to the many scholars who sadly cannot afford the pleasure of working in the extremely user-friendly National Archive in Accra. Second, as a good librarian she was aware of the impermanent nature of much of what she read. Acidic paper much loved by insects, old fashioned inks and the hot, humid climate of Accra all conspire to limit the shelf-life of this material; she thus also made a major contribution to the conservation of records. Third, her 'trawl' of the diaries was exhaustive in that she regarded no part of the Gold Coast/Ghana as marginal nor any period as more important than any other one. Accordingly, the material presented in these pages is unusually rich for scholars interested in Ghana's north, eastern and western marches, as it is for those who are as much concerned with the very earliest part of the colonial period as they are with the interwar years, the 'high colonial period'.

She was not, however, an historian by training and it is doubtful whether she was fully aware of her greatest contributions. The first of these is ways in which these diarists' concerns over time can be used to break up the monolithic idea of the colonial period. The earliest of these contributions betray all the earnestness of first encounter, of mutual discovery and the sense of recording the previously unrecorded in written form; routines are being established and rules of engagement are being drawn up. As time passes, the entries are more about the maintenance of routines and, incidentally, about the mismatch between routines and reality. The colonial period in the Gold Coast was never a seamless fabric but was, rather, a sequence of different but usually frustrated expectations constrained by African resistance and the limits of extremely varied financial circumstances.

Secondly, the diaries help us to understand that while, after 1902 at least, the Gold Coast was a colonial state, a discernible geographical expression, it comprised very different African universes. The contrasts between not only the northern diary entries, but as intriguingly between those written in the very varied parts of the Akan-speaking world are extremely instructive. The difference between the political and economic worlds within which these officers worked is as marked when daily administrative concerns in central Ashanti are compared with those in Sefwi as when reactions to the coastal environment are compared with those of the North or the Volta area. The diary extracts provide readers with an admirable vantage point from which to grapple with the interwoven historiographical problems of both period and region in modern Ghanaian history.

Thirdly, and very unusually, reading *in extenso* the words of these men enables us to do something that most accounts of the colonial period deny to us. Each of these diarists is an individual. Despite the ambitions of determinism, their origins and backgrounds do little to prepare us for their particularities. Some are sympathetic, even empathetic; some are insensitive to or uninterested in the African people they encounter on a day-to-day basis. Some are generous, others are uncaring. Some are engrossed with the worlds they encounter, while others might just as well be civil servants in the British provinces. For some, their careers are a purposeful adventure while for others it is a tough routine bordered by periods of leave.

That might highlight the significance of character but of course personality is not freestanding but is in many ways constructed by circumstance. Here again the diaries are of immeasurable value in suggesting that different generations of colonial officers had been brought up in worlds of ideas that dramatically altered over time. Obviously each of these diarists was a child of his time and those times were informed by radically changing metropolitan understandings of realities, including those of the acquisition of and then the governance of empire. Each had been educated in ways that changed over time, had read decidedly different sorts of books with distinctive and changing ideas embedded within them. These variations become very apparent from a close reading of the entries and not least from the language used by diarists of different generations.

Manifestly an unusual collection such as this, focused as it is upon what became a discrete colonial and then postcolonial state, provides an alert reader with a valuable insight into what it is now fashionable to call 'meanings'. For colonial officers every bit as much as for Africans, the meaning of colonial rule, the meaning of indirect rule, the meaning of chieftaincy and withal the meaning of the Gold Coast itself change in the sixty or so years covered by these diary entries.

The greatest strength of the volume, however, is the intimate insight into what doing the job of a district officer entailed. In much of the historical scholarship, that work is most usually made apparent in the course of a crisis. In much of the literature, the district officer is visible when he arrests someone, when he imposes a new tax, when he is in conflict with a chief, or when he is unjust. The diaries provide us with the context for the more noteworthy events of a career. It was above all obviously hard work. Few people who know Ghana and knew the extremely heavy, single-geared bicycles of the past will fail to break out in a sweat when reading about long journeys by bicycle on unpaved roads in, for example, the forest. The space-shrinking significance of the advent of motor transport is made very apparent in these pages. The incessant travelling, the long hours in court, in the office and in village meetings, and even longer hours of record keeping – including writing up these precious diaries – are very different from the assumptions of an idle, servant-supported life of sundowners on the veranda and the odd shot at a buck with the Mannlicher. Similarly, the diaries are very eloquent about the constant shadow of ill health that dogged the careers of otherwise fit and mostly young men.

But the most abiding impression to be drawn from this set of intimate accounts of the quotidian reality of colonial rule concerns the most important element of all of this. The informal record – newspapers especially – and formal records of colonial rule do little to convey what was clearly an incessant dialogue with Africans. The diaries relate a world of constant debate, oral petition, consultation and, of course, admonition. Necessarily perhaps, much of colonial rule was an oral process and manifestly this was dialogue even if one of the participants was a ruler and the others the ruled. This begs all sorts of intriguing questions about the construction of colonial knowledge. What this or that officer knew – or thought he knew – about his district was the result of information gleaned by him and his predecessors from just such encounters with Africans. Naturally, officials gave more credence to accounts that more accorded with their own or more generally with colonial policy but in turn there were Africans who benefited from that. It is hard not to read these diaries without drawing the somewhat subversive conclusion that the written record captures only a minute proportion of the interaction between Africans and those imposed upon them as their rulers.

This is a rich and remarkable collection of material that is intellectually stimulating, an important contribution to knowledge and is often genuinely engrossing reading. It deserves a wide readership. We are all in debt to Thora Williamson and Anthony Kirk-Greene for making this rich source more widely available.

Professor Richard Rathbone
School of Oriental and African Studies
University of London
July 2000

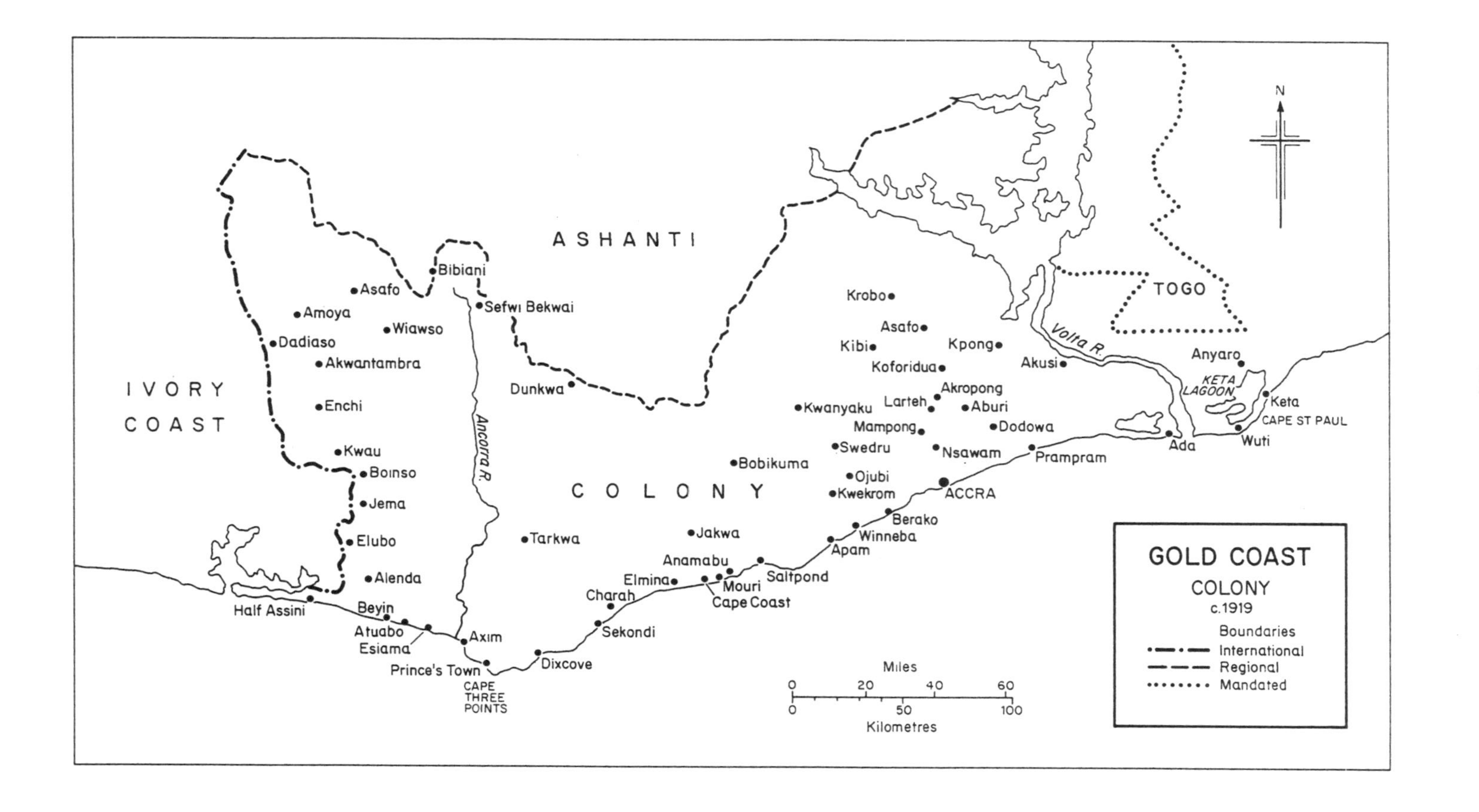
GOLD COAST
COLONY
c.1919
Boundaries
International
Regional
Mandated
N
ASHANTI
COLONY
IVORY COAST
TOGO
KETA LAGOON
Volta R.
Ancorra R.
Bibiani
Sefwi Bekwai
Asafo
Amoya
Wiawso
Dadiaso
Akwantambra
Enchi
Kwau
Boinso
Jema
Elubo
Alenda
Half Assini
Beyin
Atuabo
Esiama
Axim
Prince's Town
CAPE THREE POINTS
Dixcove
Sekondi
Charah
Elmina
Anamabu
Mouri
Cape Coast
Saltpond
Apam
Winneba
Berako
ACCRA
Prampram
Ada
Wuti
Keta
CAPE ST PAUL
Anyaro
Akusi
Kpong
Krobo
Asafo
Kibi
Koforidua
Akropong
Larteh
Aburi
Dodowa
Kwanyaku
Mampong
Swedru
Nsawam
Bobikuma
Ojubi
Kwekrom
Jakwa
Tarkwa
Dunkwa
Miles
0 20 40 60
0 50 100
Kilometres

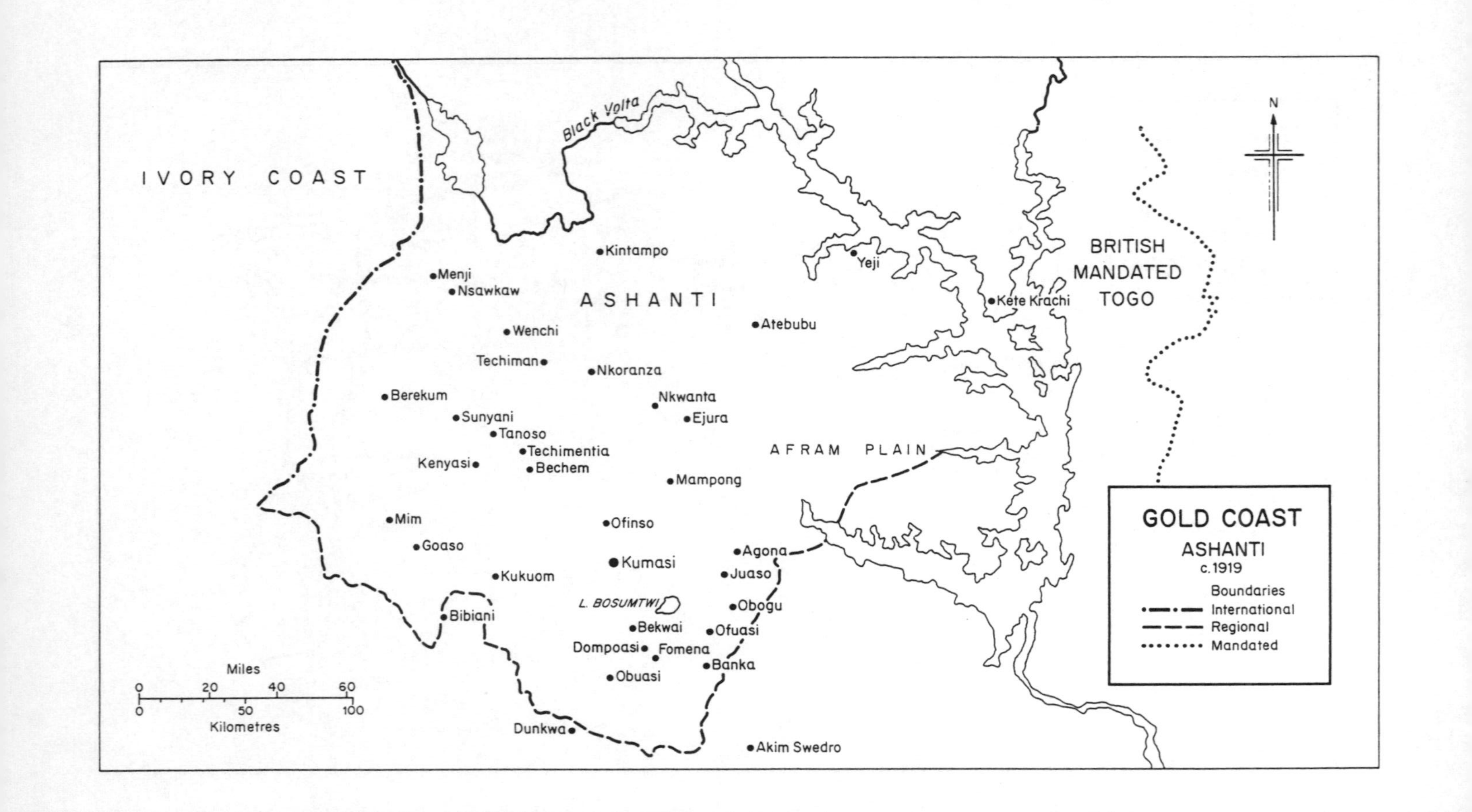
GOLD COAST
ASHANTI
c.1919
Boundaries
International
Regional
Mandated
N
IVORY COAST
BRITISH MANDATED TOGO
ASHANTI
AFRAM PLAIN
Black Volta
Kintampo
Menji
Nsawkaw
Wenchi
Techiman
Nkoranza
Berekum
Sunyani
Tanoso
Techimentia
Kenyasi
Bechem
Nkwanta
Ejura
Mampong
Atebubu
Yeji
Kete Krachi
Mim
Goaso
Ofinso
Kumasi
Kukuom
L. BOSUMTWI
Bibiani
Bekwai
Dompoasi
Fomena
Obuasi
Agona
Juaso
Obogu
Ofuasi
Banka
Dunkwa
Akim Swedro
Miles
0
20
40
60
0
50
100
Kilometres

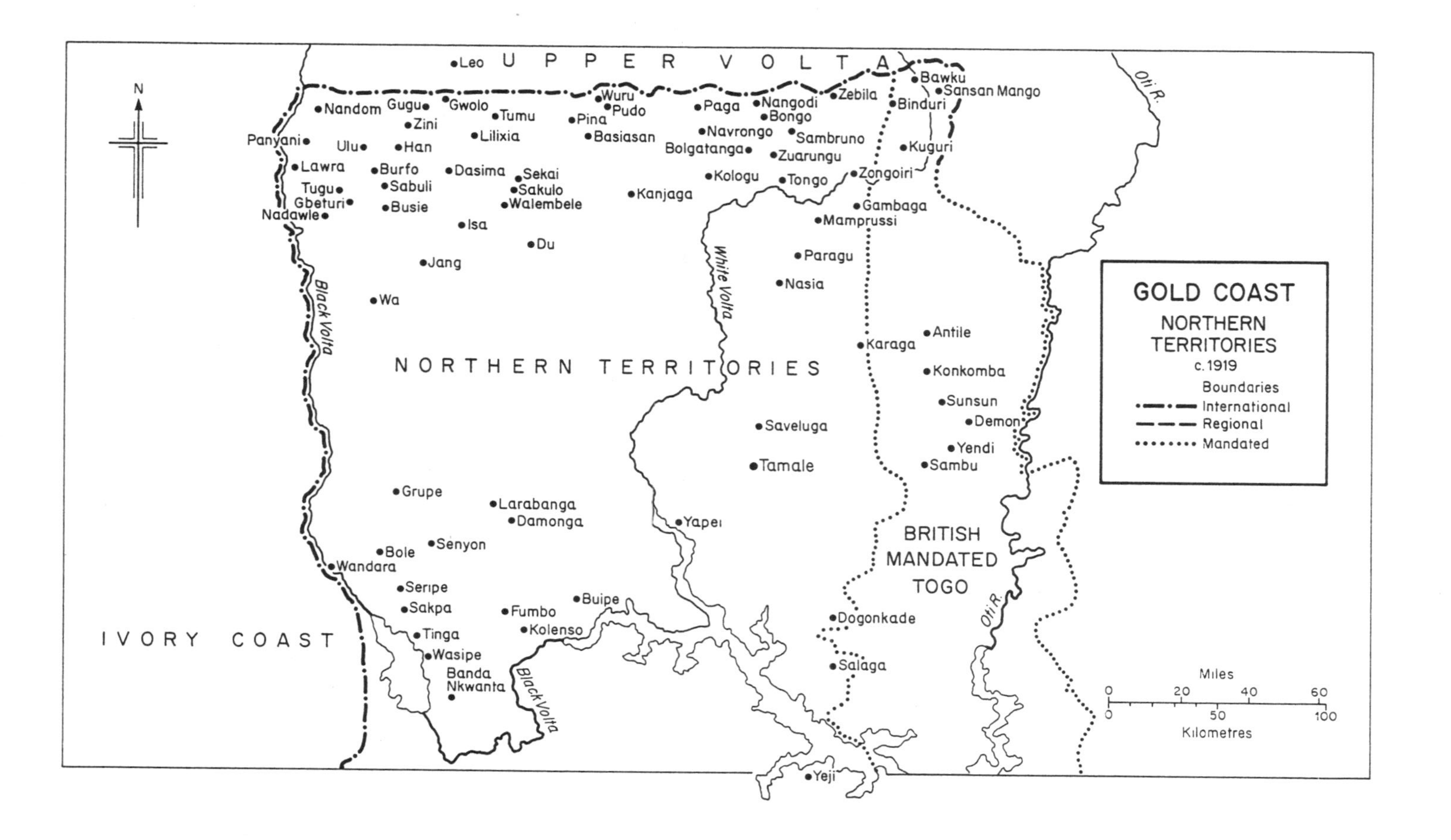
GOLD COAST
NORTHERN TERRITORIES
c. 1919
Boundaries
International
Regional
Mandated
Miles
0
20
40
60
0
50
100
Kilometres
N
UPPER VOLTA
NORTHERN TERRITORIES
BRITISH MANDATED TOGO
IVORY COAST
Oti R.
White Volta
Black Volta
Leo
Bawku
Sansan Mango
Binduri
Zebila
Nangodi
Bongo
Paga
Wuru
Pudo
Pina
Tumu
Gwolo
Gugu
Zini
Nandom
Panyani
Ulu
Han
Lilixia
Basiasan
Navrongo
Sambruno
Bolgatanga
Zuarungu
Kuguri
Zongoiri
Tongo
Kologu
Kanjaga
Lawra
Burfo
Dasima
Sekai
Sakulo
Walembele
Sabuli
Tugu
Gbeturi
Nadawle
Busie
Isa
Du
Jang
Wa
Gambaga
Mamprussi
Paragu
Nasia
Karaga
Antile
Konkomba
Sunsun
Demon
Yendi
Sambu
Saveluga
Tamale
Yapei
Grupe
Larabanga
Damonga
Bole
Senyon
Wandara
Seripe
Sakpa
Buipe
Fumbo
Kolenso
Tinga
Wasipe
Banda Nkwanta
Dogonkade
Salaga
Yeji

Introduction

Records are an essential component of any long-term bureaucracy. Over time they build up that foundation of 'case law', which helps the administrator to form opinions and put forward proposals based on precedent rather than on prejudice or spontaneity.

In the inevitably *tabula rasa* context of initial colonial rule, where the administrator's knowledge, experience and reactions were by definition limited and impromptu, keeping records was a requirement of paramount importance.[1] At the local district and provincial level, they became both an authentic repository of knowledge and a cumulative set of guidelines for all occasions. At the wider territorial and metropolitan level, such records, typically extrapolated and enhanced into an annual report, enabled the colonial government to account for its performance to Whitehall and Westminster; in turn, the opportunity of parliamentary debate allowed that stewardship to be subjected to public scrutiny.

The exact nomenclature of the multiple sources and forms of colonial reporting varied from territory to territory, yet their format displayed a widely recognizable uniformity. Analysing them in reverse order from the final product of a colonial government's Annual Report (at one stage regularly published as a Parliamentary Blue Book), the governor's report would be compiled from the annual provincial reports submitted to him from his PCs (in some instances, for example, Tanganyika, Northern Nigeria, the Sudan, these too were officially published),[2] which in turn would be drawn from the regular district reports submitted to provincial HQ by DCs. Frequently, the young cadet too was required to submit to his district officer a record of what he did and saw and met when he went out on tour/trek/*ulendo* – in his *Colonial Cadet in Nigeria* (1968), John Smith includes some 80 pages of those detailed grassroots Touring Officer's Reports.[3] Outside the Secretariat policy files, it was in the districts, looked on as the essence of colonial administration throughout the Indian and Colonial Empires, that the bulk of detailed, day-to-day records were located; and it is at this level that the post-colonial archival researcher is likely to mine some of the most valuable lodes of primary material at the cutting edge of colonial rule. Apart from the basic (but still often elusive) data of Staff and Civil Lists and territorial handbooks,[4] local documentation might include political intelligence reports, economic revenue, land and assessment reports, and administration-focused census and anthropological reports. A key item was the District Note Book (DNB), an accumulative encyclopaedia of local affairs and personalities (including the complex customs connected with chiefly succession, land tenure and boundaries) compiled over the years by successive district officers and sometimes stretching back to the inaugural years of colonial rule. Indeed, it was the unique nature of the generic DNB that was instrumental in the calling of a planning meeting at Oxford University in 1961 for a Colonial Records Project focused on an archives retrieval plan, aimed at preserving the major district records of colonial administrative history.

This survey of original documentation at the grass roots of colonial administration leaves out one further item, potentially as valuable as the rest but in no way so regular. This is the administrator's diary. Here there are two kinds of record. At its personal level, this was nothing more than a private diary. Many of these are now preserved in Rhodes House Library and other repositories of colonial records. Supplemented by letters home, some have formed the basis of a subsequently (on occasion posthumously) published notable Service memoir; for instance John Beames, *Memoirs of a Bengal Civilian* (1961) and H. M. Kisch, *A Young Victorian in India* (1957); Martin Kisch, *Letters and Sketches from Northern Nigeria* (1910) and David Carnegie, *Letters from Nigeria* (1902); or, from later generations, John Morley, *Colonial Postscript: Diary of a DO, 1935–56* (1992), John Cairns, *Bush and Boma* (1959), Sir Harry Luke, *From a South Seas Diary* (1945); and, of course, among the most famous of them all, Leonard Woolf, *Diaries in Ceylon 1908–1911* (1963) and Kenneth Bradley, *The Diary of a District Officer* (1943). At the official level of diary keeping, the Gold Coast government was one of the few to have elevated the diary to a required item of colonial administrative records, known as the DC's 'informal diary'.

Soon after the new governor of the Gold Coast, Sir Hugh Clifford, assumed office in 1912, he let it be known through his Secretariat in Accra that he had been struck by the 'scanty nature of the information'[5] about what was going on upcountry. His Excellency (HE) felt, the letter from the Colonial Secretary to the Chief Commissioner of Ashanti (CCA) continued, that apart from his statutory involvement in staff postings and applications for expenditure, 'while residing in Accra he remains almost as completely cut off from detailed information concerning Ashanti as if he had continued to reside in England.' Given his responsibility to the Secretary of State for the administration of the territory, HE had concluded, 'this is not a situation which he can regard with equanimity or which he can suffer longer to continue.' Accordingly, from October 1913, the CC would be required to keep 'an informal diary' every month. As far as possible, this was to be written up every day. It would be transmitted to Accra for HE to read, and in due course be returned to CCA 'with a copy of HE's remarks if any'. At the same time, in a move that has turned out to be of profound significance for the study of colonial administration on the ground, HE urged the CCs of Ashanti and of the Northern Territories (CCNT) to instruct their PCs to keep a similar diary, 'which at your discretion can [also] be transmitted for the governor's information'. In the event, the diary requirement was immediately passed right down to the level of DCs, for submission to their PC and often for comment or incorporation into those written by the CCs to the governor.

As to the object of this 'diary' exercise, the Colonial Secretary set it out as

> primarily to convey to the governor a general idea of the questions which from time to time are occupying your [CCA] attention, and to furnish him with a record of events which ordinarily would be regarded as too trivial for separate report, and to enable [HE] to see from day to day what is occurring in the official and political life of the dependency under your charge. Your comments on men and things, I am to add, can in a diary of this description be of a somewhat more informal and outspoken character than is usual in official correspondence.[6]

By being unofficial it was intended that the diaries would not be quoted in official correspondence or amplified with official records and statistics.

Finally, while appreciating that 'the keeping of a diary of this character will impose a certain measure of additional work', HE felt 'convinced' that CCA would appreciate the advantages that would accrue from being thus placed 'in constant and to some extent informal communication' about local administration. One suspects that CCA's reaction to such an offer of intimate contact with the capital was as unwelcoming as that of colonial governors who after the Second World War suddenly found themselves in imminent and intimate contact with senior officials from the Colonial Office or the Secretary of State himself by immediate air travel. At first the keeping of a diary was indeed looked on as just another chore, 'written — more often scribbled — in the evening when tired or overtired, after a hard day's work', to quote the description of C. H. Harper, PC,[7] but by the end of 1913, the 'informal diary' had become institutionalized as part of station – and touring – routine, by the CCs, PCs and DCs alike. It is likely that Clifford had brought the idea of the daily diary with him from Ceylon, where he had been Colonial Secretary from 1907 to 1912. There, the Government Agents and their assistants were required to maintain a day-to-day diary and send it monthly to the central government in Colombo. It was a system that dated back to 1808, when it was introduced by the governor, Sir Thomas Maitland, and continued right through to 1941.[8]

It is time to introduce Thora Williamson, whose book this is. Not only is it a unique collection of primary material; it is also, quite literally, a labour of love. Inspired by listening to the reminiscences of one of the diarists nearly 50 years on, Thora made a number of private visits to Ghana, where she copied out by hand nearly half a million words from the diaries in the national archives. The unusual story goes like this.

While working in Thame, Oxfordshire, in the late 1950s as manager of the well-known Spread Eagle Hotel, Thora (known to the family as Bunty) met among the hotel's permanent guests one [Alexander] Howard Ross. Ross, who was then approaching his eightieth birthday, had gone to the Gold Coast in 1905, first as a Supervisor in the VRPS and then from 1908 as a DC. In 1920, he transferred to Sierra Leone as PC. He was awarded the CBE in 1929 and retired in 1930. Ross found a ready ear and an alert mind to listen to his memories of life as a colonial official during the first decade of British administration in the Northern Territories (NT) and Ashanti. These had been annexed in 1902 (Ashanti as a colony and the NT as a protectorate) following the seventh (and final) Ashanti war of 1900, in which the politically inept governor, Sir Frederick Hodgson, had found himself besieged in the fort at Kumasi.

After Ross's death in 1964, Thora, stimulated by his undimmed interest in and continuing affection for the country and its people, decided to visit Ghana herself. This was in 1966, when she was nearly fifty. While working, unsponsored and at her own initiative, in the Ghana National Archives (GNA) in Accra, she came across, quite by chance, diaries written by several DCs and CCs who had regularly featured in Howard Ross's narratives, names like C. Armitage, D. Boyle, T. Fell, C. Fuller and R. S. Rattray. But it was their often dire fragility as well as their consummate interest that caught her attention. As she noted,

While some of the diaries, which have survived, are in

> hardback ledgers and are in fairly good condition, others are in loose files fastened together with much-rusted paper clips. Besides this, many have been ravaged by termites, while others are very fragile and difficult to read, due to the Indian ink used, which has rotted the paper.[9]

On returning to England, she secured a job as assistant archivist to the Oxford Colonial Records Project, which had been set up in 1963 to collect personal documentation of, by and about Colonial Service officers.[10] The assistant director was Ivan Lloyd-Phillips, who had started his Colonial Service career as a cadet in the Gold Coast in 1934. Here, Thora was able to extend her knowledge of the Gold Coast civil service by working on their donations of private papers.

By now West Africa had secured her affections. Thora had trained in domestic science and dietetics in Newcastle, and in 1939 had been employed as a cook at Girton College, Cambridge. Her other hotel management skills she had perfected at Thame. In 1969 she accepted a job as manager of the Atlantic Hotel in The Gambia. There she stayed for ten years. After retiring, first to Oxford and then to Brancaster near King's Lynn, she made a number of further visits to Ghana between 1980 and 1995, working on the diaries of Howard Ross and his seniors, contemporaries and juniors, in the GNA, as well as in the archives' regional branches in Kumasi and Tamale. In conversation, she would often express her gratitude, as a lone and unpretentiously amateur scholar, for the help she received from Judith Botchway (the 'Dear Ma' of her letters) and Frank Ablorh in the GNA.

Gradually, an idea formed in her mind: to enable wider access — especially in the United Kingdom — to the eye-witness testimony of those turn-of-the-century and prewar generations of Gold Coast administrators in their daily 'informal diaries'. So fragile and friable was the condition of many of the diaries after 60 years and longer, that her hope of the promotion of wider knowledge about colonial administrators also carried a preservation urgency to it. She taught herself how to use a word processor and, at her home in Norfolk, she set about typing up all the diaries she had copied out in longhand in the Ghana archives over the years. By the mid-1990s, the typed diary extracts had reached almost half a million words, supported by other documentation and summary historical and anthropological narratives derived from her extensive reading of the literature on Ghana. Encouraged by the positive reaction of an Oxford don, who specialized in imperialism and nationalism in Africa, Thora approached the Radcliffe Press. There, Dr Lester Crook's response was equally positive. A contract was signed in 1997 and the final text — over 600 pages of it, typed in close single spacing — was delivered in mid-1998. Tragically, in December Thora died suddenly. Though she was not to see her literal labour of love published, she was happy in the knowledge that the outcome of her conversations with Howard Ross 40 years before would see the light of day.

Three months before her death, Thora had asked me whether I would, from my vantage point as a historian of the Colonial Service, write a foreword to her book. It was thus natural that, having read through her original typescript back in 1995, I should willingly agree to the Radcliffe Press's invitation to try and edit the 300,000 word text into manageable length and shape for publication as Thora Williamson's book. Not only has she opened up an underexplored resource for the study of Gold Coast history during the early years of the twentieth century and of the grassroots work of some of the first British administrators, but she has also ensured that if the already delicate condition of some of the diaries in the archives continues to deteriorate, here at least is one success in the preservation and presentation of their unique contents.

This eventual dual management of the text, unforeseen and hence uncoordinated between the two of us, necessitates an important caveat. This is not over the primary source of the diaries themselves but over the matter of her original selection and my subsequent selectivity. Even though Thora's transcription of 97 diaries furnishes a formidable corpus, we neither know how many diaries she decided not to copy out (and why) or how far the gaps in some of the diaries are, as it were, 'theirs' or 'hers', either reflecting her judgement of the interest of the entries or else simply the not uncommon fact that not every official made an entry for every day. Add to this my editorial challenge to reduce a voluminous text by two-thirds, and a new variable, my own criterion for selection or deletion on each page of every diary, comes into play. Basically, no diarist between 1913 and 1919 originally included by Thora has been dropped by me, although — and this is the point to underline — not all entries in all the diaries have been reproduced here. The original spelling of place names and vernacular style have been retained, and only minor changes have been made to grammar and punctuation.

The enforced reduction has been made in two ways. The first is by excluding the diaries written in 1920 (Thora's cut-off point), on the grounds that 1919 is the starting-point of Henrika Kuklick's deeply archive-researched ethnography, *The Imperial Bureaucrat* (1979). This includes an acknowledged dependency on 'the unofficial diaries, which men at all levels in the colonial hierarchy were required to keep' (page 157) of the administrative cadres of the Gold Coast civil service. Indeed, such is the unwitting continuity that Kuklick, who as a sociologist argues that because these informal diaries were meant to include accounts of 'everything of interest' and not merely the matters that caught an officer's fancy 'they probably represent as accurate a record to actual behaviour as exists',[11] carries over many of the names among Thora's diarists. These include officers such as Armitage, Rattray, Cardinall, Duncan-Johnstone, Walker Leigh and Rake. The second form of reduction has been made by my own arbitrary, if not entirely untutored, excisions of certain entries, often routine or highly localized, in favour of those that seemed to me to carry a wider interest, whether for the study of Ghanaian or its colonial administrative history. In the process, other good material has often had to be ruthlessly set aside. What is important to emphasize to the researcher is that, because the diaries have undergone a two-tiered reduction process, not only are the original diary entries longer than those excerpted but also the fact that there is no entry between, say, 15 and 30 July in a diary does not necessarily indicate (though it could do) that there never was any entry against these days. Because of space exigencies, most of Thora's narrative on the early Gold Coast and the pre-colonial Ashanti and NT history, together with much of her ancillary material (including a range of letters, besides transcripts of reminiscences recorded in 1965 by Howard Ross[12] and his poem, 'The Rape of the Rock') has had to be omitted. Priority has been given to reproducing the diaries, not commentary or supplementary material. It is for this reason that we hope that Thora's complete material may eventually be lodged in some library for those who are keen to read more than it has been possible to include here.

By reordering her original chronology of excerpted diaries, I have been able to separate the five pre-1913 (the year of the inaugurating Clifford directive) diaries into a separate Chapter 2, leaving the following three chapters to present the 1913–19 diaries geographically and provincially, as well as chronologically in respect of the Colony, Ashanti, and the NT. Chapter 1, 'The Gold Coast DC', and the diarists' biographical notes in Appendix A are Thora's own work, minimally edited. The other appendices have been distilled from the considerable quantity of material that earlier appeared as historical narratives complementing the diaries or as extended notes. The reduced notes and the bibliography are an amalgam of both our efforts. The resultant book is Thora's book.

The diaries lend themselves to being read at several rewarding levels. Clearly, they can be of use to Ghanaian scholars interested in the impact of early colonial rule and in the geo-ethnic experiences and evolution of what, sandwiched at one time between the French Ivory

Coast and German Togoland (and later experiencing the tensions of the First World War in West Africa and the issuance of the Togoland mandate by the League of Nations in 1921) emerged as the framework of modern Ghana. Few DCs were able to resist a dig in their diaries at the other colonial administrations (the French more than the German) or avoid a smug self-congratulation on how 'the natives' naturally preferred British rule to that by others! Expectedly, the diaries provide useful information on wartime recruiting and Islamic propaganda and, *en passant*, on how the news of the outbreak of hostilities in 1914 and of the armistice in 1918 was received in upcountry Ashanti and the NT. They also depict the decline in morale among DCs, partly induced by the strains imposed by the wartime shortage of administrative staff and partly by the refusal of the government to let them join up and fight on the Western Front. Local historians of, say Winneba and Wenchi or Yeji and Navarro (Navrongo), may also come across fresh light on the transformation in their society. Those working on the history of colonial administration, especially its representatives and the local responses to policy during the formative years of colonial Ghana, will find in the diaries an unusually rich reservoir of data. In particular this is so for that vast majority of readers who today have – maybe can have – no idea of the physical hardships, primitive living and dangerous health conditions, and petty 'nuts and bolts' (often quite literally, as the diaries show) routine that were part and parcel of the job that went by the sophisticated name of 'colonial administration'. It is fascinating, too, to compare the dominant preoccupations in the diaries written by the DC of, on one hand, the progressively urbanizing towns like Sekondi or Cape Coast (and of course flourishing Accra) with those written in essentially rural stations such as Tumu and Zouaragu, or again the already evolving gold-mining community at Obuasi, site of the Ashanti Goldfields Corporation (1897) and still of its modern successor Ashanti Goldfields. Again, one might compare the diary entries of relatively junior DCs such as H. Ross, A. Castellain and D. Boyle, with those of seasoned administrators like C. H. Harper, P. A. H. Pott, L. H. Wheatley or E. O. Rake.

Because Thora happened to share my enthusiasm for studying Colonial Service personnel – who they were, why they joined, what they did and how they were perceived – it is among the diarists as well as from the diaries that revealing insights into the life and work of this pioneer generation of colonial administrators loom large. Indeed, the second half of Thora's scene-setting Chapter 1, 'The Gold Coast DCs', in which she illustrates the work and conditions of service of the DC, could be read as a handy summary of many of the topics dwelt on in the diaries. That the diarists were required to write 'informal' diaries – to think aloud, as it were, and imagine one was virtually writing a personal letter to one's markedly senior officer – and to keep their superiors aware of and in touch with whatever was going on in the district, all the way from policy priorities to complaints about the quality of the rest houses or the scarcity/surfeit of rain ('I trust YE will not be bored with these frequent allusions to the rainfall' – Armitage entry, 14 August 1917) means that – as is the way with the best of diarists – we can soon begin to share their experiences and empathize with the personal ups and downs of a part-exciting, part-tedious and frequently frustrating lonely life in a remote upcountry station. Many of the themes are recurring: in Ashanti, the nature of what was officially termed 'the fetish'; the capacity of chiefs to shoulder (or slough off) responsibility and to handle – then as 50 years on – the seemingly recalcitrant 'youngmen'; the building of bridges and roads, at first for bicycles (Colony and Ashanti DCs and even PCs often clocked up impressively high mileages – 'I bicycled to Kpong, 32 miles,' Harper entry 5 February 1914; 'Mr Whyte arrived having come in on a bicycle, 45 miles,' Wright entry 7 April 1917), and then, from 1915 on, for motorcars, above all the famous Model T Ford; court work and complaints; and the low-key and inevitable chores like checking the treasury, counting the specie delivery (often in nickel coins) and stamping and licensing dane (flintlock) guns. All the rural diarists display a keen concern with agriculture, including the spread of cocoa, the introduction of rubber and cotton as cashcrops, and experimentation with beeswax and sheanut butter.

It is interesting to note the importance to the DC of Sunday, the sole (along with Christmas) day spelled out in the diaries. For many it was regularly entered as '*dies non* [*est*]', while for others it was thankfully used to catch up with arrears of work. 'Sunday. A quiet uninterrupted morning working through papers,' notes Fuller (entry 20 August 1916), and, again, Harper's entry 'Sunday. Got through a heap of correspondence' (entry 2 October 1915). In Sunyani, Sunday developed into a traditional walk out to the cemetery at Odumasi. Nor was Christmas Day necessarily sacrosanct. 'Office clearing table, writing reports on roads, committee accounts' (Philbrick entry, 25 December 1916). Empire Day (24 May) was, of course, marked with multiple ceremonies and entertainment (see Poole entry, 24 May 1918), while in Ashanti 'Coomassie Day' (15 July), instituted by Fuller in 1905, was also observed (Fuller entry 15 July 1917) to commemorate the day the siege was lifted. Matters of health are repeatedly recorded, as blackwater, yellow fever and malaria struck down DCs and their colleagues in the station. In many ways, it is in the Ashanti diaries that health stands out as a predominant item, for example the collapse and death of T. Breckenridge, DC, within four days (Philbrick diary, 24–28 November 1917) and the equally distressing fatal appendicitis of Aves, DC (Fell diary, 30 May–4 June 1914). In the NT, a parallel tragedy was the death of Captain Swire (Ryan diary, 15–22 November 1913). Although a medical certificate was required for every month an officer was called on to extend his tour beyond the pre-1914 standard 11 months (see Holliday entry, 26 October 1918), a number of diarists reveal their preoccupation with whether their health will stand a protracted tour (for example, Philbrick entry 10 October 1916). But it was not only personal health that caused the DC anxiety, with common entries *à la* 'Still very shaky, but got down to court as there is a heavy mail to be answered' (Skene entry, 24 January 1917) or 'Felt CD [seedy] all day', (Poole entry, 18 January 1918) and 'Ill in bed, temperature last night 101.5' (Holliday, 7 November 1918). The fear of an epidemic sweeping across the district, like smallpox, meningitis, and of course the worldwide outbreak of influenza in 1918, also features in the diaries.

We can recognize among the diarists many of the different kinds of men who made up the colonial administrative cadres. Not all the officers in charge of a district were DCs. In the days of still rudimentary staffing, it was not unusual for a station to be run by an MO. Often he was charged to combined this responsibility with his professional duties, as we see in the almost bifurcated entries of Dr Duff and Dr Whyte and in the negative comment on this arrangement by CCNT (Irvine entry, 1 November 1913). One notices, too, the heavy incidence of military ranks held by the prewar (but post-Boer War) TCs and acting DCs as well as serving officers of the NTC. Some of the diarists reveal a preferred vocabulary of 'I ordered' and 'I instructed', while for others a clear sense of empathy and a ready recourse to a palaver or discussion with the *omanhene* or *okyeame* appeals as the more effective technique. Now and again, one comes across a downright authoritarian manner, like that of Captain B. H. W. Taylor, whose entry 'I flogged the man' followed by his conclusion that 'Truly the rule by force seems to be appreciated' (entry 9 May 1906) was calculated to raise many an eyebrow in the sensitive Secretariat. As with all effective diarists, a gentle sense of humour suffuses many of the entries.

While the diarists are, inevitably in their context, all male, it may be refreshing for readers to recall that the important female view of colonial administration in Ghana can begin to be gleaned from two linked sources. Laura Boyle, wife of the diarist David Boyle, described in her *Diary of a Colonial Wife* (1968) her record of the tour in

Ashanti in 1917/18 when she accompanied her husband, while Heather Dalton's archival collection 'Gold Coast Wives' (RHL, MSS Afr. s. 1985) comprises the reminiscences of the wives of some two dozen officials who served in the Gold Coast/Ghana from 1926 to 1963. There is, too, Lady Clifford's contemporaneous anthology, *Our Days on the Gold Coast* (1919). If wives feature so rarely in the diaries, this is because up to the 1920s a DC was positively discouraged from bringing his wife out to the Coast, both on grounds of health and because it was feared a wife might hinder his 'postability' to difficult districts (on the inconvenience of married DCs, see Armitage entry 14 August 1917).

One of the saving graces of the Colonial Service was that, while its members certainly had a strong ethos, with a disposition to speak their mind but to do what they were told, they were anything but uniform in their work priorities and their extracurricular activities. For some, town layouts and road building were the be-all and end-all of district administration, an obsession famously shared by the young ADO Rudbeck in Joyce Cary's novel *Mister Johnson* (1939). For others, it was sanitation (a frequent topic in the diaries) and latrines that were top priority. For others again, it was court work, hearing complaints, and the supervision of the treasury that spelled the best of district administration. Often it was his off-duty interests, on occasion amounting to hobbies, that helped the DC to keep his intellectual faculties alive in a situation where there was no one else in the station with whom to discuss the things he was used to talking about, like literature or music or travel, or even cricket. One notices in diaries the regular highlighting of the arrival of 'the English mail' with letters and newspapers from home, however many weeks late they might be. Similarly, every visitor passing through was a welcome intellectual stimulus – or at least a news-bearing relief – to the lone DC, and all were entertained to a meal and often accommodated too. The writing-up of the daily diary may itself have been something of an intellectual spur, calling for faculties likely not much in demand in the day's work. As A. W. Cardinall excused himself to the CCNT when stationed in remote Navarro, 'I have noticed that my diary is becoming more and more conversational and is covering ground outside its proper area. I lay myself open to rebuke, but I attribute this prolixity to solitude' (entry 4 September 1919).

Thus, we see in S. D. Nash the amateur anthropologist, an interest that new societies and customs helped to nurture in many a young colonial administrator. The same intellectual curiosity is apparent in the diaries of C. Armitage and of A. W. Cardinall ('Sunday. The whole day spent writing on native customs, but although I wrote 8000 words I did not finish' – entry 7 September 1919). A. Covey's description of an enstoolment ceremony (15 October 1902) is possibly the first account by a DC. Few, however, were able to develop this kind of research to the professional level of R. S. Rattray.[13] Sadly, Thora Williamson was unable to find any of his diaries in the archives.[14] S. D. Nash, T. E. Fell and A. W. Cardinall emerge as among the most serious and thoughtful of all the diarists, revealing an enhanced measure of concern about the implication of administrative policies.[15] Cardinall and the medical doctor, W. W. Claridge, were both destined for inclusion in the roll call of historians of Ghana and already their diaries disclose a constant interest in local history. The multifaceted Cardinall was also an amateur farmer: 'In order to alleviate the shortage of food each year, have decided to plant groundnuts practically everywhere' (entry 31 May 1918) and his later lament 'My wheat has met with disaster' (entry 15 September 1919; compare Rake entry, 13 June 1916).[16] H. A. Kortright was something of an engineer *manqué*. F. W. H. Migeod was able to indulge his study of exotic languages and eventually published works on Mende and Hausa. Both Cardinall and A. L. Castellain ('taking a load of pineapple suckers and a load of shade tree cuttings for Mr Cardinall', entry 15 May 1919) were keen on botany, while Fell was interested in fauna, keeping a pet chimpanzee called Percy. In the end, he dispatched the rumbustious Percy to the London Zoo in charge of H. Ross when he departed on leave.[17] If the diaries highlight one aspect of the life of the DC, it is that it was never a nine-to-five job.

The selection of diaries ranges from those kept by DCs, substantive or acting, and more senior PCs to those written by the two staff grade CCs. Though the original instruction to keep an 'informal diary' was addressed to CCs, it soon became the pattern for the DC to send a weekly 'informal' diary to his CC and for the CC to write a mainly 'confidential' diary to the governor. All were unofficial. Some DCs also maintained a separate 'war diary'. Not every officer wrote up his diary every day, and there is internal evidence that when the DC was away on tour his clerk sometimes wrote the diary.

There is a marked difference in format and presentation between, say, detailed and dedicated observers like Fuller and Fell, and the noticeably laconic Boyle in the opening weeks of November 1914, or Ross throughout 1916. These are countless allusions to the task imposed, for example, 'Finished typing the April diary,' 'Copied out official diary during 9th to 18th,' or throughout the diaries of Atterbury and Maxwell, or in Wheeler's significant explanation of 'I go into local questions somewhat fully in this diary, as by so doing, the diary becomes a useful guide to an officer taking over' (entry 8 April

1914). Many show evidence of having been closely read by the CC and, especially those of the CC, by the Governor.[18]

Typical of the commendatory comments are Sir Hugh Clifford's note at the end of CCA's diary for November 1917. 'I have read this diary with more than ordinary interest.' By contrast, the sharp rebuke, penned in red ink, by CCNT on E. Poole's Yendi diary in 1918 stands out: 'I have read this type-written diary with great interest, but also with the aid of a magnifying glass. I regret that you have submitted to me so shamefully a typed document, which would strain the strongest eyesight to decipher, and will request you not to repeat the delinquency.' One suspects a clash of personalities here. To judge from Fuller's comments on Boyle in his diary as CCA for January 1917, that was another case of a clash in temperament. ('He seems to have become suddenly unbalanced and capable of any *coup de tête*' – entry 23 January 1917.)

Consecutive diaries from a single station over a number of years, for example the Obuasi and Tumu diaries (1913–19), can make it clear that for all the lip service paid by colonial governors to the imperative of continuity of an officer *en poste*, short-term postings were disturbingly frequent.[19] For instance, Captain Wheeler assumed charge of Tamale at the end of March 1915, but was posted away almost immediately. His successor, Captain Dale-Glossop, was in turn relieved by Captain Hobart in mid-May. In Bole, the DC was charged three times between August and October 1916. During the war, staff shortages led to the closing down or amalgamation of several district headquarters: Goaso and Wenchi were abandoned in 1917 while Yeji and Salaga were combined in 1915, as were Navarro and Zouaragu.

Although Sir Hugh Clifford may not have foreseen it, he would certainly have been proud (and ultra-proconsul that he was, not surprised) had he known that his introduction of the 'informal diary' in 1913 would last right up to Ghana's independence in 1957. By then, mercifully for all concerned – writer, reader and researcher – the government was supplying standard 'diary books', a welcome improvement on the miscellaneous ledgers, loose foolscap sheets and paper clips the diarists used 50 years before. As an illustration of this diary continuity, the NT diaries kept by J. C. Anderson, DC, run from the 1940s right through to 1956, by which time the colonial DC had given way to Nkrumah's more political appointment of government agent.[20] What so forcibly strikes the historian is how positive the continuity in the day-to-day life of the DC is, his routine and his responsibilities, between *c.*1915 and 1955. The following consecutive entries could, *mutatis mutandis*, easily be taken from either year. In the event, while these are reproduced from Anderson's diary written in

January 1955 from Salaga and Damongo in Gonja District, they can be tellingly read alongside E. G. Dasent or E. O. Rake writing from equilocal Yeji or Bole in 1915. The continuity and echoes are uncanny, 1955 almost a *déjà vu* parody of 1915.

Salaga, January 1955

9th Sunday. I had to drive Burleigh up to Tamale this evening, as he very unluckily fell ill on his last evening in Salaga.

10th Court and Treasury.

11th The Salaga Local Development Advisory Committee met at 9.30 a.m. Mostly applications for assistance with roads.

12th On trek to Prang and went through the Council's Estimates, leaving only a few minutes before dark to greet the *pranghene* and *seriki zongo*. Prang rest house now very comfortable and well-equipped.

13th Back to Yeji and spent the day there, before returning to Salaga in the evening.

14th Court and Treasury.

15th Spent the morning in the office with the Clerk of Council, Tuluwe, going through his Estimates.

17th Drove to Kpandai in the evening for two nights' trek.

18th At Kpandai. Attended the Alfai Local Council Estimates Meeting in the morning. In the evening drove along the line of the direct Salaga–Kpandai road. For the most part this is just a cleared track, without any ditching or gravelling.

19th At Kpandai. Spent the morning in the Local Council office. Then to the Leper Settlement at Nkanchina for lunch and back to Salaga in the evening. The Salaga–Grupe road is very full of potholes.

21st Treasury and court; 24 motor cases and one assault.

26th To Yeji and Prang. Went through the Yeji Estimates with the Ag Clerk of Council, who can now start to type them. Coming back, we were held up by a tornado at the ferry, which we could not cross until the wind went down.

The research opportunities for a closer study of the early years of Ghana's occupation and of grassroots colonial administration now enabled by the ready availability of some of these diaries are extensive. The resource is at once exciting and significant, and has so far remained under-utilized. Granted the fragile state and lessening legibility of many of these diaries as encountered by Thora in the 1960s and 1980s, their availability in this excerpted form may be helpful to Ghanaian students as well as to those unable to carry out research in the GNA. In saluting Thora for her single-minded (and single-handed) enterprise, researchers will be grateful for her contribution to scholarship. *Gold Coast Diaries* is a memorial to the late Thora Williamson of which she would have, with characteristic modesty, been quietly yet deservedly proud.

I wish to thank Thora's sister, Jill Clare, for her kindness in expanding my knowledge of Thora's early years. I am extremely grateful to Professor Richard Rathbone of SOAS, University of London, the leading authority on the history of modern Ghana, for reading this introduction and helping me avoid historical and geographical howlers. His contribution of a Foreword constitutes an imprimatur of Thora's work. My thanks are also due to J. C. Anderson, formerly a DC in the NT, for allowing me to quote from his Salaga informal diary, 1955; to the Reverend A. C. Russell for sharing his insider's knowledge of colonial administration in the Gold Coast; and to Selina Cohen for her skilled and sensitive handling of the complexities inherent in reproducing these diaries. Finally, Thora herself would have wanted to express her deep thanks to Rhodes House Library for permission to quote from their collection of colonial records, especially the Fell and Harper papers, and to the staff of the GNA, Accra, for their kindness and generous cooperation.

Anthony Kirk-Greene, Emeritus Fellow
St Antony's College, Oxford
December 1999

Notes

1. See Sir Frederick Lugard, *Political Memoranda*, 1919, II, 'Books, Returns and Office Records', especially paras 6–8 and 15, 'Official Diary'. See also C. H. Stigand, *Administration in Tropical Africa*, 1914, Chapter 21. In Nyasaland, the 150-page *Resident's Handbook* (1914) was a compilation of all standing orders, rules and regulations. In Northern Nigeria, an even larger volume was *Government Standing Orders*, 1910, which the compendious *Northern Region Office Guide* 1932 complemented with subsequent amendments.
2. For example, *Annual Report of the PCs for the Year 1958*, Dar es Salaam, 1959; *Annual Reports for the Northern Province, 1953*, Kaduna, 1954; *Reports of Governors of Provinces 1925* [Sudan], London, 1926.
3. R. Heussler lists several sets of touring diaries, which he consulted in the 1960s, including those by L. C. Giles for Zaria in the 1930s and those of Kano Division in the 1920s and 1940s – *The British in Northern Nigeria*, 1968, 192–3.
4. For a survey of holdings in Britain, see A. H. M. Kirk-Greene, 'The Location of Colonial Staff and Civil Services in British Libraries: a

preliminary checklist', *African Research and Documentation*, 73, 1997, 8–29.

5. This and the quotations that follow are taken from the letter of 18 August 1913 addressed by the Ag Colonial Secretary, Accra, to the CCA (GNA, Kumasi, file D648).
6. See note 5.
7. Notes by C. H. Harper when depositing his diaries for 1904–35 in Rhodes House Library (MSS. Brit. Emp. s. 344).
8. See Leonard Woolf, *Diaries in Ceylon 1908–1911: Records of a Colonial Administrator*, 1963, Introduction Part I, by S. D. Sapraramadu, viii.
9. Letter to present writer, 16 July 1997.
10. Patricia Pugh, 'The Oxford Colonial Records Project and the Oxford Development Records Project', *Journal of the Society of Archivists*, 6, 2, 1978, 76–86.
11. Henrika Kuklick, *The Imperial Bureaucrat: The Colonial Administrative Service in the Gold Coast, 1920–39*, 1979, 159–60.
12. Among these are his reminiscences about 'Bishop' Swatson, the activist evangelist who made his way to Wioso in 1915.
13. Author of numerous publications on the Ashanti and Hausa, Oxford University awarded him a D.Sc. for his contributions to anthropology.
14. A very brief extract covering four days at the end of May 1915, from Misahohe, Togoland, where Rattray spent most of the First World War, is in PRO CO/96/559. A number of his letters are to be found in GNA 52/1/2. His unpublished notebooks are in the mss. collections of the Royal Anthropological Institute, London. See also McCaskie, 1983 and Machin, 1979, in Bibliography.
15. For example, Nash's reflections on 'I have often been asked the question of what use the NT are' in his diary for 14 October 1913.
16. Cardinall was so 'concerned of the wealth of this' that he reckoned the Navrongo area in the NT might be developed into 'a mixed ranching business' (entry 4 September 1919).
17. See Fell's diary entries for 13 May and 10 November 1914. Some 40 years later Colin Russell, by then CCA, sent ten consignments of livestock to Edinburgh Zoo. He lists these in detail in his memoir *Gold Coast to Ghana*, 1996, Appendix V.
18. Some of the Governor's (Sir Hugh Clifford) own touring diaries and observations are in PRO CO 96/538.
19. Lugard enunciated the guiding principle in his *Political Memoranda* (1906, 1919): 'I regard continuity of administration as a matter of paramount and indeed vital importance in African Administration' (I, 14). In C. H. Harper's diary, he notes from his position as PC: 'Here is a very good illustration for keeping a commissioner in one and the same district, for Ballantine, now in his third tour, has spent all his service as DC Akwapim' (entry 16 January 1914).
20. Copy of his diaries for 1943–47 is in Rhodes House Library, MSS. Afr. s. 943. That for 1955–56, quoted here, was deposited separately.

1

The Gold Coast DC

Until 1854 the British colonies were administered by the Secretary of State for War and the Colonies, but due to the increasing number of colonies and protectorates being acquired, the department was split and the Colonial Office was born. Among its tasks were engaging recruits to serve in the colonies as administrators, doctors and legal officers.

To judge by Colonial Office reports, in the 1880s the fever-ridden Gold Coast was not the most popular destination for the budding colonial administrator, but in the interests of recruitment the men on the spot painted as rosy a picture of the colony as possible. H. T. Ussher,[1] the governor of the Gold Coast, in a dispatch to the Secretary of State for the Colonies, wrote in 1880:

> I have spoken of the Gold Coast as I have found it myself. It is undoubtedly a trying and bad climate, but it is much maligned, and has to bear a good deal for which officers themselves are, at times, alone responsible. As soon as they get the ordinary attacks of fever which a visit to Aburi, or a little patience, would soon overcome, they get alarmed[2] and in many instances, leave the Coast. I do not see how officers can become thoroughly acclimatized under such conditions.[3]

In the next dispatch, written in May 1880, Ussher noted on the subject of DCs:

> There can be no doubt that a really reliable and honest African is far preferable to a European, unless the latter be of exceptional industry and physique. Unfortunately, such examples as Mr Smith, Mr Bartels, Mr Bannerman, Mr Brown and one or two others are the exception, but I try steadily, by praise and encouragement, to keep them on the right path. Mr Bartels of Winneba is very good at court work.[4]

A. W. L Hemming, in a long minute written in 1880, analysing another dispatch from the governor, felt far from sanguine about the prospect of finding recruits:

> Mr Ussher's remedy is to bring the European into immediate contact with the natives of the interior by DCs, who he says, 'must be of good mien', to reside with the kings and chiefs and rule in conjunction with them. Such a scheme reads well on paper and in theory is excellent. But, I confess, it seems to me most uneconomical and impracticable. Where are the instruments necessary to carry it into effect to be found? What man of integrity and ability would be willing or could be tempted by any conceivable remuneration to undertake such a duty? The horror of such a life is appalling to contemplate – the isolation and absence of society or companionship; the constant prospect of sickness and death, far from friends or medical assistance; being ever surrounded by foul sights and fouler sounds and smells; the monotony and weariness! If, as we so often hear, officers stationed in the Coast towns take to drink to drown their cares and discomfort, what would be the temptation of such a course to the man in Akim or Wassaw? I can hardly suppose that Mr Ussher's proposals will be entertained. The objections I have pointed out would, of course, not apply with equal force to the appointment of a certain number of TCs, whose duty it should be, at the proper season of the year, to visit the various chiefs. These officers would see and report what was going on, hear complaints and receive the taxes due from the different districts. Such a scheme would, I venture to think, be more practicable and less expensive in life and money than Mr Ussher's plan of Resident commissioners.[5]

Ussher's ideas were arguably 20 years ahead of his time. After the annexation of Ashanti and the NT in 1902, many new stations were opened and the European was brought into immediate contact with the natives of the interior, perforce residing with the kings and chiefs, and ruling the district in conjunction with them.

Hemming continued:

> Mr Ussher complains of the recent changes in the leave regulations of the Gold Coast service. The matter was well and carefully considered before the alterations were made. It was stated, by those who had the best opportunity of judging, that officers could, as a rule, keep their health pretty well for 12

> months and after that time they begin to flag. It was therefore thought better to bring men home at the end of 12 months, and send them out again, refreshed and with the prospect of being able to work satisfactorily for another tour, than to keep them on the Coast after their powers of work were exhausted and allow them to get into a condition of ill health from which six months' leave was not sufficient to restore them.[6]

As a matter of fact, from 1900 leave from the Gold Coast was generous. Only in exceptional circumstances was a DC asked to work more than 12 months without leave, and then only after a thorough medical examination. The long leave, two calendar months in the UK (the voyage to and from England did not count as leave), was considered essential to restore his health, undermined by fever and the climate, and to see his family.[7] Not until after the First World War were wives welcome in the NT and parts of Ashanti. The young upcountry DC was supposed to spend much of his spare time out and about, unencumbered and getting to know the people. Even the most understanding wife, it was argued, alone all day in a remote bush hut, would expect her husband to spend his evenings with her. Wives were tolerated in the colony, where they were not such a responsibility to government. They could meet other European women, hospital nurses and the wives of officials and other residents. The climate was considered highly dangerous to the health of European children, who were not permitted to go there under any circumstances.

In spite of Hemming's gloomy foreboding, men did come forward to serve as administrators on the Coast. During the last quarter of the nineteenth century, a sprinkling of army officers were appointed as inspectors of the Gold Coast Constabulary, established in 1874. These officers were, from time to time, called upon by the governor to act as TCs to lead missions to Ashanti and further north. There was every possibility that a temporary appointment as a TC would become permanent, with eventual promotion to DC. When Great Britain annexed Ashanti, on 1 January 1902, a handful of officers from the WAFF and the Gold Coast Constabulary transferred to the Administrative Service as acting DCs. They worked under three experienced commissioners seconded from the colony.

At the same time as the annexation of Ashanti, the NT was declared a protectorate. It was decided by the Secretary of State that a semi-military administration was the most suitable way to govern the new territories. For the first five years, army officers combined their military duties with that of DC.[8] Some of these were attracted by the country, the work and the way of life, and many transferred from the army to the Political Service when military rule gave way to a civil administration in 1907.

Until the beginning of the twentieth century, the method of appointment to the West African Colonial Service was one of patronage. By the turn of the century, a number of army officers, having survived the Boer War and anxious for further excitement, volunteered and were absorbed into the Colonial Service as assistant DCs. It has been described as 'a ramshackle system'.[9] There was no examination, and the impression the candidate created at his interviews weighed heavily. He was required to pass a rigorous medical examination. Obviously, it was an advantage to be known personally to someone in the service, who could put in a good word for him. He ought, preferably, to be unmarried: but if he had the misfortune to have a wife, he generally undertook to leave her at home for at least his first five tours. By 1908, the Colonial Office was beginning to look for its recruits from the principal universities, the regular army and Sandhurst.

Word of mouth was another fruitful source, as T. E. Fell's letters to his father in 1897 show:

> A great friend of mine, Captain Kenny Herbert,[10] who has just given up an instructorship at Sandhurst, has got an extremely lucrative and important post under the Colonial Office, surveying and exploring in Africa; and today he sends me this offer.

In his next letter Fell writes:

> I really think I had better apply for this thing. If I do not get it, I should be no worse off, and there are many and scores of better graduates than me who would give their ears to go to Tasmania instead of me. To get a chance of employment under the Colonial Office seems to me such a capital chance, and one not to be missed. The actual job seems to be mapping and surveying for trade routes. I don't see the least reason why I should let the conditions of climate and fever stand in my way. Many men have stood it before, even without the benefit of being employed by government, and why shouldn't I do so too?[11]

Sometimes a man already working in the Colony was recommended by the Governor for promotion to the Administrative Service, as ADC. Such cases were rare, and were generally discouraged by the Colonial Office, although men like R. S. Rattray and Howard Ross entered the Political Service after working for the Gold Coast government in other branches.

Over the years, the Colonial Office kept careful notes of the special requirements of the individual colonies and also of any idiosyncrasies of the Governor who, if he survived the course, normally served for five years. He too was appointed by the Secretary of State, to whom he was responsible. He had considerable latitude in the administration of the colony, and was free to make innovations and adopt his own schemes, so long as they increased the prosperity and well being of the country. If any substantial sums of money were required, for say a railway or a harbour, he could apply to the Colonial Office, and the Treasury might sanction a loan. Except in exceptional cases, each colony was self-supporting, and all the staff, African and European, were paid according to what the colony could afford. Before the advent of the submarine cable linking London with Accra in 1886, the governor might not have time to consult the Colonial Office before taking an urgent decision. Like it or not, they only heard of it after it was a *fait accompli.* At the Accra end, this delay in communication was sometimes very convenient. In 1889, the Governor, Sir W. Brandford Griffith, had written to the Colonial Office asking that barristers and lawyers should be appointed as DCs, wherever possible, because so much of the work of the colony was taken up with court work.[12] However, it continued to be difficult to find suitable barristers and a Colonial Office minute of 1898 notes: 'The Private Secretaries have now great difficulty and are reduced to applicants of dubious qualifications. I can only suggest that more effort be made to get men from the provincial Bars. In any near London, the struggling barrister finds other openings.'[13]

At the same time, some doubt as to the necessity of employing lawyers was being voiced at the Colonial Office. To quote a minute by Reginald Antrobus:[14]

> Lord Selborne[15] has talked with the Secretary of State on the general subject of the Colonial Civil Service. I was present at the discussion and at one point had occasion to mention the present difficulty of obtaining candidates for DCs. Lord Selborne said that his view was that it is now quite unnecessary to fill these posts with lawyers, and instanced the Indian Civil Service, in which men, who have not been called to the Bar, discharge functions very similar to those discharged by our DCs. I said that Colonel Burden preferred military men for DCs in Sierra Leone, but that in the colonies of the Gold Coast and Lagos it had always been considered essential to have lawyers, though I was unable to see why a good military man should not do as well, if not better, than an inferior barrister.

> Mr Chamberlain[16] then said the vacant DCships had better be filled at once, by any suitable officer in the service, and that we need not wait to find barristers. It was clear that we could only get unsuccessful lawyers and he did not see how they were better than the layman.[17]

In another minute on this subject, it was pointed out that:

> The next stage will, no doubt, be to train men, as in India, to discharge both Judicial and Administrative duties. We are making a beginning by appointing some Gold Coast cadets. But it will be a long while before we can get any class of men who are, on the whole, so well fitted to be DCs as the lawyers whom we get now.

The first Gold Coast cadets went out in 1900.

The Tropical African Service Committee set up in 1908 advised that men newly going out should attend 36 law lectures over a period of three months.

> Their duties in the colony to which they are appointed will, in nearly every case include, in the first instance, those of Justice of the Peace and Police Magistrate and their magisterial powers are subsequently increased from time to time, according to their ability and position in the service. On the whole, however, it might be said that their summary jurisdiction would be confined to petty misdemeanours and minor offences.
>
> Selected candidates will accordingly be required to study
>
> 1. Tropical hygiene and public health.
> 2. Criminal law proceedings (civil and criminal) and evidence.
> 3. Tropical economic products.
> 4. Government and elementary accounting.

At the same time, it was agreed that particulars of colonial appointments should be sent to the University Appointments Committee at 'Oxford and Cambridge as usual, to Dublin, and experimentally, to the leading Scottish and provincial universities.' It went on to remark that, in order to encourage 'the right type of young man', such as university graduates', the age of entry to the Administrative Service should be reduced from 24 to 23. It concluded that:

> Selection by competitive examination was neither desirable nor

> practicable at the present time and that no change is required in the present method of selection for Administrative, Treasury and Secretarial appointments viz nominated by the Secretary of State.[18]

Before leaving for West Africa, the newly appointed ADC had to kit himself out. He required tropical clothes, medical equipment and a large supply of tinned food. He also needed a tent, collapsible bed, bath, chair and table. Laura Boyle, who accompanied her husband to the Gold Coast in 1916, noted in her diary: 'A large number of the boxes contain food supplies of all kinds, provided in those days for many colonial officers by Fortnum & Mason, and ranging from soap and candles to tinned peaches, butter, sausages and so on. In fact, enough to stock a district officer's house for at least nine or ten months.'[19]

If the prospective DC was still enthusiastic about the job after reading the health pamphlets issued to him (see Appendices F and G), his next step was the Army & Navy Stores, Fortnum & Mason, or any of the other stores specializing in tropical kit and supplies, all able and anxious to advise him about everything he might need. They knew all about putting the groceries up in 56 'chop boxes' (the average weight of a carrier's head load).

On reaching the Coast, the new DC was told where he was to be stationed. His destination depended on the luck of the draw; or, more correctly, it was 'the exigency of the service' that decided his fate. He might be kept at headquarters for a time, to work in the Secretariat as a Second Assistant Secretary. Ideally, however, he was packed straight off to a busy district to work under one of the PCs, as ADC. There he gained experience and learned something about the routine maintenance of a government station. He spent some days in court, where he studied the PC's methods of dealing with the complicated court cases. He was encouraged to take simple cases himself. It gave him the feel of the district, besides putting him in touch with some of its people and problems. Then he might be sent on trek to a distant village to deal with a disturbance, to find out why the 'youngmen' wanted to 'destool' their chief, to enquire into a fishing dispute. In his spare time, he was encouraged to read up the old district record books.

All too often, after a very short time and long before he had mastered all the intricacies of running a district, he was packed off to another station, Ag DC to relieve a DC who might be sick or going on leave. Now he was completely on his own and the harmony and well-being of the district depended on him. He picked up the threads as he went along, gradually settling into a routine. He was always aware that, wherever he went, he was the link between the government and the people. It was his first duty to uphold the Service and ensure that the mountain of instructions and requests that arrived by mail from central government were obeyed. In reality, it was almost impossible for the DC to do all that was expected of him and most DCs became selective as they learned which directives could safely be ignored, giving priority to the work and instructions they thought important for their particular district.

A. W. Cardinall, who joined the Service in 1914 as an ADC, was immediately dispatched to Sunyani in the Western Province of Ashanti. He spent a short time there working under the PC, T. E. Fell, before being transferred to Goaso, his first station.

> I began the first of many long periods alone in the bush. There was never, at Goaso, very much work to do and I had time to study an interesting pamphlet, issued on appointment by the Colonial Office, indicative of the labour a commissioner is expected to perform. This is the catalogue:
>
> The duties of an administrative officer are of a very varied character. He is the immediate agent of the government in his district and his responsibility extends to all departments of the administration, which have not a special representative of their own at his station. Thus, in addition to his primary functions (a) of magistrate, and (b) of political officer (the officer responsible for the maintenance of satisfactory relations between the natives and the central administration), he may be called upon to take charge of a detachment of police; to perform the duties of an accountant for his district; to superintend the district prisons; to supervise road construction, the clearing of waterways or other public works. Every officer is expected to do a certain amount of travelling, in the course of which he inspects the outlying portions of his district, transacts any necessary business with native chiefs, settles disputes between individuals or communities, and generally deals with all matters requiring the personal attention of representatives of government on the spot.

No doubt this pamphlet gave the new ADC an inkling of what to expect, although, as Cardinall soon realized, it by no means covered all the ground. 'It seemed all embracing enough, but later I learned that one had to be half a veterinary, more or less able to render first aid and to be something of a botanist and a forestry man.'[20]

After three years, the ADC's appointment would be confirmed.

With a salary of £400 a year and the promise of a pension after 20 years' service, he would be put in charge of a district. He might even be temporarily appointed Ag PC in charge of a province, with his headquarters at the main town in that province. Promotion had to be earned and he was unlikely to be promoted to PC until he had served at least five years. He was always liable to be moved anywhere at a moment's notice.

The nature of his work depended greatly on location. If the DC was in an important town or district in the colony or Ashanti, he was in frequent contact with other Europeans, army officers, mine managers, representatives of the chocolate and other firms, and managers of the large West African trading companies, with all of whom it was important that he established good relations.[21] Their work was essential to the economy of the country; besides, an unfavourable report from one of them, addressed to the Governor or to the Chamber of Commerce in London or Manchester, did nothing to improve his prospects. At these stations the court work was usually heavy, with constant disputes of every description between the locals and the migrant workers, not to mention the friction that might arise between Europeans and local people. It could be tricky, with justice balanced on a knife-edge. The DC's power in court was limited: he could not impose a fine of more than £50 or a prison sentence of more than six months. Cases that, in his judgement, merited a harsher penalty were referred to the PC's court, but the governor always confirmed the death sentence. Anyone dissatisfied with the DC's decision could ask for the case to be tried in a higher court. A case in a chief's court might, at the request of the plaintiff, be transferred to the DC's court.

There was usually a European doctor at major stations. He shared with the DC responsibility for the sanitation and hygiene of the district. At some stations it was the custom to tour the town together after tea, visiting the *zongo* (the part of the town occupied by the Hausa and other northern peoples), the market, prison and water supply. The DC spent many hours in his office answering official mail, writing reports and keeping all the district records up to date. At some stations he was responsible for a considerable amount of cash; checking it and balancing the books took up much time. All the government staff – clerks, police, postmaster, PWD, road overseer, customs clerks – took their orders from the DC.

The DC was in frequent contact with the *omanhene*[22] and his 'linguists' (official spokesmen) when he listened to any complaints. All native affairs were discussed with the *omanhene*; and all orders to the subchiefs and people were relayed to them through him. The DC might tell the *omanhene* that a market should be made ready for a company of the GCR passing through the district, or perhaps inform him that carriers were required to take loads to a station in Ashanti, or require him to turn out his people, to build a new rest house, or to clean the road.

Not everyone liked these busy cosmopolitan stations, but there were compensations. The commissioner could — indeed was expected to — lead a fairly active social life. Some towns boasted a European club, of which he might be secretary. Tennis courts, and perhaps a golf course, were sometimes available, while after about 1916 in Ashanti there was likely to be a fair motor road to the coast, or at least a feeder road to the railway station. Lastly, with a European doctor on the spot and some civilized amenities, government was less likely to say no if the DC wanted to have his wife with him. At some of these stations a wife could indeed be an asset. She could arrange dinner parties and help entertain other government officers constantly passing through the district and with whom hospitality was exchanged for news of the outside world.

At the other end of the spectrum, the lone DC in an isolated bush station led a very different life. He was thrown entirely on his own resources. The nearest European might be three or four days' march away and, in stations like Wioso near the western frontier, it was not uncommon in 1915 for the DC to go three months without so much as seeing another European. For example, the Wioso quarterly reports are peppered with remarks of 'Saw one European this quarter.'

The government station, built on land leased from the chief, consisted as a rule of a bungalow for the DC; kitchen and quarters for the cook and houseboy; a courthouse and office with quarters for the clerks; a prison with police barracks and a rest house. The bungalow, often designed and built under direction of the DC, was, like the rest of the station, severely utilitarian. It was constructed from 'swish' (local earth mixed with water) with a roof of shingle or thatch extending well out from the frame forming a covered veranda to protect the mud walls from the weather. Its windows might have shutters, but certainly no glass. There was, of course, no electricity and for the DC absolutely no question of having a refrigerator, electric fan or air conditioner. His water supply was another problem. It frequently came from a well dug in the compound, perhaps augmented by a barrel to catch the rainwater from the roof. In some stations, he shared the water supply with the local people and his houseboy might walk long distances to the river to obtain a pail of muddy water, which was then filtered and boiled.

In a memorandum in 1907, the CCNT, Colonel Watherston, summarized the conditions:

> Each officer in the Protectorate has to bring up himself, all that he wants for one year's tour, including house furniture (a table and chair made from old packing cases being the most he can hope to obtain in the house he is given), and to cover this and any luxuries he may wish to bring up he is allowed 26 carriers, or 18 carriers and eight hammock men. His ordinary camp outfit takes up about 14 loads, which leaves him four loads for luxuries. On all others he has to pay £1.12*s.* from Kumasi. He is provided, at a certain reduced price, with a ration of whisky, oil, tea, coffee, flour, limejuice, biscuits, jam, potted meat etc. per month.[23]

He went on:

> Since the occupation of the country, the housing of officials in mud huts, with leaky grass roofs has been considered sufficient. Furniture of the most primitive kind exists in most stations.

Once at his headquarters, with his mud hut and leaky grass roof, it was up to the DC to make himself as comfortable as possible. In one respect, a DC in the NT was better off than his colleague in the Colony or Ashanti: he could keep a horse, which saved much time and effort when on trek.

The DC devoted much time and thought in these pioneer stations to improving the villages, discussing with the *omanhene* and village headmen all the improvements he wanted to make. Better roads, sanitation and hygiene were high on his agenda, but the DC knew he must make haste slowly. There was a limit to what the chiefs and people could be called upon to do. If they thought they were being 'humbugged' and pushed too hard, or saw no good reason for the proposed changes, they could become stubbornly uncooperative. However, a popular, enthusiastic DC could usually carry them along with him. His meetings with the chiefs and headmen played a big part in all his schemes. The chief, too, walked a tightrope. If he failed to cooperate with the DC, or the government thought him disloyal, he was dubbed a troublemaker and, after warnings, might be destooled by order of the governor.

As far as possible, the DC supported the chiefs and upheld their authority. However, if his people thought he was toadying to the DC and promising too much communal labour, his 'youngmen' frequently rebelled, thus forcing his destoolment. The DC was always ready to listen to the chief and advise him about his many problems. The villagers, too, brought their troubles to the DC. These might be anything from an unfair verdict in the chief's court, or complaining that so and so had put a fetish on him, or that his wife was being killed by a witch, or a man claiming that he and his family were slaves. This was a serious complaint. Technically, there were no slaves in the Gold Coast, but well into the twentieth century many of the chiefs had their household slaves. These were usually well cared for and, unless there was a definite complaint, authority turned a blind eye. Women, too, took their grievances to the DC. One might tell him that her children had been taken away, another that her husband no longer attended to her. All accusations were carefully investigated, however incomprehensible or superficially ridiculous they might appear to the European DC.

Before the end of the First World War there was only a handful of motorcars in the whole of the Gold Coast,[24] and no motorable roads in any of the outlying districts, where a hammock road was the most that could be expected. Bicycles were popular with some DCs if the bush paths were reasonably clean and not too swampy, but much time was inevitably spent carrying them round boulders and tree stumps.

Except in certain parts of the NT, tsetse fly prohibited the use of the horse as a means of transport. Donkeys were tried and used to a limited extent, but do not appear to have been a great success. This left man as the only beast of burden and walking, bicycling, or hammocking the only possible means of getting from place to place.

The DC spent much time on tour, meeting the village chiefs and elders and gaining their confidence. He would visit the chief's court and inspect his prison, often taking the chief round the village with him to discuss any improvements the chief should make. The DC might order latrines to be dug, or stagnant pools —a fertile breeding ground for the malaria-bearing mosquito — to be filled in. Sometimes, he supervised the construction of a well, or planned the layout of a new street or market.

The DC was always ready to deal with any and every emergency. If, as was so often the case, there was no doctor,[25] he might be asked to set a broken leg, stitch an open wound, or supply medicine for anything from blackwater fever to whisky for a chief with bellyache. If the DC suspected an outbreak of an infectious disease, he would try to avoid its spread by improvising an isolation centre for the patients before sending a runner to the nearest town to inform the MO. Again, in his role as veterinary officer, the DC might, for example, suspect that the cattle in a certain village were suffering from anthrax, and impose a ban on the movement of all cattle until a veterinary officer could be brought in to confirm it.

At the turn of the century, these self-contained peasant village communities were rife with ancestor worship and fetish of all kinds. They knew little of the European and his peculiar ways. The farmers, growing barely sufficient crops for their own immediate needs, had no thought of selling surplus produce, even to the next village let alone to the outside world. The cowrie shell was the only known currency outside the main towns, and business was transacted by barter. In some villages, the market was a novelty introduced by the DC. He encouraged the people to increase the land under cultivation by grubbing up the local bush to grow alternative crops to sell. The farmers quickly saw that they would have to improve their roads if they wanted traders to come and buy their cocoa or palm oil, and many chiefs willingly turned out with their people to make and clean the roads and bush paths. The DC has been criticized in some quarters for his paternal attitude towards the chiefs and their people, but in those early days many chiefs relied on him and were delighted when a government station was opened in their village.

Although the First World War was raging in Europe, in 1915 the Governor, Sir Hugh Clifford, decided that some of the children in the upcountry districts should have elementary schooling. Trees were felled and rudimentary schools were erected with the help of communal labour. The local carpenter was brought in to make forms and desks for the boys (mostly the sons of chiefs) to sit at. By no means all the chiefs approved of education, and the DCs had often to use their powers of persuasion to induce the chiefs to send their children to school. At least one DC threatened to withhold a gunpowder permit if the boys did not attend school.

When not on tour, the DC held court and dealt with his office work. The district record books had to be kept up to date, also the informal diary, obligatory after 1913. There were guns to be licensed too, a duty rarely appreciated by the DC. His official mail, brought in by runner, appeared at irregular intervals, but when it came, it required his immediate attention. It might contain a memo from the PC asking why he had taken a certain action, or an impatient demand for the dispatch of the district map he was supposed to be making. Sometimes there was a circular warning him to be on the lookout for a new fetish, or, as the First World War progressed, an urgent order to recruit troops and carriers for service in the Cameroons and East Africa. A telegraph line worked intermittently between HQ and a few of these stations, enabling the DC to send and receive telegrams, but as a rule runners sent messages.

In spite of all the difficulties, many DCs preferred to live in these remote bush stations, where they had a more or less free hand and were happy to be as far away as possible from the Secretariat and its petty bureaucracy. They grew to love the local people, whose interests they jealously guarded and whose virtues they extolled with pride, frequently writing articles about them and their customs for *Blackwoods* or *West Africa*. One of them, Dr W. W. Claridge, found time to write his monumental *History of the Gold Coast and Ashanti* (1915) while serving in the Gold Coast as MO-cum-administrative officer.

It was essential for the DC to have an interest or hobby to occupy his leisure. He was required to study at least one Gold Coast language and often he would go on to learn another.[26] Some were interested in anthropology, while others, fascinated by archaeology, collected early Iron Age implements and other artefacts. Many loved their gardens, growing vegetables and planting fruit trees. Some lovingly grew roses. For other, especially in the NT, the excitement of big game hunting or shooting for the pot compensated for the other deprivations. As the CCNT reported in 1908,

> The rivers are infested with crocodiles, and a very large number of hippos live in them, and do much damage to native crops. I am afraid I am one of those who regret the limit put on the shooting of these animals, and also of elephants, as the damage they can do to a maize crop during one night often reduces a village later on to starvation.[27]

Some DCs were obsessed with road making and bridge building, although the bridge might amount to nothing more than a stout tree trunk thrown across a stream. Agriculture, water divining and well digging interested others. Another DC might be keen on the scouting movement and establishes his own troop. If sport was his forte, he spent hours teaching the boys and young men at his station cricket or football, and quickly had his own team. All stations held a sports day on 24 May (Empire Day), and some enthusiasts spent many evenings before the great event coaching the various teams. As their diaries make plain, all took a keen interest in the building and upkeep of the numerous rest houses.

Naturally, any visitor was warmly received, his visit affording a welcome break in the monotony. In the early days, before the advent of the wireless, a wind-up gramophone with a few well-loved records revived memories of England, and many DCs carried a 'phonograph' with them to their bush station. T. E. Fell, the PC at Sunyani from 1907 to 1915, had a large collection of light classical records, which gave great pleasure to him and the various ADCs who served under him, while Laura Boyle in her diary writes, 'We took the pathephone out to give them [their Jimini domestics] a treat in the shape of a tune or two. We turned on 'Hitchy Koo' and they all came crowding round, looking inside the box, very puzzled to know where the sound came from, still more so when we put on a Harry Lauder song and he started by laughing.'[28] Letters from home were eagerly awaited, often five to six weeks' old by the time they reached the remote districts of Ashanti or the NT. This delay was particularly hard to bear during the First World War, when all and any news from the front was anxiously anticipated. Anyone who obtained the latest Reuters news immediately passed it on, by runner, to the DC at the next station. The French political officers in the Ivory Coast always seemed to get the most up-to-date Reuters news, and, burying the hatchet for the duration, hastened to impart it to their confrères on the British side of the frontier. Many of the political officers had their favourite English newspaper or magazine sent out to them. A not necessarily apocryphal story went the rounds of a DC in a remote station, who, when a new batch of papers arrived from home, handed them to his houseboy with instructions to deliver one to him daily.[29] For this, the boy was solemnly paid 1*d*.

On the whole, time passed quickly and, after completing a tour of 12 months, it was time for the DC to pack up and make the long journey back to the Coast, then home on leave to the United Kingdom by one of the regular mail boats, likely taking with him his Ashanti stools, gold weights and perhaps a fauna specimen for the London Zoo or a flora one for Kew Gardens.

Notes

1. Herbert Taylor Ussher served in the Gold Coast as administrator at Cape Coast from 1867, under the Governor in Chief, Sierra Leone, then as Governor of the Gold Coast Colony from June 1879 until his death in December 1880. He is buried in London Market Cemetery, James Town, Accra.
2. Considering the death rate from fever and other causes, this was hardly surprising. A. W. L. Hemming, head of the Africa Department, Colonial Office, in a minute states: 'A return, which I made up a short time back for the Secretary of State, showed that the rate of mortality and permanent invaliding amongst the European staff on the Gold Coast was, for the years 1874–1878, no less than 13 per cent per year' (Public Record Office, Kew, CO/96/130). In 1872, Sir John Pope-Hennessy, Governor in Chief of the West African Settlements wrote to a friend: 'In no part of Her Majesty's Empire is one brought so constantly face to face with death as on the West Coast of Africa' (John Pope-Hennessy, *Verandah*, London, 1964, p. 140).
3. Public Record Office, CO/96/130.
4. Ibid. These DCs were all Africans.

5. Ibid. Hemming had a low opinion of the African and never missed an opportunity to minute his dislike. 'All natives are incorrigible liars' (minute of 23 February 1887, CO/96/179).
6. Ibid.
7. During the First World War, partly due to a shortage of officers and partly because of the danger of submarine attack, many political officers served without a home break for 18 months or longer. German submarines, with great loss of life sank several of the Elder Dempster mail boats.
8. Lawyers were not allowed to practise in Ashanti and the NT until the early 1930s, so the niceties of court procedure could, to some extent, be dispensed with and it was unnecessary for the DC to be a solicitor.
9. Robert Heussler, *Yesterday's Rulers* (London, 1963, p. 9). The shift from patronage to a formalized system of references and interviews had to await the Warren Fisher Report of 1930, which resulted in the appointment of the famous Ralph Furse as director of recruitment at the Colonial Office. See his memoir *Aucuparius* (London, 1962).
10. Captain Kenny Herbert was special commissioner for survey duties. In his report of the northeast NT, 1898, he is very critical of German policy in neighbouring Togoland (PRO CO/96/315).
11. T. E. Fell's letters and diaries are in the Rhodes House Library, Oxford, MSS. Brit. Emp. s. 314.
12. CO/96/203. He was Governor of the Gold Coast from 1886 to 1895.
13. CO/96/315.
14. Reginald Antrobus was Assistant Under Secretary of State, Colonial Office, in charge of West African affairs from 1890 to 1909.
12. Lord Selborne, Parliamentary Under Secretary, Colonial Office, 1895–1900.
16. Joseph Chamberlain, Secretary of State for the Colonies, 1895–1903.
17. CO/96/315.
18. The first course of lectures for recruits began in 1909. It was held at the Imperial Institute, and lasted eight weeks. It included lectures in law, tropical hygiene, surveying, economic products and accounting (see CO/96/476). Several DCs already in the Gold Coast were given extended leave to attend some of these lectures.
19. Laura Boyle, *Diary of a Political Officer's Wife* (Oxford, 1968, p. 3). For an example of tropical outfitting requirements, see Anthony Kirk-Greene, 'The Tropics and Ten the Turl', *Oxford*, May 2000, vol. LII, no. 1, 13–18.
20. A. W. Cardinall, *Ashanti and Beyond* (London, 1927, pp. 70–1).
21. The Obuasi diary 1913–19 gives a clear picture of life at the major mining station in Ashanti.
22. The paramount chief of an Akan district. He had a number of villages under him, each of which was in charge of a chief or headman. It was up to the *omanhene* to see that the village chiefs obeyed the instructions of the DC.
23. CO/96.

24. In 1909, there were 11 motorcars and 16 lorries licensed under the Motor Traffic Ordinance, which came into force in 1908. 'When the light Ford chassis was introduced it produced a veritable revolution in the transport problems of the Gold Coast' (Legislative Council debate, 1918). Heavy lorries tore up the earth roads and did immense damage, especially in the rainy season. Much credit is due to F. W. H. Migeod, DC, who was the Gold Coast transport officer from 1909 to 1919.
25. MOs were stationed only in the main towns and visits to the outlying stations, except in an emergency, were few and far between. During the First World War, many were transferred to the Togoland and Cameroons campaigns.
26. Before 1910 certain European officials kept a local woman — 'a sleeping dictionary'. It caused consternation when it became known that a senior commissioner in the Colony also kept one of these women. In London, Circular B was hastily published, forbidding this practice. In about 1928, when interviewing a cadet sent to the NT, Duncan-Johnstone, the CC, was startled to learn that when at Cambridge, being lectured by a former political officer from the Sudan, the cadets were told 'the only way to get in touch with the natives was to keep a native woman. Since then', Duncan-Johnstone added, 'they have received a copy of [the CO's] Circular B' (Rhodes House Library. Mss. Afr. s. 593).
27. *Journal of the Africa Society*, vol. 8.
28. *Diary of a Political Officer's Wife*, p. 25.
29. One recalls the tragic tale of the new ADO who disturbed the reading order of his Resident's months-old *Times* to see who had won the Test match, and paid the ultimate price, in Somerset Maugham's short story 'The Outstation'.

2

Diaries, 1900–1907: The Early Years

Western Frontier, Preventive Service

(i) T. E. Fell, 1900[1]

31 January 1900

I embarked per SS *Bakana* for Axim. Captain refused to stop but I decided to go on as ticket was made out by *Bakana* to Axim by the agents. Attrill[2] saw me off. Took with me 39 MH rifles, 40 sword bayonets, 14 scabbards, 2000 rounds 450 ammunition.

1 February 1900

On board, captain still refused to land me at Axim and insisted we disembark at Sekondi; we chartered three surf boats to convey us and luggage to Axim, but fortunately the skipper said he would stop at Axim for us.

2 February 1900

Arrived Axim. Saw Campbell[3] and stored boxes and arms in the warehouse. Came up to Morgan's and breakfasted. After breakfast went with Campbell and examined cloth and uniforms in store with invoices. Found all correct with exception of there being in excess of the invoices: 38 first-class officer caps (gold braid peak), 125 second-class officers caps (peak caps). Went and chartered services of tailor who asked 9/– for making up each suit. Refused, and after some palaver arranged for them at 5/– per suit. Handed him 336 yards serge to begin with. Gave orders for all arms to be opened at 8.00 a.m. tomorrow for inspection and cleaning, as on arrival at Axim it was raining torrents and everything got soaked. Met DC Hunt and Dr Roche. DC Lomax sick. Was struck by magnificence of the Axim town clock. Police Barracks Axim, so much heard of in the Secretariat, washed away by heavy rain.

3 February 1900
Procured oil and employed boatmen on cleaning rifles and sword bayonets all morning. Interviewed King with Hunt and asked him if the carriers could not return to their homes for five days as I should not be leaving Axim for a week and did not wish to subsist them for that period. Asked him to secure me an intelligent headman who understood English. King said if carriers returned to their homes, most of them a day's journey away, they would be difficult to get hold of again and he could not be responsible for them. Visited tailor, who has started well on the work, and inspected arms, which had been cleaned. Boatmen seemed willing to work for me. Saw Lomax, who is better and Mrs Lomax. Shot with Morgan in afternoon, but saw nothing. Played whist with Campbell, Hunt. Won 21/–. Met a native funeral by instalments yesterday and today, first the body slung on a pole and carried along merrily swinging, today the coffin in instalments being rushed through the forest.

4 February 1900
Started boatmen on cleaning arms and showed them how to do it. Had a talk with DC Lomax re methods of pay etc. Went to tailor and egged him on to get uniforms made as soon as possible. At 4.00 p.m. the *Bornu* came in and Morgan and I went on board. Hammock from PWD arrived from Accra. Shall subsist carriers from the day of arrival as King will not be responsible for getting them again at a moment's notice and do not wish to have trouble at last moment. Logs at Axim scarce and no cargo practically for *Bornu*.

6 February 1900
Went and had long talk re pay etc. of WPPS officers with Lomax. Met Deacon and walked with him to tailors to enquire progress with uniforms. He is making ten a day and cannot do more. Went to see Carew and Bennett re man Jacobs who has asked to be my headman. Heard nothing much to his credit, chief fault being debt. I have decided to keep him with me and send the customs officer overland with uniforms to Jemma and meet me there. Interviewed youth who wishes to join the force and took his name in case of emergency; seems intelligent and is a scholar having passed grade IV. Played whist with Lomax, Bennett, Cooper. Instructed Fritz to find me some chief who procures fish in quantities to see me with a view to entering into a contract for the supply of the northern stations with him. Dillon[4] and Hausas arrived from Sefwi as witnesses on a murder case.

7 February 1900
Went and bucked up tailor and tried to make him hurry up. Cannot

procure red braid in the town, so must leave without.

8 February 1900
Saw Lomax and Hunt in the morning. Also the tailor who has promised me all the clothes tomorrow evening and 30 suits this evening. Went Miller Bros and arranged for a packer to pack up into loads all clothes, arms etc. Drew advance of £50 and subsisted carriers. Held palaver with the king who finally asked for whisky, and as he procured me the carriers I gave him a bottle. Bought packing and mackintosh material for making up the loads.

11 February 1900
Arrived Esiama 1.00 a.m. and found all the carriers had stopped there and were in the chief's house. Rather annoyed as I had wanted to get to the Twin Rivers and Beyin that night. However, turned in and slept till 5.00 a.m. when carriers were started. Twin Rivers very picturesque. Arrived Attuabo 12.00 p.m. and was so hungry, owing to there having been a muddle in the morning with the boxes, that I got no chop, so I stayed there and lunched coming on to Beyin at 2.30 p.m. Had a delicious shave and bath and prepared to spend quiet evening till midnight when I intended starting for Half Assine. Road good all the way; chiefly runs along the beach; received a letter from Vere Stead;[5] Beyin fort in ruins.

12 February 1900
Arrived Bonyere 12.45 a.m. Slept on wooden bed comfortably till 6.00 a.m. On to Half Assine crossing on river in which Likman stumbled and nearly let me in. Arrived Half Assine; went to Miller Bros. Met Vere Stead and went into accounts etc. Carriers all arrived by 5.00 p.m., some having obviously drunk too much palm wine. Went and saw Preventive Station here. House undoubtedly required by the supervisor who is living with Miller Bros agent Campbell with whom I am staying.

13 February 1900
Subsisted carriers. Discharged two and dispatched five to Axim for fresh supplies of clothing. All carriers to proceed overland to Jemma. They are taking ten loads with them and the rest I am taking by canoe. Saw the four men at this station and signed an agreement. Issued them their clothing. They asked me for caps and informed them I was going to write and ask for them. Saw Ankrah, ex-warder, suspended from duty by V. Stead for changing all the men in his station and trying to make out he had not done so, and for disobeying orders. The men as far as I can hear seem to be fairly settled in this district. This house is delightful. Campbell and Daw[6] both good chaps and

Half Assine in a very fairly flourishing condition. Campbell seems full of very legitimate enterprise as far as the Western side of this Colony goes and should be supported. Plenty of logs here and any number in the lagoon.

Started 2.00 p.m. train to Creek and got canoe there, stopped at Esokrum village on the lagoon and picked up chief who built the house at Canal Mouth and is to build one at the Bar Mouth.[7] Lagoon very pretty, also railway and creek. Many logs lying in the lagoon; arrived Canal Mouth and inspected the station. Roof leaking badly and instructed chief to put on another covering as he had failed to make the house complete. Spoke with O in C Mensah. Only two men of the seven at the station intend signing on for a further period of a year. I promised them their uniforms on the following day and a rifle to the O in C. The chief wish they expressed was that they wished to go and see their friends. I told them I had no objection to them going away for three weeks, that only one man was to go at a time and that before he went he was to produce a substitute at the station who in all ways was satisfactory to the supervisor in charge of the district. I told them of HE's wish that they should clear as much ground round the station as possible without interfering with the patrols. They said they were willing to do this but they had no machetes. I have decided, as machetes are only 4½*d.* each, to buy some out of my advance and supply each station with two. Patrols at Canal Mouth I am assured have been well done and the station seemed clean. Vere Stead assured me that the men who were intending to go were worth keeping if possible, and I will do my utmost within reason tomorrow to induce them to sign on. Went down the river to Bar Mouth. Saw one crocodile and shot one diver. Went down and selected site for the station and ordered the chief to begin clearing the land tomorrow. This, after much palaver, chief agreed to and I took him and dropped him at his village and came back. Full moon and the lagoon very pretty at night. Came up the rail by a trolley pushed by the canoemen. Chop and bed, very tired. Clocks are required at the stations. O in C Bar Mouth reported French watching at Bar Mouth.

14 February 1900

Wrote up diary and received report re Tano River from V. Stead as to unhealthiness. [He] should have started with me in the afternoon, but went down with fever, so left him. Started by 2 o'clock train. Carriers etc. of course not to be found; lost my temper utterly, but finally got started. Two canoes in Creek, which I piled with luggage and started for Canal Mouth. Arrived Canal Mouth, two men signed on; long palaver with others on leave question; am seeing them again tomorrow. They all want to go away at the same time and I have told them I will allow them to go and bring their wives one at a time, provided they provide a substitute. Left Canal Mouth 7.00 p.m. Glorious moonlight, but the river smelly. The forest reflections were very fine and the water smooth with a fair current against us. Arrived Adukrum 9.00 p.m. Met no patrol on the way. Dined by palm oil light[8] off cold mutton and potted meat and felt very fit and enjoyed it. Station so far as I can judge by moonlight well kept. House built of swish. Rigged up bed etc. O in C reported French station near Alenda, another at Hania, another at Nugua. Bought 50 cutlasses at Half Assine to distribute out of advance. King of Adukrum requests palaver and I said I would see him tomorrow afternoon. Am impressing smartness on O in C and going in for elementary drill as far as possible.

15 February 1900

Sleeping soundly when roused in the night by hoarse voice of Jacobs at my door saying 'capsized, capsized'. I leapt out of bed and swore terribly at them all. Got lights and counted loads, and thankful that all the government loads of clothing and rifles, and all my own, had been saved. All the men wringing wet and most of them lost their packages, which were swept away by the stream, containing their clothes and money. Got up at 6.00 a.m. praying for a fine day to dry the uniforms and clean up the rifles. Inspected the station. House does not leak; men have begun planting cassada and as soon as the season commences will plant corn. They keep their own fowls and have, the O in C Dawson informs me, no difficulty in getting chop. Held long palaver with four delinquents from Canal Mouth. They insisted that they must all go away and bring their wives as they could not live at Canal Mouth without them. As I consider, it would be an excellent thing for their wives to come up. I finally agreed to allow them to go for four weeks after having produced substitutes who should be efficient canoemen and instructed in the work. They asked if I would engage these substitutes in the service and, as men are going to be badly needed up the Frontier, it may turn out a means of getting other recruits. Palaver over two hours in length and very wearisome.

Chief came to see me. Gave him whisky and heard his grievances viz. (1) Flag and message stick had been promised him by Rainsford and never received. (2) He had not been paid by V. Stead for roofing house of third-class officers. (3) Cutlasses and axes had been promised him by H. M. Hull,[9] but capsized on way up, and he had been promised a fresh supply but had never received them. I promised to bring (1) and (3) to the notice of the commissioners. I think a flag would be a good thing at each station. Gave the chief leave to clear away clump of bamboo in front of wharf. Gave him whisky, which they all drank, including the children. Turned out men to clear more bush, which was difficult, but they finally started on it. Patrols, I think, are too regular and would do with variation on different days weekly. Men here jubilant with their kit and requested that I would allow them to go in the canoes for ten minutes to show me. I consented and great was the delight thereof. Issued orders to the O in C re time for wearing uniform. Clock wanted here, also kerosene. Drilled the men at stand at ease and attention for a short time and told the O in C that he is to instruct them daily.

16 February 1900
Left Adukrum about 7.00 a.m. Had plenty of shots but lost the only three waterfowl I could get through their diving. Had several shots at large birds, but I think cartridges a bit damp. Arrived Takinta about 10.00 a.m. The O in C Mensah had his men drawn up and is the smartest man I have seen in the force. Station clean, also clearing. Cassava and plantains planted. Three men here will not sign on unless they have three months' leave for funeral custom. As the leave is too long, I have not signed them on but told them they could come back on the chance that men were wanted. The river journey today was ripping, gorgeous thick forest and huge trees right down to the water's edge. Sent for King of Takinta, as the station here and all the men's huts leak badly and he must put them right. Station very clean. Very little for me to do at this station; had chop and sleep for an hour. Sweet potatoes growing here; corn to be planted as soon as the season for it. O in C seems to have his men well in hand and is readily and quickly obeyed. No clock and no kerosene here. O in C has no grievances except considers that Os in C should get more salary than Assistant Os in C. Shall recommend that assistants get 1/9*d.* – an intermediate step between 1/6 and 2/–. Shot crocodile in morning at 100 yards; large hornbill in afternoon. Went out at 5.30 with gun in canoe; shot one diver and one waterfowl.

17 February 1900
Got canoes off and waited arrival of the king. King arrived 9.00 a.m. with long white beard and a face like President Kruger. Told him he had failed in his contract to build houses as they were not watertight. He said he had not been paid for the houses he built last December, so I told him he would not be paid till they were watertight. I then told the king that he should not make fresh small paths to the river and let people moor their canoes in these out-of-the-way places, but that, as the proper road was through the station from his town to the river and there was a good wharf at the station, he should moor his canoes

there. I think that canoes being suddenly taken away from the station where a few months ago they were always moored, and special paths made to these places, might mean trying to get French goods across from their pals on the other side. The king could give no sufficient reason why the canoes were removed from the station wharf, so I told him he must continue to moor them at the wharf as heretofore, to which, after much palaver, he agreed. Palaver ended as usual by his asking for drink, which I gave him, and will stop this practice in future as it runs away with too much of my whisky and I have brought no trade gin with me. Went out in canoe 4.30 for an hour with Kofi to try and get a shot at a parrot or pigeon. All flying too high. Shot one bright blue bird and a diver of sorts. Chop and bed.

19 February 1900
Vere Stead arrived 1.00 a.m. Sat with him till 3.00 a.m. and talked, then turned in. Got up 7.00 a.m. Went through notes with Vere Stead. Drilling the men, who seemed keen on it. Left 2.30 p.m. for Bulla; arrived there 7.45 p.m. Had a shot at a large crocodile about 100 yards and missed him. Lot of snags and sunken trees in the river. Stuck on one for some time. Landed in the dark at Bulla through terrible mud, had chop and slept on a native bed in a bamboo hut; no mosquitoes and very comfortable.

20 February 1900
Left Bulla 9.15 a.m. Stopped at Hania opposite French station to consider advisability of starting new station. An extra station between Elubo and Alenda is necessary to relieve patrols, also as a protection to the timber trade and to watch the French. V. Stead and self landed and hacked our way for some distance through the forest to see if we could find high land near the river where the station could be built. No success and finally decided that if authorized the station should be built opposite the mouth of the Hania River about 100 yards higher up on the opposite bank than the French station. Started on for Elubo; had an extemporary [*sic*] meal on the bank. Saw four crocodiles. Kofi great, with terrible but ludicrous yarns about 'person beef' and heaven. He is a cannibal but one of the best niggers I have met, most amusing and full of jokes. Has only eaten one white man and never chopped anyone since he came to English territory. He is a native of Dahomey. 'White man so so beef be sweet too much', he informed us. Arrived Elubo wet through. Great palaver but very annoying one over buying a sheep. Called in chief and after much talk got sheep for 8/–.

21 February 1900
Issued arms and uniforms to the officers and uniforms to the men.

Men delighted with uniforms and drew up in line at once for inspection. Drilled them for half an hour or more. They take an interest and will turn out smart in the end. Chief arrived and endless unsatisfactory palaver about making roofs of the houses watertight. This chief is a rotter and a terrible old Jew and I refused to pay him anything unless he repaired the roofs. Told him he must sell food from the village to the Customs people at the same rate as it was bought by his own people, to which he agreed. The men here seem a good lot of excellent material. Have promised that they shall have caps and have confiscated the Napoleonic chapeaux they were wearing yesterday.

22 February 1900
Started per canoe 8.30 a.m. Current strong, river low and full of trees. At two places trees had fallen right across the river and there was great difficulty in getting canoes over them. Terribly hot. Country gets hillier and scenery very fine. Arrived Boin River 4.30 p.m. Station cut out of the side of a hill and very steep road up to it. Fair clearing here and men evidently been working on it. Promised to see chief of Jemma as to letting them have plants to grow. Tried to go up Boin River in canoe, but so blocked by fallen trees that could only get a short distance. Had a shot at an eagle without effect and saw some large black monkeys. Chop and bed. House small and leaking. Awoken 9.30 p.m. by bitter cold and hurricane of wind. Torrents of rain, which for some minutes did not get through the roof and I thought I was going to keep dry. Vain illusion, for I soon found the rain beginning to pour through onto my bed and all over loads and clothes. Covered all with mackintosh sheets, put on mackintosh and went and sat in centre of room. V. Stead in same condition, so we had a whisky and soda to keep the wet out and patiently waited. My room like a puddle and a wholesome smell of wet swish.

Sunday 25 February 1900
Copied report all day and got it packed up and sent to Comptroller. In the evening, instructions having arrived to plant mahogany seedlings at the stations, went off with V. Stead trying to find them. Extremely difficult as although we managed to find mahogany trees there are dozens of different kinds of seedlings under the trees. Employed carriers sharpening all cutlasses. Interviewed carriers and told them any looting would be at once punished by a 5/– fine. No difficulty about chop at this station for the men.

27 February 1900
Men came again to mend the roof. Carriers clearing bush. Uniforms

not arrived. Chief sent for and told to supply carriers with chop. Drew out computation of total expenditure of force and sent it to Attrill to be authorized. Wrote private letter to him and home. Walked out in evening and got five green pigeons and was glad for food's sake. Worried at Mansfield's[10] vouchers to try and get them straight. Cook drunk in morning and flogged him small small, much to his disgust; very quiet and penitent in evening. Mansfield terribly rough, but a good hearted sort. V. Stead covered with a sort of ringworm and covered him with boracic ointment.

1 March 1900

Got carriers off at 6.00 a.m. Started 7.30 a.m. and reached Boinsu 12.00 p.m. Forest all the way and one or two streams and rivers to cross; one on a native bridge consisting of the trunk of a tree over which I crossed about 20 feet above the water in trepidation. Hammockmen insisted on racing Mansfield's hammockmen and we went up and down terrible places at a run with no mishap. Road fairly clean; Jemma part worst. Boinsu portion chiefly bad owing to small trees not being cut down and logs left lying. Saw chief of Boinsu, a young man, and told him to clean his road. He offered a sheep and yams and I said I would buy them when he sent them down. Went through patrol book; very difficult to prevent faking. Patrols here, according to book, take five hours, but am sceptical. All forest. Mansfield has planted beans and vegetables and they seem to do well. Have promised to ask for seeds from Aburi, which would be a boon to European travellers.

2 March 1900

Got up 6.00 a.m. Took O in C with me over patrolling roads. Road to Moisu in French territory worse than any I have yet seen. It is just possible to patrol it. In two places terrible native bridges of one log to be crossed. Two deserted villages, which are used by timber cutters. Came across one magnificent mahogany tree felled and cut into four huge logs. As it had fallen along the road, the present road lies along the top of it. Carriers clearing bush all morning and burning and shifting cut trees. The Assistant O in C's wife made us groundnut soup for breakfast and very good too. Walked out 4.30 round mahogany cutters' villages and got six young mahogany trees.

3 March 1900

Left for Mappe. Crossed the Boin River and two or three streams on the way. Mappe a fine clean village and the station the nicest I have seen. The men have cleaned and planted a lot, and all anxious to serve on for another year, and the O in C Essien seems to take a pride in the house and everything spotlessly clean. O in C told me patrol was attacked by a 'tiger', really a leopard, and were consequently afraid.

Sunday 4 March 1900
Started 8.00 a.m. with Essien and three men to inspect roads. Went first to Boin River. Boin River very low and canoe very rickety and soon found the canoe was so often stuck on logs and banks that there was more wading about to be done than canoeing. Onto one log then off that and onto another, and so on for one and a half hours till we came opposite Bamianko. No sign of a French road. Men anxious to cut one for me, but I naturally vehemently refused. Absolutely wet through was I with wading and upsetting. At one place in the river, the French had put a fishing fence right across the river and this we had to hack down with cutlasses to get our canoe up. After great struggles we arrived at the Boin River road and I walked home dripping and sweating.

6 March 1900
Left 8.15 for Kwaku. Arrived 10.00 a.m. Saw O in C. Road from Mappe to Kwaku good but very much up and down hill. Passed the largest rubber tree I have ever seen. It had the marks of being tapped on it and stands right in the middle of the road. This station house is small but nice and cosy and the O in C goes in for flowers. A fair amount of foodstuffs are grown but there is a chop palaver here and the men say it is difficult to get. The headman of the town came and dashed me one fowl, two yams, two eggs, a bottle of palm wine, and two coconuts which are a luxury here and I dashed him a tin of preserved fruit and Mansfield gave him a tin of meat, which highly pleased him. Cleaned gun up as I hear green pigeons swarm here. No seizures and no smuggling so far as I can hear. Went out after pigeons but got none. Bed 7.30

7 March 1900
Got up 5.30. Many pigeons flying about and shot three. Started 8.00 a.m. with O in C to inspect roads. Road lately been found leading to French territory through village of Yanidigai. It must be patrolled regularly. Road very bad. Passed plenty of native gold holes.

9 March 1900
Went over road to Eba Kudjo Krum. Chief, who at Sewum was ever with me, turned out his people to clean. Chief presented me with two fowls, yams etc. Gave him a lot of advice as he is a new chief and a willing one. Deputation from Kromokrum stating that the O in C of that station had collared the fetishman and his drums. He had gone over to Kromokrum to doctor some woman and [was] asking me to

give a note to the O in C to liberate him. This I refused to do and put off the case till I got to Kromokrum.

10 March 1900
Started 7.30 a.m. for Kromokrum. Road very bad, not so much for want of clearing, but very up and down, and about half way numbers of old gold holes, which necessitate getting out of the hammock. Two villages on the way. At Amassie the people were building a house and all covered with swish. They made a lot of noise and insisted on us drinking palm wine. After much talking and yelling we got away. Arrived Kromokrum and enquired into the fetish priest's arrest. O in C had exceeded his powers and, thinking there was going to be a fight, took him a prisoner to the station. I liberated him at once and warned him not to interfere in native customs again. Walked out with Mansfield through the town. The sick woman and husband and day-old baby, for whom the fetishman had come to make fetish to cure the woman when he was locked up, came to me and the man asked me to give him a feeding bottle as the mamma was *hors de combat* with pains inside. I told him he could not expect large white man to carry bottles about with him. Doctored the woman with turpentine liniment, which I told her to rub on her tummy, and gave her a bit of lint to put on top, which seemed to please her.

11 March 1900
Issued orders re patrols and uniforms. Left about 12 noon and arrived Enchi about 2.00 p.m. Mason O in C seems an excellent man and signed him, Assistant O in C Arthur and six men on for a year. Found here two prisoners, unable to find the commissioner for trial and had been left in the station for smuggling powder. Took a guarantee of £2 each from them that they would appear when called upon; kept the powder and let them go.

12 March 1900
Sent carriers Fine Boy, Singer Boy, Kwesi Donkoh, and Kwamina Awokie for last consignment of clothing, and carrier James II to Miller Bros for one case whisky, 12 stout, and a sparklet bottle. Repacked all loads and decided what to leave at Enchi as depot. Bentinto arrived to see me about 4.30 p.m. Large palaver; I gave him one month to have his roads cleaned. He gave me a sheep, some yams and a tall and old and blushing damsel for a wife, who was commanded to honour and obey me. I thanked him much but refused the wife, who I think was decidedly piqued, although I told her she was an extremely fine mammy and gave him a bottle of whisky, which I told him was what the queen drank and good for his tummy. The king is a revelation. He

is about 80, always champing as if he'd a bit in his mouth, wears a coxcomb of feathers and a coat like Joseph's. He is a very big chief, being king of all Aowin. He asked for a commissioner of Aowin as he will not go to Asafo. I informed him if he refused to go to Asafo Hausas would be sent who would take him there. I finally toppled him into Mansfield's hammock looking like the devil incarnate and sent him home. Got one green pigeon and had the capon for dinner, which was delicious.

13 March 1900
Chief sent up one fowl and another yam and thanked me for my kindness yesterday. What it was I don't know. Went over the patrol roads with Mason. Drew map of roads and got off report. Sent copies of maps I had done to Attrill. No sign of V. Stead. Sent off letter by runner to find him as I think he must be ill. Mammy came with a complaint that she wished to be divorced from the king, as whenever she preferred another hubby the king fined her and all her family. Bought a long flintlock gun studded with brass nails to take home. Tried to bargain for an Ashanti stool, but owner would not sell it at any price.

14 March 1900
Started for Yakasie 7.30 a.m. Crossed Disue River twice on tree trunk bridges. Station clean and clearing good. Sent for the chief who came in state, drums, horns, guns, flags etc. Friendly palaver and mutual greetings; no complaints anywhere. Told chief to supply men with sufficient chop to buy. Large number of land turtles bought by carriers with glee. Bought a sheep after the usual wrangle for 8/–. One carrier with bad cut on foot and another ulcer; doctored both.

16 March 1900
Up 4.30 a.m. Got off loads. Ali tried to bolt to Accra because ordered to carry bath. Had him caught and gave him a flogging. Bath and breakfast and on the march 6.15 a.m. Quesie leading sheep with great difficulty. Terrible hill about four miles from Kromokrum. Road execrable; walked the whole way. Chief a very decent chap, brought two fowls, pineapples, yams the moment we arrived. Lots of rubber in the village. Sheep arrived looking most dejected. Chief anxious to give me an elephant hunt; promised to stay and go with him on my return.

17 March 1900
Left 6.30 a.m. Passed three villages. Rested half an hour at the first and had palm wine and bananas. Arrived Dadiaso about 1.30 p.m. Chief and people came in state and dashed me a sheep, plantains and yams. He is a fine old chap and a great wit. Promised to bring me

some elephant tusks to buy. Sheep very fatigued after its long journey; have decided not to slaughter it till it has had a few happy days here.

Amoya, 24 March 1900
Saw chief at 8.00 a.m. Had a long and successful palaver. Made agreement re building house giving him 42 days to clear the land and build the house. Cautioned him about resisting customs officers who had seized two of his guns. Bought a leopard skin, a very fine one for 7/– and a sheep for 8/–. Cook drunk all day. Curry was served as soup and mock turtle soup as curry. Chief promised to start on the house at once and I told him I would help him. Went out in canoe with Crabb. Bia River very lovely and thoroughly enjoyed it. After chop tornado came on; rigged up mackintosh sheets to protect my bed and slept like a top. Fight in the town between carriers and natives; stopped fight half a dozen of one and six of the other as usual. Called out chief. Chose site for station in the afternoon with Crabb on a good hill and a fine view. Took chief and showed him place.

Sunday 25 March 1900
Up 5.30, out after breakfast with chief, people and carriers cutting down the forest. Did a grand morning's work and cleared a lot; worked hard with an axe myself. Chief working in an extraordinary brown bowler hat very ancient indeed. Got two marvellous insects, one stick insect and one stick mantis — the stick insect at least a foot long. Turned out again in afternoon and watched trees being felled.

26 March 1900
Very seedy; went out and saw chief working on the land. Wrote reports in morning. In the afternoon chief had nobody out working. Went and found chief. He said his people did not wish to work for him. Called a palaver for 6 o'clock of the entire multitude. Went in canoe for an hour, but was forced to come back and lie down. Large palaver in town. I harangued the people for a long time and got them to promise to help the chief as all they were doing was to get him into trouble. Told the rubber brokers that they must elect a headman for themselves and work too. Bed and a terrible night. Taking nothing but brandy and arrowroot.

Bonzano, 29 March 1900
Up 5.00 a.m. Had two shots at pigeons but missed both. Had breakfast and afterwards Bonzano chief came with men to work. Had palaver; thanked him for the dash. He complained that rubber people in his villages would not work for him. Promised to report on it as it is a general complaint all through the district. Tried to enter into an agreement for buying the land. Chief refused, saying the land was the

property of the Paramount King of Sefwi. I said I would measure out the land and show him how much was required by government and he could inform Atta Kwasi accordingly. He became savage and refused to remain in the place if I insisted on measuring the land. I then told him I would refer the matter to the king. Endless chop palavers with carriers. In the evening walked to Bonzano with Crabb. Whole country full of gold holes and must be heaps of gold. Had a palaver with chief who produced with pride a long easy chair. Chief sorry for morning fracas. Tornado threatened but managed to get back before it came on.

30 March 1900
Left for Kofi Eka Krum. Walked from Abuakofi to main road by short cut. Kwa Krum people cleaning road. They cannot be got to clear up the mountain. Walked to the top, about 1500 feet I should say, and a stiff climb. Very fine scenery. Arrived Kofi Eka Krum. Chief's house very nice. Took or tried to take sketch of Moorish kind of wall done in swish. Bought an Ashanti stool, try to buy a pot of native brassware but chief would not; he promised it to me if I would bring him a brass pot in exchange from England. Saw a woman undergoing an awful operation. I heard cries and thought a murder was being committed. When I went out I saw a woman calmly standing with a man slashing a carving knife into her legs at intervals of an inch from the hips downwards. She did not move but screamed and the fetishman did not so much cut with the knife as flick it in and it must have been very painful. When he had cut both legs he wrapped them up in leaves. The ailment, I discovered, for which this awful operation was practised was rheumatism! The good lady at the end of it was standing in two inches of blood in a plantain leaf.

31 March 1900
Left for Debisu. Road between Ajuafu and Debisu filthy. Chief came to see me and I made him a prisoner at once, demanding £25 as guarantee, as he has not cleared his road or built the customs house. Great row, but money came. Gave him a month to get the house done. Wrote to commissioner. Present house falling down. Town full of rubber traders or so-called rubber traders.

1 April 1900
Palaver with rubber traders. Told them to work and threatened them with eviction if they didn't. Most of them drunk and palaver unsatisfactory. Shot a toucan and a pigeon.

2 April 1900
Wrote reports all morning, had chop about 2.30 p.m. Temperature ran up to 104 or more. Went to bed and followed 'Simple Directions'

by Chalmers.[11] Had a terrible night and longed for England and comfort. Temperature normal in morning but felt a worm, so did not get up till afternoon.

4 April 1900
Temperature normal so got up and wrote for four hours copying reports etc. Had chop; bad again in afternoon. Temperature up to 103; went to bed and could not get it down. Decided the moment it was normal to leave on my downward route. In the morning staked out house. People working well.

5 April 1900
In bed all day. People working well at the house. Carriers arrived from Axim with whisky, stout and tobacco and sparklet bottle.

6 April 1900
Temperature normal in morning so started and arrived Kofi Eka Krum. Glad to see Debisu rubber people clearing Debisu portion of road. Dashed them one bottle of gin. Chief of Ajuafu working on his road with eight men. Gave him hell. Had a short walk in evening but much pulled down. Early chop and bed.

7 April 1900
Left 7.00 a.m. Hammock boys manfully carried over Kwamiano mountain. Palaver in Kwa Krum told people to clean road to top of hill. Said they would, but am sure they won't. Progress of house at Aburokoffi very slow. Palaver with Bonzano chief berated him about not working. He informed me that 'hurry-hurry work always bad but slow-slow always good'. I tried to explain that I didn't want hurry-hurry but that slow-slow did not mean any work at all, as he interpreted it. Very friendly.

8 April 1900
Much better. Any amount of pigeons about, got four and left for Krokosua and Amoya. Everything correct at Krokosua; met both patrols on the road. Arrived Amoya about 1.30. After breakfast saw chief and went over the clearing. He has done well and I marked out the house. Entered into an agreement re the land and bought it for £4. Gave him a bottle of gin. Tremendous rain 4.00 p.m. to midnight and everything soaked.

9 April 1900
Quite fit. Left Amoya 7.30 and arrived Dadiaso about 12.30 p.m. Saw chief. Doctor's house well under way. Chief most agreeable and a nice old stick. Says he likes to shake my hand because I 'play' with him. Dosed him for rheumatism with turpentine and his son for yaws with calomel. Sent eye lotion to chief of Essien.

10 April 1900
Wrote report. Superintended house building. No food to be got. Chief and people working well. Dashed them a bottle of whisky as no gin to be bought. Carriers' feet bad and did a lot of doctoring. Chief and I good friends; he is one of the best of them. Promised him a top hat when I came out from England. He asked me to bring him an umbrella as the sun was hot!

11 April 1900
Left 7.00 a.m. Luckily got a piece of ham and a tin of sardines left, which is all. Met cook watching a large troop of big reddish monkeys; pursued them into the bush and got two shots, long ones, but succeeded in bringing down one. Great joy on part of carriers for food. Arrived Akwantamra 1.30 p.m. Thank the Lord all the rest of the uniforms here and managed to get two fowls. Shall stay here tomorrow and send off uniforms to their destinations. While hunting the monkeys walked into a red ants' nest and got badly bitten. Had to undress to find them as they got in everywhere.

15 April 1900
Went over to Yakasie to make agreement with chief. Returned to Enchi; saw King Bentinto and spoke to him re roads etc. Told him he was now in the Axim District, which delighted him; bought two elephant tusks 18/– and a small deer. Cartridges finished.

Jemma, 20 April 1900
Sent four carriers to be paid off at Axim. Wrote lot of official letters. Heard first news of Ashanti rising and HE and Lady H[odgson] bottled in Kumasi. Report of Legget and Armitage being killed.[12] Hope to God it is not true, but Hull writes me that the wires have been cut and no news can be got. Heard messengers had been sent to Atta Kwasi to ask him to join, but his word has not yet been given. Sent off a runner post haste to Crabb to keep his eyes and ears open and to stop all powder and guns going into Ashanti till I heard further.

22 April 1900
Left Elubo 8.00 a.m. Arrived Allenda about 5.00 p.m. Made a great shot at a crocodile fully 200 yards and plugged him in the side with a 450. Awful fluke. Allenda station much improved. Men beginning to get an inkling of drill. Put on land patrols to Tikobo, 2nd Allenda Wharf and Allenda town. Two river patrols to be done.

Miller Bros, Half Assine, 26 April 1900
Started 9.30 a.m. by train to Creek. On to Bar Mouth, which considering the site is a well-built station. Issued uniforms to the men.

Had lunch there. Onions growing in profusion and made a feast of them. Was surprised to see amount of petty trading done by French natives with Half Assine. Left Bar Mouth 1.30 and went by canoe to Jehwi wharf on Tano lagoon. Number of villages on our side of lagoon presumably fishing ones. Landed through 100 yards of appalling mud and walked to Jehwi on the beach. About 40 minutes' walk.

28 April 1900
Waited arrival of Lomax who turned up at 4.00 p.m. No news from Kumasi except HE, Lady H and the rest shut up in the fort. Letter arrived from Crabb saying Hobart[13] and Dillon surrounded in Wam and that the Sefwis were being approached by the Ashantis – result not known. Sent code wire with news to comptroller by runner to Axim and volunteered to go up again if necessary.

2 May 1900
Paid off carriers and settled advances. Drew pay. Wire received stating leave granted, but proceed to Accra by first steamer.

8–21 May 1900
In Accra except for four days at cantonments getting statistics about requirements of WFPS with Hull. No notice taken of my wire re Hobart and, although I had just come from the place, not a question asked me. Things at Kumasi most serious. Last news received stated they could hold out till 26th instant; 20000 Ashantis round the fort. Lady H very ill with fever. Middlemist sick, Bishop Hay and Marshall killed, Armitage and Leggett wounded, Aplin and all his officers wounded and 100 casualties. Parmeter had a narrow escape, being caught at Nkoranza and after two days and two nights in the bush got to Kintampo. Low[14] has taken all responsibility on himself and has been sitting at Accra saying that his hands were so tied he could not act. Hodgson in many ways to blame as he minimized the whole affair at the start to such an extent that until almost too late no one knew what proportions it had assumed. Heard my friends the Sefwis were wavering and don't wonder as they are left with no government representative. Would willingly have gone to Atta Kwasi myself armed with £500 to give in presents, which would probably have turned them as they hate the Ashantis and will only join through fear. No notice taken of my request. Absolutely sick of the whole show and feel, unless you are allowed to do something and know something, which nobody is, the best thing is to go home. Got complimentary minutes from HE as to reports and work done by me. SS *Sokoto* arrived 21st and I embarked for England and glad too.

(ii) J. A. Crabb, 1900[15]

1 May 1900
Left Debisu for Kofi Akka Kru shortly after two. Aburokoffi officers, who had been travelling all night, met me with a letter from the O in C at Krokosua stating that the Ashantis had sent another deputation of 30 men to Atta Kwasi to say that he must join them as they wanted to break through the WFPS ports to get to French territory to buy powder, guns, etc. Envoys are stated to have said that if they did not join the Ashantis would bring 3000 to 4000 men down upon them. O in C stated above information had been given to him by a friend of his, a Sefwi rubber broker, who also informed him the Sefwis were talking of joining in and were then making ready. Attempted to reach Aburokoffi, but roads bad and carriers pretty well done up, so could not get past Kwamiamma. After hearing above news, thought it better to speak seriously to all chiefs on my way down, telling them that I had heard of the envoys etc., that Atta Kwasi would probably wish to confer with them, and that they must not allow Atta Kwasi to be made a fool of. Pointed out that Ashantis only wished to make a cat's paw of him, and also the certain consequences to them if they did join.

2 May 1900
Left Kwamiamma for Aburokoffi – which reached early morning. O in C here has confirmed what O in C Krokosua had reported. Chiefs of Bonzano and Aburokoffi denied knowledge of the deputation to Atta Kwasi, but finally owned up and also to the fact of all the chiefs having been summoned to Wioso. Ordered all powder met with, guns etc., to be seized until after the war is over and sent back word to Debisu to this effect. (This before receiving instructions re the new Ordinance.) Explained reasons to chiefs. Wrote DC at Wam, informing him of this second deputation; also to Atta Kwasi, telling him to stand fast etc. as already reported. Customs house is nearly completed, but chief does little work at it, and that spasmodically.

3 May 1900
Left for Krokosua about noon. O in C and men rather frightened and ask for rifles etc. Reassure them as well as I can and go on to Amoya. Framework of house and roof completed, but chief been doing nothing for some time. Says he is waiting for rain to mix swish. Too lazy to carry water from river. He begged to be allowed to go to Atta Kwasi and finally asked me to write a letter for him, asking Atta Kwasi 'not to be vexed with him'. Fancy this chief is not quite so anxious to join in as some others appear to be, or he would not have asked this permission, and he is evidently going to make my refusal an excuse for not going

when called upon. Rumoured in the town that Ashantis sent Atta Kwasi the customary man's head.

4 May 1900
Left for Adeyekea, my first residence here. Station, men's quarters and customs house very nice and clean. O in C keeps his men well at work here, but understands little Fanti or English. Had little or no sleep up or down this trip on account of specie and the many rumours re Ashanti.

5 May 1900
Mails arrived. Serious rumours reported by Supervisor Stead as to seizure of HE and Lady Hodgson by Ashantis and capture of Kumasi fort. Sent off above news to DC at Wam.

6 May 1900
Sent off circular to all officers in charge, warning them to do their patrols very thoroughly just now and to allow no powder, guns etc. to get past them. Sent for Dadiaso chief, and after explaining as much as seemed desirable, got him to send off two of his runners to Wioso to try and find out the worst and how matters stand there. Kerosene arrived in loose tins and all badly smashed up again, and none more than half full. Sent one tin to each station. O in C Aburokoffi reports that Atta Kwasi's messenger to DC has been caught at Aikrodia and put in irons; letter destroyed. Also that some of the mining people killed and that Bonzano chief left off work again on the customs house.

9 May 1900
Left for Amoya. Nothing more done at customs house since I last passed. I don't think it would be wise to take any steps just now to compel the chiefs to get on with the work while the country is in this disturbed state.

12 May 1900
Reached Edyekru. Mails arrived. Letter from Stead telling me he is wiring to be allowed to come up with some of his best men. Inform him that do not think it quite necessary yet. Dadiaso chief and his return messengers arrived.

13 May 1900
Two letters from DC Wam. He reports that rumours he has heard from Kumasi are to the contrary to those I sent him from Supervisor Stead. Advises me to look out and retire if necessary. Commenced fencing off station ground here.

14 May 1900
Sent mail off and April monthly report. Had carriers out cutting bamboo etc for station. Constant complaints from carriers and police

that they are unable to buy food (plantains) in the village. Have spoken to the chief.

15 May 1900
Tiger killed large bush cow close to the station. Carriers, who were cutting bamboo etc., drove him off and brought meat in. A godsend to all hands as I have been living principally upon a few pigeons I have managed to shoot.

19 May 1900
Took over specie. Mr Mansfield thinks it will have a good effect on the Dadiaso chief if he stays here instead of at Dadiaso, as the chief, in spite of all talking to, does little or no work on the doctor's house. Chief came over later to beg Mansfield to return to Dadiaso, promising to work.

22 May 1900
Left for Amoya and, as I do not think it is quite safe to travel alone with specie, have taken Mansfield with me. Men's quarters finished here. Gave orders that they and O in C are to be living on station by the time I return. River much swollen.

24 May 1900
Fined all officers 5/– for not having completed their quarters. Left for Kofi Akka Kru. Roads good. Rivers full. Was shown a most extraordinary place on the top of Kwamiamma hill. Said to be old sacrificial spot. Cliff is cut off suddenly and takes a sheer drop of at least 200 feet, I should imagine. Hear that Captain Hobart has caught grandson of late Ashanti king and also some others who had been to French territory for powder etc.

25 May 1900
Reached Debisu. Nothing has been done since I left to new customs house. Order chief to forward loads, which have arrived for DC. Says will try to do so, but is afraid as he has heard road blocked, or about to be, by Ashantis at Essaikumakru, a place one day's journey from here. Chief of this village is in town and he informs me that he and his people all cleared out four days ago, as they had heard Ashantis meant to close road to stop loads and mails passing up to DC. He says news has been brought to him by passing rubber people from Thafo or Aikrodia who were clearing out from there.

26 May 1900
Got DC's loads off, and sent him word as to rumour of intention of closing road behind him. Investigated case where O in C had seized man for Sunday gin selling. Warned him and let him go.

Quitta, Eastern Province

(i) Arthur Covey, DC, 1902[16]

30 July 1902
Arrived in Quitta[17] coming from Accra, via Akuse and Mlefi, taking eight days.

1 August 1902
Took over from Assistant Colonial Surgeon Dillon. DC Edwards then being in station, incapacitated from work.

4 August 1902
DC Edwards taken on board *Ekwanga*. Invalided to England.

22 August 1902
Waiting here for telegraph poles [which arrived on 24 August 1902]. Dismissed Inspector of Nuisances, being a worthless and useless man. The district, though on the boundary of German territory, I found to be without flags. I ordered eight to be sent and supplied one to a new flagstaff erected by Mr Wren. The flag was on the fort. One to Danoe and the remainder I am taking with me to the boundary when on tour. Gave instructions to Dr Robertson to see to sanitation and general health of officers and town and to look after scavengers. On about 13 August I had a petition sent me by the merchants of the town, praying that I would write to HE, the Ag Governor, asking for inspectors of produce to be appointed. I understand that, at Lomé, these inspectors were appointed, and the natives much resent the examination of kernel bags and had threatened they would come to Quitta in preference to Lomé. I refused to bother HE for the following reasons. (1) It was my duty to encourage produce being brought to Quitta and to do the opposite to what they had done at Lomé. (2) The firms that wrote were German firms, one English firm alone (Swanzy's) being operated by a German, the Germans being anxious to take trade from here to Lomé. I therefore called the chiefs of Quitta together and told them that I had no intention of sending the application to HE, but should do so, unless there was a great improvement in the kernels, no adulteration. The chiefs gong gonged next market day and produce has improved.

26 August 1902
Head agent of Swanzy's badly needed here. Swanzy's seemingly treating this place as unimportant. Mischief is done to British trade by having head of firm of Swanzy's a German. From enquiries made, little enough produce is brought to Swanzy's when Schemiks is here.

People boycott him. Chiefs admit that Schemiks is doing his best to get trade to Lomé.

Anyako, 17 September 1902
Stayed night, went to town in evening. Anyako full of pigs and manure. Town filthiest I have seen in the Colony. Interviewed Tengay who promised to remedy. The whole way upcountry was begged to permit purchase of guns and gunpowder. Was advised that Lomé has increased owing to natives being able to purchase there. Grumbles by natives that Germans ill treat British subjects if they try to bring produce down here. Asked for specific persons and charges to be brought to me at any time. I consider a road ought to be made right across top of boundary.

23 September 1902
DC Covey on sick list, 26th and 27th, with congestion of liver.

Generally
My activities since leaving Accra and as soon as I had gained a little knowledge of the Quitta district, its chiefs and people, was to draw the produce from Lomé to the Quitta and Danoe districts. This I have frequently rubbed into the chiefs of Quitta, who I have found most loyal, intellectual and always ready to listen to reason. I have received great assistance from them and especially from Chief Tengay of Anyako, a chief who has a deal of power having many towns under him.

Whilst in Quitta in the months of August and September, I noticed the quality and quantity of produce being brought there had improved, and so made a third tour of inspection up and across country, visiting firstly Chief Tengay, who I instructed should meet me at Dsoji in a few days. All the chiefs of this district, I may add, are the most friendly disposed people I have yet found in the Colony. They are loyal, helpful and realize all that will ultimately be for their and their people's benefit. They all have a horror of ever becoming German subjects and are proud of being governed by the British. I nevertheless think that if either of the two kings or the head chiefs in this district were at any time dealt with without using tact and without diplomacy, the DCs' orders might then become of no effect to them and the consequences of this would be general disobedience to all orders.

Before travelling and whilst at Quitta I sent out Union Jacks to be hoisted. If, in going through a subchief's or chief's town, I find anything wrong I report it to the head chief and require it remedied. If I find a chief's orders are not obeyed then I either deal with it myself or find that it is dealt with by the chief or king. My system has been that, after adopting this mode of dealing with the natives, my wishes and orders are either acted upon or obeyed; it gives the king or head chief greater powers. They appreciate the honour; one often gets from them useful information and often is advised upon native customs interfering with a wish for something to be or not to be done, which latter one might often go bald headed against. By using these means, in this district, I find there are fewer stalling cases. I have been able to get sailing across the lagoon with the produce brought down, more being brought into Quitta and Danoe and less of its going to Lomé from English territory. Further, I have all chiefs of the townships in the Quitta district doing all in their power to encourage the growth of produce for the future. All chiefs, one and all, are more loyal and more friendly disposed than hitherto, paying me the greatest respect and doing things to carry out my wishes that one could really only expect to be thought of by the most intelligent and highly educated of natives.

Speaking generally of the native of this district, he is in times of peace a farmer but in warfare a born soldier. As a farmer, he considers where he can get the best price for his produce, generally he finds at Lomé, and so goes there with it. Sometimes it's Danoe, sometimes Quitta, but the merchants of neither place appear not to consult what Lomé is paying for any of its things and advise the kings or head chiefs they will give more. Even the DC is not advised. The surf at Danoe is, I understand, nearly always bad, likewise the same at Lomé, as is not the case at Quitta and in consequence the latter can more often ship than either of the former. Many natives prefer Quitta on the other hand to Danoe, for they can get nearly all they require, excepting the everlasting requirement, namely being able to purchase guns and powder, which I have already recommended should [be] permitted on the east side of the Volta, but which [I] am told was already decided against in May or April 1901 by HE the Governor. For this district I think a DC should be appointed to travel, for there is no work to do at Quitta that a doctor cannot do; but let that DC first become acquainted with the chiefs of Quitta, and particularly Chief James Ocloo, who is always willing to help or advise.

Travelling, 7 October 1902

Arrived from Quitta at Anyako. At Aferingba, I noticed that the five-franc German piece, known as the koppre by the natives, was very much in use. Doubtless, there being no silver coin less than 3*d*., they find they have to buy more than they want, for no change can be given.

11 October 1902

I examined each [chief] as to the missing Union Jack. Baja (chief of) by name Dogble said he had sent it to Baja where he had put it up, that the German soldiers had come and taken it away. Informed him that could not be so, as he would not dare go into German territory and that the flag must be brought to me by Tuesday evening. He said he was sure he could not get it as he had sent it to the chief the Germans had put in his place, that the soldiers had really taken it away, that the chief had put it up, for he was so glad to be under that flag.

13 October 1902
Heard that the Dsoji market, held this day, was the biggest ever known. Examined produce and found kernels to be very much better. Found plenty of oil going to the Coast towns. There is an advantage in that the Germans do ill-treat their subjects in as much as the people here are most subservient, owing to the fear that they may become Germans. Or it may be that they think the British may carry out the Germans' policy, but this latter I am disinclined to think.

In evening, a carrier of mine had seized a chicken after paying for it. I was in bed and heard a rush. I went into the town to find many natives with knives, so gave an order that anyone who had unsheathed his knife was to be arrested. Three were captured and brought to the rest house, where they remained for the night, the chief of Dsoji next morning coming in to bail them out. I told him they were under arrest for intending to stab, that this was one of the things I had spoken to his king about and he had heard from his king, therefore I would send the case to be heard by the king and there they were sent. I afterwards being informed by the king's linguist and police that they had been dealt with according to native custom (fined so much rum each). The result of this was that I saw no natives for the rest of my tour with knives.

15 October 1902
Examined boundary tree, having marks as under, looking towards the southeast. About half an hour's walk from Dogplala.

BC (Boundary Commission)
German Commission (Marcus Pfeil) MP (Emil Kuster) EK English Commission (C. Rigby Williams) CRW (H. M. Hull) HMH
27 February 1892

Dogplala, 15 October 1902
Chief Ahialey having died on 10 September last, his son was previously accepted to be stooled. A ring formed by natives. Their head chief and chiefs of various towns sitting either on the ground or on a stool. First, the head chief calls upon all the persons of town to stand

aside if they agree to the new chief being appointed. He calls to them 'Do you agree?' Yes all are glad. Then the women of the town are called to 'Do you agree?' 'Yes we are all glad.' Head chief then puts to the assembly 'I am going to place a new chief over this town to be under, firstly the DC, as representing the government here, then secondly me.' Head chief then calls for a linguist to be appointed. The linguist to the late Chief Ahialey, by name Narkay, is then appointed. A stool then is called for by head chief to place new chief upon. Whilst this is coming, head chief gives new chief advice, telling him he is to belong to no fetish. Head chief, when stool is brought, calls for a tribe to be selected for the new chief. Several people go away for purpose of deciding as to tribe and who shall be his 'play mate' (from the tribe to be selected), to teach him the tribe's ways.

An old man comes to the head chief's linguist and says 'Ga tribe selects Authu To.' Head chief's messenger sent Chome to select more. A man of Addah tribe also selects Apia. This man, as others, 'to assist new chief, to give his house and family should the chief want them and to be of help to him in all his judgements'. The new chief is then put on the stool and is held up in a sitting posture, lowered and brought up again, but not to touch the stool until about the fifth time when he is bumped with it. Chief's name Gli, born at Dogplala, a son of Chief Ahialey, deceased, of about 18 years of age. Then witnesses are called up to make the final selection of the tribes selected and to hear the tribesmen appointed as councillors, who are sworn to look after the chief and do all things for his good. Then the head chief's linguist says the new chief will be blessed, and one of the head chief's tribe called Amlada is called out to bless the new chief, who he afterwards tells to keep all the rules of government. Then the head chief calls for the new chief's grandfather's name (Abofia) and the new chief is sworn on his name, that he is to be obedient and do all things good, that if a DC sends for him, he must at once start without delay. That he is to carry out in the best possible way all that the DC advises him, that he is to stop his people using knives, cudgels, cutlasses and guns and to trust some white men (note the some).

This procedure is done by Amlada standing up, the boy being seated on his stool. Amlada holding, with two outstretched hands a cutlass covered in a cloth, when all being finished placing the cutlass across the new chief's knees. Following upon this, the different tribes come and swear him in the same way. His next of kin and the next to the stool goes through the same formality, being sworn in as subchief (Koko Sey). Then the head chief addresses the tribes and councillors and tells them to obey their new chief in all things. The head chief's linguist then gets up and calls for all the chiefs of the head chief to appear before the head chief to know their new chief. [Follows list of 13 chiefs and names of their towns. Five have German written beside their names.] One by one these men have filed up. Whilst these are preparing, the new chief is greased all over by two of the priests, then the new chief is carried shoulder high with yells from all around. After being taken away, the head chief and new chief came to me and the new chief said he was placed in my hands. He intended doing all for the government, he would endeavour to prevent produce being taken from the Colony to Togoland, that he would obey all summonses and govern his people faithfully and will finally endeavour by all means to get his town, a large one, larger than Big Dogplala which belongs to the Germans and is within half an hour of the English Dogplala. The head chief asked if I would then address the new chief, which I did.

Left Dogplala that night, reaching Dsoji at 10.45 p.m.

20 October 1902

Interviewed Chief Feth of Aflao, who had written that at Halsovfei the Germans were stationed, that soldiers had come armed there to turn the chief and people out because they wouldn't fly the German flag, saying they would only fly the English. Informed him I could do nothing as they were not under my ruling. As he was chief over them, they of course might come to Aflao for protection where they would be under British flag. The chief referred to produce going to Lomé and said some must do so, for there are more stores there, and he asked for more firms to be at Danoe. From the factories heard that produce had been coming in very well indeed during the last 14 days and that it was very much on the increase. Copra is also coming in now. All seemed pleased.

Danoe, 22 October 1902

A case against the Bremen factory was this day to have been heard by me. Mr Quistu, for the factory, appeared and I told him I was by no means anxious to do anything that might prevent competition for produce coming into Danoe. He advised that cotton was of no use for the natives to grow, that only 1*d*. was given for each pound. He advised that Lomé was doing very well through cocoa, which was being planted here, there and everywhere and great results were expected, for natives were appointed to teach the people how to grow it and then these people were going about the Colony teaching others. Cocoa would, in my opinion, grow well in this district, but I do not know personally how to tell them what to do, so have not at present mentioned it.

23 October 1902

By private information Lomé merchants say that produce is not coming in as it used, and they are now going to put up prices. Hear they do not appreciate the work done by me and will be glad to see my back and a DC who doesn't travel.

Aflao, 25 October 1902
Went as far as boundary pillars, which are about two and a half feet in height. The German one stands about 33 feet off the English. Both are in oblong shape. There would appear to be no such place as Dogbor Koffi, for the chief doesn't know the name and neither does anyone else. It is hard to decide the real boundary and I should like to ask HE the Governor whether the boundary could not be properly shown by having a road cut straight to the different points where the road is. From this point, it could reach the Poglu–Wenchi Road to Danoe, and at Whengi I would suggest a boundary road being made to Dogplala. By having these boundary roads, I firmly believe we should get a lot of German produce, for the Germans could not stop their people coming through the many bush paths, that would be open, from the various villages on the German side. Moreover, nearly all the towns are under either Chief Tengay, the King of Agbosome and the chief of Aflao and these chiefs could, and would, encourage their chiefs on the German side to bring their produce here. If this was done then doubtless HE would consider the matter of having Aflao instead of Danoe as the government seat, thereby producing three produce towns on the Coast. There is no doubt that Danoe and Aflao markets hold the greatest produce of the whole district of Quitta.

Sunday 26 October 1902
Addaffia to place a new chief on stool. King of Agbosome with all chiefs and people of the town gathered in the marketplace. King says I am leaving with my councillors to adjourn and consult among us and the people of this town who to place on the stool. Adjourned accordingly to return in about half an hour. His head linguist gets up and declares to the king that they and the people have selected a chief. They consider the next heir to the stool (a boy of about four years) is not the proper person. They have chosen Sosu, who will respect the king, who will be all things good and do all things for the government. Sosu is a big man amongst the natives and has a lot of power with them, being a big fetishman. I think he has as much power as the king himself. Sosu is a dealer in produce and well known by the factories as hating the Germans and never trading with them. Several more linguists get up and declare allegiance to the king. Then the king addresses him and asks me to advise him, which I do. The king announced all was now finished. I remarked that I should wish the chief placed on the stool according to native custom.

The king came across to me and said (I think this to try my hand and see whether I was weak and could be got over). 'Many of my people are here, and they all want rum, which is necessary according to native custom.' I informed him I was not prepared to dash any persons rum, that after the chief had been stooled, according to native custom, doubtless they had a custom of rum drinking but never at the actual stooling, so he must proceed to put him on the stool. He said, 'I have been asked by you to come here, and I have come, and I want rum.' I informed him he was not asked, he was ordered, that if the chief chosen was not placed on the stool, according to native custom, I should not recognize him as representing the government, but to be nothing other than an ordinary person and not as a chief. [I said] that I knew too well that chiefs placed on the stool by the government alone did not look up to and uphold their king; neither did they respect him, neither did they obey him. [I pointed out] that the under chief to a chief placed on the stool by government did not likewise uphold that chief, [that] that chief was known as a government chief and had to refer all things to the government, [and] that he couldn't get assistance from king or chief. I again advised him to proceed, and to this he said, 'You speak right, it is true what you say. It is good, I will proceed.'

Sosu is then taken to the king by his hands. The linguist informs the king that, 'Here is the man, he places his hands in yours.' He then left and walked across to me and held both hands closed. I was asked to take his wrists. I took them and held them and he said, 'Without my hands I am no good. I give my wrists so that you possess all.' He then goes back to his seat and the linguist gets up and calls for the late chief's jewellery, stool, hat and shoes, and whilst these are being fetched the new chief chooses his tribes as follows: Batti, Towa, and Lape. Cutlass, hat, slippers and stool are brought, and the new chief is bumped into the stool. The late chief's linguist, one of his tribesmen, then hands him the slippers, holding them in his hands, and saying that these slippers belonged to the dead man and he stood with them, so you will stand. The slippers are then placed on his feet. I give you this hat. The hat is held in the linguist's hands, whilst he stands bowing. It is waved, about five times, across the linguist's face, and finally the brim is touched by the linguist's forehead and then again waved and is finally placed on the new chief's head, the linguist saying, 'I give you this hat that you may prosper. I give you this cutlass that you may look after yourself.' Then he is kissed and sworn in. Then the tribesmen, each one by one, comes and advise that where the new chief goes they will go, that they will always protect him and do all things for his good. The new chief is lifted from the stool and carried shoulder high, that he shall he shown to all people that he is chief. A song is sung of praises and stooling ends.

26 October 1902
Inspected Swanzy's factory, and find they had all things that natives were likely to want in the way of clothes, tobacco, milk, etc.

Danoe, 27 October 1902
The telegraph poles, newly erected, will soon rot, they are already cracking, and the tar can be taken off by one's nail. Addaffia chief, Sosu, came to me, and said he wanted to make, at his own expense, the road from Addaffia to Danoe. He promised to increase the produce, and do all things for the DC. That he had an idea a factory at Addaffia would do well, and he would see if he could not get one there. He seemed highly delighted he was made chief, thanking me for all I had done, and saying he would never forget what the government, and his king had done.

Black Volta, North Western District

(i) Captain B. H. W. Taylor, Ag DC, 1906[18]

29 April 1906
Arrived Wotuma at 1.30. This natural fortress is celebrated as having withstood the siege of Babatu for six months, only having to surrender from starvation. During the siege 100 towns took refuge within its walls, and in various villages I have seen survivors who have been captured and sold by Babatu to the Ashantis, who have since been able to return to their country.

30 April 1906
I marched next morning at 5.45 arriving at Mamadowki at 7.00 a.m. It was Mamadowki's first visit from a European. The people were very friendly, bringing milk and *pito* etc. for the soldiers and carriers.

1 May 1906
I delayed starting early owing to a deputation arriving from Dasima. This deputation stated they had heard that the boundaries of the different kings were being settled and that the villages of Samambaw, Gigan and Sekai would be included in the kingdom of Dasima. I informed them that this could only be done in a big palaver at which the paramount chiefs of Dasima, Walembele and Issa were present, and that I would look into the matter on my return to Wa. I marched at 2.30 p.m. arriving at Hiel at 4.15, a flourishing village in the fork of the boundary stream between Dasima and Zini. There was a prayer

ground here, but the people are now all fetish. Hiel had made the road into Jefisi. This was the village's first visit from a European. Leaving here at 4.30 p.m. crossed the other branch of the fork and arrived 5.40 at Zini, a large scattered town, excellently wooded. Very good camping near the king's compound. I was met by the king, who had only just returned to his town.

2 May 1906
I had a most satisfactory palaver at 9.00 a.m. Present the King of Zini and his chiefs, and representatives of Dua and Sugu being present, in fact every town in Zini. I explained to the King of Zini, in full palaver, the paramount importance of prompt obedience to orders, that you [the CC] had gone away without his coming to see you and that necessarily you had relegated him to a very minor position and all the big kings and chiefs had come to greet you wherever you had gone. The palaver was such a representative one, however, that I promised to use my good offices to restore him to your favour. I then preached on the labour crusade, which was attentively listened to, also the necessity of great care in appointing new chiefs. A noticeable industry in Zini is weaving, every compound having one or more looms.

I left Zini at 2.30. Arrived Nyettor at 3.45 – a flourishing village with a most friendly chief. I had talk with his people about labour, and was able to point a moral and adorn my tale by the presence of some local men in gorgeous robes who had returned from trading in Kintampo, who supported my statement as to the money to be made.

3 May 1906
I marched at 5.45 and arrived at Nandaw at 9.05 a.m. In the afternoon I had a very well-attended palaver and spoke very strongly to the king and his people about the necessity of the Dagartis coming into line with the other people of the NT. [I said] that at present they were the only people who systematically ignored the orders of the white man, and if they did not improve we would have to hand the country over to sensible chiefs whom we could trust to help us.

4 May 1906
This morning I was told that the King of Ulu had come in with his six brothers at 1.30 a.m., having decided, in spite of his people's position, to come in to Nandaw to see the white man. Kombiri the fetish king's hand being thus forced, he followed shortly after him with his adherents, thus solving the Ulu problem for me. I sent for King Seidu of Ulu and asked him how it was that he had not come to greet you at Nandaw. He said that the Kombiri people had told him not to go; that they finally had come and found us gone. I warned a palaver for

9.30 a.m. for both Ulu and Nandaw. I heard seven court cases in the afternoon, two of them being against Chipori people who had refused to obey my summons. These men, I made Nandaw send for, as it was one of his villages. He fetched them in, much against the grain and I found, when hearing these cases, that the plaintiffs had several times been to the king, but that he had ignored the complaints, the defendants being his relatives. The *limam*, the king and a large crowd listened to the hearing of these cases, which were, as usual, mostly connected with the fair sex. The *limam* at the finish remarked that the white man's law was the law of the Koran. The majority of these cases had already been brought before the king who had shelved them. I gave him the strongest warning that I would watch him very carefully and if I found the same state of things on a future visit he would be sent to Gambaga and a king appointed who would act up to his position.

5 May 1906

I had intended a night march to arrest the chief of Mankuru and the people who had beaten my messengers and sent them back to me with insults, but judged it better, having effected a peaceful capture of Kombiri and his people, to proceed direct to Ulu, where I hoped to have a good palaver. I marched accordingly at 6.40 a.m. crossing a small stream at 7.30 and arriving at a fair-sized village, Hyan, at 7.45. The chief came to meet me, and had sent his son out on a horse some way to do so. I left here at 8.00 a.m., arriving at Chipori at 8.45. Had to send for the chief who was very old, imbecile and apparently the feeblest man in the village.

Left here at 9.00 a.m., arriving at Gurri at 9.40 a.m. The people did not run away, but hid in their huts. I had to send three messengers for the chief before he appeared. I took him with me into Ulu to teach him manners, and as an object lesson for the palaver, under the heading of incompetent chiefs. Leaving here at 9.55, I arrived at Toapari at 10.45. Finding another imbecile old chief, and his heir a worse imbecile, old and with Saint Vitus's dance, I brought in the next claimant to the stool, the chief's son, who was a young man and fairly intelligent, to Ulu.

A most cheering incident was the arrival in the afternoon of the King of Zini and three of his headmen to further question me on behalf of his people about the labour for the mines, and also to report that, in accordance with my instructions, he had heard and tried a case of assault. He had fined a young man (who was drunk) for hitting an old man on the head with a stick; 10/– he awarded the old man for damages; 10/– he fined the young man for impudence to himself. He came with the assailant's father to know if he was right. I told him that I could not have done better myself. I am very pleased with this king, he has evidently taken my speech to heart and means to follow my instructions. He is a youngish man and very keen, as he himself says, 'If my people do not like my words, I am young and strong and I do not fear to walk to Wa to ask the DC if I am right.' He asked permission to stay and hear the palaver the next day.

Accompanied by the king and mounted infantry as escort, I rode round Ulu early in the morning, visiting the compounds and telling the people there was nothing to fear, but that I wished to see them all at the palaver at 10.00 a.m. Ulu is a very scattered town of large communal compounds, thickly wooded so that it was very difficult to estimate its size. It took me, however, one and three quarter hours to ride round it. I found the Kombiri's compound was, as I would have expected, the most ruinous and dirty in the town. He would indeed have been a king after the Dagartis' own heart, opposed to all order and reform, and strenuous only in his opposition to work.

The attendance at the palaver at 10.00 a.m. was a gratifying surprise, about 300 people being present. I gave it to them very strongly on the necessity of making a national effort for improvement, and also about the need for good chiefs who will be obeyed and themselves obey their king. I was able, by examples present, to show them the absolute futility of electing useless men. When I had fairly shown to them their stupidity and their danger of being swamped by more intelligent tribes, I had Kombiri marched in. I made Seidu stand up and I then asked the people to choose their king, whether they would have Kombiri the fool, who did not believe in the power of the white man until he was caught, the fool who told them to cultivate only enough for their own needs and could not see that trade meant money, the fool who would not obey the king and had made a big people into a lot of leaderless compounds, the man who lived like a dog in a broken kennel etc. etc. or whether they would have Seidu, their rightful king, son of a big king who had fought and died for them, a man who the villages would follow, who would make them again into a big people and the man who the white man would help. I told the people that the choice was theirs, if they chose Kombiri he would go free. If they choose Seidu they would have to obey him. It was rather a critical moment, as I was not at all sure what effect my invective had had on them, but they plumped for Seidu to my relief. I then told the people that having shown that they were sensible I would tell them how to improve their country. Had they chosen Kombiri I would not have wasted my time on them. Then followed the labour scheme for the mines[19] and the restarting of the Ulu market.

In the afternoon I held court from 3.30. to 7.30. The natives, the ice once broken, flocked in with complaints and summonses, they evidently appreciate a judge who can enforce his decisions. The majority of the cases were demands for restitution of head money from parents. It seems a very common thing among the Dagartis to take head money two or three times over for their daughters. The lady, only staying a short time with number one, returns to her parental roof and soon departs with number two, who also pays head money for her. In no case was restitution made to the first husband by the father. I warned the people that this must cease, as it was perilously near slave dealing, and any such cases I meet with on a future visit would be severely dealt with. I had the King of Ulu and the *limam* of Nandaw with me as advisers in native law and custom. The court was never attended by less than 100 interested spectators, and where a *cause célèbre* was on, by many more.

7 May 1906
At the palaver the previous day was an imbecile in possession of a 'locket'[20] whom, after much questioning, I found had been sent in as the chief of Karni. It was impossible to discover how he obtained the locket, who was king or what was their country. Seidu, King of Ulu, told me that the Karni people had formerly followed his father. At 7.00 a.m. I sent Lieutenant Richardson to Karni to call the people together to discover their country, history and chief. At 2.00 p.m. he returned having had a successful meeting with the Karni people. He found that the locket had been given at Wa to the king, who was a very old man and bedridden, that the representative who had come to my palaver was apparently chosen on the Dagarti plan of selecting the village idiot as chief; he had no other apparent claim.

8 May 1906
I saw the Karni headmen, chiefs and representatives of Dir, Mankpwe, Jamfuri, Izia and Jimpari. They informed me they had considered my words, that they were good. They had elected a young man, Dapwor, to act as chief of Karni, that, as a nation, they wished to return to the King of Ulu, that they had heard he was to be a big chief. This was, I considered, most satisfactory, so I formally handed them over to Seidu and invested him with the locket. The King of Ulu pleaded for the release of the nine men, followers of Kombiri, saying that now Kombiri was broken he would answer for their good behaviour. I told the people that when a big king spoke the white man listened and, in celebration of the occasion, released them. Kombiri I have awarded six months' imprisonment with hard labour and a fine of £50. This punishment is only conditional on the good behaviour of his people in

Ulu. Should they still be refractory or not pay his fine, I have warned them that Kombiri will be sent to the CC for further punishment.

I marched at 7.15 a.m. by a good made road, passing the southernmost compound of Ulu at 8.15, arriving at Darieri, a small village, at 8.50 with a weak and foolish chief. Leaving at 9.00 a.m. I crossed the boundary stream between Ulu and Sabuli, halting at Sabuli market. The chief appeared an improvement on the usual Dagarti chief, being well dressed and fairly intelligent. There is a good market here. From Sabuli to Bussie. Bussie is a large town situated on high open ridges. I found the town in a state of chaos, there having been no properly elected king for three years. The town was divided up into three sections, each section having its own market and at enmity with each other. I collected the people and told them to elect a king.

9 May 1906
Rousing the MI and guides, a successful night's march was made to Mankuru, it being a complete surprise. We left Bussie at 1.45 a.m., arriving at Mankuru at 3.45 a.m., crossing a big stream with pools of water at the entrance to the village. Here, through a mistake of the guides, we had to recross the river about a mile and a half to the east. It was here about four feet deep, the horses only just being able to negotiate it without swimming. At two isolated compounds here we caught the men who had flogged the messenger, and some others who were present. Recrossing the river, we surrounded the chief's compound, making in all a capture of 20. No resistance was offered. The men, however, were most insolent, refusing to sell or give us corn for our horses. In the morning, I found the chief to be old, infirm and blind, so released him. We left Mankuru to return to Bussie at 5.10 a.m. The effect on the natives, who were just getting up, to our appearance with 20 prisoners was amusing and I think salutary. We having passed them by *en route* to Bussie, they imagined they had successfully defied the white man. Heavy rain from 11.00 a.m. to 5.00 p.m. delayed my palaver with Bussie until that hour. In spite of the rain, there was a fair attendance of 150. I gave them my usual set speech about the backwardness and misrule in Dagarti and had the 20 Mankurus marched in as an object lesson. I flogged the man who beat the messenger, also the men of the compounds who were present, giving the chief offender an additional six months' imprisonment with hard labour and fining the village £25 to be paid in three months. Towards the end of the palaver, some Mankuru representatives appeared, bringing with them a propitiatory cow and a newly elected chief. Truly the rule by force seems to be appreciated. A soldier whom I sent to Tizza to arrest a native, who had refused the summons to the

court, returned unsuccessful, having been met by arrows. He excused himself saying he had no orders to fire. It is impossible for me to include Tizza in my tour. It is plain that a flying visit would do more harm than good, and Dr Collier, whom I hope will proceed there on my return to Wa, will be able to obtain all the necessary information for the map. His enquiries into the sickness there should gain him the confidence of the natives and enable him to hold a successful palaver.

10 May 1906

Leaving [Ture] at 8.30, arriving at 9.30 a.m. at Daffiama, a big town. At both these places the chief had to be sent for, and on arrival proved to be utterly lacking in brains. Leaving Daffiama at 10.45 a.m. a flourishing village is reached at 12.15 – Tagillipieh. The king, an old man, was both friendly and intelligent and evidently formerly a powerful king as he is in possession of treaty of 1898 signed by Lieutenant Colonel Northcott[21] and Major Fortescue. Tangisa country had belonged to him, but as they were Lobis, was given up by order of the white man. He also had several villages, which are now under Cheripon. I had a palaver here, having sent for the Nadawle chiefs. It was fairly well attended. Nadawle possesses a large, good market, which is attended by many towns. Leaving at 6.40 a.m., I arrived at Tangisa at 7.30, the path passing through farms the whole way. I saw the King of Tangisa and defined his boundary. He used to have a stormy time before the arrival of the white man, being a Lobi colony situated between two Dagarti kingdoms. Leaving at 7.45 a.m., the path crosses some rocky hills, arriving at Nanga, shown as Cheripon on the map, at 9.00 a.m. Here I found that the people, with the exception of the king and a few others, had run away. I spoke most strongly to the king. He returned in about an hour's time saying I had shamed him and that he wished to cut his throat. I advised him to collect his people and commit a national suicide in the Volta River, leaving their country clear for better people. This evidently had the desired effect, as shortly afterwards his people returned and all through the night his chiefs were coming in.

12 May 1906

I held a fairly representative palaver at 6.00 a.m., giving the people a great warning as to their conduct and then gave them the labour scheme. I am not sure that amongst such savages as these, the idea of obtaining labour is not too advanced; they must first do some work at home. All through the Cheripon country there are no industries, trade, markets, or good roads. The people, who have a paying fishing industry at their doors, not only do not fish, but many who live within a few yards of the river have actually never been to see it. From my enquiries of the previous day I found that very few of the names on the maps could be identified.

General
I enclose the map, as added to, and wish to state that the greatest care has been taken with the spelling of the names, having as often as possible got Lieutenant Stewart Richardson to check my spelling. I am glad to report that the discipline and behaviour of the escort has been excellent.

What I may call the appalling state of savagery in Dagarti has been the cause of much thought and enquiries, as having reported such a backward state of things, I naturally wished to suggest a remedy for your consideration. I at first thought of proposing a scheme of importing chiefs and of starting settlements of their tribes, but finally came to the conclusion that the Dagarti must themselves supply the remedy, and that the remedy is compulsory education. I suggest Bussie as an admirable site for a settlement of the Pères Blancs. It is a very large town, well situated with a good water supply. Failing the white missionary, I propose, with your sanction, to immediately start Mohammedan schools at Bussie, Daffiama and Cheripon, making it compulsory for the children of the chiefs to attend. The cost of the schooling to be borne by the parents. Should this scheme meet with your approval, I will submit, after consultation with the leading *malam* of Wa, a programme of the proposed school's curriculum, cost and capacity. The existing school of Nandaw could be utilized for that kingdom and the neighbouring kingdom of Ulu.

I find that the southern Dagarti is behind his northern brothers and that, though a few sensible men are to be found on the caravan trade routes, in the outlying villages it is almost impossible to find a man capable of answering a question. Cheripon and the river villages are undoubtedly the most uncivilized people in the NT. These Dagartis will, for a considerable time, require great firmness in administration, as although they show fear on the arrival of the white man, they soon recover and are inclined to be very insolent. I think I can safely promise, on the whole, a fair return of labour for the lengthy crusade that has been preached in the district, and am sure that the visit of the delegates to the mines will rekindle their interest and have excellent results.

(ii) Captain B. Mountray Read, DC, 1907

16 February 1907
At Blon I found the people were putting out sentries on their roads at night to keep a watch in the town, to prevent Dagartis from bringing the sickness to their town. There had been some Ashantis here collect-

ing rubber, but I could not find out from any of the people how much they had collected. In fact, the chief took no interest in their doings at all and had apparently let them take the rubber for nothing. I informed him that he was not to allow anyone to collect any without my permission, and that permission would only be granted unconditionally on the men I allow to collect rubber teaching the natives how it is done. I consider that much harm can be done if vines are tapped indiscriminately before the most economical method of collecting has been ascertained and taught the natives.

17 February 1907
Leaving Blon at 3.45 a.m., I arrived at Nandom at 9.15. The road for the greater part of the way ran through hills and it is in these hills that the rubber vines grow, but though I kept a careful look out I am obliged to say I saw very little of it. In the afternoon I held a palaver at which about 150 people were present and among them eight chiefs, including the two paramount chiefs of Cherire and Lambusie. Owing to the meningitis having broken out in the south of Lambusie and some of the Nandom villages, many people did not come to the palaver. I told them here, as in other places, that isolation was the best advice I could give them to prevent the disease spreading. Both Lambusie and Cherire told me that their people wanted to go down to work in the mines, and I told them I would send to them for men when they were wanted. Both these chiefs had been into Lorha and are among the very few who supplied labour willingly to build that station. The labour representatives from this part of the country are considered quite important people by their neighbours now.

18 February 1907
Leaving Cherire at 5.00 a.m. I reached Panyani at 10 a.m. and, after an hour's halt here I went on to Lorha. The site of the station is a commanding one and the only fault lies in the distance from the river, from which water has to be got. The wells that were sunk not being capable of supplying the necessary amount of water for brick and swish making. As they are at present they can be improved and more sunk, so there should be no fear of their not yielding a sufficient water supply at ordinary times.

The fort, with courthouse, stores, office, prison, treasury vault and a magazine was nearly completed as far as the brick and swish work. Taking into consideration the difficulty that Mr Jackson [ADC] has experienced in getting the natives to work, and the water difficulty, I consider that he has done very well to have got so much done in a month. The ADC's house was laid out and the walls in course of erection. It is perhaps on the large side considering the scarcity of good timber round Lorha. There are also some other villages that refuse to give any assistance, and it is necessary that Mr Jackson should himself visit these places and point out the futility of offering any resistance. In order to enable him to do this, I am sending Dr Palmer up on 1 March for two or three weeks to help him. A doctor is also required there, as there has been a lot of sickness in the station and this epidemic of meningitis may attack the town any time. During this tour I have heard of no less than 272 deaths from this epidemic of what appears to be undoubtedly cerebrospinal meningitis. In consequence of this disease, I have had continually to change my plans and have been unable to bring many chiefs in to palavers. I had hoped to have obtained promises from the chiefs to supply all the labour that will be required for the telegraph line, but I have only had about 300 promised and they cannot be collected till this disease has worked itself out, which it shows no sign of doing at present, for as soon as it is reported nearly finished in one place, it breaks out in another.

Notes

1. Rhodes House, Oxford, Mss. Brit. Emp. s. 314–18.
2. George Attrill, Comptroller of Customs.
3. Supervisor, Preventive Service.
4. Dr Dillon, attached to the army with the Hausa detachment.
5. Supervisor, Preventive Service.
6. Agents with Miller Brothers, commercial firm.
7. In 1900, the Preventive Service on the Western Frontier was in its infancy. The local chiefs and people were ordered to erect customs sheds and houses for the Preventive Service officers. They were paid for this work, but in many instance somewhat grudgingly. The houses were made of swish, local earth mixed with water.
8. A light of sorts could be improvised by filling a cigarette tin with palm oil, with a wick made from a piece of rag dipped in the oil.
9. As early as 1891 H. M. Hull visited Kumasi as Ag TC.
10. Supervisor, Preventive Services.
11. See Appendix G.
12. Leggett and Armitage had been sent to an outlying village in Ashanti to look for the Golden Stool. They were ambushed by the Ashantis, but made their way back to the Kumasi fort. Armitage was slightly wounded, but Leggett died from wounds.
13. In 1900, Captain E. H. Hobart was DC for Sefwi and the Western Frontier District with headquarters at Wam where there was a small Hausa detachment under Dr Dillon.
14. Colonial Secretary.
15. GNA Accra, Sefwi, Bekwai, Native Affairs. No 11/644. The monthly report in the form of a diary was sent to the Comptroller of Customs, Accra, who sent it on to the Colonial Secretary.

16. GNA, Accra, Adm. 41/5/1.
17. Also spelt Kwitta, Kitta and Keta. Covey began by spelling it Quitta, but very soon after his arrival the form Keta was adopted. Similarly, Coomassie later became Kumasi.
18. Both Taylor's and Mountray Read's diaries are in GNA, Accra, Adm. 56/1/50.
19. Labour recruiting in the north for the mines in the Tarkwa–Prestea area started in 1906 when the Chamber of Mines approached the CCNT about the possibility of getting workers from the Protectorate.
20. In 1899, Major Morris, Ag Commissioner and Commandant, presented lockets containing a miniature of Queen Victoria to 91 chiefs of the NT, 'sent to them by the great white Queen over the sea'.
21. Major Northcott was appointed Commissioner and Commandant of the NT in 1897. His secret dispatches to the Colonial Secretary, Accra, sent from Gambaga, NT, in 1897/8 are in GNA Admin 11/1376. Thora Williamson reported that this file was in particularly poor condition and the handwritten paper very brittle.

3

Diaries, 1913–1919: The Colony

Accra, Eastern Province

(i) C. H. Harper, PC, 1914[1]

1 January 1914

I left Accra about 7.00 a.m. for Nsawam by road, about 20 miles. The glory of the Akim road, or rather the Accra–Nsawam portion of it, has departed. Very little traffic was met with. About six miles from Nsawam I passed some women carrying loads of tomatoes for Accra market. One of the party was communicative. She said she would sleep one night before she reached Accra, that sometimes she travelled by railway and sometimes she walked, and that she expected to get at least 30/– for her load, which seemed to weigh about 70 lbs. I passed some loads of palm fruit, which must have come from the immediate neighbourhood of Nsawam. The first cocoa was seen at a village called Play and Laugh, about half an hour's cycle ride from Nsawam. The road between Accra and Nsawam offered no difficulties and held few traps for the unwary cyclist. But certain portions of it required clearing and were in a state that would not have been tolerated on a chief's road.[2] The villages *en route* have lost the prosperous appearance they had some years ago and are now some of the dirtiest I have seen. I am instructing the DC to call in certain of the headmen and to impress upon them the duty of keeping their villages clean. The DC should later inspect these villages.

The rest house at Nsawam has a much more attractive appearance than when I saw it last. The front has been planted with Bahamas grass, which flourish exceedingly, and is pleasant to the eye. A vegetable garden should be a success. The quarters are usually occupied by the doctor and the TC, but if either is away, the vacant rooms are at the disposal of any visitor. The water tanks have not yet been supplied, though requisitioned, I believe, 12 months ago. Water is brought from the tank at the court in the town about a mile away, a not very satisfactory arrangement. In the afternoon I walked round the town with the TC. It has a bustling prosperous appearance, but though exceedingly clean and well kept is unsightly from the scours made in the streets by the rain. Many yards of cement drainage will be necessary to lead away the rainwater. The dustbins have never been used. A certain number of houses have been destroyed to open up the town and make new thoroughfares. The market, which at one time was held in the street, has now a new location to itself and is becoming popular. The Hausa *zongo* was well kept and was full of able-bodied men. I saw a number of Hausa carriers outside a pretentious house and was informed that they were one of the gangs of Solomon, who ships direct to Europe — 'Solomon's Fermented Cocoa'.

2 January 1914

In the company of the TC I bicycled in the morning to Adeisu and back, 24 miles. We intended to make an early start, but could not get away before eight, as there was some delay in getting water from the town for our ablutions. Adeisu is a small and untidy village, but of some importance as the buying centre for cocoa. The Accra–Kumasi road passes close by, and possibly some produce finds its way to Accra by that road. I spoke to the chief's representative, who is an Akwapim man. The chief is rarely here. He leaves the village to be managed by the Akwapim 'who knows how to talk to Akwapims'. There was the usual complaint that people turned a deaf ear to the instructions of the headman. They did not help to clean the streets, fouled the drinking water and put up houses without regard to streets. Permission to build, or rather a grant of land, is obtained through the headman from the chief of Asamangkese. Some streets have been laid out by the TC, and though overgrown they have not been encroached upon. The water is becoming a difficult matter at present, as the river bed is dry and there are only a few pools. A butcher established himself in the village and kills sometimes, one or two cows a week.

A native court is required at Nsawam, but there appears no one qualified to hold it. If Kwesi Ampeh has only eight followers he is hardly likely to make a success of a court. It is an important matter and one that should be considered when the Native Jurisdiction Ordinance is being amended — how native courts are to be appointed in villages that have grown to importance in recent times, but where originally there has been no one resident with powers under native custom to hold court. The indigenous population is small and the town owes its importance to the foreign element, the storekeepers, clerks, buyers etc., all comparatively well-to-do, together with the large floating population of carriers.

3 January 1914
This morning I bicycled to Asuboi and back, 25 miles. The road is in good condition until one approaches Asuboi. I interviewed the chief, and listened to the complaints of a man weary of governing. The scholars, the clerks, the buyers ignore him; they give him no assistance. They do not help him to clean the town, and when corrugated iron had to be bought to roof the latrines, they would not subscribe. The Hausas are unruly, they use the latrines as they like and throw rubbish where they please. He had recently bought land for a *zongo* for them, but they refuse to go there. The climax came when Kudjo, next in importance to the chief, gave him trouble and made a palaver. The chief thereupon handed over the town to one George, a Lagosian and agent for the Basel Mission factory, shook its dust off his feet and retired to his farm. Apparently, he was persuaded to emerge from his retirement and Ohene Kudjo paid him pacification, part of which he sent to the *omanhene*. But troubles came not singly, for the *omanhene* refused his share of the pacification, being angered at the hasty resignation, and so is the DC, Mr Phillips, and would I intercede. I condoled with him and said I would shortly be seeing Mr Phillips and the *omanhene*, and that in ten days' time would visit the town. The chief requires some assistance and possibly it may be necessary to put the village under the Towns Ordinance. I am not altogether in favour of placing isolated detachments of police in villages, certainly not unless they are frequently relieved and frequently inspected.

4 January 1914
I travelled by train with the TC to inspect New Mangoase. It would be ungenerous to criticize the state of the place when every living soul is working at high pressure, when such time as can be spared from cocoa is spent clearing the plot one has bought, or is building a tiny shanty, when between 2000 and 3000 carriers visit the place in the space of three hours each morning, and the efforts of a gang of seven scavengers under an illiterate headman are not likely to have lasting or conspicuous effect. The MO happened to be in New Mangoase and I found him optimistic. He is allowed more scavengers this year and a sanitary inspector is to have his headquarters in the town. The MO is certain that a good deal can be done, but I am afraid he has a hard task. New Mangoase has not and requires no frills. Its importance is due to the fact that, for the time being, it is the railhead. It will still continue to exist when the railway has advanced, but will not collect produce to anything like the same extent that it does now. I spent the night with Cozens-Hardy [Chief Railway Construction Engineer]. He is marvelling at his good fortune in being able to retain 3000 or 4000

labourers on the work during the height of the cocoa season. Credit must be due to the skilful and sympathetic handling of the men by the contractors.

5 January 1914
Cycled from New Mangoase to Adawso. The going was excellent, but until permanent bridges are constructed the road will not be suitable for motor traffic. Adawso, is a clean well laid out little town. A certain amount of its former trade is being diverted at Tingkong to New Mangoase by a bush path. It is thought, however, that a considerable amount of cocoa will still find its way to Adawso from Aburi and the Mampong slopes of the Akwapim hills.

6 January 1914
The Hausa chief came to pay his respects, and to promise assistance to government in the matter of carriers whenever he should be able to help. On leaving the town I saw Chief Asare, who asked for help in maintaining the bridges on the Komfrodua road. The bridges his people make are not strong enough for cask traffic. I promised to speak to the DC about the matter.

I bicycled to Okorase, eight miles. On the way I stopped at Tingkong and spoke to some of the buyers. They all appear to be of the opinion that Tingkong will remain a buying centre even when the railway is at Komfrodua, for a certain amount of produce will come from Kpong and its neighbourhood. I shall have to revise my opinion of the value of isolated detachments of police. I was informed that the police were useful at Tingkong and that it would be a mistake to remove them. Probably therefore they will be of some use at Asuboi. Cozens-Hardy told me that he experienced very great difficulty with the long string of carriers coming down the centre of the track to New Mangoase, that they made palaver with his labourers, and were quite undismayed at the rocks and stones hurtling through the air as blasting operations were in progress. Eventually, he asked for police and, to his disappointment, only one policeman was sent up, an escort policeman. But he sufficed to turn back the stream of 3000 or 4000 carriers a day who had thus to make a detour of four or five miles to get to New Mangoase. Considering they were almost within sight of their goal, and many were carrying double loads, this speaks well for the respect which the police, or some of them, can inspire.

In the afternoon I walked to the river to inspect the bridge erected by the Larteh Planters' Union. When the river is in flood the crossing is perilous and every year there is a toll of lives. Apparently, the government was unwilling to help in the matter, so some 30 natives subscribed for the cost of the bridge. They obtained the assistance of a

Mr Islaker, who for the past 20 years has resided in Mampong, and at one time had been connected with the Basel Mission. He is an engineer and the bridge is a fine piece of work. It is a braced bridge, about 75 feet space and rests on stone and cement abutments. It is constructed of odum and is roofed with corrugated iron. It looks solid and substantial. The cost, so the chief of Okorase told me, was £3000, probably an exaggerated statement. There has been some difficulty over the charges. When the river is in flood the charge is *6d.*, and when it is low 1½*d.* At the present moment no tolls appear to be charged, being forbidden, so the chief informed me, by the DC. After leaving the bridge I went along the railway track for about a mile where I found the engineer enquiring into a palaver between his labourers, NT men, and a neighbouring farmer. These complaints are enquired into on the spot and, if they are substantiated, compensation is given to the injured party. This arrangement appears to be satisfactory. It would mean great delay if the case had to be tried at Aburi, Adawso or Nsawam. A great deal depends on the contractor, whether he has much control over his men. New gangs give the most trouble, as they are apt to look upon the farms along the railway track as fair loot.

7 January 1914

In the morning I inspected land in dispute between two farmers, and the subject of appeal from the *omanhene*'s court. As New Juaben[3] has only been settled about 25 years, one would have thought it too early for land disputes to be at all numerous. The manner, however, in which the land was taken up was not calculated to make for peaceful tenure in the future. In the afternoon I saw the *omanhene* and discussed the question of land disputes among the New Juabens, the supervision of the cocoa instructors,[4] and the chiefs' conference. Among other things he brought to my notice was an application received from the New Juabens settled in the French Ivory Coast to come over to Komfrodua and settle in the neighbourhood. Their messenger had only recently arrived in the town and he was going to take council with his chiefs the following day concerning the application. There are a thousand or more people who want to come over. I told the chief that it was a delicate question and I would give him no encouragement. He could put the matter in writing for the Governor's consideration and must there let it rest.

8 January 1914

In the afternoon I inspected the court records of the *omanhene*. They were well kept and are interesting. The records of these native courts give one a good insight into the native method of thought and into native custom. Cyclists who run down people appear to be pretty severely dealt with. In one case, the injury was described as 'to wit, did severely cut his under lip and cause two of his teeth to shake, contrary to law'. One case was of exceptional interest. The 'young-men' of Affiduase passed a bye-law that their chief and elders were not to drink strong water. A breach of the law was committed and the chief was summoned, apparently in his own court and before his own linguist. The linguist found the 'youngmen' guilty, but they appealed to the *omanhene* who reversed the linguist's decision. He found that the chief had been drinking, fined him and delivered himself of a homily on the evils of drunkenness among chiefs. The last chief of Affiduase had been destooled for drunkenness and the 'youngmen' were determined that his successor should not follow in his footsteps.

9 January 1914
The Hausa butchers came to see me to ask for a paper saying that they were the persons to kill cows in Apedwa. Apparently, the Akims from time to time kill and sell in the market. The Hausas object to this as an infringement of their rights. I informed them that I was not prepared to give them, or anyone else a paper of the sort they asked for. Their spokesman, a truculent individual, who had spent some years in the neighbourhood of the mines, complained that they would have to leave if not properly treated. It would be a good thing for the *zongo* if that person did move elsewhere. He described the chief of the *zongo* as a 'damn fool' who drank too much. He would probably have made further revelations if I had not made him keep quiet.

12 January 1914
Had an informal and interesting interview with the *omanhene*. He considers Asuboi should be placed under the Towns Ordinance. The chiefs have great difficulty in dealing with foreigners, i.e. natives who are not natives of the Gold Coast or its dependencies. They do not come within the scope of the Native Jurisdiction Ordinance and can defy the chief and his bye-laws. He desires a government school for Eastern Akim, and I think this request should be considered. I discussed with him the fining of persons for selling undried cocoa. He was aware that the bye-laws had been disallowed, but claimed that he had power to fine for 'disobedience of the lawful orders of a head chief'. Lastly he submitted some bye-laws recently passed by his chiefs. Their object is to control the alienation of Eastern Akim land. It is provided that no transfer of stool land by a chief, headman, etc. shall be valid unless approved, and the deed witnessed by the *omanhene* and his councillors. The *omanhene* again pressed his point that their land was their own and once the tribal representative had given a decision no

one else had any concern or interest in the matter. I told the meeting that I would think the matter over. As I left, the *omanhene* suggested that an appeal to the DC might be desirable, but that his decision should be final.

I much regret that my tour of Eastern Akim must be postponed. So far, I am inclined to form a high opinion of Ofori Atta. He is the only chief I have ever met who appears to understand to the full the possibilities of his position, and to have the ambition to realize them. If he can keep his head, and his stool, he will be the biggest figure in native policies the Colony has yet seen. He has taken over the sanitation of Kibbi, has his own road inspectors and, as time goes on, will take upon himself other administrative duties.

16 January 1914

Both yesterday and today I have had long talks with Ballantine over his district affairs. He has a very difficult district to manage, but I feel he has a thorough acquaintance with all its needs, and I consider he has very capably administered its affairs. Here is a very good illustration for keeping a DC in one and the same district, for Ballantine, now in his third tour, has spent all his service in the Gold Coast as DC of Akwapim.

I had an interview with the chief of Dawu. There were many indictments against him, both by his immediate superior, the *nifahene* and by the DC, for example absence from his town, neglect of his roads and his town, and impertinent replies to requests from the DC or *nifahene*. He was a better looking type than I expected, and perhaps something can be made of him. I gave him a grave warning and made him understand, I hope, that it was a warning. He explained that he had now been suspended by the *nifahene*, expressed his regret that he should have been considered impertinent, promised amendment and asked for assistance. He also added, which was quite what I expected, that his youngmen are 'proud' and would not listen to him. I told the chief to give orders to his youngmen, and if the orders were ignored to summon the youngmen to his court, and I promised that the DC should sit with him to show that the government was on his side. Lastly, I told him to go back to his town and govern it.

17 January 1914

The chief of Tutu came up this morning before me. He is never in his town, his roads and the sanitation of his town are neglected. For most of the year he has been in Accra in connection with law cases. Here again is a man we might make something of. I gave him some advice and promised to visit his town. He also told me that his youngmen were proud. I gave him the same advice as I gave the chief of Dawu. If his youngmen disobeyed him he should summon them to his court and, if he wished, the DC would sit with him.

18 January 1914
I took advantage of a day off to go to Accra and visit Manche Tackie. I spoke to him about the chief's conference. I promised to inspect the records of the Accra native courts on my next visit. And I promised to ask the Director of Agriculture to visit him and advise him as to the possibility of establishing plantations of coconut trees on his stool land round Accra.

20 January 1914
Dealt with files and correspondence. Issued a circular to DCs suggesting that from time to time they should sit with chiefs in native courts, especially in sanitary and road cases.

21 January 1914
In the morning prepared a mail for Kpong. In afternoon bicycled with the DC to Mampong. On the way I stopped at Tutu. Spoke to the chief and youngmen about their roads and the state of the town, and promised them a supply of tools. The town is very dilapidated and not to be compared with Akim or Akwapim towns. The inhabitants have not the best of reputations and the chief does not seem strong enough to do much with them.

22 January 1914
Proceeded to Akropong and on the way was stopped by the chief of Amanokrum. He complained that his youngmen do not help him to clean the roads and that he has had to hire Krepi labourers to do the work. Lunched at Akropong and in the afternoon went to Adukrum. On the way I stopped at Dawu, saw the chief, took him round his town and pointed out to him what was needed to make it cleaner and addressed a warning to the youngmen. The town is more dilapidated than Tutu and no credit to the wealthy natives of Akwapim. Returned to Akropong for the night. In evening I discussed several matters with the *omanhene*.

23 January 1914
In the morning I visited Larteh. It is the largest town in Akwapim. Its mud huts, which do duty for houses, are huddled together. There is only one street and there is no marketplace. I went round and inspected both Upper and Lower Larteh. They are not on good terms with one another. Later I had a long talk with the chief of Lower Larteh. He wished for government assistance to improve his town. I told him to consult with his elders and put forward a scheme and

show what assistance they themselves were prepared to give. He considered there was no objection to demolishing huts and no difficulty in obtaining land for building. I told him I would ask for an engineer to help him as soon as they could convince me that they were going to do something to help themselves. After seeing the town I am not surprised to find Larteh people settling elsewhere.

Returned to Akropong for lunch, and then had a long interview with the *omanhene*. He complains that his subchiefs are coming to regard themselves as independent. He can hardly get them to meet together. His remedy to reduce the pride of the youngmen is the custom of their forefathers, flogging. He complained that his chiefs did not render him his share of oath fees, nor did they communicate to him important matters affecting their districts. He was inclined to be despondent about the outlook for Akwapim. There was too much independence; his people were migrating into other native divisions and he wanted to retain their allegiance. Inspected the prison and found everything in order. Returned to Aburi in the evening. Found a letter from Phillips saying he was travelling at once to Kwaku, where trouble was brewing over the election of a chief of Obomeng, and asking if he might detain the troops in Kwaku if necessary. Sent instructions to him and to the officer commanding the column proceeding to Kwaku.

26 January 1914

Left for Dodowah and arrived at one o'clock. After lunch inspected the rest house site. It is a considerable way from the town and perched on top of a steep hill. Carriers will require 1/– a load to carry loads there. The house now rented for a rest house is, in my opinion, suitable and I have recommended its purchase. The new post office is well under way and will be a fine building. The new market site is an admirable one. It is highly desirable that the sheds should be erected at once. The Hausa *zongo*, which on my last visit was a collection of charred ruins, for it had suffered severely from fire, is gradually being restored and corrugated iron is being largely used for roofing in place of thatch. Charway, the chief, asks for a message stick and a summons book.

31 January 1914

I spent the morning in visiting the Ga *manche*'s court and looking at his records. The books were well kept. As there was an oath case to be heard, I accompanied him to the meeting in the open street not far from the market. I spent an hour there, the *manche* acting as interpreter to me. The court consisted of about a dozen members. They put many shrewd questions to the parties and witnesses. I left with the impression that substantial justice would be done. The views of the majority of the court decides the issue.

2 February 1914
Spent the morning with the DC Accra. I consider his office over staffed. I had an interview with Hammond, second-grade clerk. He is 64 years of age and all the work he does is to act as Hausa interpreter. I have suggested to him that he should apply for his pension. I also attended and gave evidence before the committee considering leave regulations for native staff. Cycled back to Aburi in the afternoon.

4 February 1914
Had an interview with the PE about public works in the province. I spoke about cocoa instructors. He had sent, the day before, two of his people to be trained by the Agricultural Department for he had heard some 'foreigners' had been receiving instruction. I explained the idea of cocoa instructors and told him to apply through the *omanhene* for his two men to be trained, and I would recommend the application. I am very glad to have had the opportunity of studying Akwapim affairs on the spot. The district is not an easy one to administer, but the government is fortunate in being able to place the same DC in the district year after year. Thanks to the increase in wealth arising from the cultivation of cocoa, there is a spirit of independence spreading about the division, which is not necessarily a bad sign. The chiefs, however, will need sympathetic support and that means the presence of a DC they know and who knows them. The position of subordinate chiefs has certainly been strengthened by the Native Jurisdiction Ordinance, and the head chiefs it may be are losing influence and prestige.

5 February 1914
I bicycled to Kpong, 32 miles. I was glad to observe at Tutu and Dawu, whose chiefs I had warned some weeks before, the towns had been cleaned up and the weeds cut down. At Kpong I met Taylor on his way back to Anum, and I discussed several matters with him. He wants imprest[5] authority to purchase furniture, permanent carriers, flags, handcuffs and so on. In most of these things I can satisfy him. He is very keen on his work and I hope to visit him shortly at Peki. No report yet from Phillips as to affairs at Obomeng, so I have decided to send bailiff, Owusu, who, I have noticed, has done long distances by cycle, to take a letter to Phillips. Owusu tells me that by leaving tomorrow, he will get to Kwaku in two days and will be back by Tuesday night or Wednesday morning. The troops must be in Kwaku by now and Phillips in a position to deal with any emergency.

7 February 1914
The MO on a tour of inspection called. Informed him I had been

round the town and, considering there were only five scavengers and the chief was absent, its condition was satisfactory.

8 February 1914
A messenger with letters arrived from Phillips. The letters had to be copied at Kibbi for they were 'spoilt' by rain, hence the delay. Phillips found things quiet at Kwaku, but the *omanhene* had evidently been alarmed. For the next few days Phillips proposes to remain at Kwaku and to keep the ring while a new chief is being elected for Obomeng.

11 February 1914
Owusu returned. Phillips has committed the *nifahene* and two other chiefs for unlawful assembly. There appears to be material still for an explosion and, until the affair is settled, it is advisable for a DC and troops to remain up there.

12 February 1914
Have been dealing with an accumulation of correspondence and at last have got to the bottom of it. Not a few applications from chiefs for Union Jacks and handcuffs; I must try and supply both. Have dealt with the opening up of the Krobo plantations. The outlet must be the railway, possibly a branch line. There is little routine work in the correspondence; most of the papers require thinking over. The stock of stationery for the province is at a low ebb and, as I suppose this year's indent will not arrive till June, some local purchases will be necessary. I consider the stationery store at each district headquarters should be checked by the auditors. Some people are careless with their stock. I sent Owusu back to Kwaku today. He was too knocked up to go back yesterday. I expect him to return about Wednesday. By that time there should be enough information to form a just opinion about the whole business and I shall go into Accra to discuss the matter. I have received from the *omanhene* of Akwapim his promised memorandum on the Native Jurisdiction Ordinance. He is very emphatic in the loss of prestige and position by head chiefs due to the grant of equal jurisdiction to all the chiefs. Many of his criticisms are sound and will be useful.

Kpong and its bungalows are a great improvement on Akuse and the quarters there, but there is practically no furniture. A bare minimum is all that is needed in view of the temporary occupation of the quarters. The rent is, I consider, excessive, but as the accommodation is pleasanter than that of Akuse I will not protest. The staff appreciate the change as much as I do. Akuse is not popular with Europeans or natives as an official residence. I have worked out the leave list for DCs. Some will have to do overtime. In any case, I shall be very short-handed after April.

13 February 1914
In the morning I made up a mail for Accra. It included a suggestion from Best that the government should complete early next year a motor road from Adawso to Aburi. I have little sympathy for concession hunters, who take up concessions off the main routes and then call on government to make motor roads to their property. I am surprised a railway was not demanded. A road from the hills to the railway is, I consider, desirable and I have written on the subject. In the afternoon I bicycled to Akuse along the Kpong–Akuse road. It is not bad going for bicycles and better than I had been led to expect. At Akuse I inspected the stationery store and placed it in charge of the senior clerk in the DC's office.

15 February 1914
The *manche* complained that Agricultural Department officers never visited his land. I doubt if much in the way of agriculture can be undertaken on the Shai plains, but I will talk to the director about it. Cassava, corn and yams seem to be the staple products. The *manche* is making a well in his compound. He asks for government assistance in sinking a well in the town and he asks for corrugated iron for roofing the public latrines. Some assistance might well be given him and I will discuss it with the DC. I saw the new prison he is building. It is higher than most of the native prisons and this is an improvement. The DC has a high opinion of the *manche*, but at present I am unable to share it. The *manche* seems to me rather helpless and weak, but I understand he gets things done.

Pram Pram, 17 February 1914
I inspected the town in the morning and found it well kept, though the four scavengers were the most decrepit quartet imaginable. They were armed with small pan brushes and made some show of industry. I imagine the townspeople themselves keep the town clean. At the last census, Pram Pram returned a population of 2200 and the number of houses at 230.

It is composed of upper and lower town, a good road half a mile in length joining them. Upper town is by far the larger and contains some large buildings belonging to the trading firms. Most of the native houses are the usual thatched mud huts and crowded together. Lower town is on the beach, and is inhabited chiefly by fishermen. There is still a fair import trade in spirits and provisions, but the export trade has quite died away. There are two customs clerks here, the senior acting as postal agent, with a credit stock of £15 in postal orders and £5 in stamps. The revenue varies. In the safe today there is about £1300, collected since 14 January. The clerk is waiting for an escort to send a remittance. He informed me his remittances have always been correct and no queries had been raised.

The police detachment consists of a corporal and two men who, except when a steamer is in the roads, enjoy a sinecure. The lockup has never had an occupant and the *manche* informed me that his court sits only once a month, 'the people are so well behaved'. The so-called fort, situated on the beach consists of two tiny rooms, perched over what at one time seem to have been cells. A large part of one room is taken up with a large safe and its concrete bed. Later in the day I saw the *manche* and his elders. They brought certain matters to my notice, not, I feel sure, because any of these matters cause a sense of acute grievance but to celebrate the visit of their PC. The customs clerk brought to my notice the need for new canoes for the ferries. The one I crossed in was a very crazy affair. In the morning I visited the *manche* in his own house. He has only just recovered from a severe illness and is still looking very weak. He is well mannered and speaks English well. Before he became chief, in 1899, he was cook to one of the government messes in the Oil Rivers. Shortly after his installation I remember reading about him in the *Sporting Times*. He was evidently a popular character with them in the River.

20 February 1914
Proceeded by lorry to Accra. We had 14 people on board. The road for the first few miles is not in good condition. We passed two lorries in difficulties. Saw the Director of Agriculture. He will arrange a meeting with the *manche* and elders about planting coconuts.

23 February 1914
Left for Dodowah by lorry at 6.30 and reached there 8.30. Sent off my carriers to Somanah and left at 3.00 p.m. bicycling. As I left Dodowah I was met by the Hausas who asked if they might build a school. Had a poor interpreter, so referred the matter to the DC.

24 February 1914
Accompanied the inspector [of weights and measures] to two stores and watched operations. I gather that he alone has authority to prosecute persons using incorrect weights and that weights can easily be faked in a few seconds. Unless, therefore, there is constant inspection, the stamping of weighing machines offers no protection to the public. As a matter of fact, the sellers have a shrewd idea of the weight of their loads and, if dissatisfied with the weight given by the buying machine, will take their load round and have it weighed on the selling machine.

Accompanied the foreman of works to inspect a well he is making in the town. He has got down 16 feet and has struck a good supply, a good sign at this time of the year. He wants to go down another two feet. I hope it will be possible to sink wells in many of the towns in the province. I also saw the roads engineer. He hopes to get the Kpong road fit for motor traffic in about two months. I saw several lorries in Somanah. Ford lorries will do no appreciable damage, less I should say than the hand trucks. They seem hardly more substantial than a perambulator and are a very paying investment.

I doubled back to see the *konor*. I spoke about the chiefs' conference. He is willing to attend anywhere. He spoke about the bank and thought an agency might be successful in Somanah. He was not quite sure that his people would appreciate the advantages and, besides, they had spent most of their money in building houses. In his opinion, the chief advantage of banking one's money was that you had not got it by your side and so could not spend it. I made no reference to interest, for the endeavours of a certain bank official to explain that subject was greeted with murmurs of Ackinnie[6] and money doubling. The *konor* of Western Krobo dearly loves a jest, even at his own expense. He had to tell me of his visit to the 'manoeuvres' and how the colonel put a string in his hand and said 'pull it'. The rest of the story is left to the imagination, for the meeting broke into an uproar of merriment, in the throes of which it was all the *konor* could do to keep himself from rolling off his stool. He tells the story frequently. The *konor* of Eastern Krobo, his rival, being put on a horse is seemingly a tame and spiritless affair compared with the *konor* of Western Krobo suddenly and unexpectedly firing a big gun. I spoke of the supply of foodstuffs sent to the regiment, and how he and his people had earned such a good name. He explained the matter, and indeed it had always been a mystery to me why the two Krobo divisions, not the best of friends, should have joined together to supply food free to the troops during the whole of the manoeuvres. It is the one instance I have known in my service of public expressions of gratitude, for the benefits government has brought the people and the manner in which it was explained, apologetic almost, that one should be called upon to explain the obvious, was not the least gratifying feature of it all. It appears that when it was known for certain, in October, that the troops were coming into the district for manoeuvres, the two Krobo divisions, under their *konor*s gathered together at the foot of Krobo Hill. They called to mind that not many years' back a Krobo man could not go into the Twi country, he would be killed at sight, that the Krobo women and children were abducted. Government came and now the Krobos can go to Komfrodua without any thought of fear. Remembering this the Krobos agreed together that without making any charge, they would provide food for the troops, as long as they are on manoeuvres. 'And only the other day', added the *konor*, 'my chiefs informed me that they would willingly have continued the supply, but the troops had gone away'. If only we could ensure now that where a man has sown the lawyers shall not reap!

There were no Krobos serving in the regiment and the *konor* said that soldiering would not be attractive to his people who were farmers. When a Krobo had finished soldiering he would have no farm or land to which to return; he would be landless for all their land was privately owned. Perhaps some young men would become soldiers, if they were wanted, and he told me what happened some years ago when the DC asked for Krobo men to go into the police. At the meeting no young man came forward, but that night several slipped away, ran to Accra, joined the police and are there still.

Reached Kpong about 12.30 to meet the usual accumulation of papers. Sent a circular to the DCs to revise the distances recorded in the 1911 *Gazette*. Some of these recorded distances are absurd.

25 February 1914

After last night my correspondence is likely to be as short as my temper. About midnight, a Hausa with his throat cut and followed by his family paid me a visit. He had a nasty gash and had bled a good deal, but as he could walk and talk he did not seem at death's door. He had a pain in his chest, he told me, so he thought he would kill himself. I picked out the biggest man in the family group and, in spite of his protests, ordered him to look after the would-be suicide until the morning. Then, about two in the morning, I had to send the corporal to stop a funeral custom in the Addah quarter. The offender was full of apologies, knew they could not drum at night, but thought there would be no objection to their doing so in the morning.

26 February 1914

The attempted suicide appears, saying he is not going to kill himself again, 'he doesn't like it, and besides he is still owed money for some sheep.' Had an interesting letter from the *omanhene* of Eastern Akim. He wishes people found guilty of robbery with murder to be hanged in the district, and he complains of the number of bad characters in his division. Sent a copy of his letter to the Chief Justice.

27 February 1914

Bicycled to Akuse. Had a talk with Swanzy's provincial agent who tells me the firm are opening 24 new stores in Akim and along the railway route. I should say there will be difficulty finding storekeepers and I will not be surprised if there are several resignations among the government native staff to take up employment with the firm. Roe, Swanzy's agent, is shortly visiting America to purchase suitable launches for river traffic above Sefwi.

2 March 1914
Were it not for the survival and revival of the three land disputes, Addah would be a sinecure. The Tefle–Sokpe case was heard before the Addah *manche*'s court seven years ago: an appeal went to the High Court and Sir Brandford Griffith gave judgement by consent. Unfortunately, the boundaries agreed upon were not cut, nor was a plan made. About 18 months' ago the case came again before the Ga *manche*'s court. There was an appeal to the Eastern Province and from him to the full court. The *manche* had adhered to his former decision and now an appeal has been lodged with me. I hope to try this case in about ten days' time. I am glad to hear that the villages along the riverside, namely Big Addah, Aggravie, Battor and others, have improved greatly in the matter of sanitation. Good work has been done by Atkinson of the Preventive Service, and the present DC and MO at Addah have succeeded in arousing among the people some pride in the cleanliness and appearance of their towns. The *manche* of Big Addah has also been inspecting his villages and has assisted in the efforts of government.

3 March 1914
In company with the DC, I cycled to Big Addah. I was very pleased to find such an improvement in the appearance of the town since I last visited it three years ago. Some new streets have recently been made and the efforts of the SI show good results. I spent some time talking to the *manche*, who we found superintending the construction of his own house. The *manche* greatly surprised me, for I did not expect much of him when I first saw him just after he had been placed on the stool. Doubtless, the reflection that his three immediate predecessors had been poisoned caused him to go warily. He asked for handcuffs, with which I can supply him, for a flag, which I hope to send him, for a post office, which I do not think is a matter of urgency and I so informed him. On my way to Big Addah inspected the contagious diseases hospital. I am not aware for what particular contagious disease it is proposed to use the two cells, which are called a hospital. It will certainly be no use in the case of an epidemic of smallpox.

In the afternoon I had an interview with Beeham, road engineer, who was passing through Addah. I am glad to learn he considers the light Ford lorries do no appreciable damage to the roads and that, if these lorries are a commercial success and are adopted generally, the problem of constructing motor roads will not be an insoluble one.[7] I was shown by the *manche* a telegram he had received from the Colonial Secretary. I gather the *manche* had been trying to arrange that Captain Poole should remain in charge of the Addah District and not be transferred to the NT.

4 March 1914
Reached Attitete at 3.00 p.m. Noticed Swanzy have a large store. As long as there is a higher tariff on the other side of the river a store at Attitete side must pay. Arrived at Cape St Paul's lighthouse where I propose to make my HQ.

7 March 1914
Dealt with correspondence. Then bicycled to Quitta.[8] In the afternoon inspected the public offices. For the HQ of the Frontier District they are not a credit. A new post office, new customs offices and a new treasury are required. I inspected the prison and looked at the books, which are well kept. I went through the record books in the DC's office and found everything neatly and carefully kept. His clerk favourably impressed me and has well earned his promotion. Left Quitta at 5.00 p.m. and returned to Cape St Paul.

8 March 1914
Bicycled to Quitta. Found Beckley, Land Preventive Service, there. He had bicycled in that morning from Dsodse, 25 miles. I swore him in. He bicycled back in the afternoon. It took him over two hours to come and he expected to do the return journey a little quicker, as the wind would be behind him. Before roads and bicycles, Dsodse to Quitta and back in the ordinary course would have meant three days' journey with 14 carriers and hammock men. I saw the *fia* in the DC's office and had a talk with him. He spoke about the *Gold Coast Leader* and of the enquiries being made by the Togoland government concerning the authorship of certain articles appearing therein.[9] The *fia* informed me his people were all planting coconuts, but I should say their main industry is fishing.

During the morning I looked at the site for the PWD store, the dispensary, post office and contagious diseases hospital. I agree with the recommendations of the site board. Further reclamation of the lagoon is desirable, but it is a formidable undertaking. The people are anxious themselves to reclaim a portion, but I do not think they realize the labour involved. A water supply for Quitta is not an easy problem. Out of six wells the water in five is brackish. The MO has suggested a large underground tank with an artificial catchment area. I am inclined to support this proposal. Something of the kind was successful in Anamabu.

9 March 1914
In the afternoon I proceeded to Awuna-Ga, the *fia*'s town, where the DC and myself arranged to spend the night. In the evening we had a long informal talk with the *fia* and Chief Agbozo, who is his great friend and adviser. There is a good deal of fetish among the Awunas and the *fia* assured us that the people would be thankful if the government could put down many of the customs and practices. He did not give many details, but he undertook to bring the matter up before his Council of Chiefs. The Quitta people are very anxious to reclaim the lagoon but are in some doubt as to whom the reclaimed land would belong. The *fia* had been to the Cameroons as a petty trader, but has seen little of this Colony. He last visited Accra in 1886. Chief Agbozo, who is chief of Jella Kofie, has not travelled, though once he visited Cape Coast. I hope to arrange for both of them to visit Accra at an early date. Both speak English well and are professing Christians, but they find themselves unable to resist the attractions of polygamy. The *fia* stated that there were no insuperable difficulties raised as to his non participation in fetish rites connected with the stool, but he found himself unable to live up to the ideals of Christian marriage.

13 March 1914
Left by launch at 8.00 a.m. for Tadjey and arrived there at ten. A pleasant looking station. In afternoon bicycled to Sukpe and Tefle to spy out the land and to warn parties to be ready for me next morning. The land in dispute is about six miles from Tadjey and is barren country. Returned at six and informed there is no drinking water and that it is obtainable only from Addah. As I have no filter, the outlook is not attractive. Driven to bed early by mosquitoes. The mosquitoes gave me no peace during the night, despite the room being mosquito-proofed.

14 March 1914
Left at 7.00 a.m. to inspect the land. Spent four hours walking round the boundaries. Reached Tadjey at 12.30. After being plagued by mosquitoes by night and flies by day, I fled to Addah for the weekend.

16 March 1914
Left for Akuse. About 30 to 40 passengers on the launch. Arrived at Asuchari at 2.30. As the launch cannot at the present moment proceed further than Asuchari because of the low river, we have to tranship here. As the next mode of conveyance for passengers and baggage was one surf boat, the majority of us walked the six miles to Akuse.

17 March 1914
Had a long talk about Akwamu and Peki with Taylor. Telegram from Colonial Secretary instructing me to come to Accra as soon as pos-

sible. Enquired from the Basel Mission factory if they have a lorry going from Kpong to Accra, but not likely as the road is under repair. Shall bicycle to Dodowah and catch a lorry from there on Thursday morning.

18 March 1914
Lewis raised the question of persons bringing dane guns[10] from east to west of the Volta. Apparently at present there is nothing to prevent persons doing this and the issue of permits for dane guns is, in the neighbourhood of the river, a farce. Left for Dodowah at 2.30.

26 March 1914
Returned to Dodowah with Lloyd last evening. In the morning I climbed the Mamfe, the prettiest walk imaginable. At Akropong I called in to see the *omanhene* and found him looking very ill. He is under the treatment of Dr Muller, medical missionary. The *omanhene* is dissatisfied with the action of the DC in stopping the headman of Konto trying cases, although he has been deputed by the *omanhene* to do so. I explained the matter and told the *omanhene* that if he wished the headman to try cases he should give him a stool. In that case, the jurisdiction of the headman, or *odikro*, under the law as it stands at present, would, except as regards appeals, be as extensive as that of the *omanhene*. The *omanhene* told me he had summoned a conference of his chiefs, but that they made excuses not to attend. I am afraid he has little hold over them.

26 March 1914
I discussed various matters with Taylor, among them the treatment of chiefs and the fines imposed on them. Taylor wished to be appointed a marriage officer in the place of the Bremen missionary at Peki, who is going on leave, but it seems only missionaries can be appointed marriage officers.

29 March 1914
In the afternoon I left for Somanah. I called on Mate Kole, who wrote asking to see me. He wishes to obtain 250 guns and a supply of caps for his people. I told him, under existing conditions, this was not possible. But I told him I would grant permits to single individuals to import a cap gun and caps, if he wished especially to recommend any person, but not more than ten.

30 March 1914
Arrived Komfrodua at noon and found the Director of Surveys there and DC Ballantine. The former showed us the plan of the town. The best site for the government bungalows seems to be about a mile and a half along the Adawso road.

31 March 1914
I had an interview with the *omanhene* and discussed with him (1) the Juaben settlers on the French Ivory Coast. We could not approach the French government on the matter, but if any of the families come over to settle in New Juaben territory we would not drive them away; (2) the conditions of his enstoolment, which he wishes to bring to the notice of his chiefs; (3) cocoa instructors, which he said were doing well; and (4) the layout and development of the town by government, and the payment by the people of a contribution towards the expenses.

Cape Coast, Central Province

(i) J. L. Atterbury, Ag DC, 1915–16[11]

25 July 1915
I arrived at Cape Coast by steamer and landed at 7.00 p.m. I was met on the beach by Mr Taplin and a number of officials.

26–31 July 1915
Spent the mornings and afternoons taking over from Mr Taplin and attending to current matters. In the evenings we discussed special cases and affairs generally of this province.

31 July 1915
Received a visit from Mr Allen, agent for the West African Mahogany Company at Axim, who informed me he wished to hire or purchase the SS *Liberia*. Mr Allen was accompanied by Mr Van Eadan. Mr Allen is an energetic man and I should guess him to be of American birth, he thought he could arrange the whole matter in the office with Mr Van Eadan (who I understand represents the Board of Trade). I did not sell him the ship. Took over the province from Mr Taplin. The *omanhene*s of Cape Coast, Nkusukum and Aburi, the *ohene* of Commenda and the Hausa chief have called to pay their respects and I was agreeably surprised at the warmth of their welcome.

2 August 1915
Mr Taplin left Cape Coast this morning on SS *Elmina*. The *Elmina* arrived at daybreak and left at 8.00 a.m. I thought Mr Taplin looked tired and worn and I hope the sea voyage will soon put him right again.

5 August 1915
Met Dr Wade MOH and Mr Chatfield with Mr Bates (European SI). Made tour of town and inspected points arising at next meeting of Town Council. Re Aboom wells, I think it will be a great pity for the government to lose control of these wells. They are very popular both

for drinking water and for washing, and if they get into other hands a charge will be made for their use. Re site for girls school, I consider £12 an acre a very good price for the site. It is useless as farming land and is very difficult as building land, requiring a deal of levelling.

13 August 1915
Had an interview with Mr Jones, the president of the Gold Coast Aborigines' Society. Mr Jones informed me that his Society would hand me £1500 on Monday for a first aircraft to be called the Gold Coast Aborigines' Aeroplane, that they had a further sum of nearly £500 in hand and hoped shortly to have sufficient for another aircraft.

19 August 1915
If I was permanently stationed in Cape Coast I should seriously consider getting a small car. It is a nice run downhill on a bicycle but a horrid climb up. We have a boy to meet us first and help us up.

23 August 1915
Inspected the prison. I think the prison food is costing too much. It is 4¼*d.* to 4½*d.* a head. At Tarkwa it only costs 3¼*d.* a head. I have requested the DC to enquire into it on his return. European Club general meeting. This club is now on a fairly sound financial footing and thanks are due to Mr Aitkin the Secretary. The club rooms have been done up by the PWD (under 'castle repairs'). There is a membership of about 20.

Wednesday 1 September 1915
I had a long interview with Appinaries, the *omanhene* of Assin, who came to see me in state with a majority of his subchiefs and people of importance. I have written asking YE to confirm his installation. I was not favourably impressed with the *omanhene*. He is an oldish man and does not look to be a teetotaller, but there is no opposition to his election.

6 September 1915
A deputation from the Cape Coast ratepayers attended in my office to protest against summonses being issued to collect outstanding rates. I pointed out to them that rates were in arrears for the years 1912, 13, 14 and 15 and that the town council had no wish to go to court in order to enforce payment. After some talk I agree to give them the whole of this month to pay their arrears. Gong gong is to be beaten in Cape Coast to explain this. Mr James Young, Mr Watt and Mr D. M. Abadoo (senior) of the Scottish Wholesale Cooperative called to see me. It appears that their European agents have not been entirely satisfactory and one, Mr Poly, is reported to have gone away, with a

considerable amount of money, dressed in a Hausa gown. I referred them to the police. The Reverend Fisher called to see me about repairs and alterations to Christ Church. Mr Fisher is not asking for government to pay for the new organ chamber and vestry. He has collected the money and only wants YE's approval.

7 September 1915
The MOH and myself motored over to Elmina. The roads very bad and I have closed it against motorcars for repairs. The SMO (Dr Harper) informs me that Mr Poly (Scottish Wholesale) is in hospital. It appears his carriers set on him and nearly killed him and left him for dead. He was found and brought down here. Mr Harper thinks he will live.

8 September 1915
The Commissioner of Police (Captain Thomas) is away at Winneba so I spoke to Superintendent James this morning to enquire about Mr Poly and was surprised to find that, although the superintendent had heard of the attempt made to murder Mr Poly on Monday night, he had not yet taken any active steps to effect an arrest and no police had been sent upcountry. I have wired the COP at Winneba. Superintendent James did not salute when he entered my office, or when he left.

11 September 1915
Sent my carriers off to Anamabu and attended office till 11.30. I left Cape Coast (bicycle) 2.50 p.m. and arrived Anamabu 4.20 (13 miles). The road to Akritutua is good, but after that bad, with one or two stretches of sand. Inspected the town and called on Omanhene Amowoo, an old friend of mine.

Sunday 12 September 1915
6.30 a.m. I went off in a canoe to visit SS *Liberia*. The sight is a very sad one, and it is difficult to believe that a ship can look as dirty and old in such a short time. 7.45 a.m. Mr Heathcote arrived from Saltpond and after breakfast, we had an interview with the *omanhene*. The *omanhene* informed me that Chief Sam owed him a large sum of money for feeding the mine agents and that he was taking action in court, but he seemed to think that if he failed to recover his money from Sam, that the government would repay him.

Left Anamabu, arrived Saltpond 9.55 (five miles). This road is very bad in places. In afternoon we played tennis and I met a large number of the merchants of Saltpond. Interviewed with Ag DC Heathcote the Hausa chief, who came to pay his respects with about 50 or 60 followers. He had no complaints. The Hausa chief said he had heard of me from his brother in Tarkwa, and wants a Hausa *zongo* in Saltpond. I promised to enquire into the matter and report to HE, but explained that he might have to wait some time for his *zongo* because of the war. I believe YE is in favour of Hausa *zongo*s and shall go into the matter and write to Accra. Inspected new native hospital, which is nearing completion. I called on Mr and Mrs Dowdall. Their bungalow is in a wretched state. I wish the new type B bungalows could be completed at once.

16 September 1915
Left Saltpond at 7.00 a.m. and arrived Tantum 11.00 a.m. (18 miles). The beach road is fair, but could be much improved with a very little trouble. I met DC Lamond at Tantum. Held palaver. There are a number of Fanti-Mohammedans here and I think the idea is spreading. I first met the Fanti–Mohammedan idea in Saltpond district about six years ago. It was then under Chief Sam, who was reported later as having died in suspicious circumstances. The rest house at Tantum is a very good one with two boys' rooms and a kitchen. A latrine is being erected. The chief told me the building cost him £166 and he produced receipt, which showed £128 paid for materials and £37.3*s*. paid for wages. He says DC gave him £4 for the job. It is nicely match-boarded inside, with corrugated iron roof and cement floors. I think the chief should be given a further dash.

Appam, 18 September 1915
I held a palaver with reference to the election of a new chief of Appam. All interested parties were present, or represented, as was the *omanhene*, Kujo Nkum of Gomoa. The present position is that J. P. Swatson has been elected to the vacant stool, but there is a considerable amount of opposition to him on the part of the acting chief, Arkorful, members of some of the royal families, and the two companies. The *omanhene* and the *tufuhene*, Quaye, favour the election. Both Arkorful and Quaye are scholars and the dispute is really between them. I did not think the time ripe for me to take any decisive action and I have left them to endeavour to come to some settlement. The *omanhene* has promised to use his influence and I have promised to see them again as soon as ever they are agreed. I left Appam at 4.40 p.m. and arrived at Winneba at 6.20 p.m. I hoped to find a hard beach for bicycling, but I had to walk most of the way and arrived very tired.

Saturday 25 September 1915
I left Winneba at 8.55 on the government lorry with OC and Mrs Lamond and arrived Soades (15 miles) at 10.05 a.m. Here I met ADC Thomas. Interview with the *omanhene* of Nsaba and *ohene* of Soades

at the rest house. The most important matter brought up was the question of surveying and laying out of the towns of Nsaba, Nyakrom, Soades, Kwanyaku. The *omanhene* complains that he cannot get permission to build his houses in these towns. DC Lamond says the towns have been surveyed and the plans are at Accra. He asked that the actual laying out of the towns might be done, so that he can grant building permits, which are at present held up. Interviewed the Hausa chief who had no complaints at all.

I left Soades with Lamond and Thomas at 1.50 and arrived Nsaba 2.40 p.m. (ten miles). The rest house is started and the contractor says will be finished next month. I doubt it. I inspected the *omanhene*'s prison and found an old man from Anamabu there. He had been in prison 29 days and was still untried. I instructed Mr Lamond to enquire into the matter.

2 October 1915
The DC Saltpond, Heathcote, has written me suggesting an export tax of 1/– a load on cocoa. Mr Heathcote advocates that the tax should be used on the roads of the district from which it is collected. The question of export taxes is an old one, but I should be glad to know YE's views on the subject today.[12]

Sunday 3 October 1915
Got through a heap of correspondence. I regret to say that the relationship between DC Heathcote and Dr Dowdall is somewhat strained and I think Dowdall is entirely to blame. I have written to PMO on the matter and I hope I shall not have to trouble HE with the correspondence.

4 October 1915
Captain Thomas (Ag COP) left on SS *Lakja* for Sekondi in charge of Mr Poly (Scottish Wholesale), who has recovered from his injuries and has been sentenced to six months imprisonment. Mr Poly pleaded guilty.

5 October 1915
At 4.00 p.m. a large meeting was held outside the castle gates to offer up prayers for the success of the allies in France. Chief Colai was chiefly responsible for the gathering, and addresses were given by Chief Colai, Reverend Fisher, Reverend Gibson, Wesleyan, and others. I did not attend.

12 October 1915
The Ag DC Saltpond is away on tour for a week. I understand the MO, Dr Dowdall, refused to take over the station and on my

instructions the DC (Heathcote) handed over to the Officer in Charge PWD, who will not sit in court but is required to do anything important in the office. I am afraid I will have to report the whole matter now. I wonder when we may expect a judge at Cape Coast.

Sunday 17 October 1915
I often wonder what we should do without Sunday in this Colony and Service. I worked on official stuff from 7.30 to 11.30, with a break for breakfast and only stopped on the arrival of Dr O'Hara May, who came to lunch, and later Mr and Mrs Long, Mrs Heathcote and Mr Rickaby drew up in a new four-seater Ford car, also to lunch.

1 November 1915
Assizes opened at Cape Coast. Judge King Farlow does not like the High Court too well as a residence and I hope to arrange for him to go into the new bungalow or Government House quite soon. We held a general meeting at the tennis club after our game.

3 November 1915
I discussed the question of the lighting of Cape Coast with the MOH and the matter is on the agenda for the next meeting of the Town Council. We propose to give the contract to Mr Seemans (a native). It will cost about £700 a year.

Saturday 6 November 1916
Government girls' school, requisition of site. I attended the High Court with reference to claims for compensation. Government valuation £60. Claims £3700.14*s*.6*d*. Court adjourned to inspect site. Lunched with King Farlow.

8 November 1915
Cape Coast Town Council meeting 4.30 to 5.30. Business not finished and adjourned to Thursday. We spend a large part of our time at these meetings examining and checking accounts. I propose to ask the auditor (bank manager) to audit it monthly for two guineas instead of annually for 15 guineas. This will cost the Council an extra nine guineas, but will save a lot of time.

12 November 1915
Re boy scouts. I shall be glad to hear HE's views on this movement. There is a tendency in the Winneba district to include others than boys and they are used by the chief of Agona as something more than policemen. I am instructing the DC that boys over 16 should be discouraged from joining.

13 November 1915
Left Cape Coast and took the government lorry to Akititua. Here carriers met me from Saltpond to take my luggage. I bicycled into Saltpond. The road from Anamabu to Brewa is now open. It is interesting to note that Mr Abecham took a large motorcar from Cape Coast to Saltpond overland. He carried planks with him, which were repeatedly used. I am staying at Swanzy's bungalow. I have five land appeals to hear. Mr Heathcote and Dr Dowdall called to see me during the day.

17 November 1915
The *omanhene* of Esikuma died nearly a year ago, and a new chief has now been elected and installed. I intended going to Esikuma today and had arranged a palaver at 8.30 a.m. At 6.30 Mr Heathcote called for me with one of Swanzy's Ford cars and we started off in heavy rain, but hoped it might be local. Three miles out of Saltpond (Mr Heathcote was driving) we had a skid and went into the side ditch, but no damage was done and we got the car out fairly easily. At about eight miles we had another skid and this time we were not so fortunate, as we went down a 20-foot bank and landed in a dirty pond with the car on top of us. The native driver and my orderly and boy were in the back of the car and they were able to scramble out, but Heathcote and myself were pinned down and could not move until the orderly had collected 12 or 15 boys who were able to lift the car off us. We were a little bruised and shaken, but otherwise unhurt. We undoubtedly had a very lucky escape. The roads were very bad indeed. I returned to Saltpond and went to bed for three hours. I woke up feeling much better, but rather sore.

18 November 1915
Interviewed the Hausa Chief Maemoh on the subject of Fanti-Mohammedans. I always thought Chief Maemoh was against this movement, but he informs me that he and his people are in favour of the conversion and are prepared to receive the converts into their church.

19 November 1915
Attended to court and office work. Mr Rushton (Swanzy's transport) called with reference to the road. I shall open it again tomorrow morning. I opened the Saltpond–Esikuma road as from tomorrow, but at 7.30 p.m. in consequence of heavy rain all the afternoon, I cancelled the order.[13] I was surprised to find Mr Redeker of the German WA Company free and walking about Saltpond. Mr Redeker holds a pass signed by Captain Collins, the Inspector General of Police. I knew Mr Redeker at Saltpond in 1909, 10, 11 and did not like him.

25 November 1915
I instructed the police to take some action against the lorry drivers for fast and reckless driving in Cape Coast.

30 November 1915
It was quite a blow when I heard that I had to stay out till May or June. It had been assumed that Taplin was to relieve me in January or February and this will be a second disappointment to my wife (who went home last July). I should not mind if my wife were able to come out again, but we cannot afford the expense. I suppose the government won't help to pay my wife's passage.[14] I wonder if HE has considered the pay of Ag PCs. At present in Cape Coast the following officials draw more pay: judges, SMO and MOH. The following draw equal or nearly so: the DC and Engineer of Roads. I have nearly completed seven years in the Gold Coast Service and it has cost me £300 of my own money up to date. Cape Coast is much cheaper living than Tarkwa.

8 December 1915
I hear the banks are short of money and find difficulty in getting any. This will affect the cocoa market. Could we start paper money out here?

9 December 1915
I went to bed at 8.00 p.m. feeling rather seedy and with a temperature. Took ten grains of aspirin.

10 December 1915
I stayed in bed. Dr O'Hara May came over to see me and advised a morning in bed. I did not leave the house till 5.00 p.m. when I felt very much better. Dealt with some important letters.

Saturday 11 December 1915
I am much better today, but have a slight headache. I do not wish to complain, but it is hard work with the DC away. ADCs Smith and Freeman arrived in the Colony today. Smith will go to Elmina, I have plenty of work for him to do there for a few months, and Freeman will go to Saltpond. I want the roads there improved. When Hanson comes out next month I shall bring Thomas to Cape Coast and send Hanson to Winneba to help Lamond. With Thomas to help me I shall be able to hear about ten land appeals, which are pending. Then Thomas must go on leave.

17 December 1915
I left my house at 7.30 in a motorcar and took Dr O'Hara May and ADC Smith over to Elmina. I had called a meeting of the elders and councillors and companies for 8.00 a.m. to discuss the installation of

the new *omanhene*, which had been fixed for Monday 30th. The Elmina people were not ready and most of the members of the companies were away, out at sea fishing. I ordered gong gong and drums to be beaten to call them in and postponed the meeting to 9.30 a.m. At 9.45 my clerk came to tell me that the meeting was ready. I held it in the courthouse. I was in uniform.

Everyone unanimous in favour of I. H. Condua, the *omanhene* elect. He is at present confined in a room and comes out on Monday. I inspected all the company flags[15] to be exhibited at the installation and no objection was raised against any except Number 10 Company's flag. Number 7 Company objected to the crown on number 10 Company's flag, as they had one on their flag. It was not a serious objection and eventually number 7 Company agreed to allow the flag to be used. I pointed out to number 7 Company that the crown belonged to the King of England. Having inspected and approved the flags I made a list of the emblems and they were all approved by the meeting. I then took a bond of £500 from the elders and councillors. I have given them a pass to install their *omanhene* and carry out the custom for one week from Monday. I have also given them a permit for ten kegs of powder. The acting chief of police is aware of the date of the event, but I do not anticipate any trouble.

25 December 1915

I attended church service at 9.30 and read the first lesson. Lunched with Dr O'Hara May and Mr Bogg. There was a good deal of drunkenness in Cape Coast, but no serious disorder.

29 December 1915

I received a cable from my wife today to say she was sailing from Liverpool on 12 January. I went to the lighterage to see Mr Makinson to enquire what he could do to get my wife's boat to stop at Cape Coast. His wife is also coming out about this time and Mr Makinson has cabled to her to sail on 12th and he is asking Liverpool to stop the boat at Cape Coast.

30 December 1915

A schoolboy had received a £1 note and he took it to the post office and asked for 20/–. The postmaster reported the matter to me and asked if he should cash it. I said certainly. I sent for the boy and explained everything to him and bought the note myself.

31 December 1915

The old fort at Mouri is rapidly disappearing and one wall is certainly dangerous. I shall ask the PE to report on it and if necessary have it pulled down. If it was to fall it would bury a number of houses in

Mouri. I should like to know HE's views on this fort. I would suggest having it demolished where it is dangerous and, in time, a stone or pillar could be erected to mark the spot. I returned to Cape Coast and went to the office where I heard the awful news of the SS *Appam*.[16]

4 January 1916
Mr Chevalton (bank manager) called to see me with reference to the new paper currency. I subsequently had a meeting with the Cape Coast regent, his elders and councillors, which Mr Chevalton attended and fully explained the new money and the reason why it had been found necessary to issue it. The regent remarked that in time they would become accustomed to it.

7 January 1916
I left Cape Coast at 7.30 a.m. on board the French boat *Esterel* and arrived Accra 4.30 p.m.

17 January 1916
I lunched with Dr Harper and was examined after 13 months' tour. My throat is much better, but not well yet. Dr Harper is giving me a tonic.

Sunday 23 January 1916
I stayed in bed all the morning and got up in afternoon. I think all ADCs should be given a duty allowance of £60 per annum. Many ADCs draw £80 as Ag DCs but it sometimes works unfairly. For instance, at the present time Mr Thomas is in my office — no duty allowance. Mr Smith is Ag DC Elmina, £80 duty allowance. Mr Thomas is senior to Mr Smith. It is more convenient that Mr Smith should be at Elmina and Mr Thomas in my office. Mr Thomas ought not to lose by this arrangement, but he does.[17]

26 January 1916
The old Hausa chief, Chief Musa, called to see me to complain of the action of the MOH. It appears that the Hausas have a custom that consists in killing a sheep on the eighth day after the birth of a child. The sheep must be killed in the house of the father of the child and the blood is buried in the yard of the house. The mutton is given to the chief, chief priest and assembled company. The MOH says all sheep must be killed at the slaughterhouse. Chief Musa says he has lived in Cape Coast 60 years and this is the first time the custom has been interfered with. I am enquiring into the matter. The *Apapa* arrived in port at 5.30 p.m. I went on board to meet my wife. I am glad to say I found her in excellent health after a splendid voyage out. I met many old friends on board, but, as the sea was a bit choppy, I took my wife ashore at once.

29 January 1916
Jukwa destoolment of the *omanhene*. I arrived at Jukwa about noon, and Mr Long (DC) and myself, after changing into uniform, held a palaver into the destoolment. It was an orderly meeting and a good few chiefs were present, or represented, but I was struck by the apathy of the chiefs and people. However, everyone present was quite satisfied with the destoolment and everything has been done in accordance with custom. I shall therefore report the matter and ask HE to confirm the destoolment. I returned to Cape Coast at 2.45 p.m. after a long day. Mrs Long and my wife accompanied us.

9 February 1916
Left Cape Coast at 3.15 and arrived Anamabu at 6.00 p.m. We, my wife and I, motored to Akilitea and walked into Anamabu from there, as Mr Heathcote forgot to send a hammock. We stayed the night at Anamabu castle. The rest house quarters require some repairs and practically all the furniture has disappeared. I have already reported the matter to PWD.

10 February 1916
Interviewed the *omanhene* Anamabu. I should like to ask him into Cape Coast to meet HE when he comes next month. I have promised to present the *omanhene* with a copy of Dr Claridge's book.[18] When will it be ready?

5 June 1916
I left Cape Coast at 8.00 a.m. and arrived Elmina 8.40 a.m. in a motorcar hired from Swanzy's. The primary object of my visit to Elmina was to meet the new *omanhene* (installed 20 December 1915). Mr Smith, Ag DC, met me outside the castle and I held the palaver in the castle yard. The *omanhene* assembled with elders, councillors and captains of the companies. I was favourably impressed with the new *omanhene*, Condua III, and shall shortly forward the necessary papers and ask HE to confirm him. After the *omanhene* had been introduced to me he expressed his loyalty and affection towards the English government and then swore (not on a Bible) to obey the rules and respond to the calls of the government by day or night. This is unusual as far as my experience goes.

3 April 1919
The next few months are likely to be very trying and I shall require all YE's sympathy and support to carry me through. My most urgent need is another ADC.[19]

Winneba, Central Province

(i) C. H. P. Lamond, DC, 1915[20]

19 October 1915
Left Ojubi at 6.30 a.m. and arrived Ajau (near Accra boundary) at about 10.30. This is practically a Hausa settlement. I spoke to the chief and left about 12.30 getting to Ojubi at 4.10. From Ojubi a track has been cut by the telegraph line.

20 October 1915
Left Ojubi at 7.00 a.m. arrived at Obutu at 8 o'clock. There is a possible site for a rest house on the Kwanyaku road, but it is far from water. Indeed the chief told me that at times the water supply gives out altogether. If this difficulty can be overcome I recommend that a rest house be built here, as being the most convenient halting place between Winneba and Accra. The chief is building an eight cell prison of swish bricks. The existing cell is ventilated by only two peep holes in the door. I inspected the tribunal books and noticed no bad instances of over charging. The chief was fined £50 for this last year.

Having received a complaint from the new Attole Ahama, as to this chief's insisting on bodies being brought into Obutu for burial from the villages, I discussed the matter with the chief. At the instance of Mr Taplin, he has made a new cemetery (barely distinguishable from a farm) and gave two reasons for the practice complained of (1) to prevent burial in houses and (2) to attract people to Obutu. But for the burials and the annual custom he said the town would fall into ruins. It is in fact a decayed place, and I noticed very few people about on this and on a previous visit. I would have thought that each village should have its own cemetery, but apparently there is something in what the chief says and I should he glad to hear your opinion. I left Obutu about 9.45. Stopped at Ojubi and arrived Kwa Kwo at 2.00 p.m.

21 October 1915
Left Kwa Kwo at 7.00 a.m. arrived Winneba 11.00 a.m. I have settled all the sections for the new road, with the exception of one over which I was rushed by the chief of Obutu. I hope to adjust this shortly and to submit a full report. With a little trouble the existing road might be made into a good cycling road. There are no long steep hills and no permanent water except at the Aycu Su where there is a ferry.

9 November 1915
Left Winneba 7.45 arrived Beraku at 2.15 via Kwekrom. Interviewed the surveyor. He showed me the plans of the town, which is complete,

as far as the buildings are concerned. The survey is to extend about a mile beyond the town.

10 November 1915
Interviewed the chief. Owing to the numerous pegs put in by the surveyor, he appeared to think that we intended to pull down all the ruins, many of which are still occupied. DC assured him as to this. We pegged out several new streets in the morning and connected the line of others with the plan. In the afternoon the people were slow to turn out and I put a pick in the chief's hands and made him do a little work (an ex-storekeeper, I understand); the dignity of labour did not appeal to him. He regarded my action as an affront, but it had the effect intended as there was no lack of labour for the rest of the day.

(ii) H. W. Thomas, ADC, 1915

16 November 1915
Left Appam at 7.30. At Legu, investigated complaint against *tufuhene*, Quaye, who was present. It was alleged that he had intercepted a letter addressed to me outside my office and frightened the bearer into dashing him 5/– for a bottle of brandy. I have received the letter, which relates to the fishing dispute with Tantum. I sent Quaye, under arrest, to Winneba on a charge of extortion. Received telegram re fishing palaver and, as it has not been settled, wrote to the DC Saltpond. Suggested a meeting on Friday. A new chief has been elected at Legu, but its *omanhene* has not reported it yet. Went on to Amanful. It is a small village with a large and well-ventilated prison. Interviewed chief on usual subjects. Rain in evening. Dined in the cell, being more commodious than my own house.

20 November 1915
Arrived Ogwan. Palaver with *omanhene* in afternoon. He brought out all the old excuses about the rest house. The *omanhene* does not recognize the alleged new chief of Legu — a scholar — and said that the chief of a fishing village should be a fisherman, with which I agree. The *omanhene*'s four clerks were present; none of them are paid, but get a share of the tribunal fees. No matter of importance was brought to notice by the *omanhene*. I omitted to mention that heavy rain fell last night and that the Appam section of the road was disgraceful — as usual. The acting chief will be heavily fined. I regret that the words for three months imprisonment are not included in the section of the roads' ordinance, which authorizes a fine of £50.

5 December 1915
Dies non.

Swedru, 6 December 1915
Held court in the morning. Interviewed chief of Swedru, inspected his court book and examined his prison. No prisoner in cell. I noticed the chief was taking sanitary cases. I informed him he must not do this, as his town was not under the Ordinance and all such cases must come to me. Went to village of Brofiyedu, a few miles down the Winneba road, and laid out principal and side streets. This is an entirely new village springing up on the PWD road. The chief told me he was very grateful for the help, and said he would have all the streets guttered so that the people could not build out of line. This village is about three miles from Swedru and the people have come there from Akropong to grow cocoa. Now that the streets have been laid out before any houses have been erected, it is to be hoped that the village will be built up in a fairly sanitary manner.

8 December 1915
Held court in morning, after which I received a deputation from the women of the market complaining that the chief intended levying a tax of 1*d.* a day on all holding a pitch in the market. The chief informed me that the DC had suggested it. The actual complaint of the women was that they had incurred the expense of putting up stalls, whereas at Winneba the government had put up the sheds and the occupiers were not asked to contribute anything. The women were, however, willing to submit to the tax if the chief would refund the expenses they had incurred. It did not take long for the chief to make up his mind and refuse the request. He said most of the sellers were strangers and ought to contribute to the town. In this I agreed with him, reminding him at the same time that, but for strangers, his town would be of little importance. As the government has acquired the land for a market, I am at present uncertain whether the market belongs to the chief or government. I read the CCP's letter to the chief in charge, regarding the Boy Scout movement. I then dealt with two building permits. I had to refuse one Kweku Andam, as he wanted to build a veranda right onto the street. The veranda was half made, though it was not asked for on the permit. I inspected the *omanhene*'s prison. There was only one prisoner debtor. The books were all examined and found in order. I returned to Swedru in the evening.

9 December 1915
Held court in the morning, mostly cases of drunkenness. The chief's son was sentenced to two months' imprisonment for making serious assault on a policeman. The police experience great difficulty in maintaining any order up here and a heavy penalty seems the only solution out of the difficulty.

13 December 1915
I had intended leaving Swedru early this morning in order go to Ogwan and then up to Abodom. I had previously ordered carriers at Winneba, to be here on 12th. Only two, however, turned up, which prevented my sleeping at Abodom. No carriers of any description can be obtained here and I understand that the women[21] selected to come up here refused, as they thought perhaps the loads would be too heavy for them and they would have had the walk to Swedru for nothing. This is the position one is placed in as regards to carriers, the government pay being no inducement as the people can obtain far better pay at their jobs, anyhow in this cocoa district. I took court in the morning, fining five men £10 each for digging up a corpse at Bawjeasi. It is at this village that the chief of Obutu has been making all the trouble with regard to the cemeteries. The *omanhene* of Ogwan ordered the exhumation, as is evident by the letter he wrote to me and also to the chief of the village, where he says 'I will take all the blame.' I have sent the letter to the DC Winneba for action if he considers it necessary.

14 December 1915
No carriers have yet arrived. Mr Banson was sent down to get more yesterday afternoon. Later, I managed to get some carriers after some difficulty and arrived at Nyakrom in order to take an investigation for murder against one Tsia.

16 December 1915
At Nyakrom. Depositions continued and finished. Petty assault cases at 3.30 p.m. On looking round the town I noticed that a house next to the Basel Mission, which was building without a permit, had not been pulled down. There is no reason why the house should not stand, if there is a permit and both ends are cut off, as there is only a distance of three feet at present from the next house (at both ends) The SI was to have served a notice. The owner should be prosecuted now in court. Heavy thunderstorm commenced early in the evening and continued through most of the night.

17 December 1915
Inspected the cemeteries – the one on the Abodom road is only partly cleared, and a lot of plantains are still growing. The one on the Kwaman road is again full of bush. The last time I was here it was clean. One Benjamin Kwesie, a boy of about 12, complained that all his cocoa trees had been cut down when the cemetery was made. The number of trees is 120, he says. There are certainly a great number of stumps of cocoa trees. As the Chief Kofi Tawiah, who gave the land

to the government, was not at Nyakrom (being away at Cape Coast) I was unable to ascertain whether Kwesie's statement is correct. If it is, I think the chief ought to be made responsible for the compensation, as he was continually asked, the registrar and the boy told me, to give other land and said he would, but asked for time to consult with his elders. The plots for the Hausa *zongo*, which I marked out have not been built upon, and the land is all overgrown.

I left Nyakrom for Bobikuma at 11.30 a.m. The road was fair in parts, but a mile not yet guttered. The Nyakrom people being responsible and the Kwaman section is uncleared. I also told the chief to see that the streets in his village were also guttered, as at present there are watercourses right across the main street. This is a town that is increasing in size very greatly and I hope next time to spend a night there and lay out some streets. The town was dirty and smelt. Pigs were roaming about. I ordered the owners to pen them at once, outside the town. The Bobikuma section was clean. I interviewed the chief; nothing of importance was brought to my notice. As I arrived here about 1 o'clock I thought I would push on to Ajumako the same day. The Bobikuma section to the Okyeso boundary is good in parts. The chief told me the road had been divided up into sections for different sections of his people to clean; and this was evident, for some parts of the road were not guttered at all, while a little further on there was a good portion and so the road continued to the boundary.

22 December 1915
Fanti examination [at Cape Coast].

(iii) W. Hanson ADC, 1916

10 January 1916
Arrived Swedru from Winneba 4.30 p.m. Occupied the building originally intended as a rest house, but which, according to my instructions, are assigned to me in lieu of any others in the district. They are unfurnished and as water from the tank, after boiling and filtering, is still yellowish in colour and unpalatable I am forced to use Perrier at 7*d.* a glass or thereabouts. These matters recorded not so much by way of complaint as to state the facts. If two aluminium water carriers were officially supplied to me, I could have them filled with good water at Winneba and sent up here periodically.

Abodom, 16 February 1916
Held court, one conviction for assault. Inspected the town. The market women still sell in the roadway, as in previous years, and the Hausa butcher under a veranda in the main street. The site I chose for

a market in 1914 is to be used until a better is found. Linguist told to arrange with owner of an open space, south of Nyakrom road, and in the meantime to move women and petty traders from the main street, which they have made filthy. Later inspected the rest house. It is only a few feet high, but the walls are well built of burnt bricks. I called the bricklayer, as well as the linguist, and work is to be resumed as soon as there is any water available. In the absence of the chief, it was not possible to fix the boundaries of the land or draw up a conveyance. The site apparently must be quarter of a mile square to comply with regulations, but I will verify this. On my return, I had one hole, filthy beyond description, filled in with swish (near the main street). Also inspected three rum shops. Two are recommended. I should mention that I inspected the Boy Scouts and saw one man of 35 to 40 in uniform. He knew no drill and I hear was drunk last night. The linguist complained that scouts did no road cleaning and they announced that the chief wished them to have the duty of collecting stragglers and informing him of persons disobeying orders to attend road cleaning. Yesterday they discharged no such duties, but only went to the road playing their band and with many flags. I warned them they would catch palaver if they acted as police, that they must clean the roads like other persons (only better), and must only recruit boys in future. The chaplain was the Wesleyan schoolmaster.

18 February 1916
Left for Swedru. On the way I selected a site to be cleared for a cemetery, well clear of the town. I will inspect it next time and suggest where the fences dividing it into Christian and other factions be erected. The Wesleyans agree, though originally they wanted a cemetery for themselves only.

Sekondi, Western Province

(i) John Maxwell PC, 1914–15[22]

17 January 1914
HE and the Duke of Mecklenburgh[23] respective suites arrived from Accra per SS *Dakar*. HE and HH were met by officials of English merchants, German merchants, chiefs of Dutch and English Sekondi, prominent natives, chief of Hausas and Lagos chief. Engaged all morning attending to details of HE's visit. Accompanied HE and HH and respective suites to recreation ground where a cricket match was in progress, which HE and HH honoured with their presence. Afterwards returned to Government House. Dined with HE.

29 January 1914
Held a long palaver with *ohene* of Mansu and his councillors and spoke to him regarding roads, agriculture and sanitation. Chief complained about paying a portion of his rents to the Mpantie school fund and receiving no return. *Ohene* also complained that a Sierra Leone man had taken away one of his children to Sierra Leone. Requested *ohene* to send DC as full particulars as possible of the man and the child so that investigation could be made.

Inspected town and pleased to note that Swanzy's have erected a large and substantial factory here. The town fairly clean. Travelled from Mansu to Bensu by rail. Inspected native prison at Bensu. Two untried, seven convicts, four debtors, two female, one with a child. One complaint, on investigation later in the day found there were grounds for same and advised the regents to liberate the man, which was done. Promised to make enquiries concerning incarceration of women with children. Prison much too small for 17 prisoners and ordered that six be transferred to Sekondi forthwith.

Inspected school and was much surprised by the large attendance, 59 scholars present, including two girls. Average attendance 64, 79 on roll. The school was restarted on 7 July last by the Reverend Mr Aquash of the Wesleyan Mission, Sekondi, and, under the valuable management of Mr Akeampong and his assistant, is doing excellent work and promises to be a great success. The school has not yet been inspected and is not on the assisted list. The boys come from all parts of the district and are boarded in the village by the regents. The *omanhene* attends the school and the teacher reports that he is making good progress. It was started by Sir Matthew Nathan [Governor] in 1903 and it is pleasing to note the complete reversal of the attitude to education. I am communicating with the Director of Education on the subject.

Had long palaver with the regents (*omanhene* present), usual advice regarding sanitation, agriculture and roads. Also spoke regarding his prison and promised to send him plan of model native prison. Regents requested permission to allow their messengers to go round the division to collect oath fees, as some chiefs collect these fees and never account for same. Advised regents to continue present practice and to deal with any chief who did not account. Also advised chiefs that they should travel themselves to see what is being done in their division. Regents requested that Abina Gaidua (the Queen Mother) and the late *omanhene* be transported. Informed the regents that, as the case against these people was *sub judice*, their request could not be dealt with. Request received that agriculturalist should be sent to assist in laying out school garden. Promised to do so.

Asikama, 3 January 1914
Chief complained that Essu Kudju had beaten gong gong that plantains had to be sold in Tarkwa market at the rate of 12 for 3*d.* and that formerly the price was 3*d.* for six. Expressed the opinion that 12 for 3*d.* was a reasonable rate. Tarkwa, inspected government buildings. Interviewed acting Secretary of Mines and discussed mining matters and companies at work etc. with him.

2 April 1914
MOH and assistant engineer harbour works called regarding sites and houses for Kroo labourers and arranged to meet them this afternoon to inspect the same. Chief of Dutch Sekondi[24] called regarding extension of building plots at Ekuasi, payment of land acquired by railway and site of proposed new market. Informed him with regard to Ekuasi that I would inspect same this afternoon and that the railway and market were receiving my attention. Inspected town, including Ekuasi and found, much to my astonishment, a new village of about 100 houses being erected on a hill behind Ekuasi. Interviewed the chief and headmen. Informed them that all building operations must stop forthwith, that engineer would visit site tomorrow to lay outbuilding sites on sanitary lines. Interviewed chief on land and arranged with him to grant government land for two years to build houses for Kroo labourers at harbour works. Attended meeting regarding proposed fancy-dress ball at Easter. Routine work in office.

4 April 1914
Hausa chief called regarding proposed extension of *zongo*. Informed him no reply from Accra yet. Deputation from cooks in town called regarding the privilege said to be given to certain traders of purchasing fish on beach and they not being allowed to do so. Informed them I will enquire into their complaint.

8 April 1914
Inspected town along with the Honourable H. W. Grey, MOH and sanitary engineer. Attended committee meeting re fancy-dress ball and decided to have a band from Coomassie. Routine work in office.

9 April 1914
MOH and Ag PE called. Went over with them, on plan, lands belonging to government in Sekondi and advised action to be taken regarding removal of native huts on segregation area. Assistant Commissioner of Police (Massey) is called regarding murder of the late Mr Grey and admissibility of his dying statement as evidence. Advised him to communicate with COP and obtain the opinion of the law officers. Visited Kojo Kram with the General Manager, Railways, MOH and Sanitary

Engineer and there met chief of English Sekondi. Went over value of houses to be demolished with chief, who agrees to accept £150. Visited site of proposed new village and discussed laying out of same.

22 April 1914
Called on bank manager with reference to proposal by regents of Binsu to borrow money to liquidate their debts. He requested definite proposals in writing and promised favourably to consider same. Along with MOH and Mr Grimshaw inspected proposed extension of cemetery, when I expressed my disapproval of same. Engaged all afternoon with Mr Grimshaw and MOH and Ag TC going carefully over draft estimates for 1915 and making notes on same.

1 January 1915
Chief Briama (Hausa) called and requested piece of land for farming. Afterwards, inspected land with chief and informed him that I would make enquiries of land acquired for government purposes. Assistant Commissioner of Police called regarding spirit licences. Informed him that as his reports were unsatisfactory I would personally inspect all premises myself this afternoon.

2 January 1915
Engaged all morning superintending issue of spirit licences. MOH called regarding Board of Survey on prison stores. English gaoler called regarding a complaint that a prisoner had been put on hard labour who had not been sentenced to hard labour.[25] Attended military sports during afternoon. Great success; £22.10 subscribed by Europeans. Major Walker Leigh, DC, NT, arrived from England, reported himself to me.

18 January 1915
Assistant Commissioner of Police called regarding police stationed in Wioso and Aowin districts. Discussed matters with him prior to his proceeding there on inspection. 4.00 p.m. left for Ajua *en route* for Dixcove, Axim and Apolonia.

19 January 1915
At Ajua, inspected town. Town in a very unsanitary condition and requires more attention from sanitary authorities. 7.20 a.m. Apowa. Inspected prison, requires whitewashing and more ventilation. Asked MOH to report on same. Held palaver with new chief, Amu Gebru — quite an intelligent looking lad and I was fairly impressed with his appearance and bearing. The destooled chief is living in the village, but everything is quiet, the ceremonies in connection with the enstoolment having been carried out peacefully and no trouble in the division.

25 January 1915
At Dixcove and unable to leave owing to no carriers being obtained. Interviewed both chiefs regarding supply of carriers and telegraphed to Sekondi. Inspected Chief Hima Dickie's native prison – fair condition, but needs whitewashing.

26 January 1915
At Dixcove, carriers arrived from Sekondi. 6.10 a.m. left Dixcove. Arrived Akwida. Held palaver with chief and spoke to him regarding sanitation, roads etc. Chief's only complaint was a request for handcuffs. Left at 8.55; 10.30 a.m. Cape Three Points lighthouse. Inspected lighthouse, stores and new rest house in course of erection. *Ohene*, Kudjo Atta of Akwida, came in to see me and raised the question of compensation payable for the land on which the lighthouse and adjoining buildings erected, and complained that he had never received compensation. Considering that the lighthouse was erected in 1875, I do not think that compensation has been paid. However, it is rather late in the day to make this claim and I so informed him. He also complained that his road dues had not been paid, and wanted a permit to purchase gunpowder. At 2.10 p.m. left Cape Three Points; 4.00 p.m. arrive Princes. Inspected town, chief ill and unable to accompany me. Princes is the most insanitary town in the province. As Princes is within three hours of Axim, I think the MOH should be instructed to inspect the town.[26] Also inspected German fort.

27 January 1915
At 6.20 left Princes; 7.40 Ajemra. Held a long palaver with the chief and inspected town with him. On my last visit to Ajemra, August 1913, there was a fetish crocodile in the lagoon behind the town, but the people no longer feed the crocodile. It appears that a Christian Krooman[27] passed through this part of the province eight months ago and demanded that the people should give up worshipping jujus and fetishism and destroy all such things. Most of the people appear to have obeyed the voice of this evangelist and all jujus were burned in the various villages that were visited by the preacher. The chief solemnly informed me that he and all his people were now Christians, some Roman Catholics and some Wesleyans, and that if any person fed the crocodile he would die. This evangelist is now, I am informed, in the Ivory Coast. I shall make further enquiries regarding this gentleman during my present tour.

28 January 1915
Mr Shaw of Miller's and Swanzy's called and I discussed with him proposed beach railway at Half Assine, roads in province and spirit

licences. Mr Shaw takes the keenest interest in the province and is well informed. It is a pleasure to have a talk with him. Chief of Bamiankoe called and spoke to him strongly about his long absence from his division and the neglected state of same. This chief's sole idea seems to be to collect rents (£300 a year at least) and spend them on litigation[28] and other amusements in Sekondi. A repetition of the absent Irish landlord.

10 March 1915
Assistant Commissioner of Police called re police in Sefwi, complaints against whom having been made by DC Ross. Mr Prevost had promised to visit Sefwi and investigate complaints in January last, but nothing has yet been done. These officers must travel to supervise their own men, and the sooner instructions are given to this effect the better. Chief Briama called re complaint that TC threatened to fill up his well. Investigated same and ascertained that TC wanted him to erect a pump.

18 March 1915
COP called re quarters for German POWs. Ag SMO called re nursing sister's quarters.

30 March 1915
Dr Gush called to make enquiries re rumours calling volunteers for war service. Held long meeting with SSO and his junior and discussed with them sanitation of Dixcove and other coast villages between Axim and Sekondi. SSO dissatisfied with condition of some, but admitted that since his last visit there was an improvement, that he had just seen the villages under the most unfavourable conditions on account of the rains. Butcher called for payment of price of two bullocks. Again telegraphed Ag Colonial Secretary for vouchers.

3 December 1915
Mr Balstone of Customs called re importation of copper rods and gunpowder. Requested him to write me. Have submitted this matter to the Colonial Secretary for HE's information. It appears that large quantities of this war material are being imported when, in both Mr Balstone's and my own opinion, every ounce is required at home. Held a long meeting with the chiefs of Dutch and English Sekondi and settled with them the price of land acquired for the railway workshops. Held a long meeting with guardians and councillors of Hinian stool when they signed agreement re government paying their stool debts by retention of their concession rents. I shall submit a full report of this by next mail. After many interviews with these people, I honestly believe that the guardians and councillors are making a

strenuous effort to get rid of their incumbency. They informed me that Mr Casely Hayford had made many attempts to get them to refrain from coming to see me as he wants to draw 'the deed'. I do sympathize with these people as they did not incur the debt, although the stool is responsible and they have no idea of the large amount of money involved. In a recent interview, they stated to me if they could not get their debts paid they would run away and leave the land.

4 December 1915
Chief Efwiha (Sefwi) called to pay his respects. Had a long talk with him regarding affairs in Sefwi. He informed me that the Sefwi people now liked the DC living at Wioso.

8 December 1915
Various applicants called for passports. Mr Laurie of Dunkwa called re Mr Reynard's nationality. Informed him that matter under consideration of government. I am writing again on this matter. My own opinion is that Reynard is a German subject and the onus of proving otherwise rests with him. He has had more than enough time to prove his nationality and has failed to fulfil his promise to produce documentary evidence. Mr Trafford, Ag DC is also of opinion that he is a German.[29]

(ii) H. E. Bartlett, Ag PC, 1915–16

21 December 1915
Mr Maxwell finally handed over charge of Western Province to me and went on board the *Abrusi*. Several chiefs present on the beach to wish him goodbye.

26 December 1915
Spent morning going through the file of papers and telegrams relating to cable censorship from the time I went on leave in June and obtaining information from assistant censor as to the censorship. In consequence of 'clear the line' telegram received from Honourable Colonial Secretary directing that Mr Watt, Ag DC, should proceed at once to Coomassie for duty with GCR without waiting for arrival of relief, dispatched special runner to bring him in, he being on tour in his district. In evening walked round *zongo*, Ekuasi and Accra town with sanitary engineer.

25 March 1916
Reception of native chiefs by HE in morning. *Ohin* of Dutch Sekondi brought up the question of the trouble raised by his malcontented subjects. He had prepared a petition and explained his position to HE.

He requested me to inform the recalcitrants that no action would be taken over their grievances, nor would any further communication from them be attended to unless and until they had referred their complaint to the councillors in accordance with native custom.

The malcontents, before the meeting, approached with a petition to HE and wished me to submit it. This was drawn up by Mr F. A. Williams, a barrister, who appeared to be their spokesman. I refused to hear him, but spoke to them and promised to bring the copy of the petition to HE's notice, which I did. It is worthy of notice that the four companies whom the malcontents claim to represent were at the reception, drawn up behind the position occupied by the *ohin* and not with the four malcontents. They had powder issued to them through Anaisi and showed no lack of enthusiasm afterwards in firing their guns. I have not, up to the time of writing, heard of any friction whatever, though I must admit that when issuing the powder I felt some qualms. Mr F. A. Williams [above] is a new practitioner here and I fear is not unwilling to take an active part in native affairs, nor, as far as I can see, to the benefit of anybody except himself.

The *ohin* of English Sekondi brought up the question of the removal of Essikados, which has again been delayed owing to the financial stringency. I have always considered that these people have a very great claim to sympathy. Permits for new buildings at Essikados are refused and, though their part of the town is kept clean, not unnaturally no more is spent on it than is absolutely necessary for the bare requirements of health, while, as they very forcibly pointed out, they are still required to pay rates. I considered the statement made by the *ohin* very good, though most temperate and loyal. And, after hearing what they had to say, HE decided that permits should be given them in future to repair, and that the question of a grant for further urgent improvement should be considered by HE.

The Tacorady representatives talked about their everlasting feud with Amanful. I have heard nothing of it for two years now and think it was brought up more for something to say than for any urgent reason. The remaining chiefs were complimentary. HE and Lady Clifford and party honoured me by lunching at my bungalow. After lunch, HE discussed with me various questions I put before him and gave me his directions.

11 June 1916

At Chamah. Had long interview in the morning with the *omanhin* and councillors. The Ag DC, on his last visit, had reported unfavourably on the working of the native court here and I went into this matter with them. I too have noticed that their fines seemed to be getting heavier from their returns. I went through their books, which appeared well kept. I think the Ag DC has been a little too exacting in his standards, but a little shake-up will do them no harm. I also went into the question of their sanitary arrangements, on which the MOH has reported unfavourably and had complained that he could get no assistance from the chief and elders. They are, however, digging pit latrines in accordance with his instructions.

(iii) John Maxwell, PC, 1917

11 August 1917
Mr Trafford called to announce his arrival. Talked to him about affairs in Enchi district when he informed me that everything was quiet, that the question of French immigration would settle itself if Mr Brew was removed from his office on the frontier and that, owing to the extraordinarily heavy rains, it was practically impossible to travel. Mr Trafford proceeds on leave tomorrow.

27 August 1917
In Coomassie. Had a long meeting with the Hausa chief and the head butcher of Sekondi (the latter of whom accompanied me to Coomassie) in the presence of the CCA to enquire into the present shortage of cattle, complaints regarding which had been received, not only from Sekondi, but Dunkwa and Prestea. The reason for the present shortage is because of the quarantine at a place called Dore in the French territory, and of the heavy rains, which have rendered the country practically impassable. The reason reported to me at Sekondi was that the butchers in the Colony owed so much money that the dealers in Coomassie decided to give them no further credit. I was glad to find that this was not so. Before leaving Coomassie, the butcher was able to purchase three truck loads of cattle. I hope, with the assistance of the CCA and the CCNT, there will be no further complaints. Another reason for the present scarcity is the large purchases by the Cold Storage Company, Tarkwa. Along with the CCA, inspected the Agricultural Station and European segregation area. I was much impressed with the latter and only wish Sekondi was so easy to lay out. Along with Dr Lorema, inspected native town, Hausa *zongo*, slaughterhouse, market etc. Coomassie is far in advance of anything we have in the Colony. I was particularly impressed with the water supply and the many small refuse destructors. Since my last visit to Coomassie in 1906, the town and district have undergone a radical change and excellent work has been done. Afterwards, along with Mr and Mrs Fuller, motored to Ejura. The road is completed for motor traffic four miles north of Ejura. It is a wonderful road and I could

not have believed such a fine road existed in West Africa. It may have cost huge sums of money to construct, but I think the money will be well invested.

Wednesday 29 August 1917
At 6.30 a.m. left Coomassie for Dunkwa. Found DC Lloyd Roberts on sick list. Consulted with Dr Lorema, who advised that he should be taken to Coomassie for medical attention. Took over treasury and DC's office. In DC's office all afternoon attending to urgent matters.

30 August 1917
In DC's office all day. Held court and attended to various callers. The Hausa and Wangara chiefs called to pay their respects. Inspected the town. Notwithstanding the heavy and continuous rains, I have never seen the town in a better sanitary condition. At Dunkwa, as at Sekondi, the greatest complaint is the lack of beef and mutton and the dearness of all European foodstuffs. Fowls and eggs are as dear at Dunkwa as they are in Sekondi, but native foodstuffs are cheaper.

Sekondi, 1 October 1917
MOH called re water supply in town and wanted me to take steps to have supply cut off owing to unfavourable analysis received. Informed him that it was a very drastic step to take and, before doing so, I must be satisfied that the water was having an injurious effect on the people. Enquired if the MO had reported any sickness due to the use of water and also enquired from my own clerk the opinion amongst the people as to the water. He informed me that the people were drinking it and they liked it. Informed the MOH that I was unable to carry out his wishes except on instructions from HE. Mr Holliday ADC left today for Lomé; I shall miss him very much. He is a most conscientious and hard-working officer and always respectful and obliging. English chief called to report the high prices demanded for corn and other native food stuffs. These prices I regret to say are increasing pretty rapidly. The chief reason is that Swanzy's have a contract with the mining companies to supply quantities of native foodstuffs of all descriptions. Routine work in office.

Sunday 7 October 1917
Engaged in forenoon with Mr Atterbury discussing Axim district affairs, particularly route of new pioneer road from Ancobra River to Half Assine. Engaged all morning in bungalow with arrears of office work. On my return from my recent trek to Wassaw, I found piles of papers waiting for me and the trek taking more out of me than usual I have not been feeling too grand. In fact, I am beginning to think I should go on leave as soon as possible.

9 October 1917
Dr Williams, Prestea, called with an order from the divisional court for a railway pass to Prestea and stated that he had been at the transport office, but neither the European nor the native was in attendance. I was informed, Saturday last, that the ATO was on the sick list suffering from I know not what. He certainly wasn't taken into hospital, but of course this is in the discretion of the MO. Anyway, if he is unable to carry out his duties now that the TO has returned to the Colony, Mr Holterman should be stationed at Sekondi. I certainly am unable to attend to transport work in addition to my own and, I venture to think, HE does not expect me to do so.[30]

Chief and councillors of English Sekondi called and informed me that they had obtained loans to the amount of £200 and wanted a loan of that amount from government to pay off the debt. £100 of the loans received was from the Colonial Bank, who were pressing him for payment. Informed the chief that I would see the manager of the bank and ask for a short delay. If the proposed acquisition of the European segregation area is proceeded with, the chief will receive ample funds to liquidate his debts. I am, however, glad that he went to the bank for a loan and not to moneylenders. Afterwards had an interview with the manager of the bank, when he readily consented not to press for payment at present.

12 October 1917
In office all morning and finished off arrears of work. At 10.30 a.m. left Sekondi by SS *Akabo* for Accra to attend committee meetings and opening of Legislative Council when HE read his address.

1 December 1917
Several people called at my office during the morning to enquire about the *Apapa* and I received the official telegram about 11.30 a.m. The news is very sad. I have arranged with the Bishop of Accra to hold a memorial service at 9.30 a.m. tomorrow.

Notes

1. Rhodes House Library, Oxford, Mss. Brit. Emp. s. 344. Some of the following notes are from Harper's own notes.
2. It was the duty of chiefs and villages along these bush paths to keep them open for carrier traffic, and they received a small yearly grant from government to assist them. They had to keep the paths clear of overgrowth and fallen trees and to maintain native bridges. In some cases, for ten miles or so from a port, a better type of road was constructed by government, and along it cocoa or other produce would be rolled in large casks or drawn in hand trucks. It was one of the major concerns of

government to provide or improve means of communication between the cocoa-growing districts and the ports. The age-long mode of transport was by head load. The government load was from 50 to 56 lbs, but for double pay a carrier would cheerfully pick up and carry a double load. When they got to the firm's compound, the carriers, to show off, gave a sort of dance with their loads still on their heads. We weighed the loads, the lightest was 180 lbs, and the heaviest 221 lbs. With such heavy loads they would only walk, or rather shuffle, a few miles a day, but it might be over the roughest and steepest going. Often they would be preceded by a friend playing a pipe or flute, and, as soon as the warning notes were heard, other wayfarers would draw to the side of the path to give the heavy load plenty of room. A jostle or a jolt from a passer-by might upset the careful balance of the load and, as it tilted off the carrier's head, might dislocate his neck (note by Harper).

3. The Juabens were Ashantis, who left during civil war. Most of them were settled in Akim by government, who purchased land for them there. Other Juabens migrated into the neighbouring French Ivory Coast.
4. Government instituted a system of selecting locals as cocoa instructors. They were trained at the headquarters of the Agricultural Department and then returned to their homes to advise the farmers in the neighbourhood.
5. An authorized cash float.
6. Ackinnie was leader of a gang of money doublers.
7. The advent of the light Ford lorry opened a new chapter and redeemed large numbers of the population from servitude as beasts of burden. Government now got underway with a construction programme of roads in and to the cocoa districts, suitable for light motor traffic. Chiefs and people too joined enthusiastically in the work. Luckily, the cocoa crop was harvested in the dry season when the roads could stand up to the traffic.
8. In 1907, the governor of the Gold Coast received a memo from the Colonial Office asking that place names of antiquity should not be changed. Keta reverted to Quitta.
9. This Gold Coast newspaper published articles critical of the German administration in Togoland.
10. Flint lock guns.
11. GNA Accra 21/6/1, 21/6/2, 21/6/4. The diary, handwritten in four foolscap size hardback books, begins in January 1914. It contains brief entries for January and February, but there is no indication as to the author. Then there is a gap until 25 July 1915, when J. T. Atterbury took over as Ag PC. There is another gap from 1916 until 1919.
12. Note in margin by HE: 'I have had it under consideration for some time.'
13. In 1915, nearly all the roads in the Colony were simply made of earth, with the worst of the tree stumps and boulders removed and perhaps a gutter to carry away the rainwater. These roads were quickly wrecked in wet weather by cars and lorries.

14. Note in margin: 'Alas I fear not. HC' [Hugh Clifford].
15. The large coastal towns divided up into wards and the people living in these wards formed themselves into companies. There was much jealousy between them. Each company had a flag displaying its own emblem.
16. Sunk by German submarines.
17. Note in margin: 'He does not lose, he simply does not gain. HC.'
18. This was his *The History of the Gold Coast and Ashanti.*
19. Note in margin by A. R. Slater, Ag Governor: 'You know you may count on it. As I have told you before, you shall have one of the first batch.' Later (15 April) the PC declared ten officers to be the minimum on which to run the province, a figure that prompted Slater to minute in the margin: 'As at present advised I am inclined to think this staff excessive. ARS.'
20. The Winneba diaries are in GNA, Accra, Adm. 28/5/1.
21. In the Colony, women were frequently employed as carriers. There is no mention in any of the Ashanti or NT diaries of women being used for this work.
22. GNA, Accra 26/5/1 to 26/5/16. The PC's diary, Sekondi, was started 1 January 1914. It is handwritten in a series of hardback, foolscap exercise books, 20 in all. Where Indian ink has been used, the paper is very brittle and rotted by the ink. A line has been ruled down the centre of each page, right-hand side for the diary, left hand side for HE's observations and directions. These are few, and never amount to more than a few terse words.
23. The Governor, Sir Hugh Clifford, and his guest, the Governor of Togo who was paying a visit to the Gold Coast.
24. During much of the eighteenth century the English and Dutch each had a fort at Sekondi. Even after the Dutch fort was transferred to Britain in 1872, there continued to be a Dutch and an English section of the town.
25. The Ag Governor A. R. Slater, noted: 'I should like a special report on this please.'
26. HE noted: 'It must be realized that the sanitation of these villages is primarily the responsibility of the chief, who should be kept up to the mark by the DCs. The MOs have, after all, advisory not executive powers.'
27. This was probably the 'Prophet' Harris or 'Bishop' Swatson, both of whom tried to evangelize the people of the Western Province of the Gold Coast and the coastal district of the Ivory Coast. There is correspondence between H. Ross, DC, the Commissioner of Western Province, Colony, and the Colonial Secretary, Accra, in March–April 1915 on the 'Bishop' Swatson affair, in GNA, Letters WP (Conf).
28. Litigation in the Colony seems to have been a popular pastime, encouraged by the legal profession for whom it was a rich source of revenue. Many of the stools ran up huge debts.
29. Note by the Governor: 'What has been done about this man?'
30. Minute by the Governor, 'Of course I do not.'

4

Diaries, 1913–1919: Ashanti

Kumasi, CCA

(i) F. C. Fuller, 1916–17[1]

14 August 1916

Arrived Obuasi on the up train where I was met by Cutfield and a police guard of honour, Superintendent Coppin in command chief's representation; school children and boy scouts were also there to welcome me. Coomassie[2] at 6.00 p.m. No WAFF guard owing to shortage of men. The chiefs gave me a hearty reception. Found fort looking exceedingly smart and clean.

15 August 1916

Took over from Philbrick and worked through papers all day. Office in good order and correspondence up to date.

16 August 1916

Bishop O'Rorke called in afternoon with reference to the church's plot. All correct, but he had lost his copy of the lease and asked for a certified copy. Tried my car in afternoon. Ignition has to be attended to, evidently tampered with in packing, otherwise in excellent condition.

17 August 1916

Interviewed Messrs Holloway and Craig, representing Fry and Cadbury, with reference to the plot of land they have jointly taken. Held a large meeting of chiefs who came to salute me on my return. Then a meeting of the Coomassie Council of Chiefs.[3] Most important of the discussions was cocoa. The native merchants and clerical community presented me with an address of welcome at 6.00 p.m. Spontaneous, genuine and unexpected. I was much touched. Ran 14 miles up the Ejura road. Car running beautifully. Norris in from Ejura.

19 August 1916

Spent the whole morning listening to the complaints of the Kumawu malcontents.[4] Shall finish hearing them on Monday. I shall have to hold a large gathering of the clan somewhere out of Coomassie. Visited the prison, police barracks and hospital (native) in the evening. We badly need more prison accommodation. In fact, a new up-to-date prison is required. It is no good tinkering at the old building. Collins has included this item on his list of public works. Police barracks quite good, but will soon have to be enlarged. The native hospital is excellent. It is just what, in my opinion, it should be. Small improvements are of course always to be found, but the general lines of the scheme could not be bettered. Doctors Adams and O'Brien showed me round.

Sunday 20 August 1916
A quiet uninterrupted morning working through papers. Read through three diaries from the Western Province. All well there, I am glad to say. Ross is energetically pushing on road building. Wood has being doing good work in this direction in the Wenchi district. Went over reservation and gardens, both looking well, but the former looks deserted with so many finished bungalows lying empty.

21 August 1916
Long palaver with the Kumawu 'youngmen'. Finished hearing all their complaints, which, if correct, amount to a strong case against the *omanhene*. I told them I would convene a general meeting at Efiduasi next week.

22 August 1916
Native palaver day. Heard innumerable minor complaints, nearly all bearing on the matter of allegiance of subjects towards their chiefs. There seems to be a general tendency on the part of the petty chiefs to throw off allegiance. This, I suppose, was only to be expected with greater prosperity, but must not, in my opinion, be encouraged without just cause.

23 August 1916
Owing to a wire I receive from Colonial Secretary re export of powder and lead to French territory, have temporarily stopped all issues of both. All PCs communicated with. Western and Northern PCs told to take every measure to prevent export.

29 August 1916
Palaver day. Nothing of importance, mostly applications for permission to import double-barrelled guns, all of which I refused. All prosperous cocoa planters think that they should be allocated to possess sporting guns. Addressed the native high life of Coomassie at 6.00 p.m. in connection with Red Cross.

8 September 1916
Civil court from 9.00 a.m. to 1.00 p.m. Office in afternoon. Read through several diaries. All quiet. Kobina Foli is anxious to build a motor road between Akrokeri and his capital, Fomena. As we have no funds, Philbrick proposes to let him advance the timber and skilled labour and repay him next year. A good idea if I can get motors to run on the road as soon as it is ready to receive them.

12 September 1916
Interviewed Kwamin Afram. He was extremely dignified and moderate in his demands. He is willing to abdicate provided the stool is kept in his family, to which it has belonged since Osei Tutu's time. I fear that this will not prove agreeable to the opponents, in as much as they have got heavily into debt with one Kwaku Boaten, a Kumawu man, who if given the stool will wipe off the amount. But this is only conjecture on my part. The chief also asked that the Queen Mother might retain her stool and a general amnesty for his adherents.

14 September 1916
Interviewed the Kumawu malcontents. I believe I shall succeed in making them accept Kwamin Afram's conditions. If so, the whole problem is solved.

15 September 1916
Civil court. Three appeal cases, then a long interview with the Kumawu malcontents. They will not hear of nominating a successor from Kwamin Afram's family. I feared so, but I still hope I can come to satisfactory terms. I shall have to go to Kumawu to settle it. Unfortunately, I have no one to leave in charge, but I shall manage somehow.

22 September 1916
Sent Cutfield to meet Prouteaux[5] at Nsuta–Bechem boundary. Unfortunately, he does not speak French, but I have no one else to send.

26 September 1916
Office up to 11.30, then motored out past Bantama to meet Monsieurs Prouteaux and Cutfield. We have for the former, out of courtesy, a small guard of honour and a nice welcome by the chiefs and people generally. The boy scouts were conspicuous and very smart. The whole of the front of the fort had been decorated in tricolour by my wife, Mrs McKay and Mrs Owen. It really looked astonishingly pretty. Prouteaux was more than pleased with his reception. Indeed, you could see he was quite touched. He is a charming type of French official and very eager to see and learn all he can. It is a pleasure to show him things.

27 September 1916
Showed Prouteaux the police barracks, prison, market, school, Miller's garage and post office. He was more impressed with the school than anything else. The children are extraordinary bright and contented looking.

2 October 1916
A heart-broken private letter from Norris.[6] I am extremely sorry for him, as he means well and is extraordinarily keen, but he is tactless and impetuous. My wife and I left Coomassie at 4.30 when we said goodbye to Monsieur Prouteaux. I think he thoroughly enjoyed his visit. His tour of service so far is 59 months and he does not expect to obtain leave (unless he falls sick) until the end of the war. He much prefers the open country to the forests from a health point of view.

3 October 1916
Starting at 7.00 a.m., we reached Kumawu at 11.30. It is exactly a four-hour march, as I palavered for half an hour *en route*. Heavy rain. Skene arrived yesterday. Excellent reception in spite of the weather, it poured all afternoon. Feeling seedy. I discovered I had a temperature of 101, so turned in.

4 October 1916
Too seedy and full of quinine to hold a meeting, so remained in bed all day.

5 October 1916
Held a mass meeting, which lasted from 9.00 a.m. to 2.00 p.m. Everything is going as well as it can under the circumstances. If the nominee as Kwamin Afram's successor had to be out of the family, I would as soon have Kwaku Boaten as anyone I know. Had a private consultation with Kwamin Afram and Kwaku Boaten in the afternoon and collected all stool regalia from Kwamin Afram's house. It is now in my possession. Skene did this for me very well.

6 October 1916
Announced conditions of destoolment at a mass meeting this morning. Satisfactory as the conclusion of this affair has been, I fear it will encourage other divisions to try and get rid of their chiefs. The chiefs throughout the province feel most uncomfortable and fear the worst.

7 October 1916
Handed over all stool property to Kwaku Boaten in the afternoon and gave all parties much good advice.

14 October 1916
Office and meeting re motor traffic. We must get a special policeman to supervise the main road. Cars can do what they like.

17 October 1916
Two long land cases between subchiefs of the Central Province. Of course, boundaries had never been determined by the native authorities and I had to fix upon the most equitable limits. Now that land has become so valuable, owing to the cocoa industry, everybody is crying out for definition of boundaries. These cases give more trouble and take up more time than all the rest of my duties, and they are most harassing in as much as both sides can, and do, produce any evidence they like. Had a long talk with Ross on Western Province matters. Everything seems to be running very smoothly there. I feel sure he has done excellent work in connection with the province generally. He is one of the best type of administrative officers. Clean, straight and fearless. I much regret his departure. Perhaps YE will entertain his desire to return to Ashanti some day later on.

18 October 1916
Civil court. Goaso, Sunyani and Wenchi returns, including diaries, read through. All well. Boyle[7] amuses me. He writes: 'Nothing of importance occurred except that my wife and I were nearly killed by a mad cow on the Kintampo road.' I should have thought that rather important if it had happened to me. The Coomassie Chamber of Commerce in the shape of Mr London (president and head of Swanzy's) and Mr Owen (head agent of the African Association) wanted to know why the issue of powder had been stopped. I told them the reason and pointed out a fact they had completely overlooked, that is that the issue of any ammunition is a privilege and not a right. Sharman [PWD] came to my office with plans of the new market, for which YE kindly said that £1000 would be provided in 1917. The plan will, of course, be submitted to the DPW. The sheds are large and practical, but the scheme is hardly as ambitious as I should have liked.

19 October 1916
With regard to Prouteaux's visit, Boyle writes: 'To Sunyani. We arrived at 12 o'clock amid a perfect *feu de joie* and hearty welcome. The whole thing was wonderfully stage-managed and the singing of the Marseillaise, quite distinctly phrased by the school children, was a revelation of what they can be trained to do.' The same thing happened in Coomassie, and I don't yet know where they got the French words. I hear that Prouteaux has incurred his governor's displeasure

for coming on to Coomassie and absenting himself so long, but it will all be condoned by the heartiness of his reception. French courtesy will not be able to prevail against it.

20 October 1916
Heard by telegram from Colonial Secretary that the government dentist could not alter his programme and visit Coomassie. But why did his programme not include Coomassie? He has never favoured us that I know of. Several government officials will now have to proceed to Seccondee. Loss of time and cause [of] unnecessary expense against this one man's journey and no loss of time and work. It appears to me both foolish and unfair that a place containing such a large European population should be systematically overlooked by this man.

21 October 1916
Mail from Accra kept me busy all morning. Young Dasent in from the north. He has done an 18-month tour. Sports again in afternoon and jumble sale and raffles of all sorts. No sooner had my wife finished doling out prizes than it poured with rain. Exceptional luck to have got the two days' sports over without rain. A grand ball in the treasury building finished up the Red Cross programme.

23 October 1916
Civil cases occupied all the morning. Kofi Mensah, Nsuta representative at Ejura, reported by Norris for being drunk and for violent behaviour in court. This man is one of the cleverest Ashantis I know. He has been gradually acquiring more and more power and has of late been practically running Nsuta Division. He needs a lesson badly. I have suspended him for six months.

2 November 1916
Dr O'Dea reported a case of anthrax among the cattle at the experimental farm. Should it spread, strict quarantine will have to be enforced.

6 November 1916
Read through diaries of three provinces, Ashanti, Akim and Ejura. Districts all quiet. Rains damaging roads. Crime is extraordinarily quiet just now throughout Ashanti. Not being tied down by court work enables the DC to travel about a good deal, which is much the best means of developing a district.

7 November 1916
Weary land cases all morning. If crime is on the decrease throughout the dependency, land cases are certainly not. In fact, they must be said to constitute 50 per cent and more of a DC's work, the number will,

moreover, tend to increase rather than decrease owing to the economic value acquired by land in recent years.

8 November 1916
A second case of anthrax reported at the experimental farm. There is not much danger as long as it does not break out among the cattle in the *zongo*, as the herd at the farm is well isolated. More land cases. Inspected gaol and police barracks. Found all correct.

14 November 1916
Motored back to Coomassie early. Held court then office. Boyle in his diary says: 'The large number of French emigrants from Segu and the Senegal Niger country seems to point to some heavy taxing, forced recruiting, or other difficulties up there.' I expect they are having a good deal of trouble with recruiting, but this is the first I have heard of large-scale emigration. I shall keep YE informed should further developments ensue. Another entry is interesting: 'I find that Osman, the young third-class clerk, draws over £11 this month with mileage. I cannot conceive that this mileage system is a fair one. It is a great drain on the transport vote and surely was not contemplated when bicycles came in? Why not pay the clerk a bicycle allowance and stop the mileage. As it is, the juniors are overpaid and waste their money on European clothes; £4 salary and £7 allowance.' I pointed this out in my letter when proposing a sliding scale. The disparity between salary and mileage allowance appears to be out of all proportion. Why not halve it for both Europeans and natives?

16 November 1916
Administered the oath of allegiance to the *omanhene* of Ejisu. He seems a nice youth and very popular with his people.

23 November 1916
On to Abofo, six hours' actual marching. Motors can go as far as Amowin (about four miles beyond Offinso); after that the gradient becomes too steep and strong bridges don't exist. Had the usual palaver in the evening – nothing of moment, cocoa and roads practically the only topics discussed.

24 November 1916
On to Nkinkansu (18 miles); the first half of the road is undulated and wooded, the latter half flat and through more or less open country. I am agreeably surprised with the possibilities of this road and hope to do a great deal with it. Nkinkansu is a fine large village. The old Ashanti type of house is being discarded and large square compounds are the fashion.

1 December 1916
I fear I must discard my idea of making the Subiri stream the provincial boundary, as I find there are several Western Province villages north of the stream on its flow westward to the Tano River. A great pity as the boundary line will have to be an arbitrary one. I must have more topographical detail, however, before I am in a position to lay down the line. Mr Pott will obtain the information for me as soon as he can spare the time to do so.

Tekiman, 5 December 1916
Held the usual palaver this morning. Nothing of moment discussed. The *omanhene* asked several questions with regard to the cocoa market. He is very pleased at the prospect of a motor road through from Coomassie. Visited the town in the afternoon. Many new buildings are in progress. Inspected the Wesleyan school, which has much improved of late. It now numbers 77 pupils.

25 December 1916
Christmas Day, 20 to dinner.

26 December 1916
The chiefs came to wish me their Christmas greetings.

1 January 1917
Heavy thunderstorm in the night. Discussed the recruiting problem with Elgee.[8] His suggestion that the DC should accompany recruiting parties is the only practical procedure as regards Ashanti, and even then I doubt if more than an insignificant number will join.

18 January 1917
Rather an amusing episode has occurred in connection with an application of Miller's for a small plot of land, close to their present compound, for the purpose of erecting thereon a cinema theatre. Various Europeans saw me inspecting the plot and I have since been inundated with protests from neighbouring tenants on the grounds of noise, sanitation and other absurd pleas. The Basel Mission authorities have a legitimate grievance and are much more restrained in their protests. I convened the sanitary committee, inspected the land with them and decided it was not suitable for the aforesaid purpose. A storm in a teacup, quite in keeping with a cinema show.

19 January 1917
After office, motored out to Mampong for the weekend. I wish to see the *omanhene* on several small matters. Mampong is at least four or five degrees cooler than Coomassie, as it should be, it being 600 feet higher. The air here is delicious and the change is most noticeable.

20 January 1917
Had a long talk with *omanhene*, Osei Bonsu. He asked me to explain to him the working of a new rubber coagulator, sent out to him by a European who is trying to work up a syndicate at home. Simple and effective. Bonsu hopes to turn out some good rubber. But the danger is that the natives will mix several different kinds of latex together if they possibly can, so as to increase the volume.

23 January 1917
Queer rumour that Boyle is about to apply for leave, on urgent private affairs to see his wife home! I think he wants to get back to Europe at all costs. He seems to have become suddenly unbalanced and capable of any *coup de tête*.

24 January 1917
Poor Chief Frimpon (*adontenhene*) lost six cars and much petrol by fire last night. He seems to be dogged by ill luck in his enterprising venture. Worked out the year's road programme with Sharman, also inspected plans for new Coomassie railway station site. The new general manager must acquaint me of the exact amount of land he requires for railway purposes.

26 January 1917
It poured from 8.30 a.m. to 1.30 p.m. and was so dark that we had to have artificial light in the office to work by. Have never known the need of this before, especially in January.

29 January 1917
Had a long talk with some of the Coomassie chiefs re recruiting.[9] They say that their youngmen insist on the old national custom of following their chiefs into battle. Naturally enough, the Ashantis have always looked upon the soldiery as their enemies and prejudices die hard. Had permission to recruit been granted years ago, when General Morland and I recommended it, this feeling would long since have died out. But recruiting was only thrown open to the Ashantis since the outbreak of hostilities – scarcely an ideal time to join an alien and hated body of men, as all the northern races composing the regiment undoubtedly are to the Ashanti.

30 January 1917
Sent off a code telegram re Boyle who has applied for leave on urgent private affairs, because, forsooth, he wishes to accompany his wife to Europe. I have rarely come across such a piece of impertinence. It is, I feel sure, only a trick of his to get home. He has worked himself up into a restless and unbalanced state.

31 January 1917
Am receiving several reports re the dissatisfaction caused by rumours of compulsory service among the Ashantis. Of course, all these rumours are caused owing to some over zealous chiefs who have tried to compel their people to enlist. They will all evaporate when it is understood that no compulsion is intended.

5 February 1917
Criminal court and busy settling matters before leaving. Took afternoon train down to Bekwai. Took a stroll round the town. It has expanded and improved beyond recognition.

6 February 1917
Inspected land for government reservation. Sharman down from Coomassie with plans. We have found a most suitable plot for the government station. As the place is sure to develop, I agreed with Philbrick that it would be wise to forestall matters by reserving the best site for administrative purposes. The whole scheme will be submitted in due course.

7 February 1 17
Marched to Peki. Good rest house, but sandfly plague.

9 February 1917
To Mansu Nkwanta — 16 miles over good roads and through densely wooded rich undulated country. Good reception by the *omanhene* and all his chiefs.

Mbeim, Sunday 11 February 1917
Attended to correspondence. This is a quaint little place with a most unexpected palace in it. [It is] the best chief-owned European house I have yet seen — large, airy, well built with clocks that go and lamps that burn, a complete surprise.

13 February 1917
Walked to Akrokeri, five miles over a broad motor road as yet unbridged. Philbrick and I then inspected the Akrokeri–Fomena road. Bridge work proceeding most satisfactorily under the supervision of Harvey, the foreman of works. An excellent road. After lunch spoke to the Akrokeris concerning their unsatisfactory interior economy. They seem to spend their time intriguing against and destooling their chiefs.

14 February 1917
Akrokeri enquiry. Destooled the chief. They are a poor lot and lack pride and cohesion.

18 February 1917
Held a big palaver and spoke at length on recruiting. The fact of their having to go overseas frightens them off. At best, they would only be untrained levies.

24 February 1917
Held a large palaver [at Kokofu] after calling for recruits. I settled a dispute between *kokofuhene* and several Ashanti chiefs concerning the lake. Heat intense.

Coomassie, 4 March 1917
Went through a mass of accumulation, diaries and returns. Pott reports unfavourably of the insanitary state of Berekum and Wam, but this is only due to lack of inspection. Skene has an interesting entry, messengers reported that a clerk from Akwapim, suspected to be Basel Mission, has been telling the Juaben 'youngmen' not to enlist as Germany is winning the war. Gave them authority to arrest him if he can be found. A rumour is also rife that rice will be the only food over in East Africa, but these are all excuses. The truth of the matter is that the Ashanti will only fight in his own way and under his own chief. He is very highly strung and nervous (to put it delicately); all other reasons given are leather and prunella.

10 March 1917
More or less square in the office again. I have my court cases to wipe off before I can really settle down to the annual report. Excellent cinema show in evening. A series of Mampong views are particularly good and must have required excellent stage management.

13 March 1917
Civil and criminal court all morning. Issued letters to chiefs concerning recruiting and calling for 50 men from each head chief.

Sunday 18 March 1917
All sorts of alarming rumours [are] about concerning the attitude the Ashantis will adopt if coerced to fight. Sedition appears to emanate from Mampong.

25 March 1917
HE in Coomassie recruiting.

4 April 1917
One of my houseboys has been ailing for days. I sent him up to the hospital with a polite note. The MO, without vetting him, replies (1) constipation, (2) fit to work. Next morning, the boy had high fever and yesterday morning his temperature was 105 degrees, whereupon I

report the case to the PMO who attended the boy himself. This is the third case that has come under my notice of the callousness and lack of sympathy displayed by Dr Dugan in his treatment of natives. I shall speak to the PMO.

23 April 1917
Discussed sundry matters with Rice [PMO]. He assures me that I am wrong about Dugan, that he chose him purposely for his tact and sympathy with natives. This may be so. It is practically impossible for a layman to be positive on such a point, as he does not witness the patient being treated and I quite own that the law of coincidence made me jump to wrong conclusions. All I can do is keep in touch with the pulse of outside native opinion and note whether their attendance decreases or not, for it would be a thousand pities if the excellent work of predecessors, such as Le Fanu and O'Brien, were undermined for lack of the right man.

28 April 1917
Learned the sad news of the loss of the *Abosso* on 24th instant. It has cast a gloom over the whole place.

3 May 1917
Held meeting of Coomassie Council of Chiefs who were most interested in the war news and wanted to learn all about the *Abosso*, so talked to them at length on the submarine situation. They called the Germans murderers to make war on women and children.

8 June 1917
Several Coomassie chiefs to see me with regard to a third aeroplane. As Kobina Foli (of Adansi) has subscribed £1000, they wish to make up the difference.

16 June 1917
Long interview with Armitage over the appointment of an itinerant judge. We both concluded that, sound though it might be for Ashanti, it was a premature measure for the NT.

19 June 1917
Left Coomassie at 10.00 a.m. for Peki to inspect land in a boundary case. I am most pleasantly surprised to find a magnificent wide road all but completed for 11 miles. With a few bridges, this will make an excellent motor road, the intention being to connect Bekwai with Coomassie so as to enable Bekwai cars to run in to be repaired etc. A few more months should finish the whole line. I must say that we occasionally obtain more than our money's worth out of these native road overseers, appointed on no technical qualifications because none pos-

sess any, but haphazard because they are likely or handymen. Such a one is the overseer who constructed this Coomassie–Peki portion of the road. His pay £4–5 a month; price of tools and bridging will be all that this road will cost the administration for 12 miles of motor road.

21 June 1917
The lack of surveyors in this country is one of the greatest obstacles to a satisfactory and prompt dealing with these ever increasing boundary disputes. Commissioners have not the time to spare to study topographical details and certainly I can only do so on rare occasions. As a consequence, verbal evidence (invariably interested) plays much too important a part in these cases. An ADC with a working knowledge of survey work would be quite sufficient, but let him devote his whole time to plotting out disputed areas and perform no other duties.

25 June 1917
Civil court and office. Rather a curious case occurred the other day. Chief Kobina Kufno of Nkawie complained that a youth had become the paramour of three of his wives and had actually rendered one *enceinte*. A few years ago this would have meant death. Unfortunately, our law overlooks the criminal aspect of the case and the chiefs are very sore at our light treatment of such cases. To leave the youth at Nkawie was out of the question for his own sake. I solved the problem by obtaining an order of banishment from Nkawie territory, signed by the full native tribunal, and, as Armitage was just about proceeding north, I asked him to take him up with him — a better fate than the boy deserves, but rather a happy solution I thought.

28 June 1917
A long weird Mampong case over a fetish, which two sides laid claim to. I interviewed the Queen Mother of Agona to try and ascertain the trouble, which is in connection with an alleged witchcraft case. Roughly, the facts are as follows. An Appolonian fetish priest was supposed to have sought the hospitality of the Queen Mother of Agona. He repaid it by denouncing five females as witches — three elderly women, one girl and one infant in arms. Medicines were administered and two died, but whether death was caused by poison, natural causes or by violence, is unknown. Of course, the priest is nowhere to be found. A conspiracy of silence shields him. The bodies have been exhumed, with what results I know not. The police are doing their best, but they have very uphill work. If true, this is one of the worst witchcraft cases I remember.

29 June 1917
Broke up the school for one-month holiday. Usual singing decidedly good, but songs badly chosen to my mind.

4 July 1917
Back in Coomassie [from Seccondee]. The coolest and shortest journey up I ever remember. Lucky, as my wife, who has been quite seedy for some days, had to lie on a camp bed the whole time. She went straight into hospital on arrival.

5 July 1917
Heavy court. Civil cases and a gruesome accumulation of papers to wade through. I fear my wife has contracted dysentery; how or where, goodness only knows.

Sunday 15 July 1917
'Coomassie Day' [when] 30 of the men in the regiment during the siege took possession of the fort at 10.00 a.m. for one hour, during which time the gates were shut and they ate grass. Regimental Sergeant Major Amedu Grunchi headed them. A fine lot of men. We drank to them and to the memory of the departed, after which each man receives a ration of rice and bully beef. A pretty ceremony, which I was lucky enough to institute in 1905.

23 July 1917
Long criminal court. Heard the sad news of the deaths of poor Crowther and Greville. The former's death came as a great shock. I did not even know he had been ill. His loss to the Colony will be keenly felt — 1917 has proved a sad year for the Civil Service.

25 July 1917
Heard from Kortright. He is hard at work bridging the Nkoranza–Kintampo road. Since meeting Sharman at Nkoranza and realizing that the road from Ejura was about to become an accomplished fact, he has developed a great keenness for road building.

2 August 1917
Heathcote to Juaso to relieve Skene, who has been anxious to get home for some time. I think he wants to do war work of some sort.[10] Heard of the sinking of the *Karina*; no details yet.

7 August 1917
We motored out to Mampong. I have come out here for a few days to give my wife a change after her recent illness. It is several degrees cooler than Coomassie, specially at night. From here, I can keep in close touch with Coomassie and motor in any time.

9 August 1917
Returned the chief's call. So far, Osei Bonsu has been a great success as *maponghene*; his elders like and respect him. He is inclined to

charge heavy court fees – heavy according to our idea, not to theirs. We forget that, generally speaking, the *omanhene* depend upon these fees to keep up pomp and circumstance.

10 August 1917
A long talk with Osei Bonsu with regards to court and adultery fees. He appears to be quite reasonable in the matter.

13 August 1917
Interviewed the Ashanti and *zongo* chiefs. Complimented them on their road work and told them they would reap their reward on the enhanced importance of Ejura as a distributing centre owing to the new roads. No complaints of any sort were brought to my notice. Young Wilson is doing quite well. He is keen and conscientious. The district generally is quiet. The *atabubuhene* is reported to be drinking heavily. Have told Wilson to caution and watch him.

15 August 1917
Have succeeded in apprehending the fetish priest in the Agona witchcraft case. I at once sent him to Coomassie under arrest and called upon Ballantine to hold an exhaustive enquiry.

Ejura, 1 October 1917
At Wilson's request, I interviewed the young *atabubuhene* and reproved him for drinking too much. The elders reported him to Wilson and asked that he should be reprimanded. They told me he was very popular, but no cases could be heard while he was under the influence of alcohol. I warned him that if he continued drinking to excess I would recommend his destoolment. He swore the great oath in my presence, that he would mend his ways. I have my doubts. A pity, as he is a very prepossessing youth and well liked by his people.

3 October 1917
The old Queen Mother, after having been ill for months, is up and about again. I was very pleased to see the old lady again. Her congratulations at our escape from the perils of the deep (for she had not seen us since the *Appam* affair) was sincere and graciously delivered.

14 October 1917
To Nkwanta by the best native road I have yet seen. On to Wenchi in afternoon, a good reception.

(ii) A. J. Philbrick, 1917 and 1919[11]

1 November 1917
The Ag CCship devolves on me today. Mr and Mrs Fuller left for

Obuasi this morning. Their departure was private, but most Europeans and many chiefs and natives attended. Moved into the fort from the Colonel's house, where I have been lodged up to now owing to the fort being full. Spent morning and afternoon working on papers in the office.

3 November 1917
Migeod[12] advised me of a chance to get to Ejura, which I jumped at. In spite of the abnormal rains, the road keeps fairly good, but there are many places with guttered and washed-out surfaces. I noticed a great increase in inhabitants along the road. Interviewed Osei Bonsu at Mampong, and the *omanhene* of Agona. Met Wilson at Ejura. He seems well; the station was in excellent order. The DC's bungalow and garden have been much improved.

Sunday 4 November 1917
Worked in office in morning to clear table.

5 November 1917
Morning spent in correspondence. At present, the work here is light and much less than usual. Inspected stock of stationery, which is low. The greatest care will have to be used. More heavy rain, which, I fear, is doing immense harm to the roads. Attended a successful Red Cross concert, and took the opportunity to thank the native committee for their labours.

7 November 1917
Very little work and hardly any complaints.

9 November 1917
Two land cases came in this morning, both begun. Potter [East Kent Regiment] called re recruiting. Ashanti to date has sent 943 recruits, but Potter tells me over 200 have deserted. Collected the chiefs and impressed on them the disgrace of permitting deserters to go unpunished. They promised again to send in all they could find, also to supply boys to learn motor driving.

15 November 1917
Resumed hearing of Chief Kufno's claim to subjects at Tuntuma. Dr Duff, who wished to pass the final proficiency exam in Twi, attended at my invitation to act as interpreter. He declared the test as being unreasonably hard. Wheatley reports a disturbance at the lake over the fishing rights. All the lake youngmen, headed by the chief of Banso, came to Kokofu to maintain their arguments by force; but Wheatley wired later on that he was able to quiet them, temporarily at any rate.

16 November 1917
To Bekwai for the day to see the Wheatleys who are there now. Wheatley gives me a reassuring report on the lake troubles, but states the settlement will need delicate handling. Interviewed the *omanhene*, who has now finished the DC's house, an imposing two-storey brick structure with iron roof that compares most favourably with the PC's quarters at Obuasi.

18 November 1917
A motorcar would be a great boon. At present, I have to go cap in hand to Migeod or the PE, who are both very good but of course make a favour of lending me their cars. Personal encouragement is absolutely necessary to natives who are giving free labour and I am trying to visit the roads in progress as often as possible.

19 November 1917
Cozens-Hardy [General Manager, Railways] at my request met the sanitary board and myself to show and explain the new railway project in Coomassie town. I was amazed at the growth of the scheme since I handed back to Fuller in August 1916. It is now proposed to take more than double the land then suggested, and that in the most crowded part of the town. I am afraid compensation will be enormous and that there will be dissatisfaction amongst those dispossessed of good business stands and driven out to the less profitable neighbourhood, also among the chiefs whose free plots will be taken.

24 November 1917
Breckenridge [DC], who was coming in today, down with fever at Ejura. Case of yellow fever reported at Saltpond. Lorema called in as to precautions to be taken.

27 November 1917
Breckenridge, who should have reached here last week, was brought in from Ejura at 10 o'clock last night. O'Dea warned me this morning he was very ill. At midday he was evidently dying and I tried to talk to him, but he was too far gone. At 1.15 he died. O'Dea tells me it was yellow fever, and it looked precisely similar to the very many deaths I have seen from this. He seems to have contracted the infection at Yeji or north of it.

28 November 1917
Attended Breckenridge's funeral in uniform. Full military honours were given him and all passed off well and impressively.

1 December 1917
News of the loss of *Apapa*[13] with terrible toll of life. Accra again seems especially unfortunate.

4 December 1917
After a morning spent on papers, left at 2.00 p.m. in a touring car, hired from Miller's, for Ejura, for the purpose of opening the Ejura–Nkoranza section of road. There I met Migeod and Wilson. I inspected the *zongo*, which is growing and was busy with cola. A rice growing industry has sprung up here, which may lead to better things for Ejura. The rice is reddish and very sweet to eat.

8 December 1917
Got instructions to arrest the Germans at the Basel Mission and factory. Sent for the whole staff and went through papers. Lipps is the only ostensible German. Put him under arrest in an empty bungalow, his wife and children with him.

12 December 1917
Received reply about Prempeh's mother[14] and communicated the news to linguist, Nuama, who said he would guarantee no special trouble in the market or elsewhere. Wilson had to go into hospital. O'Dea says he is malarial and should go home. Took 30 grains of quinine myself as [my temperature] was 102 last night. Walked round reservation with Heathcote. He admired the avenues a great deal.

To Koforidua, 21 December 1917
At 11.00 a.m. I drove in Swanzy's lorry to station. Found a very busy scene. A surprisingly long train [was] filled with passengers. Noticed especially the neat houses of the railway workmen and the pretty type of post office. Was met by Applegate, who did the honours with enthusiasm. The town is well laid out. Looked at the cocoa sheds, which could easily be improved. The rest house is a most comfortable and up-to-date building. Got a wire telling me of Kortright's breakdown.

[On 3 October 1919 A. J. Philbrick again took over as Ag CC Ashanti.]

1 November 1919
Ross very bad in hospital, feared to be liver abscess. Called on him. O'Dea says he will have to go away before he is fit to resume work. Probably this illness accounts for his petulant and ungracious demeanour lately.

6 November 1919
Took Ross for a drive. He had a narrow escape.

15 November 1919
The butchers crowded into the fort yard this morning to beg again for silver. Gayton wrote in to say he would lose all his labourers north of Attabubu unless he could get silver. Every native, even those from the

bush, is insisting on silver so as to sell it at 5/– in the pound profit. Messrs Light and Talland paid a flying visit. They could promise no relief in the currency situation, which gets worse daily. At Obuasi, there has been no meat for three weeks as the butchers cannot get silver. The European miners are losing patience.

29 November 1919
At Obuasi, where I had a long talk with Watkins on the cocoa rent claimed by Kobina Foli. He agreed to the proposal to collect the rents on behalf of corporation and to pay them over after deducting the cost of collection to the head chiefs. The corporation is having difficulty with its labour owing to the shortage of silver. The Secretary of State has agreed to their paying wages in gold coin, and Watkins is now expecting £2000 a month in gold. I have induced him to offer it first to the head chiefs in return for silver. The distribution of gold coins, worth nearly double their face value, will cause unrest amongst labour and will attract everyone to the mines from other work.

30 November 1919
At Obuasi recalling memories of other days.

Obuasi, 4 December 1919
Kobina Foli looked well, his illness is diplomatic, I think. His fetish has told him not to live in Obuasi. He offered at once to take £2000 in gold in exchange for silver, so he at least is not very poor.

11 December 1919
Tried a murder case, a simple but savage *crime passionnel*, the accused glorying in his deed.

14 December 1919
Water situation is getting serious. Prempeh's well is running dry and the scenes at Odum wells, where women wait all night for water, is pathetic. A pipe-borne supply will be a real blessing.

Juaso, Central Province[15]

(i) A. W. Norris, Ag DC, 1916

8 June 1916
To Mpraeso. Although all the chiefs knew I coming no one came to meet me, or salute me in any way. At Akwaihu was informed that the *adibme* is at Accra where he has been for about two years. It seems that Mr Hobbs knew this.[16] It will be impossible to do any work here I am afraid, but I am glad to have seen such a beautiful station. Talks with *kwakunene* about oaths being sworn on Obo land in Ashanti.

Can get no help from Mr Hobbs in this. He is antagonistic and is working to get the boundary changed. These Coast DCs do not understand the Juaben people.

13 June 1916
Further talk with Mr Hobbs about the Afram plain dispute. In a way got him to see the difficulty of fixing some imaginary line as a boundary. Suggested that all plain, as regards human hunting, should be thrown open to Agogos, but that as regards fishing certain pools or stretches of the Afram should be allocated to the various parties. Mr Hobbs does not quite like the idea, but I think agrees with me that it might be used as basis of a settlement of the dispute. Had a talk with the *omanhene* about various matters. He remembers me when I was OC troops at Mampong in 1902 and again when I was Ag DC Coomassie.

14 June 1916
Left Abene 6.30 a.m., arrived Onemisu 1.30 p.m., a very rough bush path through belts of forest with patches of open country. Could not bicycle at all. Had to walk all the way.

15 June 1916
Left Onemisu arrived Agogo 10.15. Met by the chief and elders outside the town. At 5.00 p.m. sent for the chief and talked to him, trying to get him to agree to the Kwakus having fishing rights. Could not get him to entertain the idea. In effect, his answer was the *kumawuhene* and I conquered the land and we will give up nothing. The government are our masters and if they use force well and good. The government has the strength. He agreed to go off and talk the matter over with his elders and answer me tomorrow, but I doubt any favourable answer. I used every threat I could think of by way of persuasion.

20 June 1916
One of the *omanhene*'s nieces died at noon. Funeral custom all the evening and night. It was interesting to watch the *omanhene* rush down the town and pretend to catch strangers. Doubtless, in olden days there would have been some killed.

2 July 1916
Dispatched mails and two police left for Coomassie with £200 specie. Office morning. Checked cash three times found deficit of £4.3*s*.2*d*. I cannot understand this. I must have made some payment and forgotten to enter same. Shall replace with a cheque and send to Coomassie as a remittance between chests. The special runner returned at 7.00 p.m. (good going) with letter from CCA saying I was to be at

Coomassie on Thursday next and that I am to be transferred to some other place — where and when not mentioned.

(ii) C. E. Skene, DC, 1916–17

18 July 1916
Took over the district [from Norris]. Checked cash.

19 July 1916
Civil cases and appeal cases of which there appear to be a great number. Went through letters of complaints, which are unfortunately almost always against *amanhene*, and not between private parties. Put two unpaid bailiffs under £50 bond with two sureties. The road Askori–Akotoase is in very bad condition. I stopped on the way and turned out the villages under Askori to clean. The road to Domeabra is heart breaking, and there are no bridges to be seen over any of the streams to Juaso. I understand that they are broken as soon as made by cask rollers,[17] but certainly something must be put up.

20 July 1916
Court and complaints. There appears to be a vast number of native palavers, as against court cases and appeals.

21 July 1916
Court and complaints re desecration of fetish house. Inspected town. The buildings are in good condition but the roads are badly washed out.

22 July 1916
Office. Inspected prison and heard prisoners' complaints. Sold stamps and postal orders.

24 July 1916
Court and numerous complaints, as anticipated by Mr Norris.

29 July 1916
Court, sale of stamps and pay day as I am off on trek on Monday.

Sunday 30 July 1916
Office with monthly returns and vouchers. Heavy official mail arrived.

31 July 1916
Left for Obogu over a very muddy road. The stretch near Obogu is good, but bridges are conspicuous by their absence. Nkwanta is a very clean village and was in excellent condition. Court at Obogu. Drew up cocoa bye-laws. Inspected town in afternoon. *Omanhene* anxious to expand the town and establish a Hausa *zongo* for the cola trade. He also asked for an English school, complaining that the Basel

Mission schools pay more attention to Twi than English, and do not discipline their scholars. This I agree with from what I have seen of those schools. Promised to ask for an assisted school and also to open a temporary lockup for criminal prisoners, similar to the one I started at Mampong, which is a great convenience to the DC when travelling. Some ruins in the town to be pulled down and rebuilt.

4 August 1916
Court. Continued land case, but could only get frankly biased evidence from the *omanhene*, which was worthless. Apparently, the same plot of land has been given to both Dampon and Wenchi, in different cases, by Mr Norris, according to the evidence. Am writing him. Spoke to the *omanhene* about helping to build a temporary Wesleyan schoolhouse, providing that it will have to come down, if it interferes with the future railway station.

3 August 1916
Court at Bompata. Numerous complaints, including two connected with bad medicine. Criminal summons issued in one case of this. The *bompatahene*'s flagrant display of favouritism and dislike is the cause of many quite unjustifiable decisions, which call for reversal on appeal. A very painful night with a jigger, which had got right in beneath my big toe nail.

Domeabra, 4 August 1916
Good cycle road with a few dirty patches, which are now being cleaned. Two big bridges are wanted. Chief wants to build a rest house and one should be built here as it is a place constantly visited. More appeals from Bompata, which follow me about with unfailing regularity. Fortunately, however, I do not think the *omanhene* resents having his decisions reversed. It is all part of the game.

7 August 1916
Bank holiday. Office and mail. Saw *juasohene* and *apamfo* about school and dispensary for Juaso, and also about Kwakoko's stool palaver with Efiduasi, about which I had received a letter from the CCA. The *odikro* came in and refused to drink fetish[18] to Efiduasi, fearing a heavy fee, I think. Have written *efiduasihene*, but the whole affair has been settled by CCA and the stool handed over, so there is nothing for him to do but bow to the inevitable. I will try to get reasonable terms for him.

21 August 1916
Heavy criminal day, including a case of shooting, which I took as negligently causing harm. As the gun was unlicensed, the total sen-

tence was six months. Messrs Holloway and Craig, representing Fry and Cadbury came to see me, retaking an option on plots of land in Juaso and Konongo.

24 August 1916
To Juaben along bush path. The *juabenhene* is to make a proper road for his section here. Court at Juaben, Wusu's palaver settled, but the *omanhene* takes any decision against himself very badly and talked about spoiling the youngmen. I gave him a talking to in the evening, when he came to see me and explained the folly of wantonly alienating a hitherto loyal subject and rousing the youngmen against himself. He was inclined to be truculent at first, but showed much more amenity later.

Juaben, 25 August 1916
Court and complaints. The *omanhene* showed a malignant disposition to pursue grievances to the end and tried to get Wusu Atta, a drum beater of his, sent away. Wusu seems a very quiet decent fellow and only wants to be left in peace. Queen Mother reported death of a stool servant and said she was suspicious of cause.

2 September 1916
To Obogu and back in morning. Enquired into death of *omanhene* and succession to stool. Found that the elders had already selected a second chief, Humuwo, to the stool, and taken satisfaction money. Gave them a rating for this and told them they could only recommend a successor. Money handed back to Humuwo. Stool, umbrella, swords etc. handed in to me and put in locked room in charge of Banso chief and elders. Humuwo forbidden to allow fetish to be drunk to him, as yet, and town put in charge of elders. Kofi Fofie, the *omanhene*, to recommend a new second chief. He is of the same family as late *omanhene* and Queen Mother. Afternoon I made up final cash returns. At 10.00 p.m. a letter came from CCA telling me to come to Efiduasi as soon as possible.

4 September 1916
To Efiduasi. Stopped to see *juabenhene* and dosed him with quinine. Met CCA holding Kumawu palaver with Mr Gale, COP. No final decision yet as to *omanhene*. Discussed several matters with CCA and lunched with him. To Juaben in afternoon. Heard complaints. Saw *juabenhene*, who was better, and left him some medicine. He is to consider whether he will have back the exiled *ankobrahene*, Boaten, who has appealed to return.

12 September 1916
Court. Kwakoko chief given last chance to behave sensibly. He refuses

and will be destooled and sent away with his brother and son, who also refuse. Nearly all except his own family have drunk fetish to Efiduasi and will return to Kwakoko. Have sent for remaining ornaments and the people to come in and have matters explained. Mr Straw of association to see me. Apparently, the price to be offered for cocoa this season by all the firms will be low and, if the export tax on cocoa and the rise in railway freights come into operation, the price will be so low that I am afraid the people will not take the trouble to bring in their crops. This will be extremely unfortunate, as last year's big prices instilled keenness into the native farmers.

4 September 1916
Sent for a dozen of the Kumawu rioters to come and give their guns a turnover. A lot of them are being spoilt by white ants.

16 September 1916
All the Obogu elders up and there was a long talk. The elders have chosen one Kwame Appiah, the grand nephew of the late *omanhene*, for second chief, but the *ohimba* and one elder of his family protest against it. They say that the stool belongs to them, that Yaw Wusu's family had never held the stool before and that Mr Norris allowed Yaw Wusu to hold it because he offered to pay the stool debt. This is all true, but the fact of Yaw Wusu having held the stool makes his family royalty, I take it, and if the elders want a man from his family, it is quite in order. The *ohimba* should have made her fight to prevent Yaw Wusu's coming on at all if she wished to protect the succession. They are to discuss it again and give me their final unbiased choice.

Sunday 17 September 1916
Mail arrived. Powder issues stopped.

19 September 1916
Dispatched mail. Court and complaints.

20 September 1916
Court. Final discussions with Obogu elders. Ahunuwo contends he was deceived when Yaw Wusu was put on the stool, as he was told then, by Mr Norris, that after Wusu's death the stool was to go to his family for all time. This is not so, according to the paper signed by them. At any rate, the elders all want Appiah for second chief and I shall recommend him. Ahunuwo and the Queen Mother agree to waive their objections of necessity, and the stool debt is to be shared out among the elders.

25 September 1916
Court. The cocoa export tax is passed and also the 50 per cent rise in

railway freights. Luckily, the tax will not make too great a difference in the price, but it will bring it down to 13/– a load. The *juasohene* and the *konongohene* say their people will not sell at this price and will hang on to their cocoa. Rumour brought in by *juasohene* that they get 30/– a load in Koforidua. There have been several attempts at burglary in the town, presumably by Moshis, of whom there are a good number doing nothing. I have warned them that if another attempt is made they will all be turned out of the Ashanti houses where they are now living, till the *zongo* is made.

27 September 1916
Court. Moshi chief from Coomassie to see me. He is recruiting labour for the mines, and I have told him to take as many as he can get from Juaso.

3 October 1916
CCA and Mrs Fuller arrived at 11.00 a.m. and went to the rest house, as *omanhene* is to be destooled.

4 October 1916
CCA down with fever. Palaver postponed till tomorrow. Held court, more assault cases, mainly due to repressed excitement in the town. My mail arrived post to post.[19] The West African currency notes are in. Showed the notes to the Kumawus who seem to like the idea, but I have explained there is no wish to force them upon them. I explained the advantage over silver in the matter of bulk, with which they agreed.

5 October 1916
At 9.00 a.m. the CCA arrived and held a long palaver. Kwamin Afram is to be destooled, but generous terms are to be given him in consideration of his former loyal service to government. The opposition have nominated Kwaku Boaten as his successor. After the palaver, I collected stool property and went over the compounds claimed by Kwamin Afram and the *ohimba*. His people complained that the opposition said they would beat them and drive them out when they got the stool, also that they were to pay half the stool debt. I recalled the CCA's remarks to them and they promised to serve the new *omanhene* faithfully.

6 October 1916
Court. CCA a addressed the people and published the terms. Kwamin Afram to leave to lay stool property handed over. House to go to *ohimba*, Afram's wives to go with him and an amnesty to be given to Afram and supporters. Boaten to take over the stool assets and liabilities on one year's probation. The Moshis said they had been

threatened with expulsion by Boaten's party. Reminded them of conditions of amnesty. I talked to the leaders of the 'youngmen' who promised that Kwamin Afram would not be molested or insulted on his departure. Have sent for stool property to come in tomorrow. Kwamin Afram went off at 2.30 p.m. under escort of two policemen as the stool ornaments have not yet come. The people behaved very well in the town and kept their promise not to insult him. All his wives went except three, who are ill. I have been through his palavers and given the private ones to the *ohimba*. Stool ornaments arrive at 2.30 p.m. Sent a message to Efiduasi to take the guard off Kwamin Afram.

7 October 1916
Bicycled to Efiduasi to enquire into the shooting of a burglar by Hansen, Fisher's agent. Had to bring it in as manslaughter and arrested Hansen. Back to Kumawu. CCA handed stool property to Boaten and gave the people a final address.

17 October 1916
Have allowed several appeals from *agogohene*. All the 'youngmen' are in for the stool debt tomorrow. I see from Messrs Boyle's and Norris's diaries that they usually run to bush. Went through *omanhene*'s court record book and reduced one judgement. Inspected town, which is remarkably clear of weeds. The road needs repair and this is in progress throughout the town.

22 October 1916
The 'youngmen' and women mentioned in the *ohene*'s list have now run away, in spite of the chief beating gong gong, and I have warned the people that, if they do not appear to say whether they paid or not, I will recommend that they be treated as defaulters, and they will pay the tax. Visited the Basel Mission station and went through their minute book. The children sang to me for quite a long time. Visited Basel Mission station by request to see a football match, which was distinguished by a frank disregard of the rules.

24 October 1916
To Bompata. Talked about cocoa and showed the currency notes. A wrangle about Christians swearing oaths was discussed. I have ruled that in future any Christian who comes down from the station for palaver in the town and swears the *omanhene*'s oath shall pay the full oath fee to him. And then I will take the case in my court. I trust CCA will not object to this. The Basel and Wesleyan pastors agree and the people have been warned. The Bompata elders have arrogated too many cases to their courts, I think, and are inclined to resent my

taking cases or allowing appeals. I have told them I want all native palavers, for example marriage, adultery, abuse etc., to go to them, but I reserve, to all parties, the right to ask for an appeal.[20]

25 October 1916
To Juaso via Wenchi through the bush. A new road is being made here. [There are] three streams waist high without bridges. Found on arrival Mr Hesse, my clerk, lying with what appeared to be a broken arm sustained a week ago. Sent him into Coomassie in a hammock. Explained the German attitude towards the Islamic propaganda to the Hausas and gave them copies. They will tell all the Moslem people in the district. [At Juaso] car from Coomassie came in. I am glad to hear that a further £2 is to be spent on the main road by PWD.

3 November 1916
The price of cocoa is going down every day and the government advises holding up, but plenty of cocoa is coming up from the Coomassie villages and my farmers are in danger of getting left. I have advised the people now to sell their cocoa at once. I am awaiting an official answer from CCA before circulating the *amanhene*, but I have explained the whole matter to the *apamfo*. They realize their danger and the danger of the stores shutting up their stores in this district and refusing to buy cocoa. At present, the government attitude is proving a failure. If these farmers had sold three weeks ago they would have got 13/– to 14/– a load.

4 November 1916
As the Agogo people have not come in, I am writing up the case to CCA and recommending that they be called on to pay. This solution would agree with the strictly legal view and it will be a lesson to them to obey gong gong and not run to bush whenever the DC visits their town.

12 November 1916
To Mpraeso over a good broad road, a very pretty station. Had the misfortune to sprain my ankle rather nastily. Put on the sick list by the MO. Letter from Mr Lewis, the Adventist missionary at Agona, asking me to write the *kumawuhene* to start a school for him. As I have not seen the *omanhene* about it, I cannot accede to his request immediately, though I am in favour of helping any mission in addition to the Basel Mission on account of the latter's unpopularity with the natives.

17 November 1916
To Juaso. I am cutting deviations in the road to avoid the worst hills

and the road is generally being widened and made up. There is no reason why cars should not run through with a little more work being done on the road. Marked out streets for two new villages and showed Asamkare chief what kind of a rest house I want – not the Ashanti type but three-roomed type.

30 November 1916
Issued road notices and wrote to CCA. Made up accounts and paid salaries. Wrote to Blackmore, inspector of schools, who is to discuss the new government school at Juaso with me. I am very glad it has been sanctioned.

14 January 1917
Left for Boankra. Road has been spoilt in many places by careless cask rolling. I turned all villages out to make up narrow banks, ruts etc. Tornado with heavy rain. Letter from CCA re Europeans with military experience. There is still a chance.

23 January 1917
A very bad time with fever, my third attack in six months. As I never see any mosquitoes here, I can only put it down to the ravenous sand-flies, which are not supposed to be malarial carriers as far as I know.

24 January 1917
Still very shaky, but got down to court as there is a heavy mail to be answered. Hear that the Ag Governor and CCA may be coming down this way, recruiting.

25 January 1917
Court. Clearing for school nearly finished. I will put in the foundations on Sunday, if approval of the site and plan arrive from CCA. Mail arrived with recruiting posters.

31 January 1917
A fight at Juaso between Moshis and Ashantis. Not a very serious one. All parties fined.

5 February 1917
To Banso. Messengers report that a clerk from Akwapim, suspected of being from Basel Mission,[21] has been telling the Juaben 'youngmen' not to enlist, as Germany is winning the war. Gave them authority to arrest him if he can he found and bring him to me. Gave them messages for the 'youngmen' explaining how the war is really going.

14 February 1917
In the evening, a messenger arrived from Agogo to report a fight between the two parties of 'youngmen'.

15 February 1917
Message in the morning that the fighting had been stopped by the *frydemhene*, to whom great credit is due, and to the other *omanhene*, but one man has died. Went up quickly and found that there had been a nasty riot, though no guns were used. Arrested all those on both sides who had any wounds and the leaders of the fight, including the chief's clerk. The Agogo and Domeabra chiefs were wearing their war tunics, but were laughed out of them. As I explained, the only war I knew of was that with Germany. Destooled the *kyidomhene*, who has stirred it all up, and sent him away today to wait at Juaso. Saw the dead man and arrested the man who killed him. Have sent to seize all the guns of the rioters, but they have left the town with them. Also shut up the gin store here. Am getting a list of rioters' villages and I am going to take their guns. In the evening, another house-to-house search produced some guns, mostly loaded, some of which, being unlicensed, were broken up and the others kept by me.

18 February 1917
The Queen Mother says she wants to resign her stool and go away to Kumawu and take the 'youngmen' with her. They refuse to make peace with the chief. I have forbidden them to go.

20 February 1917
At last got a written statement of the complaints of the rioters. Talked to them a long time and said if they made peace with the chief I would put all their complaints right and they would not be charged for drinking fetish. However, they all said they wanted no further palavers, but could not stay with the chief and wanted to go to Kumawu and leave all their farms and houses. I said they could not be allowed to go to Kumawu, but I would see if they could settle in Bompata, as the *omanhene* wished. They all agreed. Juaben states that his youngmen will not volunteer, but wants to subscribe £400 instead. The Ashanti Akims are *en train* to be known for ever as a race of cowards. None will volunteer, though they will join the police. They openly say they are afraid to fight.[22]

23 February 1917
Court. Afternoon knotted up by a sharp attack of ptomaine poisoning with high fever.

24 and 25 (Saturday and Sunday) In bed.

27 February 1917
Called down to see Adamfo Yaw Boakye, who was unconscious and moribund when I arrived with what seemed to be pleurisy. It was too

late to give him medicines and I could only poultice the sore spot and keep him warm.

28 February 1917
Boakye died in the night, a great loss in Juaben and Ashanti Akim affairs. Rated the chief and elders soundly for not telling me he was so ill before, so that he could be got into Coomassie.

1 March 1917
Court. Made up list of prices of native food.

2 March 1917
Dispatched mail. The Hausas and Moshis are refusing to work on the Wenchi road, although they have been hired by the *juasohene* to do so. Sent police down to collect all who disobeyed the *seriki zongo* and warned them; they have all gone to work now.

Saturday 3 March 1917
Superintended prisoners re making road to town.

Sunday 11 March 1917
Back to Juaso. Stuck in ditch a mile outside Konongo and had to walk home, arriving late.

14 March 1917
Left for Atuindia. Stopped at Kumesu, dragging the big beams and hauling all to riverside. Banking also beginning and all is ready to drive the piles tomorrow when the bridge must be finished. Post to post letter from CCA to the four *omanhene* re recruiting, will be distributed early tomorrow.

15 March 1917
On the bridge early. I finished the fences on both sides for the bridging, which is fairly high owing to the unusual height of the water. Got the piles across, measurements taken and the big beams over. Finished nailing the planks and the protecting ends and wings and the banking half finished by 5.30 p.m., which is fairly rapid going.

30 March 1917
HE, the Ag Governor, the CCA, Colonel Haywood and Mr Newlands (PS) arrived at 11.15 and held a recruiting palaver, the *amanhene* being invited to speak. HE inspected Juaso buildings and agricultural station. The government school at Juaso is to be built as soon as possible.

4 April 1917
Marked out and pegged site for school, to get foundations put in

tomorrow and ground re-levelled. Enrolled another 18 recruits, having to reject three for medical reasons.

7 April 1917
To Coomassie for medical for extension of tour.

10 April 1917
Back to Juaso. Found that owing to a mistake of the police, the recruits were being marched into Coomassie without orders and had had a fight with the Odumasi people. Stopped at Konongo to look into it and ordered the recruits back to Juaso.

11 April 1917
Court. The Odumasi palaver seems to have been as much the fault of the recruits themselves as the townspeople. Complaints are coming in about the conduct of the recruits, who are trying to extort money on the strength of enlisting. I will get them into Coomassie as soon as possible, but the OCT cannot take more than some 20 at a time. Meanwhile, I am keeping them as much as possible in Juaso.

17 April 1917
Find the recruits going into Coomassie have been asking for money. Forbade the chiefs along the road to give either gin or money, only food and water being required.

21 May 1917
Received six spring balances, confiscated by Mr Inman (inspector of weights and measures). The new regulation making the circular balance compulsory will be very hard on the farmers, as the firms do not sell them. The present balance is much easier to carry and suffices for the farmers' needs, which are merely to make up the 60-pound load. Inspected prison and ordered shingles to repair roof.

2 June 1917
Turned prisoners on to making shingles for the school to relieve the *juasohene* of providing these.

4 June 1917
Sent draft of £100 to CCA, being donation from the *juabenhene* to war fund on account of his Konongo boys deserting in Coomassie. He states it is almost impossible to get further recruits.

(iii) G. C. Heathcote, Ag DC, 1917

4 August 1917
Took over station and district from Mr C. E. Skene, who left for Coomassie by motorcar.

5 August 1917
Settling down in my quarters.

6 August 1917 (Bank holiday)
Heard complaints for the recovery of debts. Chief of Juaso sent in a dash of a sheep, yams, etc. A good day, which is badly wanted.

Sunday 12 August 1917
Heard complaints. Visited the *omanhene*'s model farm. The rubber plantation is clean, but the cocoa plot is very dirty and some of the trees appear diseased.

13 August 1917
Stopped at Oyoko and arrived in Kumawu 11.30, being met by the linguist to the *omanhene* with brass band and drums at the *zongo*. The latter part of this trek was very hilly, but the scenery is very fine. Stayed in *omanhene*'s house, which is of three storeys built of stone and cement – the first native house I have seen of three storeys. It is a really large house. Heard a few complaints. The scenery from the top floor is very fine.

21 August 1917
Inspected the school, which is going on slowly. Spoke to the chief, who said he would have all the bricks and shingles ready in a week. After that, the people are to work on the Coomassie road for a week. Met the chief of Juaso about getting eggs and fruit and meat. He says since beating gong gong that people were to sell eggs at six for 3*d*., no one will sell. He is going to sell fruit every other day and meat whenever a hunter brings it in, as the butchers are not getting any now. They say it all goes to Seccondee by rail. Small bundle of letters received from CCA by car.

28 August 1917
Came to office feeling rotten. Seem to have poisoned myself with medicine. Heard a complaint or two. Wrote to Dr Lorema to prescribe for me. Dispatched mail by two runners with orders to go to Coomassie with it and, if they saw our mail carrier, they were to go on but send him in at once. I went to bed at noon.

29 August 1917
Stayed in bed all day. Mail arrived about 11.00 a.m., having been opened and robbed by two Moshi men at Konongo. We have one in custody, one registered letter lost. The carriers with the outward mail, on meeting with the mail carrier, returned with him, so that mail was delayed and opened by the robbers.

30 August 1917
Came to office. Feeling better. Signed all pay vouchers and paid officials. Stopped all work on schoolhouse, *vide* CC's minute of 14 August 1917. Estimated expenditure to finish it £14.11*s*. Amount already spent £52.9*s*.1*d*. Seems a pity to stop now; besides, the carpenters have to be paid. Hope it may yet be finished.

3 September 1917
Very busy day getting returns made out. Chief of Juaso very anxious to get the school finished. As he says, and very truly too, if it is not finished, all the work on it will be wasted, as rainfall will wash it all away.

5 September 1917
Sold a number of old guns.

11 November 1917
Left Kwahu Prahsu 7.35 a.m. and arrived Obo rest house 11.25. A very stiff climb to the plateau. Scenery fine, although the clouds very low. The air is most exhilarating. Met the *nifahene* of Obo.

16 November 1917
Left Onemisu 6.00 a.m. Had to ford two large streams. Crossed by a small tree. I took 30 minutes to get the carriers over. Heavy rain from 9.45 for rest of day, with small dry intervals. Reached Agogo 11.15 a.m. The worst day's trek I have had in West Africa. Carriers were falling badly too.

17 November 1917
Heard complaints. One man has leprosy; I ordered his isolation.

21 November 1917
Heard news of a woman having arrived at Juaso. Mail came in 2.30 and Mr Osei informed me, as the key of my bungalow was in the hands of the gaoler to tar the rooms, he had put the woman in my bungalow, the coolest piece of impertinence I've known out here. I imagine he hopes to get a little of his own back.

8 December 1917
A French Swiss gentleman, Monsieur Ryff of the SCOA, arrived last night and reported himself this morning. He is travelling with a white valet. [Heard] 27 cases of refusing to clean weeds from round their houses in court today. Inspected school and town. School progressing well. Town not very clean.

10 December 1917
Proceed to Coomassie for examination in law of evidence.

Saturday 24 December 1917
Sat and heard complaints and civil cases till 2.00 p.m. Afternoon licensed guns. I have completed 130 licences.

25 December 1917
Heard complaints. Left for Kwaman, a somewhat tiring journey 35 minutes downhill and about an hour uphill and 20 minutes along fairly even ground. This redeeming of people, who are the ancestors of those pledged years ago, seems to be a big question and will require a definite ruling soon. I returned to Kumawu at 2.50 p.m. At 4.15 I sat and heard complaints and one civil case. Packed up at 6.15 p.m. Very tired.

(iv) C. E. Skene, DC, 1918–19

20 June 1918
Took over the district. The station is very much overgrown owing to Mr Heathcote's long absence at Kamawu. Prison walls fallen down and unfortunately my memo asking for suggestions for estimates 1919 was not answered. I was verbally told by the CCA to include a new prison wall in the 1919 estimates.

21 June 1918
Sat and heard the accumulation of complaints.

22 June 1918
CCA, Mr Sharman and Dr Lorema arrived to lunch. I am to have £40 for a new prison wall and £100 from the PWD to fell trees on the main road, if it can be spared.

24 June 1918
CCA back to Coomassie. Long day of complaints and cases. Arranged to begin the wall and there is no cement in Juaso. I have sent to Coomassie. Cleaned out the well and there is a hole in the bottom, which lets out the water; sent mason to repair it. A letter from *kumawuhene* to say that some of the 'youngmen' want to seize him at Efiduase. Told him to stay in Kumawu till I come.

5 July 1918
To Juaben, road beautifully clean, though the bridges are broken. Cordial welcome from the *omanhene*, though I fear he has been drinking again, certainly this morning. Sent him away to attend court tomorrow at 9.00 a.m. He was not offensively drunk, but garrulous and unfit for court. Told Agyeman to warn him privately that if he appears in that state tomorrow he will be fined and reported to the CCA.

Kumawu, 8 July 1918
Went round town to see if any guns were unstamped as *omanhene* had beaten gong gong every day without result. As the houses were mostly locked, instructed clerks and orderly to go round tonight. Collected some unstamped guns and sent them to Juaso.

16 August 1918
To Juaben. Long talk with Mr Bona. I think he means to try and improve his work and I must say he knows more of it now I have explained things in detail to him and shown him why treasury rules are made, and he has promised to do his best. Cordial welcome by chief and *ohimba*; all the Juaben chiefs are in. Court. Read proposed agreement to the *omanhene* and assured him that no disobedience was intended by his 'youngmen'. Told him to collect contributions to Red Cross. Warned *ohimba* to get the model farm clean for my inspection.

21 August 1918
Court. Went through pending cases and complaints first. Last night a small packet containing a black powder was found in the house, apparently a Hausa charm to prevent the truth being told. Told the *omanhene* publicly that I would take no notice of this nonsense, but that for the insult in his town I returned his presents and those of the *zongo* people. Went through nine of the 18 charges against him and, to my surprise, found that they were literally ridiculous with far less sworn than even those brought against *agogohene* in his trouble. Some were so foolish that a mere reference to DC's court record dispelled them, and I myself could deny certain of them. Probably the accusers hope that someone would be sent up from the Colony who had not personal knowledge of these complaints.

22 August 1918
Finished hearing rest of the charges: the decline from the serious language in which they are couched to the actual facts is laughable. I found nothing particular against the *omanhene* and accordingly arrested the two leaders, who signed the letter and drew up a decree of banishment against them.

23 August 1918
Court. Civil cases and complaints. *Omanhene* asked that the increased market price for bush meat should have effect on the tribute paid to him in lieu of a shoulder: that is quite fair and I made an order to that effect.

Sunday 15 September 1918
Complaints all day in bungalow. Mail arrived.

21 September 1918
To Bompata. The *omanhene* has been ill since his journey to Coomassie, which was too much for him, and could not meet me. I went to see him and found the old man looking very old and ill. Told him he need not attend court.

21 October 1918
Influenza has claimed three more victims last night and nearly all the Juaso women are attacked. Court. The Kumawus now say they wish to serve the *omanhene*. Down to town to select a site for a kitchen for the school teacher: school infested with white ants. Am sending down tar and kerosene.

25 October 1918
Down to town to inspect the sick, four deaths last night. Sent to Coomassie for brandy. Disease is spreading rapidly.

12 November 1918
To Juaso, three more deaths in Bompata, six at Wenchi, five more at Juaso.

17 November 1918.
Mail with great news of Armistice with Germany.

23 November 1918
In the evening down to *omanhene*'s house at his request to warn his wives against disobedience to him and leaving the palace without permission.

2 December 1918
Court. Bompata elders in to ask for Boaten's stool to be returned, as he has apologized to me and to the *omanhene*. I returned it. Koranten of the agricultural again in trouble about a woman: I shall have to ask for his removal if he does not pull up, as the women are afraid to go to the gardens for firewood. From 22 to 30 December in Coomassie.

13 January 1919
To Coomassie for HE's visit and investiture of chiefs with medals.[23]

22 January 1919
To Obogu inspecting a farm half way to decide on whose land certain oath was sworn: there is no defined boundary between Juaben and Obogu land. Part of the road completely blocked by an extraordinary fall of tangled trees, some of great size, nearly 200 of them, due to a tornado in November, ascribed by the *omanhene* to resentment of their fetish at their working on a Tuesday – an illogical act of resentment as they now have to work every Tuesday to clear it.

23 January 1919
Court and complaints. Warned the Christians again about obedience to their chiefs. I am afraid Nelson, the Roman Catholic minister, is rather shaky about the question of obeying oaths.

7 February 1919
Advance of one month's salary paid to clerks on account of war bonus. I hear also that there is an increase to Europeans under £500, but have not got official notice.

5 April 1919
New scale of war bonus for native staff in accordance with their position. Wrote to *agogohene* to finish rest house and to refrain from bringing medicine from Kwaku to poison fish, and to stop shooting small elephants.

18 April 1919
Mail arrived with letter from CCA. No hope of leave at present.

25 July 1919
To Bompata. Walked over a new trace cut by Dryden for a motor road and took time levels; it is not practicable, some of the grades being as steep as one in four. I fear it is quite impossible to make a motor road there as the hill range stretches right from Agogo to past Domeabra. The cocoa on the road is in excellent condition, though rather thin yield. The people have kept their farms really clean this year.

26 July 1919
A curious case from Wenchi. It seems that any Wenchi 'youngman' may call any Bompata woman 'wife' in public without paying satisfaction for the insult. I consider this most unjust and useless unless there is a good reason for the custom.

6 September 1919
Vaccination of children finished. Mura Mura elders in to nominate new chief. Told them to explain to all chiefs along their road that any complaints against the troops were to be made to the officer in command, and warned them against frivolous complaints.

10 November 1919
Talked to the chief about trying to get a gang of NT labourers, otherwise they must turn out on the road themselves. Domeabra in to ask that his people should all drink fetish to him after the riot: allowed it, but advised him to be very moderate in his demands.

12 November 1919
The *juasohene* finds it impossible to get any NT labourers at all: they

are all carrying cocoa, so I must turn out the Ashantis and give them a dash.

18 November 1919
The *omanhene* [of Kumawu] is in great straits for stool wives: his elders were told to replace those taken away by Kwamin Afram, but the substitutes are small girls of about seven and the *omanhene* is getting on in years. Told him to select older girls from the families who are unmarried.

13 December 1919
Court, criminal cases. SCOA cannot spare a car. The firms are ready enough to criticize the road, but do not offer the slightest help in any way. I cannot gravel the road and shift heavy material for bridges without a lorry.

14 December 1919
The meat shortage here is acute as the dealers refuse to accept currency notes.

Sunyani, Western Province

(i) A. H. Ross ADC, 1911–12[24]

28 July 1911
Tried two cases of nuisance, fined them 2/6*d*. Complaint as to insufficiently buried body — buried near wall of a house. Ordered body to be removed and town to be cleaned thoroughly. Wade [MO] vaccinated children. Went on to Nkwanta.

29 July 1911
Nkwanta at 7.30 a.m. Nomo, the clerk, brought in Yao Yeboa (sword bearer to the chief of Nkwanta) with his left hand shattered to the bone and part of his stomach and groin shot away. This, Nomo said, he himself had done as the result of a gun accident when he was showing his new double-barrelled gun to Yao Yeboa and his brother. The man, Yao Yeboa, appeared to be dying. Wade bandaged him and I helped, but there were no proper medical appliances handy. The thumb of the left hand was amputated. He exonerated Nomo from all blame. People rather excited and wailing and shouting outside the rest house. We kept the injured man inside. I held formal enquiry in which the whole accident was explained. Wade stayed in charge of the injured man. I proceeded to Tekimentia. Saw chief and Hyde Cooper. Chief presented a sheep, eggs, plantains and yams. Inspected town with Hyde Cooper, who is engaged in cleaning it and making it sani-

tary. At 7.00 p.m. my orderly, whom I had left at Nkwanta with Dr Wade, arrived with two Moshi men who accused him of stealing their fish. Wade sent a note to me with the orderly, as the orderly appeared to be the cause of the disturbance in the town.

Tekimentia, 30 July 1911
Tried case against my orderly and made him pay 17/– compensation to the two Hausas he had ill treated. Road palaver with chief and his elders. Upheld chief's oath and ordered 15 'youngmen' to pay fines. Wrote to the Nkwanta chief.

Tekimentia, 31 July 1911
Inspected mission school and heard the children read and questioned them on various subjects. They showed marked intelligence. Set out for Dema 8.25 a.m. Arrived Dema 11.30 a.m. Saw chief who presented fowls, eggs, etc. Sent two sureties in to sign his bond for a gun.

2 August 1911
Left Dema at 7.15 a.m. and spent entire day in forest visiting various rubber camps in connection with the land dispute.

5 August 1911
Left Dema 7.00 a.m., arrived Sabranu. Very hilly and road bad and slippery. This is a great fetish town.

6 August 1911
Talked to Sabranu elders and chiefs re cleaning town. Appointed new linguist and warned people of disobedience to chief. Directed certain houses to be pulled down, rubbish pits and latrines built. My letters to England returned to me here in error.

8 August 1911
At Bechem trying court cases and hearing complaints. Read PC's letter to chief. Town in a very filthy condition. Went round town and directed new sanitary improvements.

Dema, 11 August 1911
Offinso reports and papers dispatched to CCA.

16 August 1911
Started cutting new road by compass through the forest from Kojo Mensah's village to Tanosu. Returned Sunyani 5.30 p.m.

1 September 1911
Went with prisoners, compass, sketch, cutting road to Tanosu.

2 September 1911
Opening up road through Sunyani town.

3 September 1911
Court varied by a murder case, which lasted three days.

26 September 1911
Cutting road with compass from Tano River to Sunyani.

29 September 1911
Went to Nkwanta. Met carpenter re construction of bridges and heard chief's palaver.

Chirrah, 6 October 1911
Inspected cocoa farms and saw Martineau explain diseases of trees to natives. Selected site for new rest house.

7 October 1911
Left Chirrah 6.55 a.m., arrived *zongo* on road and had lunch. Arrived Nkwanta 2.45 p.m. Open orchard country and fan palm forest.

8 October 1911
Arrived Wenchi 9.30 a.m. Saw various chiefs concerning repair of rest houses. Tried one case. Inspected town.

12 October 1911
At Wenchi, court cases. Dispenser from Veterinary Department, Coomassie, arrived to report on cattle disease around Menge. He examined cattle here and reported no disease at Wenchi. Road making.

13 October 1911
Had Wenchi chief up and instructed him to warn his people about rubber adulteration.

Sunyani, 6 November 1911
Preparing for CCA and wife who arrive at 11.00 a.m.

7 November 1911
CCA Court, palavers and deputation of chiefs. Mail arrived.

9 November 1911
Lunched and dined with CCA. Court cases held in house as CCA and wife occupied courthouse.

27 November 1911
Court. Sent one murderer to Coomassie and two rape cases to Wenchi.

25 December 1911
Xmas day. All dined – Ford MO, Skelton OC, Fell and self.

2 January 1912
Court and licensing etc. Making up judicial returns.

4 January 1912
Statistical returns (annual).

(ii) T. E. Fell, PC, 1914–15[25]

Sunday 1 March 1914
Fuller and I had a long talk with HE.[26] Very satisfactory and I am sure HE appreciates our needs. Walked round lines. Fixed site for magazine.[27] Saw clerk's house etc. With Governor in evening.

2 March 1914
Biked with HE to Techiri, lunched there. I bicycled on to Nkwanta. Excellent rest house. Chief of Tekimentia met us, no palavers taken.

3 March 1914
Biked to Bechem, HE and Fuller hammocked. Good reception. HE inspected town and rest house. Short palaver with Bechem chief. Bicycled to Abisewa and said goodbye to Governor and party. Returned Bechem, several palavers in afternoon. Arrested extortioner from Kosu and sent to Wheatley to collar others. Went with Ekner, town overseer, and showed him where to mark out streets and plots before pulling anything down. Naish of Swanzy's dined. A nice fellow, he promises tools for town work.

4 March 1914
Biked from Bechem to Sunyani, 30½ miles in 4 hours 40 minutes. Counted loads *en route* Coomassie, 750 up to 11.00 a.m. and many more in the afternoon. Joined Ross, Duncan-Johnstone, Barker, Leat, Storey[28] and a new colour sergeant. According to native accounts every one much impressed with HE. Set a man to count all loads through station for four days. Reported, traders did not travel when HE passed, sitting down in village till we had passed.

5 March 1914
Dealt with correspondence and drafted many letters. Complaints from Odumasi as to pulling all houses down. Arranged to go there the following morning; unnecessary to plot the whole town if sufficiently wide streets are driven through. Visited town, saw linguist. Ross doing accounts, Johnstone court in morning. All the station dined with me.

9 March 1914
Busy day. Issued warrant for Kellock, Secretary of West African Trading Company, as absconding debtor. Bad business.

12 March 1914
Left with Ross for Atroni, bicycling impossible, but wheeled bike for

cyclometer distance 16 miles. Branch has given Astroni people useful cocoa advice.

13 March 1914
On to Ntotroso, cyclometer distance 11 miles. Much cola and young cocoa. New rest house nearly finished. Promised ridging for roof from Sunyani. Dealt with civil action against the chief. Long case, gave common-sense judgement. No one satisfied but myself. Much cocoa and cola. Ross heard Moshi–Ashanti assault case.

14March 1914
On to Hwidiem, four miles. New village in course of construction. Chief stated some cocoa commenced bearing, got 60 bags, 13/– per bag. On to Nkassaim. Excellent new rest house and money, say £5 each, will be required as 'dashes' here and at Ntotroso. Ask for more money from rest house vote. Palaver with chief. Few cases. Village dilapidated. Cocoa reported dying, but crop of over 100 bags. Branch to come here. Attention drawn to a forest bean, having most of the properties of shea butter used in cooking. Supply plentiful. Branch to make careful enquiry and possible new industry. People keen on improvement, but 'tired'.

15 March 1914
On Goaso, six miles. Much cocoa. *Omanhene* of Ahafo met me. Station site excellent, house excellent, prison construction and kitchen site going on well. Extraordinary good work. Garden roses, doub grass, box etc. doing well. Much more advanced than Wenchi and, considering Ross has only been here for 14 days, little short of marvellous. Long palaver re future of Ahafo with *omanhene* and chiefs, keen for development. They ask for Ross to come back. Promised to try for it. Remarkable, as he hasn't spared them as regards work.

16 March 1914
Wrote official letter, as strong a one as I dared, on police, prison staff etc. Ross settling up building accounts. Settled palaver re Tano, Dumasi and Jirasu. Stools and fetishes to return to Kobina Kupror within two days. Branch [Agriculture] arrived, but only for six weeks before going to NT. Believes much of this country to be very rich soil etc. Visited cocoa farms with Branch. Arranged for demonstration *abeko* [butternut tree] tomorrow. Arranged for chief to plant cocoa farm on station clearing.

17 March 1914
Conducted experiment with Branch on *abeko* nut oil. Nut pounded,

slightly heated, mixed with a few shreds of plantain stalks and oil expressed in wooden mortar with fufu stick. Seems fine quality of oil.

20 March 1914
Ross taking court, many cases. Left for Kukuom after lunch. Immense amount of work done on road, much unnecessary. Road being made up to 20 feet wide, 12 feet sufficient. Arrived Kukuom 4.00 p.m. Inspected town with *omanhene*. Rotten condition and practically wants rebuilding.

21 March 1914
Successful palaver with *omanhene* and chiefs re Christians, native courts, roads etc. Wesleyan Mission opening in Kukuom. Missioner asked to catch fish in Tano River. Told him he could do so at his peril.[29] He asked me to order people to school, refused but enlarged upon advantage of education. Went to Nobekaw. Fair village, people send their produce to Coomassie. Some cases for DC to see about on arrival. Returned Kukuom, trivial palaver with *omanhene*. Refused to allow alteration in Nobekaw satisfaction fees for adultery, unless agreed to and uniform for all Ahafo. Very favourably impressed with *omanhene*, quiet and dignified and takes advice well. Missioner Williams, ex-railway clerk, wanted to rejoin government service.

25 March 1914
Long court morning in Bechem. Many cases and palavers. Visited school in evening. Basel Mission making little headway in school or converts. Marked out two more long streets to be constructed. Bechem clamouring for flag promised by HE. Storekeeper of Swanzy's said his trade increasing. First place in province where one can buy beer outside Sunyani. May many more arrive.

26 March 1914
To Jemma, much northern trade met – hides, cocoa, cola, two donkey caravans. Jemma large village. Cola plantations largest I have yet seen. People most hospitable. Road bad. Palaver in evening, Jemma anxious for town overseer to mark streets. Anxious for Nkwanta–Tekimentia main road to pass through Jemma. Probably not much further and can arrange it.

27 March 1914
On to Tekimentia. Much cocoa and cola. Stayed Basel Mission compound. Examined school children, 14, quite smart. Palaver with chief. Saw rest house being built. Chief wild for corrugated iron. Promised all transport, labour, timber free if I would buy the iron. Agreed, but it will come out of heaven knows what vote. Many north country

traders and much market trade, crowds of donkeys. Announced road to Nkwanta would pass through Jemma. Idea not popular, jealous of Jemma trade. Chose site for *zongo*. Town much improved, very large village for this part. Heard Rickaby had reached Wenchi in a motor.

30 March 1914
Mail arrived. Busy day. Deplorable muddle in cash and books. Money we took to Goaso not shown anywhere. Books about £30 out in cash. Failed to spot errors and being given a lot of worry and unnecessary work. Handed over Percy[30] to Leat. Visited *zongo* and town, lot of building going on.

1 April 1914
Board of cash reported surplus of £42. Odd. Unable to find error. Owusu made Barker an April fool. Said 'he thought it was done in the highest circles.' Got severely told off.

2 April 1914
Took court. Two long criminal cases. Kortright arrived. In a lucid interval, discovered Johnstone's cash error. Carrier robbed by soldier on Fiapre road. Barker blew alarm, one man missing. Station carriers had a fight and irritated me immensely.

3 April 1914
Busy morning with Kortright and Branch who arrived. Branch had a successful journey — is under the impression natives do not do enough for government officials and should be gladder to see them. His ideas are of the type that might be called 'young'.

6 April 1914
Set Johnstone onto accounts. Mail. Rumour of resignation of Colonial Secretary. Yost Basel Mission, arrived.[31] He addresses one at two yards and behaves as if addressing a meeting.

8 April 1914
Naish of Swanzy's arrived. Very interested in *abeko* oil.

10 April 1914
Holiday. Copied March diary, long job too. Dispute between two chiefs of Odumasi.

11 April 1914
Court, accounts, mail leaving. Specie arrived, 12 boxes. Bicycled to Odumasi with Johnstone. Long palaver. Chief Peyso stupid.

12 April 1914
All European hands turned to and checked the specie.

14 April 1914
Assessed *zongo* rents with Storey.

16 April 1914
Johnstone left for Praso. Took £100 imprest. Cleared up correspondence and took court.

17 April 1914
Court all morning. Inspected senior classes in school. Not so bright as usual, possibly being taken on too fast and forgetting their grounding. Got off report on Ahafo tour. Found no action taken to select two cocoa learners. Got one from Sunyani and wrote Johnstone to select one from Ahafo.

18 April 1914
Court and correspondence. Got off cyclometer distances to intelligence officer.

20 April 1914
Heavy court morning. Dealt with Berekum, the witch doctor who gave medicine to ladies to induce childbirth and generally had connection with them himself. Gave substantial damages. Court returns, signed by me without checking, sent back from Coomassie. Johnstone mainly responsible. Very annoyed about it. Tornado blew off school roof. Went round town and *zongo* with Storey to fix best method of disposing of sanitary money.

24 April 1914
Divided stationery for Goaso and Wenchi. Arranged for land to be cleared for para-rubber plantation. Branch and school children planted out 20 trees to demonstrate correct method.

29 April 1914
Surprise survey on post office stock. Found it correct.

1 May 1914
Court and accounts. Berekum on their knees begging me not to take the light of my countenance from their water works and withdraw tools.

3 May 1914
Colonel and Hornby arrived. Bicycled from Coomassie in two days. Sent hammock to Tanosu to meet them. Kortright arrived for medical examination. Got off escort with two prisoners.

4 May 1914
Busy day, several cases – unsatisfactory ones. All station dined with me. Staked out rubber plantation with Kortright. Decided to visit

Wenchi with Colonel, as intend stationing two companies, GCR, and battery there. Question of sites.

5 May 1914
Court and accounts, a busy day. Dined with Colonel. Left per bicycle – Colonel, Hornby, Kortright and self arrived Chirrah noon. No palavers, people away snail hunting.[32] Chief sick.

7 May 1914
Bicycled Wenchi with others, 27 miles. Somewhat trying, and tired on arrival. Got there noon.

8 May 1914
Visited new *zongo* with Kortright. Well laid out and satisfactory progress. Arranged market extension. Visited brickfield, nearly 30,000 ready to be burned, made by Ashantis. Went shooting.

12 May 1914
Busy morning. Handed over to Breckenridge at Wenchi. Epidemic of meningitis (probably) reported from Sikasiko. Arranged to get Storey off next day. Wrote letters to French and chiefs. Lent Storey two bicycles.

13 May 1914
Percy, the chimp, bit off top joint of child's finger. Everyone satisfied with dash of 7/–.

Wenchi, 15 May 1914
Balanced books and checked cash. Some court palavers. Natives reported sudden death of a young man, pains in head etc. Death in 24 hours, sounds suspicious. Got isolation hospital finished. Warned chiefs to be on the lookout and report suspicious illnesses. Wrote Wam and Berekum on the subject. Visited town. Big funeral custom, lots of alcohol drunk. Got Johnstone's imprest ready.

17 May 1914
Rain in evening. Gaol safe with £600 in it, jammed and unable to open it.

23 May 1914
Celebration of Empire Day. Saluting flag, speeches, recitations etc. in school. Chiefs of Sunyani and Odumasi there. Children did very well. Sports in afternoon. Clerks had a 'garden party' at night.

25 May 1914
Court and correspondence. Storey returned from Sikasiko. Practically certain had been an epidemic of meningitis at Debibi and Sikasiko. Went round town and *zongo* with Storey. Johnstone having palaver

over Obo fetish. Johnstone should not be without police. Ashie came in *en route* Tekimentia. Kept him to plant rubber farm.

27 May 1914
Planted out rubber. Kobina Fosu told me probable objection of Mim seeing the Obo fetish was that white men spoil the power of fetishes and there might be gold in the Obo rock.

28 May 1914
Trying to straighten out tool book. Picks and shovels all practically worn out. Sent off five loads of tools to Tekimentia for road. News I have won all prizes in the Derby sweep with the *Field*.

29 May 1914
Johnstone sent up one convicted prisoner under charge of hammock boys. Started schoolboys planting para-rubber for school farm.

30 May 1914
Paying out all morning. Aves [WAFF] worse (appendicitis). Doctor wired for. Sat up with Aves all night, much better. All station feeding with me till Aves better.

31 May 1914
Watt, MO, arrived having done journey in 24 hours by bicycle from Coomassie. Fine performance. Aves bad again.

2 June 1914
Aves bad night, doctor anxious to operate, patient refused. Busy court morning. Saw Aves after lunch and persuaded him to allow operation, very ill. Gave up my house to doctor for operation and to stay in. Busy getting things ready for operation at 3.00 p.m.

4 June 1914
Aves condition hopeless. He died at 9.20 p.m.; had been practically unconscious for two days and throughout suffered little. The first officer who has died at this station.

5 June 1914
Selected cemetery site and started boys and men clearing. Everyone busy arranging funeral. Aves buried at 5.00 p.m. Military funeral. Read burial service, arrangements went well.

6 June 1914
Court cases. Had house scrubbed from end to end. Infant school falling down and unsafe. Arranged to roof new school at once.

8 June 1914
Court, accounts and odds and ends. Lunched with Storey. Watt left.

Very annoyed at post office orders delaying our mails two days in Coomassie. New order that all mails leave on Saturday no matter what day they arrive. Reams from Johnstone. Evidence in Ntotroso case volumes, but quite good. Biked Sunyani, road almost clean.

9 June 1914
Answered Johnstone's letter. Mail arrived, got off mail to Wenchi and Goaso, also police pay. Asked Kortright if he would stay another month owing to Cutfield's illness. Heard from Robertson[33] querying my drawing full pay on leave. Trouble in the *zongo* and very nearly a riot — Wangaras versus the world.

10 June 1914
Zongo case. Wangaras, headed by Mamadu, very obstinate. Had men confined to barracks in readiness.

12 June 1914
Suggested rules for *zongo* management. Wangaras unreasonable. Postponed further palaver until Monday. Mamadu tried to oust some people from a house almost causing a riot. Lost my temper with him and cowed him. Letter from Johnstone. He is by no means having an easy time, but is struggling hard.

13 June 1914
Went hunting, got within 15 yards of a bush cow in thick grass and stampeded it without getting a shot. Grass very heavy.

16 June 1914
Wire from Ag CCA. Kortright not to stay. Arrangements for Pye to Wenchi. Hardly think Pye should be out of touch with MO. Appeal from Wam court. Bicycled with Barker to see work on Odumasi road. Heavy rain. French administrator asked me to arrest escaping prisoners. Sent six soldiers to Johnstone to assist in getting in his prisoners.

20 June 1914
Civil Wam action, sensational evidence of husband catching wife *in flagrante delicto* after much tracking.

21 June 1914
Post arrived by military runner. Pye ill and heaven knows whether Kortright will get away.

24 June 1914
Little work. Court slacking off with the rains. Walked Fiapre. French prisoners arrested in Coomassie pending extradition. Sent runner to inform Bondoukou.

28 June 1914
Busy all day relicensing guns, 500. Scene pandemonium, all anxious to get done at once and pay their 2/–. Issued powder permits. Seedy at night.

29 June 1914
Guns again, 200. Demonstration of rubber boiling. Very successful, people said they would do it and experiment themselves. Went round town in evening. Several minor palavers.

30 June 1914
Returned Sunyani with Baker. Astonished to find Pye, as previous letter said very seedy. No wire announcing his departure from Coomassie. He is far from well and may be a source of anxiety. Paid station and did official palaver with Johnstone who seems well and keen.

2 July 1914
Pye left. Fairly well, but not fit to be alone. Busy morning counting and taking cash. Johnstone's affairs getting more and more surfeited with station routine. Trying petty cases and sitting at the receipt of custom.

17 July 1914
Bad frontier incident with two French police. Two people stabbed, one perhaps seriously. Sent for him to be brought in. More guns to be stamped.

22 July 1914
Fined a man £5 for forging a stamp on a gun.

23 July 1914
Got transport account and imprest accounts squared. Somewhat puzzling. Prepare *abeko* oil for Levers and Maypole Dairy.

25 July 1914
Delivered long and equivocal judgement in Odumasi case. Very annoying palaver. Both in the wrong and, after getting into a mess, give me the trouble of getting them out of it. Several other cases. Heard from Pye, not very fit.

27 July 1914
Odumasi chiefs up again. Case misrepresented to *omanhene* of Berekum, whose judgement I 'tempered', not upset. Refused to hear another word. Chief Peyso said he would live on a farm. Told him good riddance. Dealt with military police on move of military to Wenchi, an expensive amusement and will cost us at least £2000 a year more in police etc. Wrote letter on antiquated report on *abeko* oil. Glad I sent some to Levers and Maypole Dairy on my own.

30 July 1914
Paid office staff. Code wire arrived afternoon, some European crisis, very vague. Precautionary measures to be taken. Regiment mustered their reserves and became ready to fight any nation.

2 August 1914
Order for half company of GCR proceed to Coomassie. Presumably war with Germany. Sent runner to Bondoukou.

3 August 1914
Crockery and stores arrived, sent carriers straight back. Could have raised 150 carriers on the spot if necessary. Telegram France and Russia at war with Germany and Austria. England apparently not yet embroiled. English diplomacy must have been first class and we should be in a strong position. Strange that what the Balkan war failed to precipitate the Austrian murders have done.

4 August 1914
Little news. Germany and Russia definitely at war. France only a question of a few hours. We are in a fine position, no alliances, strong ententes and a free hand to crush anyone. Obviously we must come in, as Germany must trust to her first burst and cannot afford to let France and Russia cripple her while we remain untouched. Hope she insults us to rouse popular enthusiasm. Runner to Bondoukou with latest news.

5 August 1914
News of war between England and Germany. Sent off to Johnstone and Pye and chiefs. Collared available stores in town and, as difficult to seal them there, put them in an empty store in the fort. At it till dark. Leat, Ramsden dined. Bumpers to the King, success France, Russia, engineers, doctors, GCR and others. Three days' bank holiday ordered to celebrate commencement of war. Feel confident of success. Started separate war diary.

6 August 1914
Ramsden had a parade and I addressed local chiefs. All promised loyalty and support. Several rolled up during the day saying they would go anywhere. Censorship on letters in Coomassie. No news from Europe. Dreadfully irksome expecting it and not getting it, but perhaps better to get reliable news than the rush of inventive journalism doubtless appearing by the million in special editions in London.

7 August 1914
A horrible out of it kind of feeling. Wire afternoon, Barker demanding

surrender of Lomé. Evidently mean to occupy German colonies, or the wireless installation is the bait. Biked to Odumasi. Krepis elated over English occupation of Lomé.

8 August 1914
Decided to check private stores of Europeans, as stores may be unobtainable in Coomassie and Johnstone and Pye may want helping out.

9 August 1914
Exciting news from Bondoukou, much more than from Coomassie. Germany–Belgium at war. French Senate acclaims England, Russia, Italy, Belgium.

10 August 1914
Several cases. With one's mind full of enormous events it is very irksome trying appeal cases involving 4/–. Troops leaving Coomassie for Togo.

11 August 1914
Great news from Bondoukou. Belgians checking Germans at Liège. French invasion of Alsace.

12 August 1914
News of German prisoners in Coomassie. First wire read 20 prisoners, ten generals. Repeated as ten females. Read lecture on sanitation to Sunyani elders.

13 August 1914
Chiefs keep coming to see me for news and to 'compliment'. Loyal letter from Berekum. Orders to release sealed stores and resume PWD work. Must mean big naval victory.

14 August 1914
Allowed traders to take back their stores. Johnstone in pursuit of a fetish crime. Pye in Tekiman; talked to him on telephone with difficulty.

15 August 1914
Lot of news from Bondoukou. Saw chief of Sunyani re native Wesleyan parson's application for a plot to build a church, a dreadful person. Chief did not wish it. Told parson he would not be allocated a school as government school sufficient for all requirements. He wants to take advantage of the government school to proselytize among the scholars.

23 August 1914
Chief of Tanosu came in to 'compliment' and see bungalow. Immensely impressed with latrine on the veranda. Hope similar style of architecture will not become fashionable in Tanosu.

26 August 1914
News of capitulation of Togo. Told chiefs; gave schools a half holiday. Linguists, on hearing of capitulation of Togo, asked now to join us to drive the French out of Bondoukou! Alliance again explained, and they said if it can't be done now I must bear it in mind. Amusing.

28 August 1914
One criminal case. Gentleman given to borrowing things from his friends and selling them. One month. No war news.

1 September 1914
Several cases. Mail arrived. Reuters papers up to 4th. Very exciting. Sent off to Johnstone and Pye. Former to come in for medical certificate. No war telegrams except from Bondoukou giving some details of Togo fight.

4 September 1914
Wrote zoo about Percy, who will go home with Leat.

8 September 1914
Opened school, large number of people and chiefs. Addressed them and school children. Gave one hour's entertainment and gave them a tea fight in afternoon. Cardinall, new ADC, arrived. A much-travelled man. Disappointed with our forests.

9 September 1914
Johnstone took court. Heavy rain, first for over two months. Farming position for natives serious. Pye says farmers attribute drought to war. All dined with Leat and Percy. Percy's behaviour unimmaculate, over ate and over drank. Preferring jigs and caviar to fish and meat.

14 September 1914
Mail arrived. *Daily Times*, *Spectator*, *Truth*. Bicycled Fiapre over land palaver. Chief most unwise to have brought the case.

15 September 1914
Court and correspondence. Went round town with Hyran. Water getting scarce; had to arrange hours for town and *zongo* to use our spring. News from Bondoukou; Germans apparently a few miles from Paris.

19 September 1914
Ramsden got orders to go to Coomassie with half company. Probably *en route* Kamerun. Bicycled Fiapre over land case. Said could not undertake to fix boundaries on farms between a chief and his subjects, too petty. Subsequently gave injunction to both parties restraining them from cutting palm trees. The *casus belli* on a certain farm.

20 September 1914
Took over military affairs, 19 reservists; 11 lame ducks of D Company to follow when recovered. Arranged for reservists to do guards only, others to keep lines clean.

21 September 1914
Enlisted one recruit. Some court cases.

22 September 1914
Inspected school. Cardinall took infants. Progress distinctly good. Philbrick sent up interesting account of Togo operations written by German sergeant POW. Another reservist joined.

23 September 1914
Went with Hyran and Lincoe to arrange fixing well pumps, site or incinerator etc. Reservists brought reasonable application or issue of second pair of trousers. Recommended itself on sanitary grounds; recruits also deserving every encouragement.

24 September 1914
Appeal case from Wam settled. Chief K. Koran arrived with corpse of very big leopard wounded in gin trap, it had mauled five people. Two probably will not recover; asked Hyran to go and see them. Went with cocoa pupil to demonstration on Kobina's farms. He is most intelligent and should have much influence.

25 September 1914
Wire refusing reservists' trousers. Wrote for reconsideration. Wire for remnants of D Company to Coomassie. Wired to know if women to go, if not, how to subsist. Advanced, on wire, £1 to soldiers' wives to proceed to Kintampo.

26 September 1914
Court. Much bother in getting off five lame ducks of D Company. Chief of Esikesu said *omanhene* of Wam assembled his chiefs on outbreak of war and all expressed willingness to join us in 'getting heads'. Walked Odumasi, caught in rain. Reuters and wire from Ramsden; land campaign satisfactory, but loss of three cruisers by submarine. European ghost reported in Cardinall's house.[34] Amusing episode.

28 September 1914
Finished up court cases. Packing up to join Philbrick. Pye sent in to say he was so unwell he was sending an urgent application for military service in the Kamerun. Such are the incongruities of neurasthenia! Linguist Sechi of Berekum again in trouble with *omanhene*. Running with the hare and hunting with the hounds.

3 October 1914
Pye has written telegram. He has applied for war service in the hope a stray bullet might end his troubles. Pathetic.

22 October 1914
Wire from CC, Boyle to relieve Johnstone. Boyle to go direct to Wenchi from Coomassie, if possible. Think this best course for service, as I don't think Boyle would hit it off in Ahafo at all. Long Tekiman extortion case. First-class lying.

28 October 1914
Long day over murder case. Decided to send to CC for advice. Ordered destoolment of chief for inciting to riot.

29 October 1914
People sent up to say linguist, Kwaku Kwateny, was dying. Faithful old government attaché. Sent regrets. He died in afternoon. Great custom for Kwaku Kwateny. Dashed a keg of powder.

10 November 1914
Left for Tekimentia. Young men had three bicycles to anticipate road. They complained when they rang the bell no one took any notice. If they touched anyone they were fined palm wine or gin. Told chief to reserve procedure, but like to hear of bicycles among Ashantis. Licensed guns. Went down Nkwanta with sharp dose fever, in bed all day. Mail arrived, terrible perfomance of Percy in England.

4 January 1915
Long criminal morning. New interpreter a disappointment. Finished juju case. Burnt jujus. Some 330 guns for 1914 brought.

13 January 1915
Court. Pye left for Coomassie on leave. Sorry to lose him as he had much improved in health and happiness lately.

22 January 1915
Court. Dangerous lunatic appeared — an epidemic of them. Fighting like a wild beast. In irons in guardroom.

6 February 1915
Rest of Odumasi burnt, including Kobina Fosu's two-storey house. Very sorry for him.

7 February 1915
Biked Odumasi. People drowning sorrows in drink. Serves them right with grass so near the village.

13 February 1915
CC arrived in morning. Went round *zongo*. Fuller surprised at signs of progress. Boyle's incinerators quite good.

15 February 1915
Palaver with chiefs. Some complaints against Boyle's administration on account of pressure of work. *Omanhene* stated Boyle's treatment of him lowered his status amongst his own people.

16 February 1915
Boyle admitted being over strenuous. Gave him some good advice in semi-official letter. Boyle certainly a worker. Went shooting, three-and-a-half brace of bush fowl.

25 February 1915
On Nkassaim and Goaso. Ross arrived. Delighted to see him and hear he has done so well. Sounds like too much searching for undercurrents of native intrigue, not properly understood and spying on the people with native spies. Inspected Goaso station. Disappointed with work in village. Cardinall making useful maps.

26 February 1915
Several cases and palavers. People all expressed pleasure with Cardinall compared with Johnstone. Don't think Cardinall gives them anything to do. Round town in evening.

27 February 1915
Visited Kukuom, biked, road excellent. Ross returned Sefwi. Several palavers, nothing important. Some streets knocked through, but little progress since October. Cardinall does not do enough tail twisting.

Sunyani, 9 March 1915
Dealt with correspondence. Water scarcer than I have known it and town pump broken down again. Lincoe had stupidly cemented top of well. Ordered him to open a manhole.

17 March 1915
Heard from Boyle re large immigration of French and perturbed state of French command. Issued instructions to try and induce them to return and give Bainard every opportunity of seeing them with Boyle at Sikasiko. Heavy rain, badly needed.

31 March 1915
News from Cardinall; Mim threatening row with Kukuom over a land case. Cardinall had seized guns and appeared to be master of the situation. Extraordinary rainfall March, nearly ten inches. In three previous years only totalled six inches for that month.

1 April 1915
News of sinking of *Falaba*. Sent runner to Cardinall with instructions. Further report from Cardinall [that] all quiet and normal.

5 April 1915
Walked Adaye camp. Missed bush buck. Saw herd of six water buck. No chance except at a doe and fawn, which was vexing.

7 April 1915
Two bush buck. Afternoon burnt grass. Saw nothing. Jolly camp. Too many mosquitoes. Cardinall wants to force Obo fetish by visiting Mim *mohan* for guns. Wrote him to do no such thing.

8 April 1915
Back in Sunyani. Much correspondence from Cardinall. Everything settled down, no more drastic action required pending case against Mim chief. Answered his letter.

10 April 1915
Court and accounts. Letters from Boyle. Sent him avocado pears, rain trees and custard apples for distribution. Acrimonious correspondence with Hyran over prisoners' excreta. Boyle reported French road open except for oil products. What are they?

12 April 1915
Court. Yost, Basel Mission, arrived from Berekum. Said he was the only Basel missionary allowed to travel. Others, being German, not allowed to leave Coomassie.

19 April 1915
Engaged Moshis for £2 to clean station road. A maze of intrigue over butchers and condemned meat. Humorous side, as Palfriman and I had eaten the best fillet steak we had tasted.

20 April 1915
Meat palavers. Sherlock Holmes required. Everyone appears to be in conspiracy. Great touch of humour. Round town.

26 April 1915
Palaver with chiefs. No complaints, arranged for temporary removal of whole market pending improvements. Selected site for temporary market. Showed them idea of new improvements. Miller's selling in small store. Prices exorbitant.

8 May 1915
Sent off 30 carriers for Rew's loads. Biked Odumasi, progress slow. Ordered Odumasi road to be cleaned.

10 May 1915
News of sinking of *Lusitania*. Makes one's blood boil.

11 May 1915
Biked Nsoko and back by 10.00 a.m., 22 miles. Gave them rough talk re town building. Fined Odumasi £10 for disgraceful portion of road, 14 sticks across it. Finished monthly accounts and marked new street in Sunyani with Hyran.

14 May 1915
Marking compounds in town, very hot. Gun carriers with Rew's loads arrived. Got return loads ready. Tornado in afternoon. Vivid lightning, Attafa's house struck and set on fire.

18 May 1915
Sentenced one man to a month for assault. Rew wired might be kept on as OC, GCR. Ready for anything, but very unsettling.

19 May 1915
Prisoner escaped and was shot by the warder, Kwaku Vi, through the shoulder joint. Warder very alarmed, gaoler said, because he had disobeyed regulations by not shooting him in the legs. Think providence guided the bullet to hit him at all.

22 May 1915
Letters from Boyle and deputation from Jaman chiefs. French immigrants' palaver nasty, and has all the elements of trouble between English and French Jaman. Boyle coming in.

25 May 1915
Court etc. Accra mail. Boyle arrived. French immigrant case may be difficult. Decided to keep Boyle pending Kwamin Kosson's arrival. Boyle paid in £150 war money.

27 May 1915
Court. Several cases. Wire, Rew commanding regiment. Wheatley to come here. Wired stating must probably go to Jaman before leaving. English mail. Many papers. Mrs Wheatley coming. Saw Leat re altering house arrangements for her.

30 May 1915
Marking out town. People not ready as per orders. Put chief in guardroom. People worked like mad and got him out.

31 May 1915
Marking town. Good progress. Paid station with Boyle. Rew sent gun carriers for his loads – stores for me. Dog gave me a toss off

bicycle – bruised my knee. House improvements for Mrs Wheatley put in hand

3 June 1915
King's birthday, but held palaver to let Boyle get away. Long palaver with Jamans – made parade of it – K. Kosson made abject apology for Sikasiko disturbance. Ordered production of stools in six days – some demur. Arrested K. Kosson; subsequently Drobo, Wirime and others guaranteed production. Let him out. Told them they could put their case to CC after I had possession. Poor things, they don't understand our point of view.

4 June 1915
Boyle left with plants and all he could take we did not want.

5 June 1915
Court. Theft case. Dismissed truculent fellow. Drobo waylaid me with a letter secretly offering me or the government any money to keep the stools. Told him off. Understand Jaman thinks Boyle was 'got at' by the French on his visit to Bondoukou in the middle of the case. I thought they would. They say he gave the French chief a 'smiling' face and K. Kosson a 'frowning' one at Sikasiko.

8 June 1915
Court. English mail. Many official letters answered. Round village with Ingram. Line down and no news of Wheatley.

9 June 1915
Moved out of house. Getting it ready for Mrs Wheatley. Complaints of Boyle shooting cow at Sikasiko and destroying guns. Wrote him officially, otherwise everything all right and people apparently happy. Gave one more day for production of stools. Boyle sent down notes of bad case of ill treatment of prisoners by a policeman and others. Told him commit one case and deal with other two.

10 June 1915
Some cases. A gin-selling case in which suspect bribery and corruption. Remanded in custody. Finished off accounts. Letter from Wheatley; he and his wife will arrive from Nkwanta tomorrow. Finished curtains in house.

11 June 1915
Wheatleys arrived from Nkwanta in time for lunch.

12 June 1915
Postponed palavers. Walked round station with Wheatleys in the evening.

13 June 1915
Marking town. Wheatley lunched and Ingram and I dined with them. Enjoyable evening. Walked to Fiapre in afternoon.

15 June 1915
Handed over cash to Wheatley. Court. CC wired if Boyle could take charge Kintampo for two weeks while Kortright meeting his wife. Sent to Boyle. Carriers and prisoners on tennis court.

18 June 1915
Going through papers and books with Wheatley. Some palavers. Arrested gin seller brought in from Wam. Chief of Esikesu handcuffed by mistake. Good progress on tennis court.

23 June 1915
Made the *omanhene* sit with me and told him he would remain my guest till guns came. Many arrived and I stamped and marked off between 400 and 500. Tired to death of them. Saw water dam; it has held well and supplied water all the dry season – water of a kind, of course.

24 June 1915
A few guns. *Omanhene* behaved well and really tried. Left for Sunyani. Biked in in two-and-three-quarter hours. Short palaver Nsoko. Planted seeds in flower beds with Wheatleys.

25 June 1915
Packing stores, kit etc. Palaver over official matters with Wheatley. Palaver with Jamans over stools. Stools to go to Coomassie with me, also wounded prisoner. Taking escort, Wam had sent in, to 'beg'. Affair creating much too much attention. Wrote to the French.

26 June 1915
Handed over *in toto* to Wheatley.

(iii) L. H. Wheatley, Ag PC, 1915[35]

26 June 1915
Took over province from Fell, busy with him all morning. Walked round station in afternoon and counted the chickens with Fell.

28 June 1915
Went through papers and letters and heard four cases and settled a few small complaints. Told the chief of Drobo I wished to introduce him to my wife tomorrow. Also notified the chief of Sunyani that I wished to introduce him and his elders to my wife at the same time.

30 June 1915
One unimportant assault case. Busy practically all morning making payments and doing treasury accounts. Paid the reservists. I had the Queen Mother of Sunyani and the chief women up to the bungalow to be introduced to my wife.

1 July 1915
A good morning's work going through office papers. Heavy rain all day. Mail from Boyle who sent in four prisoners committed to CC's court for robbery of £140. Depositions unsigned and returned to Wenchi for necessary signatures. The government school 'broke up'. No ceremony. Soaking wet day.

2 July 1915
Spent a long time over the treasury books. My wife and I walked round the village and *zongo*.

Sunday 4 July 1915
Sent for the butchers to enquire why they were not killing. Too little meat is thought owing to the small requirements of a limited population to allow of beasts being killed daily.

7 July 1915
Treasury and routine work. Two of the escort who accompanied Fell returned. No sign of returning station carriers!

9 July 1915
A few court cases. Busy getting off monthly returns. Station carriers returned. Exceedingly heavy rain all afternoon and evening. Unable to inspect lines and village with MO.

10 July 1915
Made a surprise survey on the post office. Found the accounts correct. Inspected reservists' kit. They are sadly in need of a new issue of clothing. Some barely have sufficient to cover their nakedness. Inspected WAFF and carrier lines with MO.

Sunday 11 July 1915
A slack day. Walked to Fiapre and back with Ingram.

13 July 1915
Saw the *omanhin* of Drobo and Kwamin Kosson and informed them of CCs decision – K. Kosson elected to return to French territory. I gather from private sources that he intends to endeavour to placate his *omanhin* and, through him, the French *administrateur* and, if successful, to recover the fetish stools and flee with them to Wam in English territory. I doubt whether the French will let him remain at liberty and

K. Kosson has been instructed to return direct to French territory without delay now that he has made his choice.

14 July 1915
A long morning paying the reservists and counting my cash, which happily balances. Run to Fiapre and back, breakfast.

15 July 1915
Celebrated the relief of Coomassie.

(iv) A. H. Ross, Ag PC, 1916[36]

15 March 1916
Wheatley left for Coomassie. Going through papers and filing cases. Destroyed a number of old flintlock guns. Went round station and fort. Got installed in PC's bungalow. Convict escaped. Turned out detachment of GCR and townspeople.

16 March 1916
Convict recaptured. Court cases. Inspected hospital, prison and outbuildings. Interviewed Hausa chief and chief of Sunyani. At 5.00 p.m. went through town and inspected layout, condemning some houses after consultation with chief. Gave village overseer instructions. Heavy rain.

17 March 1916
Court cases; completed and dispatched mail. Clearing out office. Destroyed a number of anteaten and useless books and papers and cleared out shelves.

18 March 1916
Parade of detachment of GCR. Inspected clerk's quarters and arranged repairs.

Sunday 19 March 1916
Planted seeds, correspondence. Walked to Odumasi.[37] Mail arrived from Goaso.

20 March 1916
Case of alleged murder in bush near Tekimentia. Court cases all morning, rape and theft. One clerk entirely employed checking and licensing guns. In afternoon, inspected all five standards of government school. Attendance not up to mark. Pressure on parents required. Went on with town planning in evening.

21 March 1916
Court cases and gun licensing. Inspected water supply and slaughterhouse. Treasury accounts.

22 March 1916
At 3.15 a.m. aroused from sleep by clerk calling me to tell me two Wam traders had been murdered on Fiapre road. Called out sergeant and sent five soldiers. Case appears to be robbery. One of the assailant's thumbs was found severed, lying on the ground. The two travellers not dead. Badly cut about, one will probably die. Took depositions and held enquiry.

23 March 1916
Had chiefs of various villages in and lectured them on sending children to school. Telegraph line reported in working order – an unusual occurrence. A flood of belated telegrams arrived, no mail from Coomassie for ten days.

24 March 1916
Court cases. Enquiry into murder charge. Treasury work. Interviewed chiefs re school children. Planted seeds. Inspected progress of clearing ditches in town during morning. Telegraph line still up.

27 March 1916
Court all morning. Dealt with a riot in Mim. No mail of any kind from Coomassie for 14 days. Line restored.

31 March 1916
Paid staff. Squared up treasury accounts and regimental accounts. Had parade of Gold Coast Regiment reservists. Telegraph line in usual condition – down.

Sunday 2 April 1916
Marked out new lines for reservists and arranged demolition of old houses.

3 April 1916
Monthly court and treasury returns. Mail from Wenchi. Started 'case' system in this office. Filing papers etc. Telegraph line down all day. It is now past all hope and I have told postmaster to report when it is up and not when it is down.

7 April 1916
Treasury accounts. Every item entered in cash book here is done by PC. Inspected school. Good progress. Prepared to leave for Wenchi. In evening walked to Fiapre and saw chief.

Tekiman, 13 April 1916
There is a decided progression in 'youngmen' movement here, which has resulted in a serious split between the chief and his people. Held enquiry, which lasted all morning.

14 April 1916
Went to Tanosu and to provincial boundary. Gave instructions to overseers and allowed the people working to go to their farms. *Omanhin* has named a child after me to celebrate the occasion. No objection if name does not imply responsibility for origin.

15 April 1916
Returned to Wenchi. Very hot, lunched at Nkwanta. Mail arrived. Shot five brace of bush fowl.

Wenchi, 16 April 1916
Wrote report on new Wenchi–Coomassie road to CCA. Wire arrived in afternoon stating 'PMO Coomassie, OC Troops, and PE all proceeding Wenchi via Sunyani.' Made hurried arrangements to postpone my arranged tour through Jaman and Wam and to proceed to Sunyani.

18 April 1916
Went to Sunyani. Road palaver *en route*. Great cry for tools. Everywhere lack of tools. Treasury accounts afternoon.

22 April 1916
Sharman, O'Dea, McPherson[38] arrived. Inspected fort, armoury, military stores etc. Held parade of detachment of reservists.

26 April 1916
Party arrived Wenchi 9.00 a.m. Met Wood, Ag DC, at *zongo*. Went immediately into water supply with MO and PE. Went on to upper ridge above Wenchi and inspected possible sites. Wrote part of report and made rough plan.

27 April 1916
Spent day at Wenchi looking for sites for various military quarters. Range parade ground. Marked out same. MO and PE at water supply.

18 June 1916
Went with Ag CCA to Wenchi and inspected all roads *en route*. Made arrangements for cutting Nkwanta–Chirrah portion.

23 June 1915
Went to Sunyani. Inspected new road *en route*, now nearing completion. Crabb, Ag DC, here. A few palavers in office. Inspected Sunyani town. Progress.

29 June 1916
Court and office. Inspecting making of new school flagstaff and town improvement plans. Progress in latter very good. Town should be finished in six weeks.

3 July 1916
Inspected water supply and pumps. Court and office.

4 July 1916
Inspected prison. Court and gun licensing.

5 July 1916
Mail arrived and dealt with. Court cases. Planted trees. Received permission to accept invitation of Administrateur Bondoukou to attend celebration at Bondoukou on 14 July.

14 July 1916
Went with escort to Bondoukou for *Fête république française*. Met by Monsieurs Prouteaux and Chaumel. Great demonstrations on a very grand scale lasting all day and night. English flag much displayed. Slept at Bondoukou. Telegram from Governor, Ivory Coast, welcoming CWPA to Bondoukou.

15 July 1916
Monsieurs Prouteaux and Chaumel came with me to Sikasiko and stayed to lunch and dinner. They returned by moonlight.

16 July 1916
At Sikasiko. One civil case of long standing. Wrote mail. Shot brace of partridges (approach to English variety, not seen here before). Sent them to Monsieur Prouteaux.

17 July 1916
Went through Kokwan to Saikwa. Linguist either wilfully insolent or drunk. Arrested him and arranged for him to go to Sunyani.

Sunyani, 24 July 1916
Court and office. Started on new street drains with sanitary fund.

28 July 1916
Office. Court cases. Started work on sanitary improvements. Drains to market from stream.

7 August 1916
Preparing to leave on trek. Treasury and court work.

8 August 1916
Mail arrived. Held court in morning. Left for Tanosu 3.00 p.m. Inspected work of laying out of new town. Gave time limits.

11 August 1916
To Jemma and Tekimentia. Palaver and court at Jemma. Arrived Tekimentia 11.30 a.m. Court lasting all afternoon. Many cases and

palavers. Tekimentia growing large and prosperous, much cocoa. At 5.00 p.m. round town and inspected commencement of new rest house. Not a very good site, but best available. Settled site for new *zongo*. Wrote out instructions.

12 August 1916
To Tanosu via Nkwanta, arrived Tanosu. Demolished part of Techiri town and arranged new main street. Measured out new plots at Tanosu. Overseer a useless invertebrate.

19 August 1916
Wood, Ag DC, arrived after handing over to Boyle. Latter brought wife.[39]

14 September 1916
Line up. A volume of telegrams arrived. Permission to flog prisoner arrived from CCA. Am not sure after consideration that he should he flogged, although I recommended it. Arranging matters concerning reception of Prouteaux.

15 September 1916
Arrangements re Prouteaux and reception by chiefs. Complaints in court. Superintending work on market stream, main road. Town inspection and *zongo*. Possible now that Prouteaux may go on to Coomassie at CCA's invitation.

18 September 1916
Town registration. Court and office. Arranging reception for Prouteaux, school children, sports etc.

19 September 1916
Squaring up some matters in court and office, and arranging labour re new road in Sunyani town. Town practically finished now and all houses numbered. Main watercourses completed.

20 September 1916
Prouteaux arrived. Big reception by assembled chiefs and by school children. All went off very well. Went round station in evening. All lunched and dined with me.

21 September 1916
Prouteaux went with MO to visit hospital. Went round town in evening. French flags displayed by all the people in their houses.

22 September 1916
Court and office. Prouteaux came and sat in court and afterwards went through some matters relevant to some Frontier incidents. In afternoon sports by school; all chiefs attended.

24 September 1916
Went to Bechem and Nsuta. Prouteaux had a big reception at Bechem. There must have been 400 guns present. Went on to Nsuta; met Cutfield, DC, and handed over Prouteaux to him.

27 September 1916
Court and office all day and clearing up accumulations. Wam rest house finished.

29 September 1916
Squaring up treasury accounts. Received by hand CCA's special post containing letter about new cocoa export duty and Supreme Court revised tariff. Inspected town and house numbers register.

6 October 1916
Explained to representatives of Sunyani and Tanosu new currency notes, which they examined and seemed to appreciate.

9 October 1916
Preparing to hand over to Pott. Treasury etc.

(v) P. A. H. Pott, Ag PC, 1916[40]

10 October 1916
Took over from Ross £1370 specie, which was checked by a board. Inspected town and station. Heavy rain.

13 October 1916
Paraded reservists and read *Gazette* re operations in East Africa to them. They ask for issue of clothing. Heard case against recalcitrant sent in by *omanhin* of Wam, sentenced to one month hard labour for assault on a woman. He was fined £16 in *omanhin*'s court. An excessive amount, which he is not now to pay. Wam needs a visit. Complaints of robbery at Tappa by chief's policeman. Directed his arrest. Inspected teacher's and clerk's quarters with MO. Conditions very good.

15 October 1916
Telegram to mobilize all reservists.

17 October 1916
Mail arrived from Coomassie. Observed sealed correspondence from CC's office addressed to DCs Goaso and Wenchi. Wired CCA to ask if he approved. Reply routine only.

18 October 1916
Civil and criminal cases. Case from Tappa interesting, as showing how strong and influential NT communities in Ashanti are becoming.

There appears to have been a riot at which an Ashanti policeman, on leave from Accra, was the alleged cause. To Odumasi on bicycle with MO in evening. Road just as it was four years ago; Odumasi laid out, but little building going on.

19 October 1916
Appeal from court of DC Goaso, which I returned as I am not aware of any ordinance permitting appeals from DC's court to those of PC's. Heard appeal from Wam native court. Surroundings of Sunyani court-house insanitary and unsavoury. No native latrines, and thick grass adjoining. Spoke to MO who agrees that a latrine is necessary; but doubts if prison labour adequate for emptying more latrines.

20 October 1916
Commenced case of assault on Ashantis by two Hausas. Bechem chief asks that all Hausas may be cleared out of Bechem. Went through 'Hints for Guidance of DCs', for the first time and made notes.[41]

21 October 1916
Paraded reservists and inspected rifles. The question of aliens in Ashanti is every year becoming of more importance. They commit at least two-thirds of the crimes. Rinderpest reported in NT.

23 October 1916
Ten old soldiers from Wenchi, of whom only two were reservists. Parade and inspection of rifles. Inspected progress of *zongo* latrines with MO. Wrote CCA Crowther's notes cannot, in my opinion, be adopted to Ashanti needs.

27 October 1916
Inspected school and listened to mental arithmetic exercises. Fair average intelligence shown. Methods appear good.

28 October 1916
Board on £600 specie to be sent to Coomassie. An application from chief of Tekementia for £10 for doors, hinges etc. for rest house, which he says Ross promised him; but I doubt it, as there is no vote from which this can come.

2 November 1916
Fine clerks and carriers for sanitary offences. They have laboured under the delusion that the government is responsible for the surroundings of the quarters they occupy.

4 November 1916
General office work. *Zongo* being cleaned up. Absolutely no foolscap paper in office.

14 November 1916
Mail from Coomassie. Heard complaints and promised Wam and Nkwanta to visit Boma, if possible, this week. Discussed points of procedure in native law and custom. The chiefs up here appear to proceed in any way that seems expedient for the moment and regardless of their own customs.

16 November 1916
Monsieur Prouteaux has gone on leave. A courteous letter from his successor, whose name it is quite impossible to read. Prouteaux writes privately he hopes to be back in May.

17 November 1916
Gave final orders as to work in my absence. Handed over to Duff [MO] and left after lunch for Tanosu. Inspected Tanosu new village laid out by Ross; his style of compound smacks strongly of a *zongo*; I doubt if it will prove suitable for Ashantis, although offering excellent accommodation for travellers and a great improvement on the old dilapidated dwellings. Rest house 100 yards from village.

18 November 1916
Tanosu to Nkwanta, bicycle all the way; road clean but rough, which can't be helped. Improvements going on and road overseer, Ashie, superintending. In evening, held a palaver at Nkwanta and talked over matters of general interest with chief. Gave him permit, one pound of powder per gun licensed in Nkwanta and warned him it was only for use of those who have licensed guns. Spoke to all chiefs recommending them to extend their cola farms. Crop this year poor. Not much traffic on road. Three donkeys coming down for cola. A number of loads of *dawa dawa* from French Moshi country.

20 November 1916
Warned Chief Nkwanta that village must not extend further in direction of rest house. Palaver re Boma lands for an hour, then made a chain and compass traverse down Boma road to Donkoto stream, which Boma claims as their boundary. Heavy rain when returning. In evening, a long talk with head linguist of Wam concerning affairs of that division.

21 November 1916
A hot and unsavoury morning over latrines, rubbish pits etc. Then to Jemo, very good road. Met by chief and people, no complaints. Lunched and on to Tekimentia. Met by the worst band in the world, I should say. Reverend Jost had just arrived from Bechem. Asked him to tea and talked on roads, trade etc.

22 November 1916
Inspected rest house, which consists of some very rickety and unsafe walls, the town and *zongo*. Spoke to chief and heads of *zongo*. They are to deposit £35 as a guarantee that work will go on steadily in connection with the building of the town and *zongo*. The Nkwantas are still lazy and a disobedient set of people. Tried to find a better site for the rest house than the present one, which is between the town and *zongo*.

4 December 1916
Left Tanosu 7.15 a.m. Reached Sunyani 9.30. Went through papers in office awaiting me. Paid staff and others, took over cash from Duff; inspected town with him in evening.

11 December 1916
Mrs Boyle reported ill at 7.00 a.m. At 10 a.m. Duff left for Wenchi. Seedy in afternoon; retired to bed.

12 December 1916
On sick list, but kept routine work up to date from my quarters. I licensed 70 guns from Chirrah. Went through old papers relating to Akwaboa stool, a Coomassie stool, taken at Ahafo after the 1900 rising, the chief of which has been oscillating between Mim and Coomassie since 1907. He recently laid a claim for subjects before CCA. In 1914, he professed to be permanently settled as one of Beditor's captains.

18 December 1916
To office for an hour, then to market. Three stalls selling meat, four or five cloths, in the open. Dried fish, salt, mankenie, garden eggs and a few groundnuts, plantains, but not very much of anything. Prices seem lower than when the troops were here. On to Chirrah in evening, inspected rest house. The only thing to be done with the partly built rest house is to knock it down. It is, as the natives themselves admit, bound to fall down. The village overseer has also made an awful hash of Ross's instructions for laying out the town. Two months' work has been wasted. Stopped in old rest house, Ashanti type, built three years ago.

20 December 1916
Moved to Wenchi. Met by Boyle and *omanhin* and heads of *zongo*. Gave Boyle *viva voce* in Instructions to DCs etc. In afternoon a written paper on law of evidence, while I went through letter books, palaver books etc.

Wenchi,[42] Western Province

(i) A. H. Kortright, DC, 1913[43]

1 October 1913
Rained last night, which means that the walls of the house will not have dried at all. Got mail away, with accounts, at about 3.30 p.m. Finished preparation of small farm for experimental purposes.

2 October 1913
Spent morning in court. Civil and criminal cases. It is noticeable that there is no local crime whatever. All offences are committed by north country people. They are usually sheep stealing, stealing in dwelling houses and occasionally stealing from a farm. Heavy rain in afternoon and at night.

3 October 1913
Spent morning in court. Dismissed one criminal case. No rain during the day or night; such a thing has not occurred for a month. Eighteen loads of galvanized iron and one of nails and washers arrived from Coomassie by local carriers.

4 October 1913
Interviewed *zongo* re cleaning up. Now wall up to top of doorway eight feet eight inches, the side of one room complete with rafters. Two corner rafters in and eight on southwest side. Trouble with permanent labourers who apparently refuse to work unless I am present. Took steps to prevent repetition of trouble. No rain by day or night.

8 October 1913
Court in morning, civil cases. Heavy rain in afternoon and fierce tornado at night. Planted out trees behind new bungalow and planted road up to bungalow.

9 October 1913
No court. Spent morning at bungalow. Progress improves considerably when I am present. Planted out potatoes in farm.

11 October 1913
Interesting conversation with *omanhin* and Kobina Janh respecting contagious diseases and fetish. Planted out more fruit trees around bungalow. Rain in evening.

13 October 1913
Rain in the morning. Civil cases. Continued building kitchen. Carpenter dressing veranda fencing. Planted out Barbados pride.

18 October 1913
Cycled to Debibi. Found excellent site for rest house. No palavers. Road nearly all the way from Wenchi to Debibi requires attention.

19 October 1913
Returned Menge. Lion taken two more cows. Informed he has his bush at certain place. Went to see with rifle, not there. Told people to wait till 4.00 p.m., would go again to kill. Someone shot him about that time.

20 October 1913
Nsoko [Nsawkaw]. Find threepenny bit smallest coin in circulation. Spoke re penny and tenth of penny. People wishing to have them and say they will arrange their market. Doubt it. They will have to deal with suffragette population.

21 October 1913
Bicycled from Nsoko to Wenchi, 21 miles. Sprained finger on way. Road very bad in places. No mail. Three carriers deserted.

23 October 1913
Court in morning. Spent afternoon at bungalow. Wrote up this journal; unable to write before owing to finger.

24 October 1913
Spent morning checking cash, preparing vouchers and at bungalow. Got part of galvanized roof on. Got in the three carriers who deserted.

28 October 1913
Toby [mason] still unable to work. Putting on more batons and iron. Making out voucher forms. Have already given instructions along Sikassiko road to have roots and stones removed, as I understand HE rides a bicycle.

(ii) D. M. Boyle DC, 1914[44]

3 November 1914
Inspected station with Captain Pye. Took over office, station and district. Inspected water supply in afternoon.

4 November 1914
Cleaned and rearranged office, papers etc. Pye left for Sunyani.

6 November 1914
Went all round town, new Wangara *zongo* and Ashanti town. Roads dirty and ditches choked. Inspected new prison.

Sunday 8 November 1914
Spent two hours round the town. Inspected roads and new streets; measured and advised.

9 November 1914
Court work and complaints all morning. Explained question of voluntary war contributions to all head chiefs. Office, guns registered. Stormy.

10 November 1914
Made up and dispatched mails; more received. After lunch inspected town.

11 November 1914
Complaints etc. Made up list of old soldiers now resident here in case they might be wanted. Town clean at last; people back to Tainsu road.

12 November 1914
Office. Bad thunderstorm in afternoon. Visited water supply. Also met and talked to various Fulani cattlemen re kraal.

13 November 1914
Jimini chief and people (the first) brought a small contribution to the relief fund.

Sunday 15 November 1914
Spent three hours laying out town and inspecting results. Getting on well.

18 November 1914
Supervised new courthouse site. All the work to be redone. Court lengthened, bricks brought up.

21 November 1914
Big palaver with chiefs re war etc.

23 November 1914
Round town with Sharman and CWPA. Selected site for slaughterhouse, and butchers' stalls, market generally, European stores, cattle kraals etc. Also visited prison. Palavers re Wenchi and Tekiman substool. In afternoon inspected water supply.

24 November 1914
CWPA and Sharman down early to dig out water source. More town planning. Office etc.

25 November 1914
Sharman left for Sunyani. CWPA and I to Tekiman; road good. After tea inspected the *zongo*. The best kept and cleanest of any I have seen.

1 December 1914
From Tainsu to Nsoko. Good road and well kept. Nsoko rest house and town beautifully clean and cleared. Held small palaver with chief re war etc. Wave of drunkenness in afternoon including my own boy.

2 December 1914
Up before light and off to try to catch meat on the road. No luck. Long tiring march to Seikwa and did not get in till 4.00 p.m. Villages on the way mostly half deserted. Road well cleaned.

Seikwa, 3 December 1914
Office work and then palaver with chief and people. Spoke re war etc. Inspected new rest house site, work getting on well, and will be ready in a month. Marked out kitchen and boys' quarters. Town very clean. People seem simple and nice.

4 December 1914
To Kokwan. Meant to go on to Sikasiko but too hot and tired. Fair-sized village evidently cleaned for my arrival. Good herd of cattle. Most primitive people and very full of superstitions. Prosperous farms everywhere.

6 December 1914
Over to Bondoukou with the CWPA. Had a great reception by the two French commissioners. Most interesting town in the oriental style and fine avenue of trees.

10 December 1914
To Pulliano via Jinim. Road fair and latterly through extensive rubber forest. Pulliano people are making a most excellent village as laid out by Kortright. If it goes on as well as it has begun, they will deserve great praise.

13 December 1914
To Seikwa. Before leaving Goka chose a place for a rest house and they will start at once. Road at first through thick forest. Road then goes close to the big range of hills on left and has a few isolated hills on right, in all about four hours' march. Road fairly clean and can be made into a hammock road.

15 December 1914
Stayed at Bedukurom. Four sheep and a goat taken by leopard last night. Vain search for elephants. Tied up for a leopard at night, but he defeated me, though had a shot in the dark.

18 December 1914
Very heavy office work, paying off carriers etc. all morning. In

afternoon inspected town work in progress with clerk, Eckener. Wangaras have done quite wonderfully – must be 30 new houses at least and many streets now opened out. Hausas, as usual, have done nothing and Eckener finds absence of any desire to straighten their drains etc. The *malam* is quite useless now as regards power, whether because he is ill or otherwise I know not.

19 December 1914
Very long morning and afternoon in office, court and complaints. Serious charge by Wangaras, Moshis, butchers and general traders; also brought up by Eckener (clerk) that Hausa carrier headman has been stopping all travellers at Akete, outside here, and charging *6d.* a head. Result: no cattle arriving and many Moshis gone.

Sunday 20 December 1914
Spent early hours painting signposts, then inspected prison and arranged for cell windows. After breakfast, spent three and a half hours laying out Wangara town, allotted site for mosque, 20 feet square, and inspected all the work. The progress is extraordinary and Eckener deserves great credit; not a word, however, to the people themselves until they have finished, or they will sit down and pat themselves on the back. Mail arrived 2.30, having only left Sunyani yesterday at midday.

21 December 1914
Office, civil and criminal cases from 8.00 a.m. and accounts in afternoon. Wangaras hard at work. Hausas doing nothing and the Yorubas, under them, anxious to break away.

22 December 1914
Busy morning in office. Then down to Ashanti town to fix signpost for Nsoko road and instruct Eckener and Benson re work while I am in Sunyani. Dr Hopkins, PMO, arrived noon. Round town with him in afternoon.

26 December 1914
Boxing Day. Did a little account work with CWP.

29 December 1914
To Nkunsia. Small bush fires beginning. Strong harmattan.

31 December 1914
Very busy paying out December wages. Messrs Shaw and London of Miller's arrived re site for stores. Gave them lunch and then chose site with them.

Summary: a month of great progress everywhere.

(iii) D.M. Boyle, DC, 1916

10 August 1916
Left Coomassie for Kwaman, 13 miles. Rest house good, and clean. To Chickiwere, 18 miles. Road clean till Chickiwere portion was reached, which, as usual, was dirty beyond description, as also the village.

12 August 1916
To Sechodumasi. After leaving Chickiwere portion of the road, it became excellent, specially near the village of Eyemasu. Sechodumasi was good also and I found Hagan, the road overseer, there doing some fine work in the main street. People very keen on a motor road to Abofo to join Offinso road. Cement wanted for broken rest house veranda.

13 August 1916
To Nkoranza. Thanks to excellent hammock boys, we reached Nkoranza at 2.30 p.m. (in spite of an hour for lunch at Nkwanta). It could not be quicker. Welcomed by the *omanhin* of Nkoranza in great style.

14 August 1916
To Tekiman. Road almost impassable in places and only arrived Tekiman 4.00 p.m. after leaving Nkoranza at 6.15 a.m. Fifteen miles in nine and three-quarter hours, less one and a quarter hours for lunch. Great welcome from the *omanhin*, Hausa chief and the school children, who had made great progress under a new teacher (Wesleyan).

Tekiman, 15 August 1916
Carriers, like General Sordet's cavalry on the retreat from Mons, too tired to move. Round *zongo* in morning, very clean. Palavers with Tekiman *omanhin*. Told him of Fuller's safe arrival. Apparently, several people, aided by Yao Ankama (a very bad hat), have been trying to spoil the *omanhin*'s power, but I said of course that no past events were my business. Visited Ashanti town in evening and also peeped into school where the children seem very happy.

16 August 1916
To Wenchi. Found great work on the road, which, for the most part, has been widened to 24 feet, though I cannot conceive the number of cars likely to pass each other really need such width. Arrived Wenchi 11.45 a.m. and had fine reception from chiefs with bands, horses etc. New room, alas still unfinished, but money is apparently short these days.

17 August 1916
Took over office and all affairs from Wood. Garden overgrown and

bush around so dense as to be almost dangerous from a health point of view; mosquitoes plentiful, a thing that has not been before. But, I am told, all energy and spare time has been employed on road work, which seems to have made wonderful progress.

18 August 1916
Wood left for Goaso via Sunyani. Cleaned office files and generally readapted to suit myself; we all have our own likes and dislikes. Round town in evening. Greatly struck with the cleanliness and generally prosperous appearance. Ansah, the town clerk, seems a good worker and has done well, but is overpaid at £3 plus £1 from the chief. Government clerks compare badly.

19 August 1916
Did a few jobs in the office, but chiefly employed in settling into the house.

21 August 1916
A long, interesting court morning. All the principal chiefs and *malams* welcomed me. I told them of the war, of the CCA's *Appam* adventures and the good progress to be seen here on all sides. Several complaints and odd letters. Read up files etc. Down to the water supply in the evening, which is apparently in good order now and has excellent roads out of it.

23 August 1916
Petty cash and complaints all morning. Complaints about cattle road diverting trade. Established system of approved drovers getting passes to go unmolested down the road, provided they too played the game and kept off newly-made pieces. Cases and complaints all morning. Guns in afternoon. We need a gun clerk here for the months of March to September just as much as any other district. With a total of 4000 odd guns in widely scattered parts, [there is] only one clerk for the increasing clerical, treasury and judicial work to do it all.

25 August 1916
Heavy morning's work. Stealing, civil cases and complaints. Dispatched mail to Sunyani. Letter from Sunyani arrived in the afternoon with CC's telegram re powder to French country. Have long suspected trade being carried on in Jaman, but never succeeded last year in finding it, though I employed a detective. Hard to get a detective who won't either give it away, or try to make a hit himself. Some rain and warmer.

26 August 1916
Court all morning. Gun work all afternoon.

28 August 1916
Court all morning. Boys' houses and orderly's wrecked in storm. Started rebuilding. Leopard took gaoler's monkey.

29 August 1916
Started bush clearing and road in rest house compound. Round town, thoroughly inspected latrines, vacant sites, market, mosque etc. Very little fault to find. Draining of water after heavy rain is rather a difficulty. Started planting flamboyants in the new town.

30 August 1916
Court and correspondence. Mail arrived. Two weeks of English and various Sunyani letters.

31 August 1916
Dispatched local mail. Prisoners complained re quality of rations, looked into and found it justified. Have given stringent orders on the subject and they had a topping good dinner today as a result to start with. Busy on accounts and treasury work all day.

2 October 1916
A busy morning finishing up September account and statement for the mail, which was finally sent off at 11.30 a.m. Did some mapping in afternoon and planted flamboyants round the new rest house in evening. Big storm at night.

5 October 1916
Worked at office, maps etc. in morning. Local mail arrived in afternoon. Round town, progress good.

6 October 1916
Good deal of rain. Finished going through office files. Gun books and everything up to date.

7 October 1916
Very heavy morning in court. Three and a half hours' cases, and two hours' office. Sunyani mail. Prouteaux not coming. Great disappointment. Some 46 cows and 150 sheep killed for the feast! Tremendous celebrations all day. Sudden rainstorm, 20 minutes only, with almost an inch of rain.

9 October 1916
Dispatched Sunyani mail. Court, civil cases etc. Had to inform the people that Monsieur Prouteaux could not come after all. They are very genuinely disappointed, particularly the *omanhin*, who said: 'Our town is now the finest in the world (*sic*) and we wanted to show the French.' Probably, the fact that he had invested in a cow as a present

would accentuate the grief shown. I showed them the treasury notes sent on approval from Lagos. Ashantis rather doubtful of the scheme, but Wangaras think it good. 'Numbered, so not likely to be stolen.'

10 October 1916
Out early round town, 5.45 to 8.30 a.m. Very hot after the recent heavy rains, good chance of burning and town outskirts getting well cleaned up. Office and court fairly slack.

11 October 1916
To work on new Ashanti town site. Inspected slaughterhouse afterwards. Held a 'garden party' in the afternoon to celebrate the big Mohammedan feast.[45] About 1500 people came. All the *zongo* chiefs etc. and danced, sang and played from three to six. Cola nuts, cigarettes and scent were distributed. Apparently, it was a great success.

12 October 1916
Out again 7.00 to 9.00 a.m. to new Ashanti town work. Also inspected *zongo*, latrines, market etc. Heard a report of murder on Sunyani road. Sent out at once to investigate.

13 October 1916
Continued assault case from 9.30 to 2.45 p.m. when adjourned. Lies, lies, lies. Very hot and thundery.

18 October 1916
To Nchira (Kintampo road). Met 129 Moshis between Wenchi and Akete, where the NT road turns off; about same number arrive every day now for the cola season.

19 October 1916
To Wufoma. Pleasant little march. Wufoma village and rest house good and clean as usual. Cocoa here now increasing. Owing to low prices in Coomassie they are hanging on to it.

Wufoma, 20 October 1916
Palaver in afternoon. Wufoma people now planting more cocoa and want Mr Evans, or some other Agriculture Department man, sent up to help them. Good country for it.

21 October 1916
To Tuobodom through Boyem, the prettiest little village in the country. Arrived Tuobodom about 11.30 a.m. No preparations. Marked out rest house site; large town now.

22 October 1916
To Tekiman through Takofrano. No complaints. Court at Tekiman

on arrival. Several cases and complaints. In afternoon, [went] to see cattle kraal – all wrong – instructed to rebuild. Then saw the Wesleyan school garden, very neat and creditable.

24 October 1916
To Wenchi. Inspected Ashanti new town and then through town. New market shed finished and all clean. Court 10.00 a.m. to 12.30. Office in afternoon, round town again in evening.

25 October 1916
Very hot. Usual work. Tekiman messengers with a present of £10 for Mrs Boyle! Told them this is not permissible and strongly to be deprecated, though perhaps the feeling that inspired it is good.

26 October 1916
Rains seem to have ended now and kites herald the dry season. Mails from Sunyani and home. Cattle disease notifications. The large number of French emigrants from Segu and the Senegal Niger country seems to point to some heavy taxing, forced recruiting or other difficulties up there. Out all morning at Ashanti town site. Small court and office after.

28 October 1916
In court 8.00 a.m. to 12.30. Explained cattle disease to the dealers and have established an observation post at Akete on the Northern Territory road. A bad fetish case cropped up in a civil suit and suitably dealt with.

Goaso, Western Province

(i) L. W. Wood, Ag DC, 1917[46]

1 January 1917
Public holiday. Stopped prisoners fetching water and prohibited anyone but myself from using water supply as advised by MO. One bullock slaughtered.

4 January 1917
Court and palavers. Gunpowder case. Rearranged clerks and own office and all papers and books therein. Mail and English mail arrived. Inspected work at water supply and on station.

5 January 1917
Court and palavers. Gunpowder case finished. Extraordinary amount of court work and palavers have come up since return from Sunyani. Fixed timetable for this, which will keep me fully occupied until 20th.

Completed rearrangement of office. Case of man attempting to commit suicide at Sienchem. Gambled with some 20 men and lost £10. Gamblers dealt with by Kukuom elders for violating the late *omanhene*'s oath re gambling in his division.

13 January 1917
Sick prisoner and alleged lunatic sent to MO Sunyani, the latter for observation pending enquiry into the fetishman's complicity. Finished Kyniase stealing case. Two men convicted, but others had to be released on account of lack of evidence against them. Whole of stolen money recovered.

26 January 1917
Investigated a complaint about the high prices charged by the local butcher. Significant that my investigation was synchronous with reduction of his price to reasonable level.

27 January 1917
Inspected work at water supply. Quite a large number of sheep have been killed this month. Hardly ever has there not been fresh meat each day.

2 February 1917
Office returns. All trees have now been removed from streets in Goaso village.

5 February 1917
Mail and English mail arrived. Instructed to close down Goaso station and proceed to Sunyani.[47] Court and palavers. Office.

6 February 1917
Dispatched mail. All prisoners transferred to Sunyani. Prison and treasury returns. Office.

7 February 1917
Closed down prison. Bain to Kukuom for a couple of weeks to finish marking out new town. Explained to *omanhene* and elders about the closing of Goaso station. Various other palavers.

10 February 1917
Dispatched mail. Office, completing books etc. for closing station.

16 February 1917
Completed packing and listing of government stores. Formally handed over station buildings and stores to representatives of *omanhene* and gave instructions as to cleaning etc.

Obuasi, Southern Province

(i) A. J. Philbrick, DC, 1913–14[48]

18 November 1913
Took over province from Mr Pott and instructed Mr Johnstone who had been doing the DC's work, to proceed to Coomassie, as soon as possible. Found the office in good order, all work up to date as far as I could judge. The bungalow is in a deplorable condition, owing to dry rot, and fungus on the white paint. Went round town with Mr Pott, the surveyor and doctor missing appointment. Streets clean and well kept, but the bush not cut down and earth drains largely choked up. Inspected gaol. No complaints. Building clean.

19 November 1913
Get gang of prisoners to clean bungalow. Engaged four more station carriers to clean up hill. Attended to correspondence.

20 November 1913
Palaver day. Principal matter the application for detoolment of Queen Mother of Adukwai. Adjourned for further evidence. Inspected town in evening.

21 November 1913
Court. Few civil and criminal cases, but evidence so copious that all morning was occupied. Sat until 12 o'clock and adjourned five cases to Monday.

24 November 1913
Court day. Nuisance, criminal and civil case. Forestry inspector Chipps arrived from Ayenum. Inspected Wawassi and upper part of Obuasi with MO and SOV. Found streets very clean and well kept, but surrounding bush overgrown. K. Foli's wash-house drain to be extended. Gave permit for his new store, which has been approved by MO.

25 November 1913
Palaver day. Many small complaints. Decided the dispute between Adansi and Bekwai re the claim by Adansi to the descendants of Appiah, a Dumasi captive in the Adansi–Bekwai war, in favour of Bekwai. I relied on a judgement of Sir Donald Stewart, which seems definite. Went carefully into sanitary committee accounts to devise methods by which treasury accounts and the SOV's should correspond closer month by month.

26 November 1913
Complaint from a discharged European that the place he had to work

in, in the Ashanti mine, was unhealthy. Made memo to get inspector of mines to examine it.

27 November 1913
Interview with the Wesleyan minister, Barnes, re building new school and mission house and enlarging chapel. Left pending for committee. Visited post office. Found conditions much improved.

4 December 1913
Interesting point raised by Akrokeri as to liabilities of stool servant who became Christian to get out of stool service.[49]

5 December 1913
Report by a Hausa that two of his companions had been shot at and killed at Jacobo near Akrokeri. Man vouched for by Hausa headman. Sent superintendent and two men to investigate. Court in morning. Inspected village with MO and SOV. Not quite satisfied with bush round Wawassi.

6 December 1913
General correspondence. Superintendent returns and reports that murder at Jacobo only exists in imagination of informant. Order him to be kept for a few days under medical observation.

8 December 1913
Left by 9.20 train for Bekwai. Palaver with head chief Bekwai. Explained new scheme for educating local cocoa instructors. He promised to choose a suitable man and present him on Wednesday. Palaver at Kokofu with head chief who complained (1) that his watchmen had been suppressed; (2) that his prison had been suppressed; (3) he wished to concentrate all cocoa selling in his head village; (4) application for 40 new guns. Answered as to (1) and (2) that enquiry should be made; as to (3) refused, and (4) refused until all gun tax collected.

9 December 1913
Kokofu to camp on Lake Bosumtwi at Isansi. Time two hours' fast walking. Houses at camp ambitious in design but badly built. Would be dangerous in tornado, roofs leak and walls and floors not finished. The chiefs concerned have promised to put them in order at once.

10 December 1913
Left camp, reached Bekwai in four hours, talking with all the chiefs on the road. Held Dengyase boundary palaver at Bekwai.

Sunday 14 December 1913
Gave permission for Roman Catholic torch-light procession.

15 December 1913
Court work. Prisoner who escaped recaptured and given three months. The Hausa man who invented the story of his companions being murdered was brought up. MO put on certificate that he was imbecile, but not dangerous. Handed over to his people to be sent back to Sokoto, his birthplace.

17 December 1913
Court in morning. Application by West African Mahogany syndicate to be allowed to cut trees in Nkwanta Division by arrangement with chiefs.

18 December 1913
Witnessed agreement between West African Mahogany syndicate and head chief Nkwanta, and chief of Karaga. Syndicate gets right to cut trees for two years at £1 per tree.

19 December 1913
Court sat until 12.30. Police discovered what looks like far-reaching gold frauds. Remanded accused for further enquiries. Inspected village in evening. *Zongo* clean.

25 December 1913
Public holiday. Attended matins at mines' chapel.

27 December 1913
Bishop of Accra from Coomassie. Discussed with him the attitude of natives who declared themselves Christians suddenly in order to avoid tribal service.

29 December 1913
Long morning dealing with disorder resulting from Christmas holiday. Superintendent reports much drunkenness.

2 January 1914
Court day. Important gold-dealing fraud, which took all morning and was unfinished. Dealt with licences and yearly accounts. Board on treasury. All correct.

5 January 1914
Heavy court. Finished gold-dealing case by committing for trial. Serious ramifications implicating prominent Adansis. Issued licences — spirits, gold and trading. Inspected town.

6 January 1914
Palaver day. Long and busy morning, summoned all the headmen of local courts. Read over to them the rules governing their conduct,

explained them and answered their questions. Lectured all assembled in court on methods of fighting cocoa pests.

9 January 1914
Left for Formanah at 8.30 a.m. Road much improved and fit for bicycles in most places. Stayed in new house built by the chief for the trading company. The village completely transformed, being now laid out in a square. Many good huts and houses going up.

17 January 1914
Moved out of quarters and prepared for HE's arrival in afternoon, also Captain Adams's, with 28 police for guard.

18 January 1914
HE with the Duke of Mecklenburg,[50] Captain King and Lieutenant Ave Raven, an ADC, a DC and Director of Railways. HE and Duke in PC's bungalow. English staff in bush huts in garden. German staff in assistant engineer's bungalow. All chiefs at station, also school children and European and native staff.

19 January 1914
HE and party went round mine in morning. Lunch at mine. Dinner given by HE at PC's bungalow.

21 January 1914
Discussions with chiefs. They all seem satisfied and report their divisions to be flourishing. They want light railways and free guns.

10 February 1914
Major Rew arrived Obuasi to take over the province from Mr Philbrick. [Philbrick spent the next eight months in Kumasi as Ag CCNT.]

14 October 1914
Left Coomassie 6.30 a.m. Found that everything in the house and office was apparently in good order. Dined at the mine.

16 October 1914
Sat in court and took palavers. Everything seems very quiet, as always happens when commissioners are changed.

17 October 1914
Was examined by Dr Grave for my 11-month certificate. Resumed the pleasant habit of Saturday dinner at the mine. Had many callers in the afternoon.

26 October 1914
Travelled along the new road ordered by Major Rew from Nkwanta to Bekwai via Dengyase. This is instead of the road via Pelalia, which

1. ABOVE. Howard Ross administering medicine to boat crew, Krachi, Volta River.

2. RIGHT. T.E. Fell. Halt at village near Sunyani, Western Province, Ashanti.

3. LEFT. Kwamin Tano, Omanhin of Sefwi.

4. ABOVE. Kwamin Tano on his palanquin under his state umbrella, preceded by his gold sword bearers, 1915.

5. LEFT. Sefwi sword bearers and drums.

6. RIGHT. Fetish children at Wioso.

7. BELOW. Fetish woman dancing in the street.

8. LEFT. 'Tiger', Howard Ross's steward.

9. BELOW. Crowd outside D.C.'s court, Sunyani.

10. Howard Ross in his old age.

11. ABOVE. Back from the shoot.

12. LEFT. Drs Wm. Graham and C.V. Le Fanu, Gambaga 1905.

13. RIGHT. Pte Kofi Grunshi, 2nd G.C.R.

14. BELOW. H.E. presenting medals, Gambaga 1906.

15. ABOVE. H.E.'s parade, Gambaga 1906.

16. BELOW. Alhaji Bukari's mosque in Salaga.

I was having made. It was altered by Major Rew. It is much shorter, but goes through a very difficult country, which is not nearly so well inhabited. It has given rise to some boundary palavers in the Nkwanta division, which I endeavoured to settle as I went along it. The chief is very deaf. I am bringing him in for medical examination, to get him an ear trumpet.

Sunday 1 November 1914
Wrote letters and paid my monthly bills. Called in at the club and renewed acquaintance with the mine staff.

2 November 1914
A meeting, with the manager AGC Ltd and the various chiefs from whom he wants a timber concession. Manager offers £50 down and £5 per annum. Chiefs want to exempt mahogany from the bargain. There being a deadlock, I could do nothing. Swore in seven more volunteers, but I do not yet know the actual situation with regard to this force. Checked over Wood's criminal returns. Find him exceedingly careful — will not do anything rash.

3 November 1914
Left Obuasi on 3.00 p.m. train for Bekwai, and went straight through to Kokofu. Able to cycle all the way. Stayed in the head chief's two-storey house! Palfriman was on the train, going to relieve McLeod.[51]

4 November 1914
Left early and marched to Eduadin station. Met Chief Frimpon there. He showed me his boundary with Dadiasewa. To follow it, we waded for a mile down the Oda.

5 November 1914
Got a touch of the sun and feeling upset. Head chief came in, in evening, and had a long chat. He is feeling very depressed about the low price of cocoa, but seems as loyal as possible. Told him all about the war.

6 November 1914
Wrote a copy of my October diary and sent it in to the CCA also my judgement in the Frimpon–Toto case. The case of alleged finding of gold dust here was brought again. Four months ago decided there was no evidence of anything at all being found. Now, the finder retracts his former statement and avows that he did find the gold and handed it over to one Acquah, who has stolen it.

7 November 1914
Took all parties in the gold-dust case in to Obuasi, under arrest, and

signed a search warrant. Tried a manslaughter case at Bekwai and gave the guilty man a year. Got back to Kokofu at 6.00 p.m. Cycled each way from Bekwai in one hour.

8 November 1914
Left Kokofu at 3.00 a.m. and walked to Tepeso, a camp on Lake Bosumtwi. The road has been made up and ditched, but it is too up and down for cycling. The camp is looking neglected, only one house being finished. The Kokofu house is still too pretentious and one wall is again falling down. A lovely sunset.

9 November 1914
Left Tepeso early and walked along the southern part of the lake to Ankase. The road was well cleaned all the way and the cocoa farms looked very good indeed. Stayed in the compound of the fetish house, where I put up my tent. Had a raft formed and went out a mile towards the centre of the lake, the depth gradually increasing to 150 feet. In the evening, bathed and had races. The men showed marvellous dexterity on the logs. Saw their method of catching fish, which is most ingenious.

10 November 1914
Continued walking round the lake to Konkuma, then turned eastward to Biposo and thence to Isace and Belayease. This latter a filthy village, full of pigs and sheep. Put up my tent outside and, as luck would have it, was drowned out in the night and had to take refuge in the village after all. The chief, who is under Ofuasi, has promised to put up a rest house at once. I selected an excellent site. Promised to send chief papers re war contribution.

13 November 1914
To Brofu Yedru. The rest house at Brofu Yedru is finished and is most comfortable. The village getting quite large. Miller's now have a big store and bungalow. Cocoa was coming in in large quantities all along the road and brokers were buying at the outlying villages.

14 November 1914
Got back to Obuasi in afternoon. Found all well. The road near Obuasi has not been finished; am summoning the village headman. Found instructions to put all Germans under close arrest. Did so by putting sentries on their quarters. Had to withdraw the two Germans working on parole at the gas plant.

15 November 1914
Wrote private letters. Called on the Germans and explained the new conditions to them.

16 November 1914
Worked in office, picking up details of what had transpired during my absence. Ordered a quantity of road tools and put on new road overseer for the Dengyase road.

18 November 1914
Began trial of Acquah for stealing the Kokofu gold dust and two others for perjury. Most intricate case with lots of false evidence. A Mr Jackson came from Akrokeri complaining that his boys were besieging him in his bungalow, as he could not pay them their wages for timber felling. Granted the boys a free summons. Got a boy to climb the flagstaff and put in new halyards, so the flag now flies again. Heavy rain falling each afternoon.

19 November 1914
Continued hearing the gold-dust case. Spent afternoon over the Native Jurisdictions papers.

20 November 1914
Gave judgement in the Axim mahogany case in favour of the boys for their wages and telegraphed to Seccondee to seize any logs that might be there. Further hearing of the gold-dust case.

2 December 1914
Up to lunch time spent the morning in writing letters, diaries etc. After lunch I walked to Banka, where I held a palaver with the chief. A large English mail arrived for me in the evening.

3 December 1914
Leaving Banka early, I walked back to Tepeso and thence struck out northwest to Insutim. The road had been cleaned for me, but evidently had not been touched for months before. The country was flat, well watered and extensively planted with cocoa. Nsuaem is a big village, with at least one good house. I was informed that no DC had ever been there before. I held a meeting in the evening and spoke to them about roads, village improvements etc. I fined one Kojo Ashanti 40/– for felling trees over the road when making his farm and not clearing them away.

4 December 1914
Leaving Nsuaem at 6.30 a.m., I reached Abodom after a six-hour march. The roads excessively steep, going over what must be one of the highest ranges in Ashanti. For two hours the up grade was very heavy. Abodom, where I slept, is much improved. The chief has done very well and the village is clean and prosperous. He has promised to put up a rest house and I selected the site.

5 December 1914
Leaving Abodom at 7.00 a.m., I passed through Dadiaso at 8.00 a.m., Ahuri at 9.00 a.m. and reached Tepeso camp at 11.00 a.m. Dadiaso looked neglected. This chief is a very important one, now under Kokofu. I censured him on the state of his village and the road and he promised reform. He was told to meet me at Kokofu on Monday. Ahuri was clean and prosperous. This village has a large Friday market attended by people from all about. And, it would be easy to make a motor road here from Bekwai.

Sunday 6 December 1914
Was idle during the morning reading papers etc. In the afternoon walked into Kokofu and was met by a large brass band in the most startling uniforms I have yet seen. Each one was different and each more gorgeous than the other.

7 December 1914
Held a palaver at which all the principal Kokofus were present. I was asked whether one Kokofu could claim the 1*d*. per tree tax from another. I decided that he could not do so, as both contributed to the stool expenses, but a small rent, which in this case I fixed at £2 should be paid. One, Viney, was brought in. He had been impersonating a road overseer and alleged he was appointed 13 months ago by Major Rew. Sent him to Obuasi to be tried. Walked over to Esumaja in evening and had a talk with the chief. He is now always argumentative and seems to be getting foolish with drink, a pity as he was a good man.

8 December 1914
Left Kokofu at 7.00 a.m. Went through Eduadin, Kintincheri and Peki, trespassing a short way into the Central Province. The country was all full of cocoa, and no disease. The site for the new rest house has now been cleaned. The building is to be on a new plan, which I hope will be successful. The chiefs all along this road have been selling spirits on 1913 licences. Wrote to Wood about their prosecution.

9 December 1914
Leaving Peki late in the morning, walked into Bekwai. At Bekwai had a long talk with the *omanhene*, who was too weak to rise from his mat. Held court and sentenced a clerk to three months for unlawful entry. There being no lockup, I shut him in the goods shed at the station and he escaped during the evening. Two more men were brought in charged with impersonating road overseers. Sent them to Obuasi for trial.

10 October 1914
Walked from Bekwai to Jacobo along the old main road. This is the first time I have been along it. The villages are large and appear flourishing. The cocoa all along the way was in first-rate condition. At Jacobo met Mr Hunter of the Agriculture Department. He expressed himself as pleased with what he had seen of the Southern Province. He gave an interesting lecture in the evening to the villagers. The rest house is not yet finished and is of a plan that will not be good in the rains. I have had several trees planted along the avenue near the rest house, which I hope will grow.

12 December 1914
Returned to Obuasi and found all well. Watkins met me on the platform with particulars of an alleged series of gold frauds on the mine. The harmattan is beginning and, in consequence, the dust from the new plant is very bad. For the next three months it will be very unpleasant. Dined at the mine.

14 December 1914
In court and office. Miller's agent came down to get agent in several debt cases. The clerk who escaped from Bekwai surrendered, explaining he had only escaped to arrange his private affairs.

19 December 1914
Passed the day writing and walking about.

20 December 1914
Taplin and Moore, Ag DC Saltpond, came in at 11.00 a.m. They had an escort of ten men. Head Chief Kobina Foli, with all his subchiefs and about 200 followers, arrived at 10.00 a.m. and Swedru, with hardly any followers, at 3.00 p.m. A palaver followed, but from the beginning it was evident that Swedru would not abate his claim to the river and it was with difficulty that a riot was avoided. Kobina Foli behaved well, but both sides began hurling insults at each other and the palaver broke up in confusion. Taplin and I discussed the affair after and there are still hopes of arranging the matter without declaring the ferry at Nsese a government one, a course I do not want to advise owing to the difficulty of administration. The Bogesangos, who are still in Ayinase in Akim, were present, but it was impossible to discuss their business owing to the state of temper of both sides.

25 December 1914
The town was very quiet. Discovered that the office was broken into yesterday after it was closed. Nothing but some gin, which was on exhibit, was taken.

29 December 1914
Work in the office. Police reported that there had been very little drunkenness and rioting. Much less than usual, but that burglaries and gold stealing had taken place. Attended the Christmas staff dinner at the mine.

31 December 1914
Took palavers, but very few natives came in. Took opportunity to begin correcting the mileage scale, which needs revision.

(ii) P. A. H. Pott, Ag PC, 1915

14 January 1915
Took over province. Went through letter book etc.

15 January 1915
Mr Philbrick left for Seccondee. Read up this diary for the year and sundry other papers. Inspected carriers' work on hill and rest house. Dust from mine very bad at this time of year, and it is impossible to keep the bungalow clean. It also affects one's throat and eyes. Hunting accident reported from Bekwai.

26 January 1914
Long palaver with Adansis re Kokufu boundary dispute and many other matters. They still retain their reputation as unblushing liars.

Bogesango, 10 February 1914
Had palaver with chief of Bogesango and explained I could do little for him with reference to the people who refused to leave Akim after having drunk fetish at Fomena. Discussed many other matters. Caught ten men who have paid no gun licence for years and fined them £2 apiece.

Betinkor, 11 February 1915
Chief of Dadiaso and a number of followers arrived. I commenced by informing them that I had heard the Adansi side of the question and explained it to them. I was rudely interrupted several times. I then called on the chief of Dadiaso to state his side of the case. He said he would not allow the Adansis to take his land from him and behaved in so extraordinary a fashion that I thought he must be drunk. I told him to return to Dadiaso and that I would send for him when I was at Obuasi, where he would await my convenience. At once, what was obviously an organized riot arose. The Bogesangos or Adansis were beaten. Guns were found on the road at a little distance and it was apparent that many of the Dadiaso were armed with knives. I affected to treat the matter lightly and, after a time, with the assistance of my escort of three policemen, I got the Dadiasos to return to Tapeso.

15 February 1915
Sent letter to chief of Kokofu and *omanhin* of Bekwai. Adansi chief brought in a list of names of Dadiasos implicated in riot. Stated they were interfering with travellers on Banda road. Asked Adansi to send out two constables. Sent coded wire to CCA. Accident reported in mine. Native killed.

16 February 1915
The natives are keeping Bekwai very clean and have bought £20 of planks for their culverts. Palavered with Bekwais till noon. They pressed for a general decision as to cocoa tribute between subjects of subchiefs living on another subchief's land. Promised to consult CCA and quoted arrangement made by Philbrick in Kokofu case. Then, on to Kokofu. Road clean and good. Of this too Rickaby complained. He wants a motor road, or at least a barrel rolling road.

17 February 1915
Spoke to *omanhene*, Queen Mother and elders and explained to them what the chief of Dadiaso has done and its effect on the peace and administration of the province.

25 February 1915
A long morning, complaints and palavers. Learnt that the chief of Dadiaso had written a lying letter to the *omanhin* of Kokofu who, in response, wrote an impertinent one to me. Arrested chief of Dadiaso and wrote for *omanhin* of Kokofu to come in and explain.

16 March 1915
Tried chief of Dadiaso and others for Betinkor riot. All parties now behaving well, but having regard to the disturbance the offence created, substantial fines were inflicted.

Dompoasi, 20 March 1915
Destroyed four useless guns – unlicensed. At Obuasi, was met by complaint about boundary pillars, settled by Cutfield but not yet put in right place. At Akrokeri, chief and elders met me and begged me not to take them to Fomena, stating that they had sat up all night and settled their differences. I gave them a month to show signs of real improvement.

29 March 1915
Visited spot that a Christian, an ex-linguist, is said to have farmed in contravention of native tradition, as to its being a burial place of Kwissa chiefs. Found he had done so and encouraged others. He had refused to go before a native court and written a grossly libellous letter to the *omanhin*. He was brought in and fined, in all £10, and

sent into Obuasi to stand trial for criminal libel, saying he would divulge many secrets.

Brofu Yedro, 1 April 1915
Short palaver with *odikro* and Muslim headman re *zongo*, which chief wants to build. Encouraged the idea, but pointed out that if the Ashantis persist in housing north country people, they are not likely to build houses for themselves. Came into Obuasi. Arrived about 3.00 p.m. After a short talk with Wood, went up to change. CC passed through with Mrs Fuller in afternoon train, though not expected till Saturday, so I missed him unfortunately.

4 April 1915
Easter Sunday. Visited prison.

22 May 1915
A complaint as to extortion by warders sent out to get food for prisoners.

24 May 1915
School children saluted the flag. I gave them a short address in the morning. Afternoon sports and tea.

25 May 1915
Long morning in complaints against warder and gaolers. Over 100 women appeared in court. Same old story about taking food and paying insufficient prices.

(iii) L. H. Wheatley PC, 1916

1 May 1916
Criminal cases and office routine. Left Obuasi for Bekwai by afternoon train. Found things fairly quiet on arrival; there had been some rioting, one man was wounded and feeling was beginning to run high. Held meeting with *omanhene* elect, chiefs and elders and all people present. Was informed by Chief Kojo Okanjon and elders that Kwami Osei Esibey had been elected *omanhene* in due form and order, but that certain youngmen, the relatives and household officers of the late *omanhene*, were vigorously opposing the election of Kwami Osei Esibey. The ringleader of the opposition informed me that their main reason for objecting was the undersize of the *omanhene* elect's testicles, which would bring shame on the Bekwais. They admitted it was no physical disability or weakness. (I fancy the real reason at the back was that Kweku Abebrese, an ex-*omanhene* destooled at the last rising, was plotting to be re-elected to the stool and had got round Yaw Bramba, nephew of the late *omanhene*, and his followers to work on his behalf.) After listening long and patiently to both sides

and reasoning with the opposition till long after dark, I was unable to settle matters satisfactorily. Yaw Bramba and his followers withdrew all opposition to the election of Kwami Osei Esibey and each stepped forward and swore loyalty to the *omanhene*. They also agreed to drink fetish, and the *omanhene* elect also agreed to drink fetish by proxy, that he bore them no ill will. No fees were to be charged. The subchiefs behaved very well after the late *omanhene*'s death and showed much patience and common sense in endeavouring to keep the people within bounds. I was fortunate in choosing the time of my visit, as matters had reached a critical point, when patience and tempers had grown short and feelings were running high, and it was only by careful handling that the custom finished without serious consequences. I have left the sergeant and four police at Bekwai for a couple of days as a precautionary measure, although probably an unnecessary one.

2 May 1916
Back to Obuasi and found all correct. Few civil cases and routine work. Informed that Awotwi is to hold himself in readiness to proceed to the Colony. A great pity that Ashanti should lose his services. He will be a loss to the office and the Southern Province, which he appears to know well.

3 May 1916
Criminal and civil cases. Correspondence.

5 May 1916
A few civil and criminal cases. Discussed Kobeda land case. A slack day. Trouble over the market arising from reduced prices, people not bringing stuff in. Sent out to bring in the headmen of surrounding villages to answer why they have not obeyed the gong gong and *omanhene*'s oath to bring in foodstuff. Sergeant and men returned from Bekwai and report everything quiet. Ross passed through, but his message only reached me after his train had gone. Sent tea down to Miss Adair,[52] *en route* for Coomassie.

Sunday 7 May 1916
Tennis at the mines.

8 May 1916
One civil case and several complaints. Busy with monthly returns. People coming into market, which was quite a good one.

9 May 1916
Routine and correspondence. Long sitting in court over cocoa tribute cases involving land ownership.

18 May 1916
Received information that four men from Praso, Gold Coast Colony, were smuggling powder into and selling same in Southern Province Ashanti, also carrying on illicit gin selling, also that a money doubler was carrying out his nefarious practices near Jacobo, on the Obuasi–Jacobo road. Sent out police detectives to investigate and make arrest if possible, if report is true. Long discussion, the third, with Adansi and Fwidiem representatives re cocoa tribute. Both parties agree to an annual tribute of £15. Agreement to be signed tomorrow. Sent round a circular asking for subscriptions towards Empire Day sports for school children.

20 May 1915
Inspected broken pipes at water dam. Also Obuasi village, which was clean. Visited prison and attended to various matters in the office.

23 May 1916
Dealt with numerous complaints and office routine. Busy preparing for Empire Day sports. Police make a large capture of smuggled powder and gin being sold without a licence.

24 May 1916
Empire Day. Gave school children tea and held successful sports for them in afternoon. Mrs Wheatley[53] presented the prizes and also badges for boy scouts.

(iv) A. J. Cutfield, Ag PC, 1916

25 June 1916
Omanhin of Kokofu reports fishing with hooks and nets in Lake Bosumtwi. Matter is receiving attention. The second-class warder sentenced to five months for using his gang of prisoners to steal cassava and then sitting down with them to eat it.

Monday 17 July 1916
Returned from Coomassie by train. Big criminal court. Kroo boys convicted of keeping a gambling house.

1 August 1916
Longish court day. A man charged with many thefts from dwelling houses. He is an old offender having three previous convictions for the same offence. I urge that sentence of flogging may be confirmed. He lives in gaol and does not like being out.

(v) A. J. Philbrick, PC, 1916

7 September 1916
Walked to Kokofu through Esuinegu. The road is very good, but there are several places where heavy work will have to be done before it is even fit for casks. I have put the chiefs on to work at once and they have promised to finish it speedily. The *omanhin* of Kokofu expressed himself as much pleased to see me again. He made great preparations to meet me.

10 October 1916
Long list of palavers in morning, chiefly complaints and appeals from native courts. Correspondence etc. Dr Spurrell examined medically for extension from 12 to 13 months.[54]

12 October 1916
Stayed in Kokofu. Urged chief to begin his road. Showed him what to do. He gave me £100 to pay for tools etc. Visited Esumaja and showed people how to ferment cocoa and pick out defective beans. All appear anxious to improve the quality, but complain the brokers are robbing them.

20 October 1916
A few police cases and palavers. The Mohammedans very much interested in the German efforts to suppress them in East Africa. They attended in a body and asked what they could do to show their support for England. I cautioned them against believing any lying rumours and told them of the progress of the war.

26 October 1916
Much cocoa picked, but they cannot dry it owing to want of sun. The price advertised in Akrokeri is 15/6*d*., but only some firms pay this in full, the others deducting 1/– brokerage, even if the farmer himself brings the cocoa to the scale. This the farmers cannot understand.

14 November 1916
The new chief of Ascuberi, only a small boy, came in in a state. Postponed seeing him until tomorrow. A crowded court, 12 criminal and 33 civil actions, mostly unimportant. A well-known money doubler was remanded for a week.

15 November 1916
The chief of Ascuberi was presented. He is the nephew of the deposed chief. I agreed to his election, pending CC's consent, for one year on probation. Spurrell, MO, examined me and passed me for another month.

2 December 1916
Visited the cocoa-buying shed. Immense quantities of cocoa are coming in, more than can well be handled. Got the first Reuters since 21 November.

Sunday 3 December 1916
Private correspondence. The usual dinner in evening.

5 December 1916
A strike began among the loco drivers in the mine and, in consequence, it was shut down for want of fuel. The trouble seems to have arisen owing to dissatisfaction with a new superintendent.

7 December 1916
Price of cocoa down again. People much dissatisfied.

8 December 1916
The town committee met Mr Wright, a sanitary officer, at 5.00 p.m. and inspected the section of drain that had fallen in. Decided to remove the ruins and reinforce the rest of the drain at once.

9 December 1916
Planted out 18 rose trees from Colchester in the PC's garden. Visited Dr Spurrell's menagerie, which is assuming big proportions.

11 December 1916
Domenase rioters came up this morning. Ten selected as ringleaders. Four sentenced to one year, five to three months and one fined £10. The chief fined 40/– for destroying a boundary pillar. Passed medical examination for 14–15 months.

12 December 1916
Cocoa still coming in fast, and all storage room is full. Much now lying out in the street under tarpaulins.

18 December 1916
Left Mbeim at 7.15 a.m. and walked over a road where none remember any commissioner going through the villages of Agoyesum, Nkuntin and Adenkyem. The country appears extraordinarily rich and fairly populated. At Edubia, I found Chief Kwamin Pong better from his wound but low spirited over the price of cocoa. He states his people are abandoning its cultivation. Explained the reason for the low price.

20 December 1916
From Mbeim to Domi, Whinisu and Odahun, where the Dengyases are disputing with the Bekwais over some land on the Oda. Visited the

spot and got a general idea of the dispute, which I hope to settle, referring to Captain Armitage's notes, when laying out the boundary of Dengyase. Had a good catch of fish in the Oda in the evening.

21 December 1916
To Odasu and Jacobo. This is quite the worst road I have been on for years and cannot think how its condition has escaped notice. Immediate steps will be taken to have it improved. The chief of Jacobo is busy working on the other side, but the other chiefs responsible have no excuse.

25 December 1916
Office clearing table and writing reports on roads, committee accounts etc. Walked through town in afternoon, all very quiet. Visited prison. Found it in order. Dined at the mine, 26 sat down.

27 December 1916
Criminal cases, which had accumulated during the last week. No special Christmas cases. The superintendent reported that there had been very little drunkenness and no disturbances, 19 civil cases. Mr Chandler, SPG, came in afternoon to hold service. Staying with me.

28 December 1916
Civil cases, including some interesting claims for pawns.[55] Found it very difficult to decide them, that is to enforce our slavery laws strictly without upsetting native custom too much.

29 December 1916
Captain Armitage passed through. I accompanied him a short way down the line as I had much to talk about. Passed the rest of the day clearing up accounts etc. for end of year.

(vi) L. H. Wheatley, PC, 1918

2 January 1918
Criminal court. Held board on treasury. Office routine.

3 January 1918
Civil court and numerous small complaints. A report brought in that the chief of Senassi has had women severely flogged who were going to dig white clay at Tetrain. Sent a constable out to bring in the men who committed the assault.

4 January 1918
Criminal court, chiefly railway prosecutions. The SSOR is still unable to attend to duty since the beginning of the year.

7 January 1918
No criminal court. Office routine. Checked court accounts for December. A slack day.

9 January 1918
Criminal court, inquests. The Moshi chief and many of his followers are brought up for making a night attack on the Lagos people at Akrokeri, armed with cutlasses etc. Sentenced the Moshi chief to eight months with hard labour, his followers to three months, and inflicted small fines on certain Lagosians. Much damage to property was done.

10 January 1918
Civil court and complaints. Had Esumaja and Ofuasi before me with their interminable cocoa tribute palavers. I made a definite arrangement for a mutual payment of the tribute between them, but I hesitate to think it will be final.

11 January 1918
Criminal court and routine. Collecting material for annual report.

12 January 1918
Office routine. Drainage work with Watkins. The work is going on satisfactorily, but we are now faced with a shortage of cement owing to its non arrival from England.

14 January 1918
Small criminal court. SSOR Coppin reports he has been granted five months' leave in the colony and is going to Lomé.[56]

21 January 1918
Saw gold weighed, sampled and boxed for Coghill. Criminal court.

22 January 1918
Civil court and complaints. The furniture for the Commissioner's house, which has arrived, is excellent and greatly adds to the comfort of the house.

24 January 1918
Dealt with a few small complaints. Out to Auwri Nkwanta to inspect the banking of the road. Found good progress had been made and gave instructions for heavy retaining sticks to be placed at the sides of embanking. Visited sawyer and found them hard at work on the timber required for the bridge, road etc.

Sunday 27 January 1918
The official mail arrived, with which I dealt.

28 January 1918
Spent a long morning enquiring into complaints laid by the chief of Esaman against his subchiefs on the lake and found, in small, there was no basis to them. Then, listened to the complaints of the subchiefs against the chief of Esaman. The main complaint was that the chief kept all the moneys and this should properly be shared. This complaint I find genuine. The subchiefs wish the chief to satisfy them and make peace, but this the chief refuses to do. I made no order as I am wishful to give the chief time for consideration. I went down with a bad attack of fever after the palaver and took to my bed.

29 January 1918
Ill in bed. The MO, Dr Carson, arrived about 10.30 p.m.

30 January 1918
The MO decides to take me through to Bekwai and thence Coomassie and hospital. Catch afternoon train to Coomassie and go into hospital [he stays there until 6 February].

Sunday 17 February 1918
Begin fifteenth month of my tour. Busy with various official papers and annual report.

18 February 1918
Long criminal court. Left by train for Bekwai in afternoon. Ag CC at Bekwai. Dined with him at PC's house. The Ag CC informs me that the Ag PC has been down to Bekwai for the day to consult as to the proposed reservation for a government station. This is the first intimation I have that the Ag PC was coming into my province. I was somewhat surprised that I, as PC of the province, was kept in ignorance of the fact and given no opportunity of being present.

(vii) P. A. H. Pott PC, 1918

23 April 1918
Took over from Wheatley. Checked cash in vault and treasury clerk's safe. Spoke to SOV as to his work. Went through files, diaries etc.

24 April 1918
The criminal case. *Zongo* elders called. Continued my search through files.

25 April 1918
Heard civil cases. Inspected police station and gaol. Took dispositions of a woman who had been murderously attacked on the road near Akrokeri and is now in mine's hospital.

29 April 1918
Commenced two rape cases. Heard number of criminal cases. A gang of pickpockets from Accra convicted. Fairey, SOV, said to be of intemperate habits. Made thorough inspection of prisons and warned warders.

30 April 1918
Held meeting of representatives and headmen and explained their duties to them. Heard number of civil cases and complaints. Checked treasury accounts. SM, Bekwai, reports he is sending in body of a labourer who is alleged to have died suddenly after being beaten by a carpenter of police at Bekwai for stealing a tin of sardines. Body arrived at 4.00 p.m. on a trolley and I viewed it and requested mine's doctor, Hamilton Hart, to make a postmortem.

1 May 1918
Interviewed Harvey and road overseer. Gave instructions for month. Finished one rape case and committed accused. Correy, assistant auditor, wires [that he is] arriving this afternoon.

2 May 1918
Went through gun books. Heard civil cases and complaints. Went into question of oath fees with Fanti headmen. One man produced a sort of printed power of attorney from the *omanhene* of Anamabu. Matter will be referred to CCA.

3 May 1918
Inquiry into death of workman at Bekwai. Finding manslaughter against policeman and a carpenter.

6 May 1918
Completed case of carnal knowledge and committed to CCA. Worked at road schedule. Not much accurate information seems to be available.

8 May 1918
Criminal cases and correspondence. A large number of gun licences to sign. Continued search through files and records.

9 May 1918
Routine. Correspondence, civil cases, complaints.

18 May 1918
Correspondence and accounts. Harvey called. Road work going on pretty well. He complains that the chief of Dadiaso has been rude to him. This chief is a worthless fellow.

Whit Sunday, 19 May 1918
The MO reports death of a native run over by a loco engine last night.

23 May 1918
Wife of chief of Dadiaso complains of ill-treatment. Tied to a tree and whipped. Granted a summons as he has done this before.

24 May 1918
Empire Day. Schools took part in a parade and a concert under their master's supervision.

28 May 1918
Sanitary conditions bad, drains holding water all over the place. Tank in Drewry's yard breeding mosquitoes by the million. Emptied it.

21 June 1918
Kobina Foli complains villages won't keep up his motor road to Fomena, saying they haven't got a car and why should they.

22 June 1918
Meeting to fix prices of foodstuffs. Found the prison had reverted to the old bad habit of sending out for food. Once more make an arrangement for the supply.

24 June 1918
Heathcote from Coomassie as ADC. Talked over his duties with him.

26 June 1918
Handed over treasury to Heathcote. Heathcote took court. Cement arrived.

29 August 1918
A talk with *omanhene* of Kokofu as to his court, and warned him that there was no general feeling of confidence in its integrity and that his clerk was not above suspicion.

8 September 1918
Troop trains passed through at 1.30 and 4.30 a.m. — 30 officers and NCOs and 900 men. We gave the officers and NCOs soup, coffee, tea, sandwiches and the troops a very large quantity of food of all kinds, kanki, fufu, fish, soup, yams, sugar cane.

17 September 1918
To Pamu and back. Road in bad condition and my instructions not carried out. Work on rest house Pamu slovenly to last degree. Dismissed road overseer. Unless a skilled overseer can be obtained the Bekwai–Tepiso Road will never be fit for motor traffic. The line is not an easy one.

12 October 1918
Town and market show only a third of normal population, if that. Nurse Yarquah the only representative of Medical Department reports sick. Servants and hammock boys are down with influenza.

13 October 1918
Fairey, SOV, reports two European miners died last night. [The] total of native deaths 37. A telegram from Harper [arrived] saying he knows nothing of Dr Hart's alleged appointment, but suggests I should make use of his services and send serious cases to Coomassie. It is, unfortunately, doubtful if any value can be attached to these services. Market and town almost deserted this morning. Attended funeral of miners in rain in evening. Saw Hart who appeared to be drunk.

15 October 1918
A few civil cases and complaints. SMO wires he has no drugs to spare for the station and suggests I should borrow some from mines. By CCA's instruction, sent out a circular requesting all head chiefs to send me a daily report of deaths from influenza in their division.

16 October 1918
All prisoners report sick. Heathcote and myself inspected them and instructed gaoler to employ those prisoners who did not seem really ill on light duty and to keep them in the air as much as possible. Put 15 sanitary labourers on latrine work,[57] paying them *6d.* a day extra.

17 October 1918
Mines' MO says he cannot supply any drugs.

18 October 1918
Shortage of food in prison reported. The market is badly supplied with food and time women are putting up prices and refusing to bring produce in. Spoke to Adansi representative about it.

8 November 1918
Harper, SMO from Coomassie, went on sick list with colic. Circuit judge wires he is down with fever and cannot come.

12 November 1918
Sent letters to chiefs re armistice, also re paper money.

14 November 1918
Inspected prison where there has been an organized protest against the food, apparently due to gaoler giving the prisoners better food than they are entitled to and then stopping it.

11 December 1918
Streams of carriers bringing in cocoa. Rode to Jacobo and back. Road very fairly good. Alaxis, travelling instructor, doing demonstrations of cocoa culture in which the people seemed to take but a languid interest.

21 December 1918
HE, Lady Clifford, CCA, and Mr Holmes, PS, arrived Obuasi at noon and were welcomed by all officials, by chiefs and children. Guard of police. At 4.30 p.m. presentation of medals to chiefs on tennis court.

18 March 1919
Civil cases and a large number of complaints. Witnessed sampling, boxing and sealed bullion for AGC.[58] Dr Ford informs me he is under orders to proceed immediately to Gambaga. When he has gone, I shall be the only European official in the province.

16 May 1919
Heard criminal cases but could not get through the list. Ag MO put me on sick list and asked for a medical board and I also applied to CC.

22 May 1919
Letter from CCA. I am to go into hospital as soon as someone can relieve me.

2 June 1919
Coomassie and went into hospital. [In hospital until 9 June.]

11 June 1919
Watkins rang me up to say there had been a fight at the mine and asked for police assistance. Instructed superintendent and all available constables to proceed to the spot and assist management. Superintendent reports the fight was easily stopped and that, at the request of the manager, no one was arrested.

20 June 1919
A talk with the chief of Akrokeri re his town and affairs. The nurse has resigned and the medical department cannot, or will not, fill the vacancy. This means the hospital will have to be shut, a discreditable state of affairs in a place like Obuasi.

15 July 1919
Appam homeward on 20th.

(viii) L. H. Wheatley, PC, 1919

1 October 1919
Mr Wheatley arrived and assumed charge of the province.

3 October 1919
Long criminal court and routine. Appointed new butcher on probation in place of Elia, who was yesterday arrested for debt on a warrant issued by the CC's court. CC informs me that Mangin must style himself ADC and that of Ag DC pending his being given jurisdiction powers.

4 October 1919
Inspected Obuasi and Insuta with the village supervisor and found both places very fairly clean. I instructed the village supervisor to send me an estimate for improvements I propose to make to the market stalls. Inspected prison and visited the post office.

Sunday 5 October 1919
Reading PC's confidential diary for the last year.

6 October 1919
Criminal court all morning. Received letter and various correspondence from one Reynard at Dunkwa that one of the barges, belonging to the Offin River Concession (in liquidation), is sunk and lying across the river and blocking navigation.

7 October 1919
Civil court and routine. Sent Mangin down to Dunkwa to see if there was anything in the report. Village supervisor reports not enough meat in the market. This is owing to the change in butchers, the new one not being established as yet. Mangin returned and reported that the sunk dredger is many miles away from Dunkwa, and he was loth to visit the spot. The Ag DC Dunkwa, however, reported that he had visited the spot and that the dredger was so blocking the river that it was only with much difficulty a canoe could get by.

16 October 1919
Sent off load at 8.00 a.m. and left at 8.40 a.m. myself, after dealing with a few small complaints. Talked with the chiefs of Dadease and Whurien *en route*. The latter told me that the brokers were paying 30/– in notes, or 22/– in silver, for a load of cocoa. Query: is this a form of discount? Arrived Kokofu a little after 11 o'clock. Held court in afternoon and discussed the alleged breach of the lake fishing rules. It seems that the villages generally are all using spun yarn nets. Instructed the chief of Esaman to obtain definite evidence and names of offenders in this province, when the parties can be prosecuted.

17 October 1919
Held court in the morning and settled various minor palavers. Began enquiry into the dispute between the chief and ex-chief of Dadease. The latter was amenable, but the former evinced such temper and unreasonableness I adjourned till the afternoon to give him an opportunity of reconsidering his attitude. At the same time, I gave him some much needed advice. Sat again at 5.00 p.m. and found the chief of Dadease in a much more reasonable frame of mind and was able to settle the matter successfully.

Bekwai, 23 October 1919
Held court in the morning, civil cases and several minor complaints. The representatives of Messrs Drewry, Nestlés, Pickering and Berthoud's called in the afternoon and informed me all their labourers had struck owing to the question of their removal to the *zongo*. Held a meeting with the labourers, which Messrs Drewry and company and the ADC attended. The labourers stated their sole objection to removing to the *zongo* was lack of house *lorsu* [capacity], which they say is insufficient and that the *seriki zongo* is trying to price them more. I inform them that the government has no wish to make them houseless and that I will visit the *zongo* with one of their numbers this afternoon to look into the matter. They then peacefully disperse. Visited the *zongo* and selected a site for the Moshis to build on, at which they expressed themselves as much pleased and promised to complete all their building within four months by working on Sundays. Call Messrs Drewry's agent. He dines with me.

24 October 1919
Return to Obuasi and find all in order. I am informed there is no meat to be had. I gather that the butcher is unable to buy owing to the currency notes being so unpopular. A heavy criminal court and accumulation of paper keeps me very busy.

27 October 1919
Still no meat in the market. Butcher said to have £300 in currency notes with him, but unable to buy cattle with them. Understand he approached the mine with a view to them letting them have some silver, but they were unable to do so. The butcher has been away for some days endeavouring to get someone to sell him cattle for currency notes.

29 October 1919
Morning taken up with criminal court. HE and party consisting of the Secretary of Native Affairs, Mr Furley, the General Manager of the Gold Coast Railways and a DC and PS arrived at 2.55. HE inspected

the guard of honour. He had the Europeans introduced to him and then inspected the boy scouts, after which he greeted the *amanhene* and chiefs assembled on the tennis courts. HE expressed his pleasure and surprise at the number assembled to meet him. Discussed various provincial matters with Philbrick during the morning, including the continued breach of the lake fishing rules. He proposes a reward should be offered for information leading to the conviction of offenders.

31 October 1919
Criminal court, routine. Began enquiry into the Mansu Nkwanta–Mbeim palaver. There does not appear to be any sufficient grounds for the destoolment of Kojo Mensah, chief of Mbeim. The *omanhene* is evincing very great animosity and appears determined not to allow Kojo Mensah to remain on the stool. I adjourned the enquiry to give the *omanhene* an opportunity to think matters over. The CC accompanied by the General Manager Railways arrived at 2.20. He was met by myself and the ADC, Mr Mangin, and a guard of honour furnished by the police.

Saturday 1 November 1919
The CC departed for Seccondee *en route* for England by the morning train after first saying goodbye to the *amanhene* and chiefs.

Abrokerri, 11 November 1919
Held court and then inspected the town. Received a complaint that five men at Odumasi had fired on a Fulani. Sent a constable out to arrest the men.

12 November 1919
Saw the chief. Neither he nor his people had any complaints. His road is still overgrown in spite of all the road overseer's efforts. Fined him £10. Sent off another constable to bring in the men from Odumasi. Held an enquiry into the attempted shooting case. There seems little doubt that the men made a deliberate attempt to shoot the Fulani. It is possible it was planned and is suspiciously like an attempted 'fetish human sacrifice'.

Bekwai, Southern Province

(i) P. A. H. Pott, DC, 1913[59]

7 October 1913
Lengthy enquiry into death of Abudu Grunshi, a shovel boy in mine. Mining rules as to signals when drawing up men evidently habitually disregarded. Negligence on part of employees of mine unknown to the

management. Manager, mine captain, doctor and others present at enquiry.

8 October 1913
Criminal and civil cases and correspondence. Unspent votes, roads maintenance, dwellings etc. Began trial of bell boy at mine for manslaughter by negligence.

14 October 1913
Completed case manslaughter by negligence in mine. Six months' hard labour. CC completed case of gold-dust stealing at Mansu Nkwanta, seven years. Complaint from Basel Mission factory, Bekwai, re Chief Edu Bobill stopping cocoa at Kokofu and refusing to allow it to come to Bekwai. £200 advance made by Basel Mission agent.

16 October 1913
Complaints and palavers. Discussed cocoa rents from strangers with *omanhins* of Adansi, Mansu Nkwanta and Dengyase. Case of girl refusing to marry chief of Ekrofuom. European, Carr, arrested on suspicion of being concerned in gold stealing. Two natives also arrested. Another European, Courtney, got away.

17 October 1913
Visited police station. Inspected box seized and saw Carr and released him under supervision of police. Box belongs to Courtney. Small gold-bearing quartz in shaving soap tube. Sent sergeant down line with warrant for Courtney. Courtney arrested with £20 worth of quartz on him. Admitted his guilt.

Saturday 18 October 1913
Investigated witnesses and accused in Courtney's case and ordered the re-arrest of two natives and of the European, Carr, alias Jobling. Manager AGC inspected stolen quartz. Serious assault on woman in market, by sergeant in charge of railway police reported. Wired Ag Commissioner of Police asking him to come down re this case and that of the Europeans. Ordered tools for road work.

20 October 1913
Adjourned charge against Europeans until 22nd. Courtney pleaded guilty to theft of quartz. Ag Commissioner of Police from Coomassie to prosecute and take charge of case. Chiefs of Mansu Nkwanta and Dengyase left for their homes.

22 October 1913
Two Europeans, Courtney and Carr, sentenced three months' hard labour for stealing quartz from mine.

27 October 1913
Wrote Bekwai re criminal case of witchcraft, Kobina Kumah. Information from *omanhin*s re genealogical tables generally useless. After much labour, Bekwai nearly complete. Subchiefs hopeless.

29 October 1913
Curious claim by ex-slaves to share in profit of a cocoa farm left to their deceased master. Complicated by the fact that one of their numbers had been rendered blind by improper medical treatment by defendant's mother. Adjourned for medical report. Visited prison 5.00 p.m. Discipline bad, gaoler absent.

(ii) A. J. Philbrick, PC, 1917

31 January 1917
Guns are pouring in in far greater quantities than we can handle. Labour is scarce, all boys having gone to bush, hearing that we are going to conscript them.

5 February 1917
To Bekwai, where I met the Fullers. They stayed in my bungalow and I in Miller's.

17 February 1917
Checked gold at mine.

28 February 1917
To Bekwai and Obuasi. CC did not require a copy of my diary.

5 March 1917
At 9.00 a.m. attendance at mine where 5400 lbs of gold were poured, stamped, weighed and boxed up. Afterwards, at 11.30, resumed court and sat until 4.30 with interval for lunch. English mail arrived. Safe in office cut into by burglars who, however, could not get the door off. Nothing missing, but safe ruined.

7 March 1917
Convicted a man of manslaughter by negligence and gave him one year. Careless shooting in the bush is much too common.

Sunday 11 March 1917
Lazy morning. Wrote home letters. To Metcalfe in evening for bridge.

12 March 1917
A few criminal cases. Several civil cases from Bekwai for recovery of cocoa allowances etc. Attended prison to try a convict who had made a disturbance. Found things very lax.

16 March 1917
Wheatley from Coomassie. Handed over to him.

(iii) L. H. Wheatley, PC, 1917

18 April 1917
Philbrick and Watkins left for England. Saw the output of gold run off, stamped, weighed, packed, sealed. This occupied all morning. Spent afternoon in office dealing with various matters and making myself *au fait* with recent happenings and state of affairs. Inspected the DC's bungalow, the keys of the bed and dressing room are missing. Inspected the flower and vegetable garden. The former very dried up and few if any flowers. In the latter, no sign of any vegetables but understand seeds recently planted.

19 April 1917
Long criminal court and a few minor complaints. Dealt with many office papers. Inspected Wawassi village. It is an absolute rabbit warren though clean, although surrounded by much long grass and weeds. This is due to the reduction of labourers on the grounds of war economy. The number of labourers must be increased when the rains come on. A new latrine is in building and I was much struck by tile quality and shape of the bricks, and the poor quality of the mortar. It appears to be a question of utilizing what is available in preference to doing nothing. Discovered the 'chicken' boy had missing keys of bungalow.

23 April 1917
Adjourned case against warder, Ansah. There seems to be something irregular going on in regard to this case. The Superintendent of Police has been tampering with a witness.

24 April 1917
Out at 6.45 and met the SE and made an inspection of the new drainage works. A good deal of progress seems to have been made since the SE returned from leave in January. About 120 yards of the main drain remain to be done and neither the Obuasi nor Nsuta creeks have yet been begun. There are several springs scattered about, which yet remain to be dealt with, and I should say that the most effective, if also the least expensive, will be to make washing places thereby, with small drains running into one or other of the main drains.

2 May 1917
Out at 8 o'clock and to the cyanide plant to see gold made into bricks, and afterwards to manager's office to check the gold being weighed

and boxed, a long process withal. Back to office and dealt with letters and small criminal court. Wire from CC informing me no hope survival of missing Gold Coast passengers ex *Akoso*. No news yet of who are missing. Went up to see how the painting of the bungalow is getting on. Good progress is being made. Found seed box, which contains hardly any seeds. Wonder what has been done with them.

3 May 1917
Long civil court and many complaints. Busy time in office. Cleared my table. Made a preliminary enquiry into what seems a particularly bad case of rape.

5 May 1917
Busy with correspondence and routine work until close on noon. I find out the reason for there being hardly any seeds left. Philbrick has given them away to both Europeans and natives. This deprives his successor, to all intents and purposes, of vegetables till next quarter's allowance. I cannot help feeling that it is most inconsiderate and a misuse of the seeds in giving them away.

10 May 1917
Civil court, small complaints, office routine.

11 May 1917
A long and trying criminal court. Office routine. Saw the chief of Amouful, together with Birri Yehoa, ex-chief of Ankase, and Kweku Amantin, an *ourisu ansah*, elders of Ankase. The two latter have proved themselves evil counsellors to Birri Yehoa and have proved themselves most vindictive and recalcitrant in the whole palaver. I have instructed the three to drink fetish to prove their future loyalty to the chief of Amouful. They demurred for some time, but eventually agreed to do so. Birri Yehoa is to pay £2.7*s*.0*d*. fee for drinking fetish, and the other two £8 each, on account of behaviour and refusal to serve any more as elders.

14 May 1917
Office routine. Long criminal and short civil court. Have rheumatism badly in my back. Have felt it for past few days, but now it is very painful to move.

16 May 1917
Civil and criminal court and complaints. A long morning. Office routine all afternoon. Bain, SF, refused to obey my instructions to vacate the DC's quarters and occupy nursing sister's bungalow. States the furniture is insufficient and that the stove is in need of repair. Bungalow contains two chairs, table, washstand and a bed is avail-

able, the stove is useable. I hold that he could well occupy the quarters without great discomfort.

17 May 1917
Bain, SF, moves into nursing sister's bungalow. He has evidently thought better of his action.

25 May 1917
Left Brofu Yedru at 8.50 a.m. and arrived Fomena at 10.20. A pleasant walk, but a stiff climb over the Kwissa hills. The *omanhene* of Adansi met me in state at Kwissa. Went down with a sharp attack of fever in afternoon. Temperature 103.

26 May 1917
Still down with fever. Temperature only slightly over 101.

27 May 1917
Temperature down to 100 and decide to push on to Akrokeri. Harvey, FW, met me on road short way out from Fomena and I thoroughly inspected the road, walking the whole way to Akrokeri. Harvey has put in excellent work on the culverts and bridges, and has also done some good embanking. I hope to retain his services for the purpose of grading and putting a 'camber' on the road, and also to make a few small deviations. I spoke to several of the chiefs *en route*, who have done little or nothing since the road was cut through. Was very done up when I reached Akrokeri. Said a few words to the chief in afternoon and settled a dispute from the *zongo*.

Monday 28 May 1917
Went out along the Jacobo road to inspect it, but was too weak to get more than half way when I had to return. Turned in and had a good rest and felt better.

29 May 1917
Took things easy as I felt rotten. Dealt with correspondence.

30 May 1917
Everyone was very peaceful. There was no hint of a disturbance. I afterwards visited the village of Jacobo and inspected the rest house. The chief informed me that both Mr Philbrick and Mr Pott had promised him a present when it was finished. It is a good little rest house and I promised to see what I could do. Got back to Akrokeri about 2.00 p.m. and found O'Dea there looking after my wife, who is really very seedy.

4 June 1917
HM the King's birthday kept. At the mines at 8.30 to check extra bars

of gold, which had to be smelted. Things went wrong and it proved a long business, taking two and half hours instead of 45 minutes, as expected. Checked returns for day.

5 June 1917
Office routine. Long civil court and complaints. Dealt with four road cases. Inflicted three fines of £10 each and one of £2. A few fines in such cases are badly needed in this province. Chiefs appear to be under the impression that a summons merely means a caution and advise to be good in future. Result: little attention paid to road work. This impression I hope to remove.

6 June 1917
Long criminal court and office routine. My wife seriously ill. I spent afternoon in bungalow. Dr Dowdall spent three and half hours with wife.

7 June 1917
Mrs Fuller[60] arrives to look after my wife, who I am thankful to say has taken a turn for the better. Heavy civil court and complaints. Engaged in office routine all afternoon.

11 June 1917
Heavy criminal court. Trial of four soldiers for stealing and assault took up all morning, when I had to adjourn till next day. In afternoon, saw Mrs Fuller off who returned to Coomassie.

12 June 1917
Criminal court till noon, finished case of soldiers, all found guilty. It seems extraordinary that they should have been sent wandering in this province without the civil authorities being advised. They were armed with rifles and full ammunition! I propose making a special report on the matter to CC. Civil court from noon to 1.00.

6 November 1917
Had a talk with the chief in the morning. He told me he had a lot of healthy cocoa, but was only getting 6/6*d.* a load. Left at 8 o'clock and lunched *en route* in the bush. The road, where it was made, was clean, but it is extremely swampy and made travelling very heavy and I did not reach Mbeim till 5.45 p.m. I was met outside by the assembled chiefs, three brass bands and two native tom-tom bands and the din was awful, but the crowd appeared to enjoy it.

7 November 1917
Held a palaver at 8.00 a.m. in regard to the election of a new *omanhene*. I find that Chief Kojo Nsia, of Abrain, and Kweku

Nimmo, of Yaw Kroom, and linguist have practically elected one Kobina Atta as *omanhene* and got the chiefs to swear allegiance to him, either before or after the event. Undoubtedly, it was arranged by these three men; the chiefs are not satisfied thereat. It is said Kobina Atta has paid out £300 to the three, a most unlikely event. The election is irregular, it being the Queen Mother's duty to produce a candidate and the electors' part to finally close. I inform the chiefs that Kobina Atta's election is irregular, and null and void and that the Queen Mother must take her part, and that they must all assemble and choose a candidate – Kobina Atta or another, in due and proper form, observing the rightful customs. After further discussion, I dismissed the meeting for that purpose. At 5.00 p.m. I hold another palaver but, after much discussion, find the Kobina Atta party have done nothing. I inform them definitely that the government won't consider any election that is not carried out in a regular manner, that I intend remaining at Mbeim and shall expect a communication from them in due course.

8 November 1917
The chiefs are all assembled holding a serious and, at times, noisy meeting in the endeavour to reconcile their differences. They were still in full discussion when the day closed.

9 November 1917
Held a meeting with the chiefs at which they informed me that they have elected Kwamin Pong, chief of Edua, as *omanhene*. The only dissentient being the Queen Mother, her reason being that she does not wish the stool to pass from her branch of the family. The chiefs ask that Kobina Atta shall arrange about handing over the stool regalia before he leaves Mbeim. I assent to this. Later, they inform me that Kobina Atta is preparing to leave without seeing them. I send to give him definite instructions that he is not to leave without my permission. Later, I find that he has left, ignoring my definite instructions. I send the corporal and two men to bring him back at once, which they succeed in doing in about two hours. I then decided to keep him in custody. I insist on Kobina Atta appointing a representative to hand over the regalia on his behalf.

14 November 1917
It is now 10 o'clock and none of the lake chiefs have appeared. I have sent off a message stick with instructions to the chief of Banso that he and the other chiefs must come in without delay. The chiefs arrived about 11.45 and the tribunal sat. About 2.00 p.m. a messenger rushed in saying there was fighting. I immediately went out and found the

youngmen from the lake villages, armed with bludgeons and sticks, descending on Kokofu. I placed the police and carriers to prevent any chance of the Kokofus advancing and I went among the lake youngmen. They were extremely excited and threatening, but at last I herded them back a few yards when I sat down and eventually got them to listen to me. I impressed upon them the foolishness of their conduct and told them they could depend on justice being dealt out to them by government should they be wrongly dealt with by the tribunal. I then, with much trouble, succeeded after an hour or more in getting them outside the precincts of the village, where they remained. The tribunal then resumed its sitting and I sat close by to prevent any further disorder.

Tuesday 4 December 1917
Heard 23 civil cases and dealt with numerous complaints. Busy in office. Six applications for the issue of goldsmiths' licences resultant on action being taken against two youngmen at Dengyase, on my last tour, who had been working without a licence.

8 December 1917
Left Bekwai for Peki. Arrived about 11.30 a.m. Talked to the people at the various villages *en route* about the best method of fermenting cocoa, which none of them seemed to know of. Held meeting with the chiefs and people at Peki. Nothing of consequence came up. The old chief is very ill and likely to die at any time. The elders asked for a permit for powder in anticipation of the event.

Notes

1. GNA, Kumasi D1116.
2. In 1907, the Governor of the Gold Coast received a memo from the Colonial Office asking that place names of antiquity should not be changed. They noted with regret that in a map from the Director of Military Operations, along with other changes, Coomassie was spelled Kumasi. 'Such departures from familiar and generally accepted forms of well-known places are unnecessary and inconvenient' (PRO CO/9G/444). This old spelling was still in use on the official notepaper of the CCA in 1920.
3. Kumasi Council of Chiefs was created in August 1905 to compensate the Kumasi chiefs for the powers they had lost.
4. The friction in Kumawu between the 'youngmen' and the chief, Kwamin Afram, who was eventually destooled, was a source of anxiety to the DC, C. E. Skene.
5. The French Administrator at Bonuku, Ivory Coast.
6. Alex Norris, Ag DC.
7. David Boyle, DC. Compare Fuller's entry of 30 January 1917.

8. The Company Commander, WAFF.
9. The War Office directed that the colonies should play their part in the 1914–18 war effort by raising a certain number of recruits as soldiers and carriers. This order was sent to the various governors. Meetings and recruiting campaigns were held by the commissioners throughout the country, with varying degrees of success. Theoretically, there was no conscription in the Gold Coast, but it seemed very like it to the chiefs and people. Each chief had to muster a certain number of recruits. Alongside Fuller's diary for January 1917 is a letter from him to HE, dated 23 November 1916. He writes: 'Owing to the action of some over zealous chiefs, a belief spread among the people that they were about to be compelled to fight. A great deal of foolish and thoughtless talk ensued to the effect that they were not slaves and would prefer to resist the government than be compelled to leave Ashanti.'
10. HE noted in the margin of Skene's diary: 'This will only be possible for the duration of his leave. HC.'
11. GNA, Kumasi Number D 1116
12. F. W. H. Migeod was Transport Officer, Gold Coast.
13. Sunk by German submarines.
14. On 7 December Philbrick heard, unofficially, that Prempeh's mother and brother were dead.
15. The Juaso diaries are in GNA, Accra no. 50/5/8. Skene's diary, 22 February 1917 to 5 April 1917, is in part taken from his monthly diary, which he submitted to the CCA. It is similar to the station diary from which all the early extracts are taken, but contains certain omissions and additions. It can be found in GNA Kumasi, 1890. The station at Juaso was opened in June 1913, but the first available diary, in a very dilapidated ledger, does not begin until June 1916.
16. H. J. Hobbs was DC of the adjoining district in the Colony.
17. Palm oil, cocoa etc. was transported in casks, which were rolled from the farms to the river or railway. They did great damage to chiefs' roads and cannot have done the casks much good either.
18. 'Drinking fetish is simply the most binding form of oath. It is usually done as a sign of loyalty and friendship of one person to another, or of subjects to a chief.' From Sunyani District Record Book by T. E. Fell, PC.
19. A messenger service direct between rural stations, not through the postal system.
20. Anyone could ask for a retrial in the DC's court if not satisfied with the decision given in the chief's court.
21. During the First World War the Basel Mission, because of its German connections, was viewed with great suspicion by the government.
22. To suggest that the Ashantis, of all people, might be known for ever as a race of cowards is a curious assertion on the part of Skene.
23. After the war chiefs were given medals for their loyalty to the government.
24. This was his first tour as an ADC. His papers are in Rhodes House Library, MSS. Afr. s. 469–75.

25. GNA, Kumasi D 612.
26. The CCA, F. C. Fuller, and the Governor, Sir Hugh Clifford.
27. From 1901 to 1906, the government station for the Western Province, Ashanti, was at Odumasi supported by a Company of the WAFF. In 1906, the whole establishment was transferred to Sunyani. This was considered healthier for Europeans, two commissioners having died in Odumasi. From the Ashanti point of view the move must have seemed inexplicable. Odumasi was more important in their eyes, being the *omanhene*'s town.
28. Ross and Johnstone, ADCs; Storey, MO; Barker and Leat, WAFF officers.
29. 'The Tano River is the principal fetish in the Western Province. Its fish are fetish and may not be caught in the river itself. They are fed at different crossings and become tame. When the Tano overflows, the fish that leave the rivers and enter the creeks can be caught in these creeks.' Memo by T. E. Fell.
30. His chimpanzee, which he later sent to the London Zoo.
31. Mr and Mrs Yost, of the Basel Mission, were held in the fort at Kumasi in 1900.
32. At certain times of year, snail hunting was the principal industry in many parts of Ashanti. Whole villages turned out and camped in the forest to collect the snails, which were considered a great delicacy and had a ready sale in Kumasi and elsewhere.
33. Ag Colonial Secretary.
34. At Akwantamra, the ghost of one Arthur Fowler was said to haunt the station. Sir Hugh Clifford wrote a short story, 'The Other Master' about these ghostly apparitions (*Blackwoods Magazine*, March 1917).
35. GNA, Kumasi no. 612.
36. GNA, Kumasi no. 612.
37. 'We had a weird habit of taking a Sunday walk to Odumasi to view the cemetery, that seems a morbid occupation, but it provided a walk and ensured proper care being taken of our dead, for Odumasi had been a station once, until it was found to be too unhealthy (A. W. Cardinall, *In Ashanti and Beyond*, 1915, p. 57).
38. Sharman, PE; O'Dea, PMO; McPherson, OCT.
39. Both were eventually to publish memoirs of their Ashanti days (see Bibliography).
40. GNA, Kumasi, no. 499.
41. In 1916, Francis Crowther, Secretary of Native Affairs, wrote a pamphlet for the guidance of DCs. The Governor, Sir Hugh Clifford, had intended to write it himself, but decided that his knowledge of the day-to-day work of the DC was insufficient and Crowther volunteered to write it (CO 96/568).
42. GNA, Kumasi 150.
43. The station at Wenchi was opened in the summer of 1913. A. H. Kortright seems to have been the first DC to be stationed there. He

spent much of his time building the station, erecting staff quarters, making primitive roads and establishing British authority.

44. Kortright was relieved by F. J. Pye in June 1914 but Pye's diary is not available in the Kumasi archives. He was followed by David Boyle who, on is return from leave in October 1914, was sent straight up to Wenchi. Boyle was there until February 1916. On Sunday 28 December 1915 his diary reads: 'At Sunyani. Medically examined by MO thirteen months.'
45. The account of the garden party here is vividly amplified by the description in his wife's memoir (see Bibliography). The September gap in his informal diary is fully covered in his published memoir.
46. GNA, Kumasi 1900.
47. The station was closed because of the wartime shortage of political officers.
48. The Obuasi diaries for 1913–16 are in Kumasi GNA 149. Those from 1917 to 1919 are in Accra GNA Adm. 53/5/1.
49. 'In 1911 a certain amount of friction was caused by Christian converts refusing personal service to their chiefs on the plea that they could not do violence to their religious feelings. This attitude was upheld by the government when conscientious scruples were involved. But the plea was often nothing more than an excuse to avoid communal or personal obligations, quite distinct from spiritual matters' (Sir Francis Fuller, *A Vanished Dynasty*, 1921, p. 223).
50. Governor of Togoland.
51. N. C. McLeod, Conservator of Forests; L. R. Palfriman, Assistant Conservator of Forests.
52. The railway from Sekondi to Kumasi, begun in 1898, reached Obuasi in 1902, and Kumasi in December 1903. Its daily arrival was a welcome break to the monotony. Every official from the NT and Ashanti *en route* to the Coast travelled on it. Some officers broke their journey there, otherwise the PC could meet his friends on the train and discuss local problems and world events (see Wheatley entry of 29 December 1916). Miss Adair was probably the matron of the European hospital in Kumasi.
53. Wheatley was senior enough to have few problems in being allowed to have his wife with him. Some of the mine officials brought their wives out, and the women were able to lead a comfortable life. The relatively traditional hardships of a life in the bush did not apply, especially as Obuasi was within easy reach of Kumasi and medical attention.
54. Prior to the First World War, leave was taken at the end of 11 months in the Colony, unless there was an urgent reason why an officer should extend his tour by perhaps a month. He was always examined by an MO to make sure he was fit to continue (see Wheatley entry of 17 February 1918). As the war dragged on, the tours were extended.
55. Pawning was the custom by which a person became the slave of a temporary master as a pledge for a debt. A man might pawn himself, or the head of a family might pawn any one of its members.

56. During the latter part of the war, European officials were encouraged to take their leave in the Colony due to the submarine menace.
57. Normally, the prisoners did the latrine and other work about the station. The MO was responsible for them.
58. The Ashanti Goldfields Corporation had its headquarters at Obuasi. It commenced operations in 1897, on land belonging partly to Bekwai and partly to Adansi.
59. GNA Accra 46/5/1. The Bekwai diaries should be read with the Obuasi diaries, as Bekwai was run in conjunction with Obuasi. Both diaries were kept up by the PC of the Southern Province, Ashanti.
60. Wife of the CCA.

5

Diaries, 1913–1919: Northern Territories

Tamale, CCNT[1]

(i) Major R. A. Irvine, Ag CCNT, 1913

1 November 1913

Wire from Colonial Secretary to say that Challoner completes establishment and that it is not proposed to appoint an extra ADC. This is regrettable as Dr Whyte will have to continue to act as DC Bawku and Wright will have to extend his tour until Wheeler arrives. It is unsatisfactory to have MOs acting for any length of time as DCs, as not only do they have little or no experience of their duties, but they cannot be expected to take the same interest in them as an experienced administrative officer.

3 November 1913

Transport officer reports that all mails will be sent to and from Coomassie and Mampong by motor. This arrangement will effect a saving of two days both ways.

6 November 1913

Visited prison. Heard no complaints. Everything in very good order. Ag PC Southern Province reports the seizure, from smugglers, of a quantity of gunpowder and dane guns by the chief of Salaga. Sanctioned the chief receiving a reward. Saw Inspector of Works re measures to be adopted to eliminate the bats from the CC's house. They appear to be increasing greatly in number. A few days' ago it was estimated that 3000 were destroyed in a small room in the annex to the bungalow. Spoke to Wright at Salaga and Branch at Yeji on the telephone about their leave. Told the latter he could go as soon as Challoner arrived and the former that, as there was no officer available to relieve him, he would, unless reported medically unfit, have to wait until Wheeler returned from leave at the end of December.

10 November 1913
In the afternoon, presented prizes to the pupils of the government school in the presence of all European officials and all the native subordinate staff. The chief of Tamale and a number of other parents were also present. At intervals during the presentation, selected pupils gave recitations very creditably and the pupils sang part songs very well. I gave a short address to the pupils, laying particular stress on the importance of pupils, when they returned to their homes, paying proper respect to their parents, performing farm duties etc. and showing, by their conduct generally, the good effect of the training received whilst at school. It has come to my knowledge that some pupils, on returning to their homes, have declined to do anything to assist their parents and had expected to be treated in an exceptional manner. This is tending to make parents reluctant to send their sons to school. Concluded my address by asking every pupil to try and bring one recruit with him on his return to school after the holidays.

12 November 1913
In the morning I inspected the town [Savelugu], which I found comparatively clean. Afterwards, I held a palaver in the marketplace at which were the chief of Savelugu and his headmen and all the chiefs who had met me the previous afternoon. I addressed the meeting on (1) cattle breeding. Advised the chiefs and people to dispose of surplus bullocks and, with the proceeds, buy cows. (2) Sanitation. Pointed out its importance to the individual native and the community as a whole. (3) Care of *dawa dawa* and shea butter trees. (4) Beeswax. Explained method of preparation and its value in Coomassie. (5) Cotton. Its importance to them as a cash crop and tried to impress upon them that, no matter how much they grew, it would be purchased by the BCGA at Tamale and that the seed would be returned to them. Caused some amusement by telling them that they couldn't expect to get cotton if they made soup out of the seeds given them to sow by the BCGA. This method of planting the seed is not infrequently practised. (6) Government School. Pointed out the advantages that would accrue to the sons of influential natives by sending them to school. (7) Leprosy. All chiefs informed me no lepers in their town. (8) Carrying of weapons in market. Ordered the chiefs to beat gong gong in their respective districts and notify all their people not to bring weapons to markets and, after due warning, to fine anyone disobeying the order. (9) Roads. Pointed out the importance and advantages of good roads. Directed the chief of Savelugu to instruct his subchiefs to supply

labourers to the native road foreman for the reformation of the Tamale–Savelugu road.

13 November 1913
Arrived at Kumbungu at 11.30 a.m., one of the most important towns if not the most important trading centre in Western Dagomba. The chief had no complaints. Had an interview with the *limam* and 18 *malams*, who appear to be a very intelligent set of men. They told me they all held classes for Mohammedan boys and at least 100 children attended these classes. There appears to be a large Mohammedan population. There are two mosques and a large number of places set apart for prayers. The principal industries in the town are dyeing and weaving.

15 November 1913
Went on to Gahho, a village of about 15 compounds and 150 inhabitants. Out of 23 women who attended the palaver, counted 17 with infants on their backs. The chief is a distinguished looking native with a marked personality. He has very good control over his people by whom he is much respected. He was formerly a freebooter and was sentenced to ten years for firing on a foraging party of our soldiers at Singa in January 1898 and killing two privates and one carrier. He was subsequently released on medical grounds by Colonel Morris, with the sanction of Governor Sir Mathew Nathan in 1903. Since then, no complaints have been made against him. He has served the government loyally.

(ii) Captain C. H. Armitage, CC, 1917

14 August 1917
Some rain fell during the night. Rode up to the Telegraph Office and had a conversation with Captain Breckenridge on the telephone. He has heard nothing further from Zouaragu, but tells me that no Mamprussi recruits have presented themselves as yet. Paid a surprise visit to the school and found attendance of 60. Several boys are absent suffering from measles and one, the son of the head mason at Tamale, died on 9th instant. It began to rain as I got back to the office and continued to do so the whole morning. Wrote a further report on recruiting and worked in the office for the remainder of the day. Very heavy rain fell at 10.30 p.m. I trust YE will not be bored with these frequent allusions to the rainfall. It is 20 years ago that I left Coomassie and arrived at Yeji towards the end of August to find the whole countryside flooded. I have never seen the Volta River reach so high a level since then. I waded and swam most of the way to Tamale

and, when I retraced my steps in the middle of November, my carriers were able to wade across the Volta at the Katakunji ferry above Yeji. The heavy rains this year have commenced in a manner that indicates a rainy season equal to that of 1897 and it is for this reason that I make mention of the rain in this diary.

Major Walker Leigh arrived at Salaga today, and I have instructed him to take over the Salaga–Yeji district from Dr Ryan. I had no idea he was bringing his wife up with him and, if I had known that he intended to do so, I would have protested strongly. If he had been alone I should have sent him either to the Navarro, Zouaragu district, or to the Bole districts, but with his wife with him I cannot take the responsibility of ordering him to either of those districts now that the heavy rains have set in and the roads are flooded.

26 September 1917

Routine work all morning. Read the outstanding diaries that I have received up to date. They form one monotonous record of unprecedentedly heavy rains, of houses collapsing in every direction, of swollen rivers and flooded country – even of traders drowned in attempting to cross the former.

30 September 1917

I paid a tribute to the memory of the late chief (Karaga) whose place it would be difficult to fill. I then wished the chiefs goodbye and shook hands with all of them. The five sons of the late chief of Karaga, who have returned from Karaga after completing their father's funeral custom, came to see me in my office. They have presented me with their father's war robe and, when I commiserated with them on their father's demise, the eldest brother said, 'now that we see you again we forget that our father is dead.' I made a further appeal to the Dagomba chiefs to endeavour to persuade some of their youngmen to enlist, or if they did not care to be soldiers to join as gun carriers, 50 of whom are required.

3 November 1917

At 9.00 a.m. I visited the schoolhouse, now being converted into the PC's house, to distribute the prizes and close the school for the Christmas holidays. There are 74 pupils on the school roll. The examiners informed me that the pupils have done remarkably well in the examinations. The officers, who had just arrived in Tamale, expressed surprise at the intelligence shown by the boys. The prizes, which I felt ashamed to distribute, were of the most wretched description this year. Watches at 39/– a dozen, imitation leather belts and hair brushes were bad enough, but when I was asked to present scraps of cotton with tawdry lace borders, which cost 2/3*d.* a dozen, to youths for proficiency in history, geography etc., I felt inclined to leave the building.

7 November 1917
Colonel Potter writes to tell me that 400 recruits from the NT have left for East Africa in the highest spirits and that there was not a single case of desertion, although they were kept five days at Seccondee before the transport arrived.

8 November 1917
The three elder sons of the late chief of Karaga came to see me. They tell me that the late chief was the father of at least 150 children.

Yendi,[2] *16 November 1917*
As soon as the chiefs and their followers arrived and arranged themselves on the palaver ground, I addressed them as follows. The great world war still raged with unabated fury and that, while many events of local importance had occurred since I last visited them, these dwindled into absolute insignificance before it. On my last visit to Yendi, I had told the late King of Dagomba to exercise patience and to await the reunion of British and Togoland Dagomba at the end of the war with confidence. This he had promised to do and had respected the promise until his lamented death in January 1917. Intriguing began immediately after his death and, not content with the appointment of the chief of Sambul as regent to the Yendi stool, the chiefs clamoured with almost indecent haste for the appointment of a new king, and brought forward the absurd argument that the people's crops were spoiling owing to the stool being vacant, forgetting that God alone controlled the seasons and their harvests. I had informed the DPO[3] that the regent could be appointed chief of Yendi provisionally till the end of the war, provided that he and the Yendi chiefs promised to interfere in no way in British Dagomba affairs, and that Abdualai was not to be enstooled with any of the ceremonies attached to that of a king of Dagomba. I then asked if these ceremonies had taken place when he was put on the Yendi stool and he replied, with some reluctance, in the affirmative, and informed me, in reply to my second question, that the DPO had warned him that such ceremonies were not to be performed. I stopped the flow of excuses and upbraided him for his folly in pushing forward, as he thought, his own little petty affairs at such a time as this. When a woman was carrying a load of millet that had been removed from the cob and a single grain fell from the load to the ground, would she stop to look for it? The millet represented Yendi, as compared in importance with the world war now

waging, with the liberty of all the people at stake. I told him that such episodes as this spoilt all the pleasure of my visit to Yendi and that his action had been that of a small boy who could not wait until the fruit was ripe, but must needs pluck it and eat it while it was still green, with the result that he suffered severely from stomach-ache. The chief admitted my simile and that my public reprimand represented the stomach-ache. I said I would overlook his offence this time, as he had confessed before the chiefs that he had done wrong.

21 November 1917
A very cold morning, which caused the carriers to be rather later than usual. Left at 6.10 a.m. and arrived Palbu 7.10 and at Tschangbani and Kuntule at 8.15. Was met outside both villages by parties of youngmen under their headman who had, however, discarded their picturesque war costumes, which include cowrie-covered and horned 'helmets' and decorated quivers, in deference to me. I requested Captain Poole to let the people of the Konkomba villages, which I propose to visit before returning to Yendi, know that I wish the youngmen to turn out in full war paint. This announcement pleased them immensely and we were met outside Sambul by a party of finely built young men in full war costume, which consists of a cowrie-studded helmet surmounted by roan, cob or other antelope horns, with strings of cowries hanging to the shoulder and nearly hiding the face, a quiver full of arrows, the quiver decorated with cowries, very elaborately, an apron of cowrie shells, on the most scanty of loincloths and, in some cases, an antelope skin decorated with cowries slung over the shoulder to protect the back. They are armed with bows and 'brain pickers' and a curved knife that slips over the palm of the right-hand. They also wear an iron ring with a long curved point, which is used in the market to remind strangers that they don't like being jostled.

The young bloods pay the greatest attention to their personal appearance. Their hair is woven and plaited into the most elaborate designs into which small brass rings and discs are introduced, the whole giving the appearance, at a short distance, of tightly fitting skull caps of intricate workmanship. Fillets of red cloth and leather, embroidered in white, are bound round their foreheads and a brass disc, with an attachment of seven-inch long strings of blood red beads, is attached to the forehead above each ear. Brightly-coloured beads adorn their necks and wrists, and cowries and brass anklets and bracelets are also worn. The whole attire gives an effect, at once barbaric and pleasing, and the sight of a couple of hundred youngmen in full war costume, dancing and chanting to the accompaniment of drums and gong gongs, is both interesting and impressive. With the exception of the Fra Fras, these men are quite the physically finest savages that I have met in this part of the world. Their womenfolk are distinctly disappointing. In the great majority of cases, they appear stunted figureless creatures with no regard for personal appearance. Their heads are clean shaven, wear few if any ornaments, and a dirty cloth wound round their middle completes their costume. The Konkombas live in round, grass-thatched huts, each family building its own compound out of bow shot of the next.

I asked the youngmen of each village if they wanted the Germans back and, when their loud chorus of dissent had died down, I told them that they must demonstrate their desire to remain under British rule by refraining from fighting amongst themselves. I told them we were not here to exploit them, as did the Germans, by taxation and forced labour, but to bring peace and prosperity to the country. All that we asked them to do was to keep their roads clean and open and to supply, occasionally, a gang of labourers for Yendi to do a few days' work in the station and on the plantation.

23 November 1917

Captain Poole proposed to take me direct to Kutza from Sambul, but I expressed the intention of proceeding there via Bakundjibi (Kunji), where the natives have been mixed up with the Najoli, Pajoli, Kanjock–Kugnau fighting on the side of the former. The track was uncleaned and canoes had to be sent down river from Sambul to the Kunji crossing. I got the carriers off very early and left myself at 6.30 a.m. along a scarcely discernible track through long, rank grass and Guinea corn and millet farms. The country is flat and still swampy in places. After walking for some time, in a northeasterly direction, we suddenly turned due west and stumbled along a narrow track, which ran along the top of the high left bank of the river, eventually emerging into a clearing beyond which was a deep gully, which cut off further progress. Here, all the carriers were assembled with their loads on the ground, but no canoes, or any sign of a crossing were to be seen. The guide, a small boy, had disappeared. Presently, Captain Poole arrived and I asked him for an explanation, when he naively remarked that the same thing had happened to him when he had taken this route on a previous occasion. An elderly native now appeared on the other side of the gully, but apparently made off during a shouting competition that ensued between Captain Poole, Sergeant Major Samba Moshi and the interpreter, while the carriers, much amused, chattered at the tops of their voices. There was nothing left to me but to sit down and laugh and await developments.

Presently arrived a Sambul elder, who took us a switch back journey over old yam farms and through tall elephant grass until we finally struck the right track, which led down a steep bank to a stretch of sand in the river bed, where two canoes awaited us. On arrival at the other side of the river, we had to climb a steep, slippery bank and it is a marvel that none of the loads met with disaster. On emerging from the dense undergrowth that fringes the river bank, a vast plain, covered with rank grass came into view, while in the distance a few tall kapok trees located the site of Kunji village. The usual crowd of youngmen met and escorted me to a quite comfortable little rest house, from the shelter of which I addressed the natives. I pointed out to them their folly in making one with the Kanjocks, to fight against their own brothers, and told them that, when a dog joined in a hunting partnership with a hyena, all went well as long as there was plenty of food, but the first thing the hyena did when a scarcity arose was to eat the dog. That was what would happen eventually to their youngmen. We parted the best of friends and I was able to use my hammock, for a broad track had been cleared to Kutza.

24 November 1917

I was up before 5.00 a.m. and got off the carriers. I left at 6.00 a.m., crossing a swampy plain. The natives have constructed a miniature embanked track, about four feet high, and between six inches and a foot broad on top, through the worst part of the swamp. It is composed of clods of clayey soil, strengthened by tough grass roots, and winds its way through still-running water, two to three-feet deep. The sure-footed carriers travel along it with ease, but it is a rather perilous undertaking for the bebooted white man who does not want to get wet. There must be excellent snipe shooting on this plain and I put up several jacksnipe when I left the track. What, at first sight, appears to be a system of irrigation proves, on closer inspection, to be a series of small dams constructed to catch fish on the subsidence of floods. Channels, through which the water can flow from one damned area of land into another are cut in the various embankments and in these are inserted long fibre baskets with an entrance placed upstream, but no exit. As the floods subside, the fish are driven into these baskets from each succeeding area. On approaching the river, the track winds through large plantations of Guinea corn and millet, and a number of small boys who followed us made them re-echo with their shrill screams as they started to drive off flights of birds, which were already at work on the ripening crops.

27 November 1917

After having read what Mr Cardinall had written under the heading

Archaeology, in the Yendi record book, I decided to visit Nafejeke and Notogu myself and inspect the wells described by this officer in his informal diary. With this object in view, I left at 6.00 a.m. and walked along a narrow track through farms and thick grass to Kunaneragu, where I received the usual welcome and addressed a large gathering of elders and youngmen. We reached Nafejeke at 9.15 and I proceeded on foot to visit Mr Cardinall's wells. We then proceeded along a narrow waterworn track that wound through coarse, ten-foot high grass, until we emerged on a cleared track that led to Natago. The headman guided me to the wells and, after a careful inspection of these, I left at 11.45. My hammock met me here and I was glad to get into it and travel down the Yendi–Sansanne Mango road. All the villages visited today are composed of widely-scattered compounds that cover a very large area of ground. The natives are of the usual Konkomba type, the men of very fine build, the women small as a rule and ungainly. I noticed that a number of the young men had smeared antimony round their eyes, presumably to give them a fierce appearance that they would not otherwise possess. The women here, as elsewhere, have a cylindrical bead, or piece of glass or stone stuck into the lower lip and protruding below it. In the evening, I walked to the *tindana*'s house to inspect the giant bracelets and thumb rings described by Mr Cardinall and alleged to have belonged to a prehistoric race of giants. I recognized their real use immediately.

30 November 1917

Left at 6.00 a.m. and travelled down the excellent main road, which is 15 feet wide, between ditches and on which doub grass is well established, to Yendi, where we arrived at 9.10 a.m. Was disappointed to find no communication of any kind had arrived for me from Tamale. I have seen no Reuters since the 20th instant. Within half an hour of my having written the above, a mounted constable arrived with letters from Tamale, one of which contained the distressing news of Captain Breckenridge's death in Coomassie on his way down. He appeared to have recovered his health completely and was in the best of spirits, and I was ill prepared for Captain Hobart's sad news. Captain Breckenridge's untimely death is the more tragic in that he leaves a wife and two small children, the younger of whom he was going home to see for the first time.[4]

3 December 1917

The chief and elders visited me in the evening, when I gave them news of the war. The chief is suffering from inflamed eyes and I made up a lotion for him, which gave him instant relief. A constable from Salaga arrived at dusk, bringing me a letter from Major Walker Leigh and telegrams from Captain Hobart. Was inexpressibly shocked to read the Colonial Secretary's telegram informing me of the fate of the SS *Apapa*,[5] and of that of so many Gold Coast officials and their wives. Accra has indeed suffered this year.

21 December 1917
Left Kluto at 11.00 a.m. and reached the Ho bungalow at 1.20. It is built on the summit of a steep hill overlooking the village and commands a magnificent view to the east. In the far distance, the Adaklu hills rise abruptly from the surrounding flat countryside. The bungalow is flanked to the north and south by plantations of teak. We left at 4.30 and arrived at Kluto at 6.35 p.m.

29 December 1917
Visited Dr Claridge in the morning and paid some farewell calls. Went on board SS *St George* at Lomé with Bishop Hummel. Captain Harpward and Chief Mate Williamson did their best to make us as comfortable as possible, but as the decks fore and aft were packed with a miscellaneous collection of natives and their belongings, sheep and goats, pigs, turkeys, fowls and ducks, and the upper deck swarmed with mosquitoes, very little rest could be got. We anchored off Quitta about 8.00 a.m.

31 December 1917
The captain kindly provided us with an early breakfast and Bishop Hummel and I landed at 9.00 a.m., and were met by the PS who took us by car to Government House.

Tamale, Southern Province[6]

(i) Captain S. D. Nash, Ag PC, 1915

9 October 1915
Enquired into two trivial cases, cases which one would have expected the chiefs to settle. Like icebergs, however, these cases may have only shown a quarter of their importance to my eyes, and it is on this account that a DC's work is so difficult. He must keep a light hand on a chief's politics, knowing everything and yet doing little and saying almost nothing. If he is autocratic and deputes power to no one, he will have quiet, obedient but furtive chiefs. Under such circumstances, chiefs are a positive danger, as they possess no responsibility and merely regard their offices as an avenue for misdemeanour. On the other hand, if chiefs are allowed unlimited authority, a DC is not master in his own district. The above cases, after being enquired into, were sent back to the chiefs for their decision and report.

13 October 1914
Many survey carriers with loads are arriving from Navarro via Zouaragu. They are mostly in a starving condition, having been given only 1/6*d*. when leaving for their long eight-days' journey with heavy loads. Such a state of affairs does not conduce to or increase our popularity or prestige. A letter to DC Zouaragu on the subject, as Ag PC was absent from Navarro when these boys left his station.

Sunday 19 October 1914
Seven carriers arrived, under escort from Bole, to bring back six boxes nickel coins and one medical load. The CC [Armitage] held a meeting in the marketplace at Tamale in afternoon. All the chiefs of Western Dagomba were present. The causes of the present European war were explained thoroughly by the CC. It was explained that the chiefs on the Coast, on their own initiative, intended to help England by presents of cocoa. This was quite voluntary on their part. The Dagomba chiefs would also have an opportunity of showing that 'their hearts were all right' and, although poor, could show in small ways their sympathy with the present crisis. The CC's speech was received with marked respect and the people showed by their manner that they would have been offended if not given an opportunity to show their feelings.

23 October 1914
The CC, accompanied by the Ag PC, proceeded to Yapei via Kawsaw. The chief of the latter place was interviewed by the CC who presented him with a long gown. The CC reminded the chief of Kawsaw that the last time he visited the village was in 1895. Kawsaw remembered the incident quite well and seemed much pleased at the visit and honour paid him on the present occasion. At Yapei, a few minor complaints were gone into, including: (1) the chief of Yapei wants to build some houses at right angle to the Yapei–Daboya road. He said that monkeys played havoc with the farms and some of his people wanted to build close to cultivated land. Given permission and informed that Mr Ogoe would come down to peg out the sites. (2) The chief complains that two men have left Yapei and have gone to live in the bush. This is probably done in order to avoid the small calls for labour at Yapei. The men ordered to return to Yapei.

11 November 1914
Interview with *limams* of Kumbungu, Diare and Savelugu with reference to our war with Turkey. They all say, 'We pray to God and obey the English. We take no interest in this war between England and Turkey from a religious point of view. We hope the English will win, as we live under them.' To a great extent, their religion is a secondary

matter. The important point is that Mussulmen in Dagomba are considered the intellectual class. Religious enthusiasm is quite absent. Most of the chiefs pray after Mohammedan fashion, but, as they cannot read or write, they do not call themselves true Mohammedans, nor are they regarded as such by the people. They are 'half in half' with a strong leaning towards paganism. We need, therefore, fear no excitement on account of our war with Turkey. Chief of Bamvim hands over £10 as his and his people's contribution to the Imperial War Fund.

12 November 1914
Held a meeting of the Mohammedan community at Tamale and explained to them the causes of the outbreak of war between England and Turkey. Peculiarly, none of them seem even to have heard of Turkey or the Sultan, although they all know of Mecca. None of them really seemed to take much interest in the matter and I don't think there is the remotest chance of any excitement arising among the so-called Mohammedans in the NT. After I had spoken to the people the *limam* of Tamale said, 'You are speaking the truth. If a man follows what is false he will fall, if he follows what is true he won't.' It must be remembered that all, or nearly all, the so-called Mohammedans are native Dagombas in this district. Their religion is therefore very mixed and pagan customs have been grafted on to Mohammedan ceremonies. And, in the same village, people will look on with interested curiosity at Mohammedans praying and at the fetish men killing a fowl and scattering the blood on the same rock as his ancestor did before him. With regard to emissaries coming down from the north, I warned the people to report to me the arrival of any of these men. They are called Larrabawas (corruption probably of Arab) and are mostly traders, but also go in for preaching and selling small Moslem charms. Most of them seem to come from Seriki Asambul, a place about 40 days north of here.

2 December 1914
Complaint from Mr Fletcher, PWD, about labour. He finds it difficult to get [at] present while he is paying his unskilled labour. The boys are certainly not the manhood of the country, in fact the majority of them are sickly looking and very weedy. Evidently, the people do not think *6d.* a day a sufficient wage.

8 December 1914
English mail not yet arrived. DC Yeji reports boys were dispatched between Ejura and Yeji, and that he is sending a full report. Strong measures would appear to be necessary to stop malingering on the

part of the transport carriers. What happens is that a day or so out of Ejura they go sick and leave HM Mails to the tender mercies of any native who is generous enough to take them on to the next village. I understand that a mail guard, consisting of one headman, is dispatched with each mail gang. Surely, he could be made responsible.

18 December 1914
Enquired into forms of oaths used by natives. The subject is intricate and no uniform oath seems to be used. For instance, a Moshi man in court today takes some earth in his mouth and says, 'I have drunk water at Tamale; I take this bit of Tamale ground and may the guardian spirit of Tamale kill me, and may the water I have drunk poison me if I don't speak the truth.' No gesticulations are used by this man.

23 December 1914
Letter from DC Yeji reporting progress of Yeji–Prang road and saying the transport officer proposes putting a Ford car, if possible, on this stretch of road. He is drifting most of the small rivers and not bridging, which I think is far the best plan. What a blessing it would be if we could get even as far as Yeji by motor transport. Took notes on tribal marks and native methods of swearing.

8 January 1915
Went into case of Mr Sam and one of his wives. Mr Sam accuses her of putting fetish under his pillow. Mrs Sam denies this, but says the trouble is that her husband has a new wife, a lady (that is one who wears European clothing), and that he cares no longer for her. Asked Mr Assam to try and settle the silly dispute, as they all come from the same town on the Coast.

17 January 1915
Great noise this morning in the bush behind my bungalow, a crowd of people drumming, blowing horns etc. and shouting. Rode down on horseback with my rifle, as I heard from my boys that the people had cornered a lion. On arrival, I found a crowd of people had surrounded a small belt of pampas grass. All the people were armed, some with spears, others with bows and arrows, whilst a few had dane guns. A fair amount were mounted. After a short while, a leopard bolted and ran a couple of hundred yards, but was headed off by some horsemen and turned back. It was making straight for the same bit of pampas grass when a warrior met it, fell on it and cut its throat. This all happened within ten yards of me, so I can vouch for the truth of it. The man who killed the leopard was fairly badly mauled about the arms and legs and we sent him to hospital to get the wounds washed.

How he tackled the beast and killed it with a knife without getting himself more seriously damaged is a mystery.

20 February 1915
Present at execution of Musa Bazabarimi held at 8.00 a.m. Held an inquest on death of Musa Bazabarimi. The cause of death was dislocation of cervical vertebrae. Death was instantaneous.

4 March 1915
People are interviewed on the subject of the registration of their guns. They reply they cannot get any powder. They are informed the subject will be brought to the notice of CC as it is really a hardship to make them pay for licences and to be unable to get powder. Chief also spoken to on the subject of bringing food to Tamale market. The general impression conveyed to me by the people was that food is bound to be dear, but that the Tamale non-natives, constabulary, carpenters etc., want to buy food on the same terms as if there had been a bountiful harvest; yams, millet, groundnuts must rise in price.

6 March 1915
Interview again with the chiefs of Karaga and Savelugu who say they want to talk about gunpowder. They evidently all want powder. The chiefs say they are willing to send their own boys to Coomassie for powder, but that the general mass of the people would like a store to buy from. They say they fired guns for HE for 30 miles along the road and were promised gunpowder in return, but have not seen any since. Told them the subject would be brought to the notice of the CC.

(ii) Captain H. T. C. Wheeler, Ag PC, 1915

1 April 1915
Attended and carried out an execution at 8.00 a.m. Held inquest on deceased.

6 April 1915
Kasuri sent his *windana* in to see me about his (Kasuri's) son going to technical school in Accra. Dilated on the benefits of technical training to the *windana*. After a little conversation, he said the chief was quite willing that the boy should go. I feel a little doubtful if the boy quite spoke the truth when he said his father was unwilling. I arranged with Mr Agbloe (dispenser in training) who is proceeding to Accra to take charge of the five schoolboys who will leave tomorrow after the prize giving.[7]

8 April 1915
On parades with CC at his inspection of NT Constabulary. A charge

is brought against a schoolboy of using the name of the Commissioner to obtain something in the village of Tolon. Caused drums to be beaten with a view to obtaining 40 volunteers to work in the PWD at 6*d*. a day.

22 April 1915
Savelugu's messenger came to say that the people of Tolon were refusing to carry out a decision of his. Sent a flag out to call them in.

(iii) Captain E. H. Hobart, PC, 1915

Sunday 16 May 1915
Ten carriers arrived from Ejura with the following loads: seven cases provisions for Captain Dale-Glossop; two cases provisions for Captain Breckenridge, Navarro; one case of drugs for Dr Allan, Gambaga. Investigated complaint and dealt with office routine.

15 June 1915
Eight horse boys, NT Constabulary, were reported for stealing corn from Dagomba farms. Being juvenile offenders, they were sentenced to be whipped. Three to 15 strokes of the cane, four to nine strokes and one to six strokes. Checked specie in vault.

18 June 1915
PMO reports that the reconstructed native cemetery is now ready. It has been divided into sections for Dagombas, Hausas, NT natives and Coast natives.[8]

18 August 1915
Chief of Tamale and caravanserai agent interviewed with regard to the outbreak of rinderpest. They were instructed to report all suspicious cases.

16 October 1915
Some 34 locally-hired carriers left today for Yapei to bring up government loads. Post Office, Tamale, issued a circular yesterday that three mailbags of the Eastern and Accra mails had been left behind. Postmaster informs me that the three bags had been left at Ejura, as the transport department was unable to supply sufficient carriers to convey the mails (14 bags). As the transport department appears to be incapable of conveying mails, it was taken out of their hands.

9 November 1915
Major B. Mountray Read, Ag CC, formally closed the Tamale government school for the Christmas vacation. Mrs Read distributed the prizes to the successful pupils. Escort left for Yendi with specie.

25 August 1916
Visited prison (condemned prisoner). Continued compiling list of seniority of chiefs and those in possession of lockets. Mail arrived this evening. It contained practically no English letters or papers.

Yeji, Southern Province[9]

(i) Captain Challoner, Ag DC, 1913

3 December 1913
Long interview with the chief of Yeji with regard to collecting of sticks and grass to make shelter houses here and at Kapilini for the Governor's visit. Started him to collect sticks at once and advised the chief of Kadua to come in and complete the work he had begun. Yeji asked me whether he could be allowed to bring some gin for his own use from Coomassie. He asked the CC about this and was told to come to me. I explained to him that the law would not permit it and that, as the law now stands, it was beyond my province to give him permission or countenance him having gin in his possession.[10]

5 December 1913
Occupied this morning with a criminal charge against one Yendi, a carrier belonging to the BCGA, Tamale, who broke open his load and stole whisky from it. Pleaded guilty of stealing. Sentenced five months hard labour. Complaints have been received by me about loads being broached on the road by carriers, so this man was made an example of.

10 December 1913
On the Yeji–Prang road in the morning. Pegged out site for dining shelter at Yeji for HE's visit. English mail arrived.

24 December 1913
Checking ferry tolls.

3–9 January 1914
Erecting a dining hall 48 x 18 x 14 feet. Superintended the erection of bridges and cleaning of road. Marking out and commencing the erection of round grass huts.[11]

29 January 1914
HE and party left at 6.30 a.m. in canoes for Krachi.[12]

31 January 1914
Paying vouchers and making up cash book. The mails have arrived here on Thursday and Friday instead of Tuesday and Saturday. No

official notification has been given to me of the change, so many letters will probably be dispatched a mail late.

10 February 1914
Held board on all penny and five-shilling tickets in stock and destroyed them.

12 February 1914
Checking toll collectors' books before dispatching counterfoils to Tamale. Counting ferry tolls. Collecting material for annual report, which is not easy as the records of this district are nil.

(ii) H. C. Branch, DC, 1914

4 June 1914
Granted pass to chief of Yeji for four days to hold funeral custom. Guns and tom-toms now. Inspected Yeji town with Salaga sanitary inspector. Town fairly clean, the new roads and streets made by Captain Pye are a great improvement. Spoke to chief about beeswax. He has now collected a small quantity, but not sufficient to send into Coomassie for sale. Made a contract for the digging of a new native latrine in Yeji for £1, out of my large vote of £2 for sanitary improvements.

5 June 1914
Engaged in office all morning. Dr Burgess arrived and returned to Makongo in afternoon. Discussed with him sanitary requirements for the 1915 estimates. Suggested sanitary labourers be increased from eight to ten, concrete slaughter place be built, similar to that at Salaga, also a concrete floor and butchers' stalls, and galvanized roofing for three pit latrines. A cemetery to be opened and marked with concrete pillars and a sum of money to be provided for drainage and improving streets.[13]

5 August 1914
Received telegram that war declared between Germany and England. Sent for Yeji chief and informed him that war had been declared; assured him that there was no cause for alarm and his people would be protected. Explained that this was purely a palaver between white men and that no native would be allowed to take part. Informed him that government relied on his loyalty to procure and furnish me with all information possible of any movements on the Togoland frontier. Instructed him to warn the chief of Chiripo to keep a strict watch on the Pajai road on the right bank of the Volta. Told him I relied on him to give me every assistance in procuring food supplies should they be

required. In answer to a question, he informed me that he and his people had practically no gunpowder. At 2.00 p.m. received wire from Colonial Secretary declaring fifth, sixth and seventh bank holidays and ordering all provision stores to be sealed up. Went down to ferry at 2.30 and took over from W. Q. Dan (the only provision store in the station) two cases sardines, one corn beef, seven dozen milk, six tins kerosene oil, eight cases beer and 15 cases sugar. Also ordered Chief Wilson to store in his compound and keep at my disposal 50 bags of native salt. At 4.30, a parade of the constabulary. Informed the sergeant that war had been declared. Issued 100 rounds ball cartridge to each man and appointed the guardroom as rallying place should an alarm be sounded. Instructed the toll collector to detain all canoes coming down river, as these will be required to cross the troops at Kafaba, should the Kintampo detachment be ordered to Salaga.

6 August 1914
Telephoned to DC's clerk, Attabubu, to send urgent message to Krachi to inform Sergeant Lake, GCR, that war had been declared. Made arrangements at ferry for extra boats to cross F Company GCR. Ordered chief to provide food for troops.

7 August 1914
Received telephone message from DC Salaga that mobilization of troops had been ordered at Coomassie and that Captain Mackesey was appointed intelligence officer. Asked DC to inform Mackesey that, should he require boats to proceed to Krachi, I could provide four with crews at a moment's notice. Wired to OC, GCR, informing him that 300 cattle were on way down to Coomassie and that I had instructed the drivers not to sell cattle on the road and to proceed with all dispatch to Coomassie. Telephoned Commandant, NTC, and asked permission to detain the 15 men due to return to Tamale. Pointed out that it was vital for our communications that the ferry should be held and the boats protected. Received permission, after some argument, to detain three men. With these I must be content.

Appo, the linguist of the chief of Yeji, came to me and volunteered to go to Togoland and obtain information. He goes to the Togoland chiefs ostensibly with a complimentary message from the chief of Yeji. I have instructed him to obtain information as to any orders the German authorities may have given to the chiefs, and of the feelings of friendliness or otherwise of the natives towards us. Should he hear of any movement of troops, a messenger is to be immediately sent back to me. The linguist is an old and very intelligent native and, by his training and calling, secretive. I am likely to obtain more reliable information through him than from anyone else. From all I can hear, the occupation of Togoland by us would be welcomed by the natives, anyway in the central and southern portions.

11 August 1914
Warned Yeji chief of the column, which would arrive on Saturday, and told him to warn the outlying villages.

13 August 1914
Corporal Shaw and Colour Sergeant Williams arrived with 82 soldiers and 220 carriers. No food of any description prepared by chief. Sent out parties of constables to several villages to bring in food. Our chief of Yeji in guardroom. Spent all afternoon in village and market trying to scrape together sufficient food for the column. Efforts now very successful. Small amount of food brought in late in afternoon.

10 May 1915
At 11.00 a.m. there was much excitement on hearing a motorcar approaching. This turned out to be the Ford car sent up by the transport to run between Yeji and Prang. The *omanhene* reports his road was in excellent condition in spite of the recent rains. The population of this village were much excited and the children spent most of the day gazing at and examining the machine.

11 May 1915
Planned out and started the erection of a temporary garage. Took the chief of Yeji for a drive, which pleased him immensely. The car is, however, only working on two of its four cylinders. It had to be dismantled for conveyance to Prang and is now in good working order.

(iii) E. G. Dasent, Ag DC, 1915

24 July 1915
Talked to the chief of Prang about the condition of his road and talked to the chief of Yeji about the state of the market and the lack of food, but got nothing satisfactory out of him as to the reason why food is not brought. I think the trouble lies with the constabulary and I am investigating. Preparing escort for taking prisoners to Tamale.

26 July 1915
Dispatched four prisoners and an escort to Tamale, which leaves me without any. Paid off the warder. Talked again to the chief of Yeji and his subchiefs as to why there was such a scarcity of food in the market. He told me there was plenty in the villages around. I have made the chief deposit £5 with me as security of there being sufficient food for the month coming.

29 July 1915
Finished paying off in the morning. Garaba reports that he cannot get labour for the Makongo road, the men say they will not stay here and work for *9d.* when they can get 1/– in Coomassie. We are at present reduced to four labourers and there is enough work for ten.

Sunday 1 August 1915
Went out shooting in the morning but had no luck. In the afternoon I went on the road with Garaba, the headman. The water has been over the embankment. It seems to me the money I have is quite insufficient to keep the road properly repaired.

4 September 1915
Work in office. Reading up correspondence and getting some knowledge of the district. Down at the ferry in afternoon. Superintending mending of steel canoe, which was leaking badly.

7 September 1915
Went round the town with the MO. In afternoon, chose two spots for cemeteries, one for the Brongs and one for the Hausas, which was sanctioned by the MO.

17 September 1915
Morning worked in office. Mail arrived from Coomassie. In the afternoon one of the labourers on the Makongo road was washing down at the ferry when he was seized by a crocodile and dragged in. His body has not been seen since. I had a shot at the crocodile, but missed. I have now ten labourers, also two carpenters, repairing bridges.

8 October 1915
In the afternoon talked to Kweku Ahih, the chief of Prang. He reported the crops as good, especially the yams. He made a complaint that he could not stop the Hausa traders and carriers from sleeping in the rest house. So told him I will send him a constable. The River Pru is considerably swollen and the chief says he is making a lot of money out of the ferry. I think there is a good deal of gin coming into Prang, but cannot locate it. The chief complains that the carriers steal yams from the farms in passing.

18 February 1916
Issuing gun licences in afternoon.

15 April 1916
The CCNT arrived Yeji at 2.30 p.m. Just when it was nice and cool and as I had a temperature of 102, I quite enjoyed standing about in the sun. All the chiefs of the district were out to meet him at 11.30 a.m.

Sunday 16 April 1916
CC met the chiefs in afternoon. The chief of Yeji brought one complaint about a decision of the Ag DC. I wonder why justice is dispensed better in a coat.

Bole, Southern Province[14]

(i) Dr David Duff, Ag DC, 1915

22 March 1915
Supervising labourers 8.00–9.00 a.m. Hospital work 9.00–11.00 a.m. and 2.00–3.00 p.m.; 3.00–4.00 p.m. completed two-thirds of new road, laying out last third; 4.30–5.00 p.m. supervising labour.

25 March 1915
Hospital work 8.00–9.30 a.m. Commenced work of laying out six new type latrines in Mohammedan town and two at caravanserai.

30 March 1915
Supervising labourers 6.00–7.00 a.m. Hospital work 8.00–9.00 a.m. Hospital work 2.00–4.00 p.m. Ordinary office routine DC's office.

13 April 1915
Supervising labourers 6.00–7.00 a.m. Hospital work 8.00–9.00 a.m. Hospital work 2.00–2.30 p.m. DC's office 3.30–4.00 p.m.

12 May 1915
Hospital work 8.00–9.00 a.m. DC's office 9.00 to 12 noon. The chiefs reassembled re recruiting palaver. Chiefs of Yipala and Kulmanso said they were willing to try to get men, if they had a 'lead' making decisions. To consider further and report to me. Yabum's attitude is one of inactivity and is ruining all prospects of gaining recruits. Stated, 'I can get men to labour in the district. I could get money, but I will not give men to be killed.'

25 October 1915
Hospital work 8.00–9.00 a.m. DC's office 9.00–12.00 a.m. Heard a complaint against chief of Murugu because he does not keep his canoe regularly on the Mambili ferry between Larabanga and Murugu. This causes delay in mail to Tamale. People of Murugu complain of a family of five lions on road between ferry and Murugu. Address given to chiefs of Larabanga and Murugu to send a man along with postman as protection. Hospital work 2.30 p.m. DC'S office 3.00–4.00 p.m. Had a case in respect of sanitary offences.

(ii) E. O. Rake, Ag DC, 1916

20 January 1916
Left Bole arrived Suripe. Chief asked permission to be absent from Damba on the grounds of sickness. Permission given. Road and rest house in good repair. Crops reported good. Chief is building a caravanserai of 12 huts on the south of the road and has been given permission to charge 20 cowries per man per night from traders making use of it.

21 January 1916
Arrived Malawey, passing Sakpa *en route*. Rest houses at Sakpa in bad repair. Orders given for their repair to be started on chief's return from Damba. The precincts of the town were in a state of appalling filth. The nature of the town – a solid block of square flat-roofed houses – makes an abatement of this nuisance a difficult problem. Suggested to the chief the advantages of building a caravanserai. He received the idea with favour, but complained of the lack of water for building purposes at this time of year. Orders given for three broken-down bridges to be repaired before the rains. No complaints at Malawey.

Sunday 23 January 1916
Arrived Banda Nkwanta, passing Tinga II *en route*. There seemed to be some doubt as to who was headman at Banda Nkwanta. The former headman seemed disinclined to continue exercising the office and had not formally resigned. I accordingly put the matter to the vote and Dari, a Dagarti, was almost unanimously chosen. Dari appears to be an intelligent and energetic man and, being head of the Dagarti section, the most numerous in the village, his election should prove satisfactory. The village seems to be increasing; besides the Dagartis there are Grunshis, Dagombas, Bandas, Fulanis and Lobis.

Banda Nkwanta, 24 January 1916
Investigated case of attempted murder by poisoned arrows and subsequent death of accused, who was alleged to have committed suicide before his apprehension. The two victims, old women, were brought up, both very sick with arrow wounds about the body. After examining a witness on oath, I was unable to find any reason for doubting the original statement of the headman who had found the body of accused in the bush. The practice of keeping poisoned bows and arrows by the inhabitants of villages is, in my humble opinion, dangerous and unnecessary, and should, I suggest, be discouraged. They are seldom, if ever, used for hunting purposes, for practically every able-bodied man appears to be in possession of a dane gun.

1 February 1916
Sent a message to Wandara to procure information with regard to refugees from French military service said to be seeking asylum there.

2 February 1916
Gave detachment practice in range firing. Interviewed headman of Wandara with regard to French refugees. Informed me that none had come in up to date. I told him to be on the lookout and give prompt information of the arrival of any, and that the harbouring of such refugees would be looked upon as a serious offence. Interviewed Dagarti chief of Bole with reference to chief of Yabum's complaint. The Dagarti said that he was too poor to give Yabum a cow and had sent instead some Guinea corn, which had been refused. This chief is in receipt of no tribute or dues of any kind, and I consider the present of a cow to Yabum rather a severe tax. Matter in abeyance pending discussion with chief of Yabum. Interview with the chief of Yabum and various other chiefs and headmen. The matter of the chief of Dagarti still under discussion. I decided that the chief of Dagarti should make a present of 15/– to the chief of Yabum as a token of his respect for him as paramount chief. This, the chief of Yabum refused, insinuating that the chief was attempting to make himself independent.

5 February 1916
Final interview with the chief of Yabum with reference to the Dagarti chief. The chief of Yabum said the size of the cow was immaterial, but according to custom the gift must be a cow, however small, otherwise dire consequences ensue and the paramount chief loses the stool from death or other causes during the year. Also, if the custom is not properly observed, the rains fail and crops are ruined. In consideration of this and the fact that Yabum and the principal subchiefs appear to show considerable feeling about the matter, I decided that the Dagarti chief should make a small subscription from his people and present the chief of Yabum with a small cow.

10 July 1916
Work in the office. Hearing complaints. Received letter from Dr J. J. Simpson stating that he would begin Bole some time at the end of the month. Was there a rest house? Also, would I have the road cleaned from Larabanga to Wandara? I imagine Dr J. J. Simpson is a government official, but can find no record in this office or his having reported his arrival in this district. He would appear to lack the courtesy that should appertain to a government official.

(iii) G. W. F. Wright, DC, 1917

5 April 1917
Mr Sherriff, Ag DC, went down with blackwater.[15] Took sworn statements of further witnesses in the treason trial. Found no entry in office diary after 13 March.

6 April 1917
Talked to Dr Whyte over the telephone urging him to get in as soon as possible. Fifteen carriers sent out to meet him. Applied to Ag CC for board on cash and ammunition.

7 April 1917
Dr Whyte arrived Bole at 3.00 p.m. having come in from Kulmanso on a bicycle, 45 miles. Unable to do anything further in office until board on chest has been held.

9 April 1917
Board on money held by Commandant, NTC.

11 April 1917
Held enquiry into alleged charge of spying against two men. Discharged one and put the other back for more evidence. Received instructions to hold a board on deficiency in cash.

13 April 1917
Sentence in Yabum treason case, prosecuted by Ag CC in presence of all the Europeans in the station, chiefs, headmen etc.[16] The chief of Bole expressed his thanks to the Ag CC for settling the rebellion and the *limam* of Bole also expressed his gratitude. Order given by Ag CC to break up the Senyon fetish. Board on deficiencies in cash book held by DC and Lieutenant Prabe. The deficiency was not accounted for. Report sent to CC.

16 April 1917
Ordered chief of Bole to get his people in for vaccination.

17 April 1917
MO vaccinating Bole people. Went through correspondence in office, found some dating back to early March had not been answered.

19 April 1917
Getting ready to move office back to its proper place. The present building used as an office is too depressing and dark.

23 April 1917
DC, MO, district clerk and court interpreter with escort and chiefs of Bole and Wandara left for Senyon at 9.00 a.m. Four miles from Bole

had a bush path pointed out to me as being the war path made by the Seripe people, the path looked like an old one. On arrival at Kyapi, saw the headman, an old man, who said he had no complaints and did not join in last rebellion – doubtful. Arrived Senyon 12.30 and sent for Kupo, the 'guardian of the fetish', a very old man. Informed him that the Ag CC had inflicted a fine on the town of £40 and told him to see about getting the money at once.

Senyon, 24 April 1917

In morning ordered Kupo to show the way to the fetish place. It consisted of a small grove with a fetish stone in the middle and a large collection of cooking pots. Was told that no one, except those intimately connected with the fetish, are allowed to use the path and the court interpreter, who has lived in Bole all his life, had never seen the place before. The chief of Yabum was not allowed to use the road, but I understand that this ancient custom was waived during the recent rising. Broke up the pots etc. and had the fetish stone carried to Bole. Had the late chief fetishman's house searched and found his official wands and war kit, umbrella, leopard skin etc. and brought them to Bole.

25 April 1917

Deserter from GCR caught on Senyon road and brought to Bole. Wire to Ag PC for instructions. Saw Kupo, who admitted that the Senyon men were hiding in the bush when the DC was at Senyon because they were afraid. Kupo was sent back to Senyon with messages that the people had nothing now to fear and, as soon as the fine of £40 was paid, all trouble would be over.

26 April 1917

Left Wandara 7.00 a.m. and arrived Buanfo 10.00 a.m., bush paths only. Two small round huts, only enough room for an 'X bed' to stand. Tornado came up about 1.00 p.m. and lasted till 3.30. Had to crowd everything into the small huts and everything got wet. Conditions were very unpleasant and uncomfortable. Saw chief in evening. No complaints and no palavers.

2 May 1917

Dr Whyte, MO, left for Wa. Hope now there will be a lull in the demand for carriers, as many have been supplied and the people want a chance to get on with their farming.

3 May 1917

No complaints or palavers. Floor of office being beaten by women from the town. Heavy rain from 3.00 p.m. and all evening.

10 May 1917
DC, escort and court interpreter left Bole 6.45 and arrived Seripe 10.15. Rest house in good condition. Two additional shelters of *zana* mats and sticks. One in state of collapse. It really is useless to put up such flimsy structures and expect them to stand tornadoes. Chief had no complaints. He states that he had somewhat of a difficulty in providing food for all the troops and carriers[17] during March and April. There was no looting, but he would not be able to provide food for any such large parties for some time.

Sunday 13 May 1917
The last two days I have travelled through the bush for 11 hours without seeing the least sign of any human habitation. The track is very little used. No rest house at Fumbo and no shelter of any kind. Tent pitched under tree to east of the village. Water good. Tsetse fly on road.

15 May 1917
Good palm wine can be had at Fumbo, Boakipi, and Kolenso.

16 May 1917
Left Kolenso 6.45 a.m., arrived Morno 12.10. Misled again about the distance. Was told that it 'did not catch' three hours. Road very bad, mostly through dried-up swamps. Struck the Volta about 8.30 a.m. and crossed it about 9.30. Quite dry at crossing and very steep banks. Passed large palm groves. Morno, a small and very dirty place. No accommodation and the tent had to be pitched in the middle of the village. Chief is under Buipe. Told him to get the place cleaned up anyhow. Very hot and tiring day. Plenty of tsetse fly along the road. Food seemed plentiful and the water was fairly good. The headman had no complaints and nothing to bring before me. He stated that his farms were backward on account of scarcity of rainfall.

17 May 1917
Left Morno 6.00 a.m. arrived Buipe 9.15 a.m. Old road Kintampo to Gambaga. Found rest houses at Buipe in bad repair and an effort appears to have been made quite recently to do them up, probably when the chief heard I was coming. Ordered him to get on with them at once and to build a wall round the compound. A tornado came up at 5.00 p.m. and the palaver had to be put off.

18 May 1917
Copied out official diary 9 to 18 May inclusive and sent copies to Ag PC, SP, with a mail to Salaga for transmission to Tamale. Awarded carriers 1/– each.

20 May 1917
Left Tolendo 6.00 a.m. arrived Busunu 11.00 a.m. Rest houses (two) in fair condition. On arrival, I was informed that the chief of Busunu and his son, Apampo, had gone to Bole. As I wanted particularly to see both men, and as the visits of the DC to Busunu are rare, I could not understand why he was not about, especially as word had been sent ahead that the DC was coming. I am convinced that Busunu and his son are hiding somewhere as they both fear arrest. Busunu's conduct has been very suspicious during the Gonja rising and his son is wanted for obtaining money by false pretences.

On arrival at the rest house I found a man under arrest. This man, who is stated to be the brother of the chief of Busunu, was seen by one of my men to empty something out of a small bag into a large pot of water standing at the rest house for my use. I had the pot emptied and found a sort of charm at the bottom and some black sticky stuff. Shall take the man into Bole to investigate the case. Shall wait till arrival at Murugu and see how things are there and write in to Tamale from there about the whole matter, but I think the chief of Busunu should be sent to Tamale for a time to frighten him, as his behaviour is most unsatisfactory and, as his town is six days from Bole, it is impossible to check his vagaries and intrigues. Just after arrival, a tornado with heavy rain broke over the town. This had been threatening all last night and this morning. Letter sent in post to post to clerk at Bole.

21 May 1917
Had the man up before me who is alleged to have put, or attempted to put, 'medicine' in the water for the DC. Of course he denied it. Am taking him to Bole.

Murugu, 24 May 1917
The headman produced £25, amount of fine inflicted on the town. He said he and his people were all very sorry for what had happened and would not have done what they did had it not been for the action of their chief. They promised never to do anything of the kind again and asked me to tell the CC this.

25 May 1917
Left Murugu 6.00 a.m. and Larabanga 10.40. Delay at the Mole River, which was unexpectedly full and a canoe had to be sent for. The first passage made the thing sink and left me in about ten feet of water.

29 May 1917
Left Grupe 6.30 a.m. Arrived Senyon 10.40 a.m. Delayed by rain. Found that the rest house work at Senyon had been thoroughly well

done and reflects great credit on Constable Sayi Dagarti, who was left to superintend. Three large, round houses have been put up, well ventilated and roofed – kitchen and boy's house and latrine. The compound has been beaten and the whole enclosed with a good wall. The bush in the vicinity has also been cut down and all the buildings and surrounding wall well whitened.

6 June 1917
At 4.00 p.m. received wire from Ag CCNT stating that Governor had pardoned Yabum and the others. This came as a tremendous surprise to me and will be a still greater surprise to the people in the district when they hear about it. It may cause trouble. Letter to Ag CCNT pointing out how unfortunate it would be if Mahama be allowed to resume job at Yabum.

28 June 1917
First complaints brought in by chiefs of Bole and Wandara as to reports of the chief of Yabum being set free in Tamale. State that Yabum's men have been going about the country saying he was coming back to Yabum and making plans [about] which chiefs were going to have trouble when Mahama gets back to Yabum. It seems that a regular system of messengers from all parties has been established between here and Tamale, and there is reason to believe the constabulary line at Tamale has been the headquarters of some of these messengers. The messengers also told the people that they now see that Mahama was not a man to be played with and that he was only waiting till the rains were over to tour all through Bole district and give his orders.

3 July 1917
The chief of Bole called up and said he had nothing to report. He promised to keep me fully posted as to what went on and said he would do exactly as I told him and would do his best to prevent other chiefs from doing anything wrong. Said he was told that Mahama was going to ride into Bole in state. Told him there was no authority for any such report and that he was to tell his people so.

4 July 1917
At work on returns. The chief of Bole called in and had a long talk. The news was that Mahama was coming back to Yabum to be head of the district again. The chief of Bole said he had been consulting with the loyal chiefs as to what to do. He said they had agreed to have messengers posted on the road to see if Mahama of Yabum was coming back. If he did come back to the district, all the Bole people had decided to leave the town and go down to Accra. The chief of

Buipe would follow them and meet them at Banda Nkwanta. I told the chief that it was no good to go out and meet trouble half way. Assured him that he would have full information as to what would happen, that he could trust absolutely that nothing would be done to injure him or his people, and that Mahama would be allowed to do nothing.

5 July 1917
Rumour brought in that French subjects are running gunpowder from Coomassie, and passing at night through Wandara and going via Konfusi and a bush path to Tantama and thence to Boma. Have sent privately to investigate.

7 February 1918
CC inspected the station and office in morning and signed up all the books.

10 February 1918
The CC returned from Senyon at 9.45 a.m. and saw the chiefs immediately. They said they had not yet decided on a new chief of Bole and the CC saw them again at 4.30, when the chief of Wandara was at first proposed and rejected by CC, on grounds of general uselessness and misconduct, and the chief of Bonfu was then put forward. He did not appeal to the CC and the other chiefs apparently did not view his appointment with approval, for they said nothing when asked by the CC. Finally, after a few straight remarks by the CC, the chiefs were told to go away and come back next day with a candidate ready.

(iv) Dr A. M. Dowdall, Ag DC,[18] 1918

26 August 1918
Took over the station from DC Wright. Inspected constabulary. Held dispensary. Inspected town and *zongo* in evening.

29 August 1918
Another very cold morning. Held dispensary — a few old deadbeats of the something-for-nothing type. External application of soap and water would be better medication than any internal dope. Ordinary office routine. English mail arrived in evening.

31 August 1918
The dispensary this morning amounted to one patient. I believe he has been attending for some time. Received letter from HPMO to remove all drugs and equipment to Wa and leave only ordinary mixtures of everyday use behind. The native nurse has been transferred to Wa, so only an illiterate and not too intellectual hospital labourer is in charge

and it would be dreadful to think of what might happen if he started to dispense a bottle of strychnine among his friends.

9 October 1918
Attended dispensary. Ordinary office routine. One constable and one carrier left for Tamale to bring £5 in nickel coins, which are badly needed as there is no small change in the treasury chest at this station. Several large droves of cattle have passed through the station in the last few days proceeding south. One small drove of young bulls from Lorha district passed through. I am pleased to notice this weeding out, as on my inspection of cattle[19] in the Dagarti, Grunshi and Lobi districts, I have remarked on the number of young bulls, in many cases comprising half the herd, which is not conducive to good cattle raising. Rain fell during the evening.

17 October 1918
Attended dispensary. Chief of Yabum, mounted on his horse and in his silk clothes and medallion, accompanied by the chief of Bole, came and called. The chief of Yabum was informed of HE's visit and expressed his pleasure at the master visiting his people. Asked as to transport, the chief of Yabum wished to know, if possible, the number required and to be given adequate notice. Food supply is plentiful. Discussed rest house, *zana* mat houses and chief informed that sites had been selected. A model *zana* mat house and other temporary buildings will be erected at Bole for guidance. The chief of Yabum had a complaint against several men that during his absence at Tamale, whilst he was under arrest, these people went after his wives. I asked the chief of Bole for a messenger to go and get satisfaction of £15 from Kamlielli who was the prime mover. Kamlielli was unable to pay, but paid £13. Constabulary had a parade this morning and employed in making targets for disappearing figure practice, which I learned how to do while at Wa from Captain Nash.

18 October 1918
Attended dispensary. Chief of Yabum, chief of Bole and *malam* called to salute me on the occasion of Mohammedan feast. Gave them a dash of 25/– from the presents to chiefs' vote.

19 October 1918
Attended dispensary. Busy with Tamale mail. Chief of Yabum called and paid balance of Red Cross collection. There appears to have been some dirty work here and the chief very careless. Yesterday he was £8.17*s*.6*d*. short and today he has brought 19/– too much. He acknowledges he never counted the money and the messenger, who brought it, appears to have thought that charity begins at home.

There are also several villages whose donations have not yet been received.

21 October 1918
Attended dispensary. Two constables suffering from bronchitis and headache, looks very like influenza.[20] Ordered caravanserai to be placed out of bounds.

22 October 1918
Two men reported died in *zongo* of influenza, doubt plenty in the town not seeking treatment. Placed constabulary lines out of bounds for townspeople and *zongo* and marketplace for constabulary. Received letter from Mr Holliday [Ag DC] to say he was coming to Bole, first information on the subject. Wrote letter to PC Wa and DCs Lorha and Tumu giving instructions on symptoms and preventive measures against influenza.

23 October 1918
Attended dispensary. All constabulary sick except two; 43 cases of influenza at dispensary this morning. Work in station at a standstill.

24 October 1918
Attended dispensary; 50 cases influenza. Mr Holliday arrived in station from Tamale at 8.45 a.m. Nothing doing in station owing to sickness.

25 October 1918
Busy handing over cash, stamps etc. to Mr Holliday.

(v) A. R. Holliday, Ag DC, 1918

26 October 1918
Took over district from Dr Dowdall this morning and telegraphed CCNT accordingly. Chiefs of Yabum and Bole call to pay their respects. Discussed HE's visit with them[21] and ordered paramount chief to call all his subchiefs in to see me on Monday next. Went round station etc. with Dr Dowdall in afternoon. I cannot help recording my surprise at being sent all this way up from Lomé, after having been out over 20 months this tour, and without being first medically examined. I fancy that the date of my arrival in Lomé from Seccondee, viz 1 October 1917, must have been mistaken for the date of my arrival from home.

29 October 1918
Sent telegram to commander reporting death of Constable Mosie Grumah. Sergeant reported a woman, wife of Constable Haragu

Kampala, died in the lines this morning. States she was under treatment by the MO for influenza. Five constables and one prisoner still sick. Found telegrams since 24th not sent off yet, despite numerous attempts to get Kintampo. Decide to send a special runner unless call answered today. After linesman had sat at instrument all morning, managed to get messages through.

31 October 1918
Work commenced on bungalow and outbuildings, but one mason and one scavenger ill and this rather delays work. Sergeant reported corporal and five men still on sick list. Corporal not so well today, cannot eat, ordered him to have beef tea in small quantities at frequent intervals. Sent off mails to Wa and Tamale.

4 November 1918
Paramount and subchiefs came in re Governor's visit. Paramount chief and chief of Bole not properly dressed, so I called them inside my office and spoke to them privately. They admitted they were not properly dressed, but offered no excuse. However, they expressed their thanks to me for speaking privately to them. Meeting adjourned till 4.00 p.m. At 4.00 p.m. all chiefs arrived properly gowned. Explained fully re Governor's visit and necessary requirements. Paramount chief states definitely would supply 300 carriers, provided influenza epidemic died out by then. Informed them will proceed to Kintampo boundary on Friday and that carriers to be provided. Paid out war bonus to detachment.

7 November 1918
Ill in bed. Temperature last night 101.5. Fancy it is influenza. Chief of Bole reported three people died in town, one of old age, two from influenza. Caravanserai keeper reported one death in caravanserai today.

Sunday 10 November 1918
Feeling much better so got up. Strolled round station and down to garden in afternoon.

13 November 1918
Telegram received from PC 3.30 p.m. with joyful news that Germany signed armistice at 5.00 a.m. 11th instant. Ordered detachment to parade and all local chiefs and people to assemble on parade ground. Attended parade in khaki field service uniform, and informed all present (about 200) of the good news and instructed them to spread it throughout the district. Three cheers for the King and our allies and much satisfaction expressed at news. Warned people not to expect to see marvellous changes immediately, even if peace is arranged.

14 November 1918
I completed tour of 22 months this morning. Inspected constabulary kit. In view of yesterday's good news gave all hands a holiday today.

20 November 1918
Visited dispensary in morning and gave hospital boy instructions about a few simple medicines in case of need. Sent off telegram to PC advising him I am leaving for Kintampo boundary this morning. Left Bole at 9.25. Started to foot it, but had to give it up and get hammock men, as I find that very little exertion knocks me out.

25 November 1918
Left Jogboi at 6.45 a.m. At Tasilima found people starting to clean up village. Inspected the village and found surroundings very dirty and that dead bodies are buried right inside the village among the houses, one body having recently been buried within ten yards of a deep well inside the village. Soil is very porous, so ordered this well to be closed instantly and another dug, and that a proper cemetery to be set apart. All future burials to take place there, under pain of punishment. Headman reported Kwamin, a youth of about 19, as a very disobedient fellow and one who defies him and refuses to obey his orders. Ordered Kwamin to follow me to Bole for a course of training in hygiene and obedience. Climbed uphill about 40 minutes out of Banda Nkwanta to get some idea of the topography of country.

26 November 1918
Headman of Tasilima brought in the youth, Kwamin, and begged for him to be let off, as he is now doing what he was ordered. Agreed.

29 November 1918
Left Malawey at 6.00 a.m. and arrived Sakpa at 10.50. Found surroundings of village in disgusting condition in spite of having given orders the other day for it to be cleaned up. The registrar informs me that Mr Wright frequently spoke about this, so I ordered the headman and ten of his people to come into Bole in one week's time for an object lesson. Arrived Seripe at 1.00 p.m. Chief reported five people died from influenza, but others all getting better. Selected site for additional quarters in event of Governor's visit and gave chief full instructions. Sandflies very bad here in evening. Shook chief up a bit about the condition of the surroundings of villages.

Sunday 1 December 1918
Country looking delightfully fresh and green after the rain. Visited guard and fatigue party.

5 December 1918
Office routine in morning. Chief of Bole brought in headman of Senyon and reported that, though he had sent to him twice and ordered him to send in men, he refused and only came in on my orders. The headman's excuse is that all his people are ill, but I have evidence to the contrary and find people of the district are trying to work the influenza business for all they are worth. Headman admits he has not cleaned his town as I ordered. Evidently, a severe lesson is necessary as these people appear to suffer from swollen heads since their fetish saved their chief in the Bole show. Headman consequently to be detained as political prisoner for 14 days, and 20 men from Senyon to come in at once.

6 December 1918
Dispatched Tamale mail. Visited various gangs at work cleaning station. Much rank grass is being rooted up by hand and the area thus cleaned planted with Bahamas grass. I consider this a very necessary precaution against bush fires in a station where every building is roofed with thatch. I propose to clean a large area round the station. A considerable amount has been done in this respect by my predecessors, but extension is necessary. Market day, so strolled round market and found very few people here and very little produce.

31 December 1918
Checked and signed all vouchers. Wanted to pay out detachment and all labourers, but felt too ill and had to go off to bed.

1 January 1919
In bed all day.

2 January 1919
Not feeling at all fit, but felt I must make an effort to close off books and hold board on vault and safe. Paid off detachment and all station hands, but by 11.30 became much worse and had to be conveyed to bungalow in a hammock. Telegraphed to PC advising.

3 January 1919
Had a very bad night but a little easier this morning. I have now diagnosed it as fever. (The NT has the doubtful honour of being the first place in West Africa to lay me out with malaria and that after a residence of a little over two months.)

6 January 1919
Still on sick list. Chief of Yabum complained his people will not come in to repair the roof of his house and asked for police to bring them in. Informed the chief I am getting tired of this request for police on

all paltry occasions and that it is quite time he learned to exercise a little more authority and control over his people. Told him to send his linguist and call the people again and warn them that if I have to send for them there will be trouble. I must confess, so far, that I am disappointed with the chief of Yabum, who appears a miserable weakling devoid of any character or authority. And the same views were expressed by Dr Dowdall and Mr Dasent during my recent visit to Wa. Whilst in Togoland I observed that the Germans had so undermined the authority of their chiefs that they were unable to enforce the slightest command without police assistance. I am determined, if possible, to prevent such a state of affairs here. The chiefs will not recognize it as a sign of weakness that their authority must be backed up by police, but regard it rather as a fine show of their authority that they are able to obtain police assistance whenever desired.

8 January 1919
Resumed duty this morning and informed PC accordingly by telegram. Went to dispensary and made up a lot of cough mixture for general use. In office all morning. Visited garden, much disappointed with the gardener's efforts. I fear he is wholly incompetent and I intend asking the curator if he can supply me with a man who knows something about it, as I am particularly anxious to start nurseries of various fruit and shade trees, which are much needed here.

10 January 1919
Hausa chief came to pay his respects and said his wife and daughter had run away again. I informed him that I had secured their return for him once and, if he cannot look after them, he cannot expect me to undertake that very doubtful pleasure. Visited work on Kintampo road in afternoon and found, despite a corporal of constabulary in charge and it under supervision of sergeant, the work had been done entirely regardless of my instructions as to direction and dimensions. The road goes off at an angle to the pegs put in by me. It seems that, if I want this work done properly, there is nothing for it but to supervise it myself and risk another go of fever by standing about in the sun.

Sunday 26 January 1919
Visited garden, market, caravanserai and inspected work on Kintampo road, which is now completed. Work has been well done. The chief of Bole exhibited great keenness in the work and I found him there supervising it on every occasion on which I visited it, which was practically daily.

27 January 1919
On inspecting prison cells found prisoners' ration and latrine pans

inside and not cleaned properly. Cautioned warder and warned him I will fine him if I find them there again.

14 February 1919
I have today completed 25 months this tour. Chief of Bole applied for permission for the people to play and sing every evening until 11.00 p.m. for one week as the heat is now so great that they can't sleep early. Permission granted till 10.00 p.m.

22 February 1919
Wa mail arrived. Dispatched Kintampo mail. Handed over to Mr Dasent and telegraphed PC accordingly.

(vi) E. G. Dasent, Ag DC, 1919

23 February 1919
Mr Holliday left for England via Kintampo. The chief of Bole came up during the morning with a dash. He informed me that he wished to erect a new market, the present site being very hot and dusty. The site chosen is more central and has some shade. Lately, in the NWP I have seen a lot of reasons given for the decrease in trade passing from French territory through that province, but no mention of roads coming from Wa to Bole. After leaving the Wa boundary, roads no longer exist. In the dim past, it is just possible some sort of road existed, that it was never drained is certain, that it has been repaired during the last ten years does not seem likely. Now the so-called road is an excellent imitation of a river bed, where when one is not picking one's way between boulders and tree stumps one is ankle deep in sand. Two to two and a half miles an hour is excellent going for carriers with light loads. If the French authorities have followed their usual policy of building good roads, it would not be surprising to learn that the traders, although it is somewhat further, prefer to follow a good road to the Ivory Coast.

24 February 1919
Various chiefs came into the office to salute. There appear to have been a lot of changes since I was here last [1915] and most of the faces are new to me.

26 February 1919
This morning the chief of Yabum made a rather tardy appearance to salute me. He made a number of futile excuses and finally stated he had not finished his work at Yabum. After being informed that his manners were those of a small urchin, he was ordered to attend the office every morning and leave when the chief left. In the evening,

made a sanitary inspection of the town and found it compared favourably with any town I have visited in the NT. My predecessor instituted a constabulary patrol which made a round of the town every morning, to which cause may be attributed the present sanitary conditions.

13 March 1919
Visited the Lobi village. There appear to be very few grown men, but a multitude of women and children. Of course, it is more than probable that the former were hiding. Their compounds are well constructed and have no ground entrances, the only way in being by small manholes in the roof. The people informed me that in their own country they spent their time in inter-village warfare and that the peacefulness of the English territory was much preferable. It was explained that certain obligations were attached to living in peace and that these were to be carried out promptly and obediently. After many false attempts and much talking, 13 labourers were collected by the Lobi headman and the chief of Bole. These then left for Kunfasi.

5 March 1919
Spent the whole day on the road. The work is much impeded by the lack of suitable tools, much having to be done with only native hoes. The completed road is drained and slightly cambered; this will probably disappear after the rains when the loose earth in the centre settles down. The chiefs are superintending all the work on the road and, in future, should be able to keep it in proper repair.

Sunday 23 March 1919
Labourers from Kunfasi arrived; 60 were collared by the chief of Bole and 24 were brought in. The idea of completely rebuilding the road has had to be given up and now only the worst places are being repaired. Labour is very scarce and the time for farming is approaching. The chief of Kulba reported that he wished to relinquish the stool. He was told to inform the chief of Yabum. Visited the town and garden in the evening. There is now a plentiful supply of water in all the water holes. The gardener excelled himself today by producing some very fine cape gooseberry plants as a vegetable. I think it would be hard to find a more complete set of fools than are the government employees at Bole.

29 March 1919
The message stick sent to Kowhisi on 18th has not yet returned.

2 April 1919
The mosquitoes here, since the few rains we have had, are numbered

in their millions and it is impossible to sit still in the evening unless one is enveloped in smoke. Have hunted all round the house and clearing, but have found no obvious breeding places.

Saturday 5 April 1919
Spent the whole evening sowing trees and shrubs in the garden. Bole is particularly devoid of shrubs and shade trees.

Tumu, Western Province

(i) Dr William Ryan, Ag DC, 1913–14[22]

15 November 1913
Captain Swire [DC] reported sick and struck off duty.

17 November 1913
Captain Swire diagnosed as one of yellow fever. Special runner sent to Tamale to report fact to PMO and Ag CC. Quarantine declared in Tumu.

18 November 1913
Captain Swire keeping well ahead of his illness.

19 November 1913
Mail arrived from England Captain Swire quite interested in his mail. Dictated some letters home. Is very hopeful of speedy recovery.

20 November 1913
Captain Swire's illness gaining ground. Towards evening condition critical. Mail for England dispatched.

22 November 1913
Captain Swire died at 5.00 p.m. All his goods, stores etc. collected under the supervision of Sergeant Kwarra Kanjarga and placed in the house under a guard.

23 November 1913
Captain Swire buried. Military funeral attended by the chief headman and people of Tumu who brought their guns and, when the firing party of the NT' detachment retired, they formed a circle round the grave and fired a last salute.

26 November 1913
Mail arrived from Wa. A letter from PC Wa asking MO to take over duties of Ag DC. Chiefs of outlying districts coming in to pay their last respects to dead Commissioner. Thanked and commended by Ag DC.

4 December 1913
Dr Coghill arrived to enquire into the outbreak of yellow fever.

6 December 1913
The chiefs of Tumu district summoned to attend enquiry into place of origin of, existence of, or other information concerning the outbreak of yellow fever in the district.

8 December 1913
Constabulary lines inspected by yellow fever commission, also caravanserai and general inspection of town of Tumu.

9 December 1913
Chief of Kupulima reported Moshis detained in his town under quarantine giving trouble. Ringleaders sent for and ordered to work on the station at Tumu.

16 December 1913
Quarantine raised. Moshis caused much trouble at Kupulima and Sekai and refused to obey messengers from DC. They were finally brought in by armed party and fined ten cows.

18 December 1913
English mail late. One cow, part of fine on Moshis, ran amok and was shot by sergeant on my orders. Dr Coghill left for Wa.

1 January 1914
Chief of Sekai and his subchiefs summoned to show cause why orders from the DC were not obeyed. He reported his subchiefs had refused to obey him. Sekai is an old man clad in a short shirt, which is filthy. He has absolutely no attributes of a chief. No appearance, dirty, no wives, no personal possessions, no authority. Lilixia, one of Sekai's subdistricts, reported for refusing to supply labour for road construction. This same district and others in the northwest of Tumu are giving trouble in refusing to accept coin of the realm (silver) in exchange for goods. These people have been punished before for taking money tendered and scornfully throwing it into the bush.

10 January 1914
Gwolu people called on for labour to finish the roofing of the DC's house. The old roof was removed by the MO after the death of Captain Swire.

12 January 1914
Called to Leo [Ivory Coast] in my capacity as MO. Left for Leo this evening. (*Entente cordiale.*)

(ii) G. A. E. Poole, Ag DC, 1914

30 March 1914

Chief of Kwapo with his subchiefs arrived and brought in 14 headmen of compounds who, the chief reported, had refused to obey his orders. A careful enquiry was made and it would appear that the accused, mostly youngmen, had failed to carry out orders, the excuse being that in the last four months they had been called upon to make roads, bridges, supply groundnut tops for Tumu horses and grass for houses in the town. I pointed out that the orders given by the chief were by him received from the DC and, as such, were government orders. The DC further pointed out that in this colony there were no taxes, hence little money to pay out for labour. Their freedom from persecution and annihilation from such as Babatu and Samory was touched upon, and expense of walled towns and warlike stories saved to them. Any little work asked of them must be willingly supplied as to set off the benefits they were daily receiving. All expressed regret at their behaviour and said that the chief would have no further cause to be vexed with them. Complaints as to the impossibility of the local chiefs being able to supply the NTC daily market listened to and the justice of their grievance recognized. In future, there will be a weekly market on Sunday, when each head chief, in turn, will supply food in bulk for which he will receive a fair price. There being 13 head chiefs, this will not be a hardship. The chief of Pina made a statement that his donkey had been shot by a European, for which he had received no compensation; the matter will be enquired into and justice done.

3 April 1914

The DC attended the first of the new weekly markets arranged for the constabulary, the food being supplied by the people of Golu, and saw that justice was done to everyone. Dr Ryan gelded the horse of Captain Poole.

10 April 1914

The weekly special market arranged for the constabulary was supplied this day by the people of Kwapo (two days' journey); the MO and DC were present. A measure was called for and filled. The sellers were asked the price and stated 1/6*d.* The constabulary, represented by their wives, objected to the price. The measure was weighed by the DC. It turned the scale at 25 lbs. The DC asked if the sellers were agreeable to reducing the price to 1/3*d.* At this the constabulary women left *en masse*. The sellers, being intimidated, offered the 25 lbs for 1/–. The sergeant was sent for and, in the presence of Mr Tamakloe, was shown the measure and reminded that the scarce season was approaching and that, even at 2/– per load, corn at this time was anything but expensive. The gravity of the constabulary action was pointed out and their attitude would automatically cancel the special market arranged for themselves, and that in future their food supplies would have to be obtained as at other stations. This reasoning was of no avail, not a grain was sold. The DC thanked the Kwapo people for their ready response to his call, 'dashed' them for their trouble and supplied them an escort to see their loads beyond the town of Tumu.

9 July 1914

Demands for the new nickel coins were made without result. The paucity of these coins in the district has done considerable harm. Their innovation upset the cowrie currency and now there is no small change of any sort available. The outcome of this scarcity of nickel will be a flooding of the district with French nickel, as Quitta is stocked with German pfennigs and English copper and nickel is not accepted by the natives there. The lack of rain is causing grievous anxiety and the farms are showing the effect of this long drought. The 12 cases of yaws, which have been attending hospital for some little time, are practically all cured. Dr Ryan states he will hand over Tumu to his successor free from this complaint. The daily attendance at hospital is good.

15 July 1914

The absence of rain still continues and is causing great anxiety. The crops are practically destroyed. Owing to lack of water, there being only two wells with any, that of the constabulary and the European, building operations at the new DC's house have been stopped. The people of Sorbella brought in their dane guns to be stamped, 24 in all.

29 July 1914

The DC returned from his tour of inspection having visited Kassano, Kwapo, Pudo, Basiasan, Dolbizan and Bujan. At each village, a meeting was held of the chiefs and headmen when their attention was called to: (1) the importance of sanitation; (2) danger of flies as carriers of disease; (3) lack of foresight in allowing indiscriminate interbreeding in cattle; (4) wisdom of planting their farms from selected grain; (5) danger incurred in the present funeral custom as a carrier of infectious diseases from village to village; (6) the lack of fidelity of the women as a class to their husbands, greatly owing to the system of elderly men taking over small girls and acting as guardians till they reach a marriageable age when they cohabit with them; and (7) the fact that security of life and property having now become established, the necessity for congregating in large compounds has passed.

3 August 1914
Monsieur Remond arrived from Leo, having been met with an escort of the NTC. At 4.00 p.m., a dispatch dated Wagadugu, 3 August, arrived for Monsieur Remond, who at once begged to be excused, stating he had received news of the gravest importance and must return to Leo immediately. From the little information Monsieur Remond was inclined to give, it was gathered that war had broken out between Austria and Serbia and the whole of Europe was in a state of great unrest and preparing for the event of war themselves.[23]

7 August 1914
An outline of the information derived from Monsieur Remond was sent, post to post, to Wa, Tamale and Navarro. The people of Pulima were accused by the chief of refusing to obey his orders, in that they would not attend the Tumu market on account of their distaste for silver, but visited the other six day markets where they could obtain cowries.

9 August 1914
At 9.00 a.m. Monsieur Bulat arrived from Leo with news dated 5th from Wagadugu, informing me of war between England and Germany and sending other news from France.

13 August 1914
At 5.00 p.m. a runner arrived from PC, Zouaragu, calling for Tumu detachment. Within an hour, two NCOs and eight men marched out, leaving one lance corporal and two sick men, who will follow in a few days with runners when they return. The wells at Tumu are giving out owing to this prolonged drought. Three were deepened this day five feet and the remaining three will be deepened in the course of the next day or two.

15 August 1914
War news was sent post to post to Wa, Lorha and Navarro. A tornado in afternoon but no rain, the crops in Tumu have failed and sheep and goats are now turned out in them.

2 September 1914
A nice fall of rain took place in the night. Monsieur Remond wrote stating Monsieur Bulat of Leo was very ill with fever and desired the MO here to be informed. Dr O'Donoghue is proceeding to Leo tomorrow.

3 September 1914
A very heavy fall of rain in the afternoon estimated at five inches, which although welcome, did a lot of damage to roads and proved that the grass roofs on European quarters were much too thinly thatched to meet such a downpour. The European well at the foot of the hill fell in; fortunately the one near the court remained satisfactory.

7 September 1914
The day broke in a drizzle, which continued all morning. The DC took advantage of the wet day to plant doub grass round the station, which had been received from Wa two months ago and which, having been planted out near the garden, had received water daily and had much spread.

26 September 1914
Dasima was in a disgraceful state, a mass of garbage, excrement and other filth, the rest house in keeping with the town. One constable was left to get the place cleaned up and another sent today with a sanitary inspector, supplied by the MO, to have the place put in order. Owing to the rain in the early morning, the DC left Dasima at 8.00 a.m. and, after much hard work and swimming two rivers, arrived Lilixia at 5.00 p.m. The two rivers were only crossed by means of a bath, acting as canoe for loads, five of which capsized, the bed among the number. Beyond the river trouble, the road proved unsafe for horse traffic. In many places the ponies got bogged up to the knees and hocks and I dismounted. The carriers sent to Coomassie for tools and Dr O'Donoghue's loads returned.

29 September 1914
Attended court all morning and listened to complaints as to the refusal to accept English silver in the local markets. Apparently, the difficulty is in the matter of change, but when nickel is sufficiently common in the country (if ever) this difficulty will be overcome

3 October 1914
The MO went on a tour of inspection. It seems to me that sanitation and cleanliness are the two first steps towards the education of these people.

7 October 1914
It would seem that the control of the prisons should be under the DCs and not the medical, as is the practice on the Coast. In olden days, the MO utilized the prisoners entirely for sanitary work, especially connected with latrines. These days, the MO has a permanent gang of

scavengers under him and a special vote to meet the expenses, so there is no necessity now for him having supreme control of prison labour. At the present time, the DC has no labour to call upon for station requirements he may deem expedient, unless he draws upon his special vote or interferes with the liberty of the people by compulsory labour, for which he has no official sanction.

Sunday 11 October 1914
Drs O'Donoghue and Oakley operated on a lad who had been in hospital for some four months with a diseased leg. They were good enough to allow the chiefs and headmen of Tumu, at the request of the DC, to attend the operation as an educational lesson, which may be of value to bring home to them the ignorance of their own medicine men. The operation was performed in the courthouse, the head chiefs of Tumu and Sorbella, and many prominent men of these villages being present.

(iii) Dr P. D. Oakley, Ag DC, 1915

2 January 1915
In office signing all constabulary returns. No complaints so was able to get on with my own returns. The murderer Musa Bazabarimi appears to be getting weaker and at the same time is showing some signs of insanity. Very persistent in his request to me, as MO, to give him some strong medicine so that he can die.

22 January 1915
Bitterly cold and everybody coughing. Have never experienced such severe harmattan before. The men working on the house are now going too fast for the brickmakers, so I have put every one onto making bricks for three days. Burnt the grass at the back of my house. The natives here seem to be a most peaceful lot and give next to no trouble.

27 January 1915
Left Tumu for Pina. The carriers did not put in an appearance until 6.20 a.m., after having been told to be present at reveille. They met with rather a different reception than they expected. Put the murderer Musa Bazabarimi in my hammock as he couldn't possibly walk all the way. Very cold on starting, but from 9.00 a.m. the sun was very powerful.

28 January 1915
Left Pina for Basiasan. The Basiasan drummers came out to meet me and drummed me in. My train gradually increased as each chief is out to meet me, and then falls in to follow me to Basiasan to meet the CC.

On the road I saw a plentiful supply of hartebeest and roan spoor. Not far from Kwanchogaw I saw two roan close to the road, both carrying very fine heads. The wind was quite wrong and I never got a shot at them. When I followed them, I came across fresh lion and elephant spoor. The latter I followed until they crossed the main road. A very big herd, I should say, with some pretty big ones amongst it judging by the way branches of trees had been ripped off high up. Heard that the CC slept at Chana last night, so he will be at Nakong tonight and here tomorrow. The chief of Basiasan did not seem at all pleased when he was told that he would have to supply food for nearly 80 men and about 20 horses tomorrow.

Friday 29 January 1915
Rode out in the morning at 6.30 to the Sisile River to meet the CC. An escort of 28 horses with drummers came to meet him. The CC and Captain Breckenridge, PC, NEP, were met and escorted to the rest house where the CC had a small talk with the chiefs. It was arranged for them to assemble at 4.30 p.m., when the CC would address them. He spoke to them about the war fund and also on the market question, and warned the paramount chief that if they were unable to supply food he could be under the painful necessity of closing down Tumu station. The chiefs were all most emphatic in their desire to supply the market. In the evening, it was reported to me that three men had gone into a compound in the absence of the owner and, besides taking groundnut tops for the horses, they took three fowls. The culprits were horse boys belonging to the constabulary and were summarily dealt with. Chief of Basiasan supplied 78 pots of food for the carriers. This is most creditable considering 80 carriers besides boys, constabulary and other chiefs with their followers and 48 horses were present. The chief of Basiasan deserves great credit for his efforts.

Saturday 30 January 1915
The CC tried Musa Bazabarimi on the charge of murder. He was found guilty and sentenced to death.

2 February 1915
The murderer, under sentence of death, made a determined effort to escape from prison at 7.30 p.m. He managed to slip his handcuffs and climbed over the wall into the next cell and from there into the carpenter's shop when the sentry caught him. He is a very thin man and when I tried the handcuffs I found I could pull his hand through them. I found that the handcuffs fitted his ankles very nicely and I do not anticipate any further attempts.

3 February 1915
Sent to Lorha to ask for a pair of leg irons.

4 February 1915
Checked cash. MO vaccinated the Tumu people. Have cut down the water supply by half, as it is getting very short.

11 February 1915
English mail arrived. Heard that Mr Tamakloe has to refund, as the vouchers have to go to the treasurer for countersignature. I wish these things would be more clearly defined and not left to the imagination. English mail closed at 4.00 p.m. Mr Berkeley and myself left at 4.30 for Leo.

12 February 1915
Arrived Leo 9.00 a.m. Met by Monsieur Remond. Certainly the house is very fine indeed and most beautifully cool. We were shown round the station. Real scarcity of water here.

Sunday 14 February 1915
Left Leo at 7.00 a.m., arrived Tumu 1.20. Found everything correct. Some good progress has been made on the rest house. Post to post from Lorha arrived.

16 February 1915
Left Tumu at 6.00 a.m., arriving Golu 2.30. The MO[24] vaccinated in the evening. It is only 18 miles from Tumu to Golu, but six carriers dropped out. This shows that 12 to 15 miles is an elegant sufficiency for any of these Issala carriers.

6 March 1915
From Bujan to Dolbizan. Road fair, rest house in fair condition, water supply bad. Told the chief not to allow the cattle to walk into the same pool as the drinking water is taken from. I rather fancy he likes the taste. No complaints.

7 March 1915
From Dolbizan to Basiasan, five hours twenty minutes, very rocky and hard on the carriers, heat something frightful. Came to a stream with two good pools of water. All the carriers lay down in it. An example that was followed by the Ag DC.

9 March 1915
Left Pudo at 6.00 a.m. and reached Wuru at 7.10. Chief had no complaints. Left 7.20 and arrived Kwapo 8.50. Kwapo very big place, but scattered. Chief stated that he had a complaint, so was told to come at 4.30 p.m. A new rest house has been made and very well

made too. The people have decorated the interior to such an extent and with such weird figures that I thought I had the 'rats' for the moment. Good water supply and food fairly plentiful. They have just begun smelting in the district. Chief of Wuru brought me some fresh fish, which was most acceptable.

11 March 1915
From Kassano to Tumu. Found that the masons and carpenter had not been doing too much work whilst I was away, so docked them two days' pay.

12 March 1915
Very heavy rain fell all night and it is still raining now at 10.30 a.m. All this rain is coming from the west. The rest house has suffered very much as this storm took us by surprise. The house will have to be practically replastered. Yesterday I was informed that there was a *malam* preaching a jihad, saying that we were not fighting against Germany but against the Mahdi. Sent a mounted man to the village I thought he would be at and managed to get him. He was formally charged with treasonable felony this morning and remanded pending the arrival of witnesses. Two women convicted for taking water from the government well. No sign of the mail yet. I expect the rain will have delayed him.

13 March 1915
Paid the constabulary for the half month. There were actually four baskets of food in the daily market this morning and about 40 women all fighting for them. The rain of yesterday has done more damage than was at first thought. The rest house has been very badly knocked about and it will take a long time to put it right. Whenever a white man does anything in this country something untoward nearly always happens. It must be a visitation of God for our numerous sins. All the so-called wells are full up to the brim with surface water and one has fallen in altogether. Lions were heard last night. An extraordinary thing how one day's rain will bring them out. No one seems to know where they get to in the dry season.

Balanced the cash book. In the afternoon, heard the case against Muley Mahama. The man makes no defence at all except that God is his witness. He was told that wouldn't carry in a court of law. I cannot help but think that this man is in the employ of the Germans. I have heard that all the *malams* at Leo have been arrested and sent to Wagadugu, presumably for the same reason. At the first opportunity, I shall visit all the villages at which this man Muley Mahama has been preaching and explain the matter to the people. I think the man

Joseph, who brought this matter to my notice, deserves some small reward, for without that information I should have known nothing about the matter.

16 March 1915
From Tumu to Sokolu. Road good. Spoke at each village explaining away the things told them by the *malam*, Muley Mahama. Sokolu in a very insanitary state and the chief was told to clean up and keep it clean. Of course, he won't dream of obeying the latter order.

17 March 1915
From Sokolu to Bowbellie. Rest house here in fair condition. Had a talk to the chief and his people in the evening. I explained that Muley Mahama was trying to make trouble, but the chief said he did not believe what he had told them. The *malam*s had put the man up for two days, but when asked about it they swore they had never seen the man. Am taking four of these gentlemen to interview Mr Berkeley [PC].

27 March 1915
A man named Mamadu complained that he came from French country to visit his brother who lives in Golu and, on arrival, found that his brother had been arrested at Golu and taken into Lorha. Wrote to the Ag DC to know if this was so and, if so, strongly objecting to Lorha constables arresting people from my district.

Sunday 28 March 1915
Received post to post from Wa enclosing a letter from the PMG. I noted that men in outstations are to make their own arrangements for the mail. I have no doubt we shall be capable of running our own post quite as well as the postal department. It makes me tired for men in Accra to sit down and write reams about a protectorate they know nothing of. I should like the PMG to come up here and have to sit down by himself, in a station, for five months and then be told that the postal department refuses any further responsibility for his mail, for that is what it practically amounts to.

(iv) Captain S. D. Nash, DC, 1916

Wednesday 5 April 1916
Left Tumu 6.00 a.m. on inspection along French frontier.

6 April 1916
Left Kassano 6.20 a.m. in drizzling rain; arrived Kwapo 11.30. Chief reports people and cattle now free of the disease reported last year, but it was still breaking out spasmodically at Wuru.

7 April 1916
Left Kwapo 6.00 a.m., arrived Pudo 9.30. Visited Wuru on the way. I saw a man there who had been ill for four days, but was now getting better, and who was said to be suffering from the disease complained of. He had a slight temperature and quick pulse with carbuncle on left side of his chest. It was difficult to say what it was, as he had it smeared over with some native medicine and it appeared to be clearing up. There was a similar case in the same compound some four weeks ago, a woman, with fatal results. They are still losing cattle here, particularly goats. I saw one that had died that morning and found the spleen slightly enlarged. I had, unfortunately, no slides with me to take blood smears, but it looks rather suggestive of the presence of anthrax. The chief was told to segregate all his sick animals and any that died to be buried entirely. He was also told to have his kraals scraped clean, the refuse buried and the clean kraal treated with fire. From what the chief said, they appear to have a periodic outbreak here every year during the dry season. The chief informed me that his people were now clear of the sickness, but an occasional goat was still dying.

21 April 1916
Interviewed a few chiefs this morning from near the French frontier and questioned them as to whether natives were crossing to our side to avoid the French orders as to conscription. None of them seemed to know anything about the matter. Interviewed natives on some of their customs etc.

Saturday 22 April 1916
Some natives from Kwapo come in to pay their respects and bring in 85 lbs of cotton, for which they are paid. Interview again with the people on the subject of their customs.

25 April 1916
Chief of Pulima comes in and says his father died yesterday and that they are going to commence the funeral custom. He was not very old and therefore the ceremonies will only last three days. Crowds of Tumu people are already proceeding out to Pulima. I don't think I have ever been in a district where so much respect is paid to the departed. The people keep their cattle and sheep for slaughter on these occasions and not for sale. I am credibly informed that six cattle were killed in Pulima yesterday to feed the people who had come to the wake, and yet no meat has been killed in Tumu market since my arrival. The relations of the dead do not supply provisions on these occasions. Each guest 'brings his own bread and butter, and his own tea and

sugar' in the shape of fowls, sheep etc. and a man who wants to put on side brings cattle. I do not see how they can find time to farm and attend to business if they are constantly running about to funerals.

26 April 1916
Checked money in vault with view to transmitting worn-out coins to Tamale. Continued pegging out the station into squares. The whole of Tumu seems to have gone to Pulima today and, taken by the general craze, I biked out there in the afternoon. Crowds of people had assembled from the four points of the compass. The place was turned into a kind of fair and much selling and buying was going on.

Friday 28 April 1916
Continued the enquiry with the people on subject of 22nd [Kopille customs]. One difficulty in this matter is the native's indifference to abstract truth, and he is at all times ready to sacrifice it to the supposed wishes of the person with whom he is talking. If he thinks that the enquirer wants a certain answer, he is willing to oblige – leading questions are therefore of no use.

Saturday 6 May 1916
A huge crowd of people has collected near the chief's house, as a man had died last night and was to be buried tonight. I looked on for a considerable time at the ceremonies. Everything was done *pro forma* and everyone seemed to know exactly what to do. The men and women kept apart and each had their separate role to play. At a shout from one of the leaders of the ceremonies, all the men would get up and advance to the door of the house where the deceased was, singing a dirge; they would then turn round, walk back and sit down. The women walked round in circles crying and throwing their hands in the air. Two dogs, a goat, some fowls and a cow were killed and were lying on the ground among the people. At sundown, the body was brought outside the compound and laid on a bench, sitting upright and completely clothed, even to a red fez. The wife and sister, I was told, lay down on the bench and the proceedings then took the form of trying to persuade these relatives that death had occurred and that burial should take place. Only the women took part in this, the men sitting down and looking on. A woman would come up, touch the corpse and turn to the relatives and condole with them. The latter would cling to the dead body. The persuasion of the relatives to allow the body to be interred went on till midnight, when the body was buried. All the young take part in these ceremonies and their minds are therefore from youth fettered with fetish and some disgusting customs.

(v) E. O. Rake, Ag DC, 1916

27 May 1916
Interviewed the chief of Golu with regard to the cattle disease that has broken out in his village. A constable was sent out to investigate. He brought back information that 21 had already died and shot ten more infected ones. From the description of the disease — coughing, swelling of the lungs, white discharge from nose and mouth — I should imagine the disease to be pleuro-pneumonia. Gave the chief instructions with regard to segregation, choice of new grazing areas and immediate destruction of infected beasts.

Sunday 28 May 1916
Inspected constabulary line.

30 May 1916
A certain Awudu came up seeking the appointment of station butcher. As there is no butcher at present, and meat is very rarely procurable in the market, he was given the appointment and promised to do his best to keep the market supplied. Paid detachment NTC.

31 May 1916
Held a meeting of all the chiefs who had come in to meet the CC with a view to drawing up a list of the petitions or grievances they wished to bring to the notice of the CC. All the head chiefs, or their representatives, are in with the exception of Basiasan and Dasima. The latter will meet the CC on the road. Took down a list of their complaints, which were not numerous. The chief of Ulu complained that he had been compelled to make the journey into Tumu unaccompanied, his headmen refusing to come in. A message stick was sent to the headmen responsible, bidding them to appear or show cause why they should not accompany their chief when he comes to pay his respects to the CC. Mail from England arrived in evening.

1 June 1916
No complaints or court cases. Office routine and end-of-month settlement. General cleaning up of station.

2 June 1916
Captain C. H. Armitage, CC, NT, arrived in Tumu with Dr E. W. Graham, PMO. All the chiefs and subchiefs, with few exceptions, met the CC on the road and welcomed him with scenes of enthusiasm. The English mail left for Wa at dawn. The CC held a meeting of the chiefs and subchiefs in the evening, thanked them for their very satisfactory behaviour in these troublesome times and for their generosity in

subscribing to the Imperial War Fund, and displayed the new medallion shortly to be distributed among chiefs who, by their good qualities and chiefly conduct, are deemed worthy of them. He finally asked them if they had any grievances or complaints.

Saturday 3 June 1916
The CC held a meeting of the chiefs to settle the election of a head chief for the subdistrict of Sakai. Two candidates appeared, Kwahai and Neyiera. After the claims of both had been heard, Kwahai was appointed on the usual 12 months probation. The chief of Pulima then brought forward his claim to be head chief of the Sorbella subdistrict. The reasons for his claim were not considered to be sufficiently strong to oust the claim of Diegri, who had already been elected pending confirmation. He was, however, given permission by the CC to bring forward his claim when further appointments of chiefs were made in the Sorbella subdistrict.

Sunday 4 June 1916
The PMO, with the Ag DC, inspected the European and native water supply, the European gardens, the caravanserai and market. The CC inspected the town in the evening.

6 June 1916
In the evening, the CC interviewed the chief of Walembele and presented him with a robe.

7 June 1916
Interview with chief in afternoon. Went into the matter of the elephant claim. Decided for the present that Elenday of Nabolo should keep the tusks, as the elephant was shot and died in Nabolo country. Ali of Walembele informed, however, that he might bring a further claim before me at Tumu. Chief of Nabolo complained that Walembele men shot over his country and did not give him a share of the spoils of hunting. Informed him I would speak to the chief of Walembele about this. A share of the spoils should, I imagine, be given to the chief on whose land the game is shot. Was informed that 30 cows had lately died. Inspected herds. Found one sick cow and ordered its immediate destruction. Examined lungs of cow, which had died during the day. Lungs, even to the inexpert eyes of the layman, very much diseased. Gave instructions as to choice of absolutely new grazing area, immediate destruction of sick beasts and selection of new cattle kraals. This herd was situated about a mile and a half away from the cattle of the main part of the village. Gave instructions to the chief about keeping his cattle strictly away from this herd.

8 June 1916
Arrived Mandamu [along] narrow bush track. Chief complained that three of his headmen refused to obey him, also refused to accompany him to Tumu to pay their respects to the CC. Ordered the men in question to appear before me at Tumu next week.

13 June 1916
Started planting the teak seeds.

Sunday 25 June 1916
Returned to Tumu via Navarro, Domasan and Tientean. Everywhere peace and quiet and the whole population out in the fields engaged in agriculture, except at Tientean, where demonic screams mingled with the beating of drums and blowing of horns. Funeral rights were in progress and the village *en masse* were gathered round the corpse. Agricultural operations all suspended for the enjoyment of what seems to be one of the few recreations of the inhabitants of this district.

27 June 1916
Complaint by a certain *abiba* of Tolon, Tamale District, that a man, Dinwah of Tientean, refuses to give up the custody of her grandson. Message sent to Dinwah requesting him to show cause why he should not give up the child.

7 July 1916
No complaints or court cases. It is now a week since anyone has come up to the court with any sort of complaint. It would appear that the population are too busily engaged in their farming operations to give any cause for complaint. During the day, the vicinity of the compounds presents a deserted appearance, the only individuals visible being the very old and the very young and disconsolate donkeys and goats in bonds. The time of freedom of the latter is temporarily at an end. They are no longer free to wander as they will and, as all the juvenile labour is at present required for the tilling and planting, there is apparently no one available to drive them in herds to the pastures. At daybreak a string of men, women, children and dogs is seen going off to the farms where, as a rule, the whole day is spent. They return in the evening, the women usually bearing enormous loads of fire wood or branches of trees with green leaves – fodder for the captive goats. Many also bring back heavy loads of shea butter fruit, for the season of shea butter making is now at its height. The manufacture of this commodity is a long and tiresome undertaking. First, the green outside pulp has to be removed; this is done by the simple process of consuming it as food. Second, the kernels are boiled. Third, the hard outside shells of the kernels are removed by pounding in a wooden

mortar. Fourth, the inner kernels are taken and pounded with wooden pestles on a flat rock. Fifth, the resulting pulp is placed in an earthenware pot without water and stirred vigorously for about an hour; now signs of the oil begin to appear. Sixth, this oily mass is taken and ground very fine between two flat stones; the result is a semi-liquid black oily substance. Seventh, it is put in a pot with water and boiled, the fat being removed as it comes to the top. This is laid aside to cool and is the finished product.

8 July 1916
A portion of the memorial cross for the late Captain Swire arrived.

10 July 1916
Complaint by Kobbogo headman that certain men refuse to recognize his authority and, when called upon for labour, refuse. In future, these passive resisters are to come before the DC's court to give explanation or excuse for their refusal.

12 July 1916
Issued four gun licences. There are still many inhabitants who have failed to take out licences and even yet they appear to be unable to understand that licences must be renewed yearly. Some have migrated to outlying villages, others declared and in some cases produced, burst guns. Spoke to the headman about the importance of gun owners notifying the DC as to their change of residence and bringing in their guns when they are spoiled for purposes of correction in the register.

20 July 1916
Left Jefisi and arrived Bellu. Heard complaint of chief of Bellu against four of his headmen who, the chief stated, refused to recognize his authority. One of the headmen has run away into French country; the others adopted an unrepentant attitude. The chief of Bellu is, in my opinion, one of the most efficient in the district. I upheld his authority by allowing him to fine the offenders 5/– each and warned the headmen that further justified complaints against them would entail their removal from the town. Collected some gun licences, but the majority of the gun owners on the register appear either to have gone into French territory or otherwise disappeared.

9 August 1916
Chief of Tumu asked permission to drink fetish to discover the perpetrator of a theft from the house of Amadu Fulani, which took place over a week ago and was never reported by the victim. Informed them that I had little faith in their methods of detection of crime and that the possibility of discovery of the thief would have been greater if they

had reported the matter properly. However, permission to drink fetish was given with the warning as to the consequences of any fatal results.

12 August 1916[25]
Nothing of importance to record. Ag DC sick with fever.

14 August 1916
Ag DC resumes. Paid detachment second week's pay.

1 September 1916
During the last five days no less than 1304 cattle have come into Tumu. This is a record for any month since the trade returns have been kept. The sudden influx, I imagine, is due to the settlement of the troubles in French territory. The amount of traders visiting Tumu during the last month has been more encouraging. There is very little accommodation for these petty traders, the caravanserai being full up, also the houses of the Hausa settlers. Billets have had to be found in the market stalls. It would be a good thing for trade, I think, to encourage the building of a Hausa *zongo* on a much larger scale. There are several Hausa settlers here and I am assured by them in conversation that more traders would come and settle if there was a Hausa *zongo* and automatically the market, which is so lamentably poor at present, would improve.

5 September 1916
Lately, the market has presented quite an encouraging appearance. Formerly, it was unusual to observe more than two or three old ladies selling groundnuts and, possibly, a petty trader or two with a small display of beads and cloth. It was seldom worth while for the butcher to kill any meat and the average monthly slaughter of cows for meat was about four. All this has changed in the last few days.

9 September 1916
Left Tumu in morning for Kassano. Bush track much overgrown and must be cleared next month. Going very bad in places, particularly at the River Kassienpur, the approach to which was a mass of soft mud in which the ponies and carriers could get no foothold and floundered about in a helpless manner. The river itself was out of a man's depth and flowing fairly swiftly. Those who could, swam it. The others and loads were balanced on top of large hollow calabashes and pushed across by a man swimming. In three-quarters of an hour the crossing was effected without mishap, although there were some exciting moments when the calabashes with their human freight got carried down the stream.

The chief reported his people all well. He has great hopes for a particularly good harvest. His only complaint was that one of his people had found a roan antelope, killed by a lion, and had refused to give him any of the meat. He was given permission to fine the man 5/– as compensation. Lions are very plentiful in this neighbourhood and the villagers get a certain amount of meat by going out after a kill and robbing the lions of their prey. No one in the village has a gun but they drive the lion off by fire and beating of drums.

Sunday 10 September 1916
Inspected constabulary lines; £200 specie arrived from Wa; carriers with memorial cross [for Captain Swire's grave] arrived from Wa.

18 October 1916
Issued passes to about a score of Wala boys who were going to French country to buy cattle etc. They had been up there before and the French commissioner had told them that it is well that they had papers, as conscription was in force. He also told them to bring dane guns with them and use them if his people interfered with their property. Some 79 Dagartis pass through for work in Coomassie.

Wuchiau, 22 October 1916
Came up here this morning, a short journey of seven miles. This is a fairly large Wala town for these parts and boasts a mosque and Mohammedan population of about 60. The census of the town is taken and the usual subjects discussed. There are no complaints except that the people ask that they may be given some time before they pay their gun licences. They are told that they have had already ten months grace this year and they must pay at once, also that their French neighbours have to pay a tax of 5/– for each compound, so they may consider themselves lucky.

23 October 1916
On leaving Dunyari, I was accompanied on my way with song and dance by an old lady of venerable appearance and surprising agility. The song, it appeared, related at some length the history of Babatu as applied to the locality and results of the coming of the white man.

Sunday 29 October 1916
[Toppo] is a large place and thickly peopled. The census is taken, showing 200 able-bodied men. As Berkeley [PC] has made frequent remarks on the difficulty of getting labour in these parts I told them I would not have amenable people like the Walas and Issalas doing all the work. They quite agreed. The chief wants a market started and says it will be a means of civilizing his wild boys, as strangers frequenting the market will teach them sense and tell them what they

do in other parts. A headman is appointed to look after the market and the chief harangues the audience on the subject and asks them to bring in food supplies for sale.

Charria, 30 October 1916
We came on to Sankana this morning where the chief of that place and Samatigu met me. Both men of striking presence, being close to seven feet tall each, and trying to get their people in order, but the material will not always bow their way. There is a large market at Sankana and it is on one of the main trade routes from the north. The census of Samatigu is taken and the usual subjects discussed with a large assemblage, amongst whom were many well-dressed men. Altogether, in spite of the lack of discipline and sense of responsibility, the people look very prosperous. They want one more tornado so that their farms may put them in the lap of luxury.

8 November 1916
Held a meeting with Mohammedans. The literature sent to me by the CC with reference to German anti-Islamic methods in East Africa is discussed. Malam Izaka says they all know that this is quite contrary to British ideas. They realize our policy is upholding of the law, encouragement of the general progress of the people, and to every class his creed. Malam Izaka then says that certain 'evilly disposed persons' were talking about the building of a school at Ja, for which he and other Mohammedans were supplying boys for work and spreading an idea that this was the thin edge of the wedge whereby their customs might vanish. I told him I was only too anxious to deal with such talkers. It is ridiculous to talk of England, who has for centuries ruled India, adopting any such foolish policy as suppressing native beliefs. Twenty-five Dagartis passed through for work in Coomassie.

27 November 1916
The chief of Dolbizan, who is very aged and sick and has not left his house for some time, asked to see the Ag DC. At the audience in his house, he informed me that he was very tired and thought that he would soon die. He wished to hand over the care of his people to Baduah, the CC's interpreter, on his death. The chief was informed that he had years of life before him yet, but that a record would he made of his wishes and Baduah's appointment considered in the event of his death.

17 March 1917
About 4.00 p.m. a plague of locusts was first seen coming down from the northeast in an enormous cloud driven apparently by a tornado, which was threatening in that direction. They passed south, only the

fringe settling at Somboro. Coming down into the valley, I rode right into the heart of the main body of the locusts. A rusty red blight was over the face of the country, as if a blast from some infernal furnace had escaped and withered everything iron red. For five miles I rode through swarms, but they were not staying. By midday, the stripped trees and shrubs, with an occasional gorged or disabled locust staggering on the ground below, were the only evidence of the visitation.

15 April 1916
The inhabitants of Dasima appeared to be very much occupied with iron smelting. There were eight forges working. A tremendous expenditure of energy appears to be necessary to produce very small results. The chief brought up one case only. The case of his runaway wife. The matter was again referred to the PC Wa, the King of Wa having already decided the case once. The chief was warned about the outbreak of smallpox at Nandom and Jefisi and given instructions with regard to isolation and segregation of cases. He appeared to think it was all a matter of fate whether the disease came to Dasima or not. The cattle at Dasima are still in fine condition. It was reported that cattle disease had broken out at Jefisi. The wretched condition of the children was especially remarkable. It was difficult to discover one who was not suffering from ophthalmia, or terrible sores and ulcers, or other infirmity. The town was, as usual, in a filthy condition and when this was demonstrated to the chief he remarked with undeniable truth that, in the eyes of the acting DC, it was undoubtedly filthy, but in the eyes of him and his people it was clean. Some attempt, however, was made to improve matters in the eyes of the acting DC.

(vi) E. G. Dasent, Ag DC, 1917–18

23 August 1917
During my tour of the northwest portion of the district, I have, according to instructions received barely three weeks ago, addressed recruiting meetings at every possible opportunity. On arriving at Tumu, received a wire stating that no further recruits are required for the present!

28 August 1917
Supervising the planting of young trees in the town.

5 October 1917
Completing monthly returns and report. Mail arrived from Wa, including English mail, the first for three weeks. I have received instructions from the Treasury to balance the cash book daily. Have received instructions to hold a board on the medical stores. I find this

somewhat of a problem as the medical ledger contains a great many signs that I do not understand.

21 November 1917
Left Tumu for Leo with the PC for a visit to Leo on the invitation of Monsieur Remond. The town of Leo is not much of an improvement on Tumu, but the station surroundings and buildings are far superior, and it is at once obvious that a certain degree of comfort and beauty may be the lot of the commissioner resident there.

22 November 1917
Left Leo for Tumu. Both the PC and myself were treated royally and with much hospitality.

30 December 1917
Ejisu to Burifo. The latter is fit accommodation for a king and situated on a fair sized hill commanding an excellent view of the Volta and surrounding country. The harmattan being rather strong, the hills in French country were very indistinct. I was introduced to the chief of Burifo, a man with many notches on his gun, as they would say in the States, who brought his people to dance for me. Having seen the performance, the word dance is a misnomer; it would be more correctly described as an acrobatic gymkhana.

31 December 1917
With regards to my remarks about the desolation of Tumu and the CC's marginal comment, I consider that Tumu has Bole beaten hollow. Taking one thing alone, the volume of trade passing through Bole is much greater than that which passes through Tumu, which alone gives it more interest; also, there is a better market at Bole and a more interesting Mohammedan population.

17 May 1918
At about 3.00 p.m. there was a great drumming and shouting in the town and a horseman came dashing up to tell me that a lion had killed a man out in a farm on the Kassano road. I proceeded there with all haste and, after following the spoor for some time, I discovered the remains of a young boy who had been partly devoured. From the condition of the body, it was evident that he had been killed in the early morning. There were no signs of his murderer, and the grass being 20-feet long made a search for him unpractical. The boy had certainly not been killed by a lion. I think he was killed by a half-grown leopard.

1 November 1918
Received information from MO, Wa, that Spanish influenza had

arrived at Bole. Put the town out of bounds for the constabulary and have given strict orders that no stranger is to enter any of the houses in the town, but to be confined to the caravanserai. Warned chiefs in district, explaining the symptoms and instructing them to at once report any outbreak.

4 November 1918
Received letter from Resident Leo that all roads into French country had been closed owing to an epidemic of *grippe* (I had forgotten this word), which has claimed numerous victims. Received wire yesterday stating that HE's visit was indefinitely postponed. I am afraid the people will now begin to wonder if there really is such a person or whether we merely invent him when we want to get extra work done. Dispatched messenger to stop all building of temporary houses.

11 November 1918
Received wire by special runner from Wa informing me of the excellent news that an armistice had been declared. The caravanserai and marketplace both very dead now that no traders are passing through. Doubt if there can be a more deadly uninteresting town in the NT – I mean towns at which there is a station – than Tumu.

(vii) E. O. Rake, DC, 1919

17 February 1919
Spent most of the day in the office reading the record book etc. and refreshing my memory as to the political conditions in the district. Vast changes have occurred in the station and district. The station is now supplied with a house worthy of a district HQ and living conditions have improved out of all recognition.

20 February 1919
After the busy days at Bawku, where every morning was spent hearing numerous complaints and several mornings a week investigating charges of sheep and goat stealing and other criminal offences, it is difficult at first to get accustomed to this peaceful district inhabited by people without guile. How does one account for it? Are the Issala and Grunshi really morally superior to the Kussi? The latter would appear to be superior in every other way. I used to think at Bawku that the sheep stealing etc. was natural, owing to the system of allowing livestock to stray promiscuously, but the same system is in vogue here and the Issalas have the same temptations. I regret the old Bawku days. At present, there is a good deal of labour supervision to do and plenty of occupation to be found in bringing oneself up to date in the office.

Later will come the pleasanter task of travelling and returning the visits of the chiefs.

22 February 1919
A good well has been completed for the natives of the town nearest the cantonments. It is to be hoped that the effect of drinking good water, after what they have been accustomed to, will not be serious in its results. This well has been dug by the inhabitants of the compounds in question with the help of a supervisor supplied by government. It is very popular and it seems strange that the people have not the initiative to dig wells for themselves, instead of being content with digging up a few drops of muddy stinking water from an old water hole that has been discarded as a washing place by humans and a drinking place by beasts.

Sunday 23 February 1919
Inspected lines and stables and marked out site for constabulary kitchen. The harmattan is in its most annoying form today. A thick haze and an intermittent blustering breeze, which brings no coolth. [French] Resident Leo sent kindly some banana suckers for planting in the station. These are most welcome as strangely enough there are no mature banana trees here.

18 March 1919
Arrived at Bellu, being met on the road by the chief with his following including, as usual, his small son mounted on a fiery steed acting as chief's galloper. All reported well, except that the cattle are suffering from lack of grazing. A tornado in evening, little rain, but sufficient to produce that most delicious of African smells, moist earth after pitiless months of a parching sun.

21 March 1919
Came via Bakelembele to Gigan. The chief had little to say at first and no complaints. He got more conversational later, touching on the subject of the depredations of lions and leopards and the influenza as it affected the marriage question. The lions and leopards continue to take an enormous toll of livestock and the hunters attribute their ill success in their efforts against these pests to the disfavour of their fetish. It appears that so many fowls have been sacrificed to appease the spirit of the victims of influenza, over 30 in this small village, that there are not sufficient left to do justice in a fitting manner to the demands of the hunters' fetish. With regard to the marriage question, the chief suggested that it was a serious matter that so many of his youngmen were without wives owing to the mortality and he was apprehensive of the future. I could find no solution to meet the case

beyond suggesting that, for the sake of the future of the race, all those fortunate people with more than one wife should give up the surplus for fair distribution among the unfortunate bachelors. This was naturally a suggestion not welcomed.

Nabolo, 29 March 1919
Received letter from MO at Lorha with news of the spread of cerebro-spinal disease and asking me to establish a sanitary cordon between the two districts. Locusts arrived at 5.00 p.m. from the west. The sky was red with them in every direction by 5.30. They appeared to be travelling in a southeasterly direction.

17 April 1919
Proceeded by a bush track to Sekai. At Sekai, the iron smelters and blacksmiths were very busy coping with the demand for new season's hoes. Strings of women and small children coming in with baskets of ironstone and charcoal. There were six forges working and it is no light labour. For a short time at any rate, no one could work harder than these natives.

Tumu, 7 May 1919
The whole population of the town, and that of most of the surrounding villages, is today gathered together to mourn the death of a young man. Yesterday everybody was very busy on their farms, today they have downed tools without a thought of their farming prospects and they will not take them up again for three days when the funeral rites are finished. This man was not a chief or a headman, but his death is the signal for a funeral holiday, with the accompaniment of feasting, drumming, music and howling. This sort of thing happens daily all over the district and might possibly be one of the causes of the annual hunger, which is always complained of at this time of year.

25 May 1919
Planted various tree seeds, vegetables and pawpaws round rest house and made a small garden. Visited CSM Seriki John pensioner, GCR, totally disabled. He was well and learning to get about a bit better on his crutches. He complained of fever and pain in his wounds and was given some quinine.

(viii) Lieutenant Colonel P. F. Whittall, DSO, 1919

23 July 1919
Took over the station. I noticed at the meeting of chiefs yesterday a peculiar apathy with regard to their affairs. Even the promise of cows to eat and unlimited *pito* for the peace celebrations did not meet with

even a politely interested murmur. The really interesting item of the day was listening to Mr Rake trying to sort out the accounts before handing over, as the clerk did not seem to have grasped the unusual situation caused by settling up for the month on the 23rd.

24 July 1919
After a night disturbed by the howling of hyenas and the baying of hunting dogs I had a final look round with Rake and he departed in quite good spirits after lunch.

11 October 1919
Arranged the remaking of Captain Swire's grave. I hope, by digging a hole 18 inches deep and two feet wider than the present grave and filling this carefully with laid stones to make a foundation, that will not fall in. It is going to be troublesome to mend the cross owing to having no tool that will drill rock.

Lorha, North Western Province[26]

(i) A. H. C. Walker Leigh, DC, 1913–14

10 November 1913
Trekked to Babile, made a surprise visit to market at Babile. Very large attendance, should say 1000 people; did not find a single bow and arrow in the market. Market shed burned in bush fire. Ordered Mohammedans, who use them, to rebuild at once. Inspected town.

12 November 1913
MO down with fever. Temperature 103 this morning. Mounted the guard. Went to hospital.

14 November 1913
Took hospital for MO who is still down with fever. Wrote Gawa[27] re yellow fever. English mail out. Three carriers sent to Tamale to bring nickel money. Getting thorns to make cattle kraal lion proof.

16 November 1913
MO still down with fever. Took hospital. Letter from French re yellow fever answered. Sent one constable to Sabuli to bring in timber, rebuilding of MO's house being delayed owing to its non arrival. Had prisoner's clothes washed.

18 November 1913
Rode out to inspect north road, found it clean. MO convalescent. Not up yet. Took hospital. Getting gradually a list of lepers in Lorha sub-division.

27 November 1913
MO writes advocating sanitary precautions on account of yellow fever. A quarantine to be established and traders medically examined.

28 November 1913
Constabulary holiday. Inspection of carbines; 198 loads of grass came in from Denyi of Nandom; 26 loads from Kokolobu. Tie-tie[28] from Lorha subdistrict, 12 baulks in from near Yaga.

Sunday 30 November 1913
Rode to Furo to choose site for proposed masonry bridge, if cement is forthcoming. Paid off carriers from Zini, who had gone sick on road. Looked at quarantine camp, about 25 people let go through.

1 December 1913
Moshis up from *zongo* to help put grass on MO's house. Letter from Ag PC Wa relating to an outbreak of cerebrospinal meningitis at Iziri and Tangisa. Diverting the caravans from infected areas.

Christmas Day, Thursday 25 December 1913
MO returned from trek. Holiday for Europeans. Sent out one corporal and one man to Arrumon to find the corpse of a murdered Moshi. Corpse brought in after dinner, beaten to death with axes.

31 December 1913
Reports and returns. Helped MO to give chloroform to Dobo while he cut off two fingers. Board on treasury 2.00 p.m. These boards may be all right for treasurers who have nothing else to do but accounts, but at the very busiest time of the year they are a great hindrance to the DC in the NT and keep the clerk from getting at his returns.

Wa, 25 January 1914
Had operation on my throat by Dr Patton.

26 January 1914
Remained at Wa to see how throat was going on.

28 January 1914
Trekked to Nandaw. Did not have enough food for my carriers.

5 February 1914
Had to get nails for the MO's house made out of old pick axes.

7 February 1914
Owing to shortage of nails, I had to send a man eight miles to look in the bed of a river, where a bridge had been burnt, in the hope of getting some. A carrier was sent to Tamale 20 days ago for a load of nails. If he arrives without any, the rain will come and ruin all the

work that has been done, as it is quite impossible to put on a roof without nailing on the baulks and rafters.

2 March 1914
Took all mounted men on early parade to try and get them into shape. Carpenter begins to pull roof off court. Bugler fined 10/– for being drunk. A man up for selling diseased meat, fined £1. Afternoon checking money and enquiry into Dorku palaver.

4 March 1914
Mounted parade in morning. Corson's carriers in, this will be 5/– a day on to my transport owing to Oakley not coming when expected. The carriers must be paid as they have no food. Have to put off my trek now owing to the same cause.

5 March 1914
Chief of Sabuli in with cotton, sent sample to Tamale; 17 guns licensed. Oakley due Saturday, so I can get away on Sunday.[29]

23 March 1914
Lion roaring at night. Shot a roan antelope. Carriers having a day off and self washing clothes.

25 March 1914
Sent message for my ponies to come. Message miscarried, so I stayed another day.

26 March 1914
Ponies still not arriving, so started on my feet to Nandaw, but luckily met ponies after walking five miles. Arrived Nandaw. No water in Kulpawn [River] here. A lioness killed in the town four days ago. She was on a donkey and a hunter managed to get his gun against her before she saw him.

13 April 1914
[DC] back on duty. One criminal case dealt with. Work on garden well and new roof for hospital being got ready. Tied up again for want of nails.

(ii) Dr P. D. Oakley, Ag DC, 1914

23 May 1914
Bought 50 lbs cotton from chief of Nandaw. Rode out to Konyekwong to inspect the place where the bridge was. Found that nearly all the timber had been stolen.

24 May 1914
Rain fell all night. Sides of new well fell in.

26 May 1914
Heard that six carriers had run away from Major Leigh and had returned to Ulu. Sent out constable to arrest them.

22 June 1914
Made preparations for reception of CC. Fined nuisance case. All mammies in the lines fined 1/– each for not cleaning.

23 June 1914
CC, Captain Armitage, accompanied by PC Major Mountray Read, arrived Lorha from Girapa on tour of inspection. All paramount chiefs turned out to meet him. The CC held a palaver at 5.00 p.m. They had no complaints and all appeared quite contented. The CC received numerous presents of sheep and Guinea corn.

25 June 1914
Sold 23 sheep belonging to the CC. Sent vouchers for £200 to Tumu by post to post. Sitting in court in morning. CC and PC left in afternoon for Kamba. I rode out with them and returned the same night.

2 July 1914
River rose rapidly during the night. Evidently heavy rain is falling up north, but Lorha seems to escape. Everything in the garden suffering from the dry atmosphere and all the farms appear to be at a standstill. The people here say that the chief of Lorha is stopping the rain and you cannot get them to think anything else.

3 July 1914
Sitting in office checking gun returns. Issued one gun licence. Very large flock of crested cranes passed close to station. Well in garden now completed, so I have to put the mason on to making bricks for the new stables for the Europeans' horses. Still working at gun returns.

7 July 1914
Inspected the town and found everything correct. The headmen from Nandaw came in and I attempted to find out who would be the best man for the stool. They said the son, Bayor, is the man, but as he is after the village idiot type, I am writing to the PC in regard to the matter.

23 July 1914
Complaint from the Hausa people at Konyekwong that the Dapola people had driven them from the marketplace and beaten them and that one woman had been chased into the river and drowned. Took

all the evidence I could get and wrote to the PC, Wa, and the French Resident Gawa. Gave orders that no French people were to be allowed in Lorha market until further orders and no English people were to go into French country. Rain threatened but passed off.

24 July 1914
Nice rain fell in the morning for two hours, but it was not very heavy.

27 July 1914
Received letter and some vegetables from Gawa. Monsieur Labouret informs me that he is proceeding to Dapola to make enquiries into the matter of people being driven out. Sent post to post to Dapola asking Monsieur Labouret to visit me in Lorha. Received letter saying he would lunch with me tomorrow. It appears that there is trouble in Dapola and that he has taken 70 soldiers with him. Planted out lime seeds in garden.

28 July 1914
Made preparations for reception of Lieutenant Labouret, who arrived at 10.30 accompanied by one soldier and the chief of Dapola. He informed me that he had fined the people nine head of cattle for compensation and the people appeared satisfied; 320 cattle arrived from French country. English mail arrived 10.00 p.m.

29 July 1914
Sitting in court writing numerous letters. Interviewed the Hausa people from Konyekwong, who appeared more than pleased at the termination of the Dapola affair. They had been given some very nice cows, many of which were in calf. The man whose wife was drowned received three head of cattle, one bull and two cows and was extremely satisfied. Heard two minor complaints. Warned a constable to be ready to start on patrol tomorrow to watch the markets and see that the Moshi people are paying good money for their food. No more rain.

13 August 1914
Issued constabulary clothing. Slight harmattan blowing, I do not think we shall get any more rain this year. Chief of Lorha is very busy offering up black fowls to bring rain.

15 August 1914
Balanced cash book. Inspected town. Heard nuisance case. Fined defendant 2/6*d*. Listened to complaints. Some 54 cattle arrived from French country. Rain threatened in evening, but although it was raining all round Lorha, not a drop fell here.

Sunday 16 August 1914
Received runners from Diebougou and later from Tumu with war news. Rain again threatened, but did not fall. Very cold in evening.

18 August 1914
Tornado broke at 6.00 p.m. and it was still raining at 10.00 p.m. Very heavy rain indeed. MO's house more like a miniature lake than anything. English mail arrived at 5.00 p.m.

19 August 1914
Chief of Lorha came up to say that he had brought the rain at last, was told to go away and not be silly. Sitting in court till morning listening to palavers.

5 September 1914
Heard case against a Moshi for stealing from a farm. Wrote to PC for permission to flog.[30] Gave Ulu some cotton seed. Balanced cash book.

9 September 1914
English mail arrived. Sitting in court answering letters and queries, no complaints. Received news that the Germans were only 60 miles from Paris, so the good reports we get from the French must be slightly incorrect.

10 September 1914
Sitting in court. Weekly letters. No complaints to listen to. The Moshi man flogged 12 lashes for stealing from a farm.

(iii) A. C. P. Duncan-Johnstone, Ag DC, 1917[31]

23 October 1917
Konyekwong from Lorha. Found seven cases of smallpox. Selected site for isolation camp downstream below the crossing, so that water will not be fouled. Put Jatto, hospital boy, in charge of the camp. This is the first real bit of work he will have had for some time. However, his enforced idleness at 25/– a month in Lorha, owing to lack of drugs, is not his fault and he is quite keen. Had sheds for patients erected, houses for those who will took after them and a latrine dug. Closed road north of Konyekwong and south of Babile by putting out patrols. Also put a cordon of mounted men round infected area. This may be in time to localize the outbreak. Sent for headman of Babile and asked him why he had not reported the outbreak of sickness. He said he thought I would hear of it at Lorha. He told me that a man had died four days ago. Rode to Babile in afternoon. I found that the death occurred in the headman's house itself. This conduct is in contrast of the headman of Konyekwong, who is alert and willing to

do all in his power. In this, he is helped and advised by an ex-sergeant of the regiment who lives here and appears to be the headman's right-hand man. Heavy tornado in evening. The isolation camp should be finished tomorrow and have arranged to have all the sick transferred there. Am handicapped by want of drugs, of which I have only quinine and some carbolic disinfectant.

24 October 1917
Passed a miserable night, washed out of my tent by a tornado. Rain came down in torrents, ruining everything. Felt more cheerful when the sun came out. The court interpreter, whom I sent to Burifo yesterday, returned and said that the sickness was reported from 80 compounds there and that four people were already dead. The son of the headman who came in said that this had been reported some days ago to the chief of Lorha. Rode over to Burifo across country, going very heavy and half the way through swamp. Selected site for isolation camp on slope of a small hill away from the compounds and near water. The disease has attacked 80 compounds, but I am unable so far to ascertain total number of cases. Also selected site for a rest house on a big bluff overlooking the town and commanding a fine view of the surrounding country. There is a spring nearly at the bottom of the bluff. Am putting up a temporary rest house of *zana* mats. This afternoon, Lance Corporal Alheri Dagarti, who was ordered by Sergeant Musa Grunshi to accompany me to Burifo, ran up and said he couldn't go as he had never had smallpox and was afraid. Sent him into Wa to be vaccinated. The remainder of my force, fortunately, do not show such a craven spirit and are very keen and conscientious.

25 October 1917
Mail arrived from Wa. Rode out to Tanchera in the morning. The people have had the 'nous' to make an isolation camp there. I found the patients, however, shut up in small stifling grass huts, the entrance closed, excluding all fresh air and sunlight, the chief enemy of the microbe. One patient, a boy of about 14, was rolled up in a mat like a corpse, already nearly dead and quite unconscious, his body a mass of running scabs. Marked out a new camp with proper houses, latrines etc. This should be ready tomorrow. Returned to Konyekwong. Have now 12 patients in hospital and they are all as comfortable as possible. Dosed them all with five grain tabloid of quinine, which is all that I have got. So far, I have found the people of Konyekwong, Babile and Tanchera very amenable and ready to follow out what is explained to them. I am afraid, however, that there will be some difficulty with the Burifo people, who have already attempted to conceal the sickness and are not at all agreeable to the idea of an

isolation camp. Have sent into Lorha for the head scavenger, a sensible man, to come out and look after the camp at Burifo. Have had the cordon round the infected area flagged with small red flags to mark it and a red flag has been placed in every infected house. It is difficult to locate all the compounds, owing to the corn, which completely hides them. Headman of Tanchera reports that the boy I saw this morning has just died. This brings the number of known deaths, so far, up to seven. The chief of Burifo's son came in this evening and reports that a girl has died there. Also that, with the exception of five compounds, the people have refused to turn out and work on the isolation camp. I don't know what we should have done without the help of the Mohammedan community of Konyekwong Hausa, Wangaras and Bazabarimas who, led by Alhajj Abdul Hamid, have turned up trumps. With the exception of the clearing, they have built the whole of the isolation camp and rest house here and today went over to help at Burifo, laden with *zana* mats.

Friday 26 October 1917
Another death reported from Burifo. This makes nine so far. Visited isolation camp here, 12 patients installed. Dosed them with Dover's powder and five grains of quinine each, to follow after an interval. Returned to Konyekwong in the evening. Have spent the last four days in the saddle and feel very fit. There is no doubt that hunger is the best cook, as the Hun says. The whole neighbourhood resounds to the beating of the melodious Lobi xylophone marking the different funeral customs. Thank goodness they don't drum.

28 October 1917
Am now awaiting an answer from the PC to whom I wrote suggesting vaccination. Can do no more at present. Rode over to Burifo camp in evening. Rode over to isolation camp in afternoon. Luckily, the sickness seems to be staying inside the cordon, as no cases have been reported outside it. There are 32 cases in camp here and 96 suspects in quarantine. The remaining 170 odd have all recovered and, as I have no room for them in camp, had them all disinfected by washing them with carbolic disinfectant and sending them home. The smell in camp is rather overpowering, as the people are very dirty when they come in. One feels most sorry for the children who are very stolid and patient.

29 October 1917
Received a letter from Ag PC, Wa, informing me that the MO left Wa yesterday and will arrive at Yaga on 30th, where I am to meet him. No new cases reported yesterday and sickness does not appear to be spreading.

31 October 1917
Dr Whyte arrived from Nadaw. He tells me that he has only enough vaccine for 200 people and that he doubts its efficacy as it is old. Disappointing. There is one thing that this outbreak of smallpox has brought about and that is it has enabled me to get more into touch with the riverside people, being continuously among them, and in and out of the villages and isolation camps, I have seen more of them during the last ten days than I could in normal times. So out of evil has come forth a little good.

1 November 1917
Went over with the MO to the isolation camp in evening. Jatto complained that some of the partially recovered patients had bolted back to their compounds the night previous. This is exactly what one seeks to prevent. But how?

3 November 1917
A woman died this morning here. She had been hidden in a compound for four days since the disease attacked her. Chief of Lorha sends me a message that one of his people has gone mad. Yesterday the man went mad and tried to run amok. They shut him up, but during the night he escaped, saying he would kill everyone he met. Some men followed him, but were unable to catch him while he taunted from a distance saying, 'You waste your time. Don't you know I am not a man but a ghost? I died a week ago from witchcraft and I am going to find out who did it.' Told the chief to tell his people to keep out of the lunatic's way until I returned. Collected about 300 people, mostly women and children who had not been inoculated or had smallpox, and got them to come to be vaccinated. After about 230 had been done, the vaccine ran out. Some of the children were very amusing and most of them very good. Mothers brought babies in wicker cradles of the type in which Moses made his first voyage.

Sunday 4 November 1917
Another case reported from Furo and one from Barewo. There are 83 cases now in the isolation camp here. Dr Whyte estimates that 95 per cent of the cases in Burifo are caused by people inoculating themselves. Mail arrived. Tornado in evening.

Monday 5 November 1917
Konyekwong from Burifo. One new case reported here. Dr Whyte inspected isolation camp, now 22 patients. Issued passes to some Mohammedan traders who wanted to proceed to Coomassie. They were all passed by the doctor and had had the disease. Passes were given to them, showing right thumb in black ink. These passes are

collected by the sentries and returned to me. Every person allowed out has to wash himself and his clothes thoroughly, under a guard, and then proceed directly without entering any house again.

6 November 1917
Before leaving, Dr Whyte vaccinated 240 people belonging to neighbourhood. Total vaccinated now 607.

Navarro, North Eastern Province[32]

(i) H. M. Berkeley, Ag PC, 1913–14

Sunday 14 December 1913
Received visit from Roman Catholic Mission fathers — both looking extremely ill, especially Father Doryon, who tells me he went up to 107 with sun fever. Marvellous how he is still alive, as he always looks as if he is at death's door.

16 December 1913
Had a long interview with the chief as to the disposal of his property after his death. He informs me he has already allotted all his cattle and sheep to various members of his family. He is also reported to have a large amount of cash buried in his compound. But this he denies. He has never been known to spend any money, even his meat and salt are obtained by being in the market.

25 December 1913
Christmas Day. Office closed.

29 December 1913
Constabulary and station staff paid off. Gauri of Navarro charged with stealing a cow, and a Moshi brought in charged with stealing from a dwelling house. The chief and headmen of Navarro came in. I am under the impression that all the funds paid to the various headmen for distribution among their people for road cleaning, bridging etc. has been taken from them by the chief, who is reported to bury all his money.

1 January 1914
Mr Addy, the only clerk in the station, left for Zouaragu to sit on board of Medical Stores. This arrangement of leaving the station without a clerk at all is most inconvenient. He cannot get back before the night of 3rd at the earliest and everything is at a standstill in the meantime. I cannot think that the Colonial Secretary, when issuing these instructions, was aware that there was only one clerk in this district for duty in the PC's office and constabulary office.

12 January 1914
Dr Allen arrived from Zouaragu. He tells me Lieutenant Magee came up from Yeji to Yapei on the river. I was not aware that this route was at present available for regular transport of Europeans. And, in consequence, carriers sent for Mr Ievers have been directed to go to Salaga. The awful trek up to these parts has now lost half its terrors; in fact, now it is quite a pleasant journey with sufficient change to prevent it becoming monotonous.

13 January 1914
Dr Whyte at Bawku seems to be having a lot of trouble with fines for carrying lethal weapons. He has been told to fine only those who carry poisoned weapons in public markets.

22 January 1914
A very long and tiresome case between a male RC convert and a pagan girl who had been married according to the rights of the RC Church. The ceremony, to start with, was not binding in any way as far as the girl is concerned and she refuses to return. She states the RC missionaries married her without first obtaining the consent of her parents, who objected at the time. She told them that they did not, but, for all that, the RC missionaries should certainly have interviewed the head of the girl's family. The ceremony itself also appears to have been very irregular. The Father Superior, according to the convert, gave away the girl, none of the responsible members of the girl's family being present.

24 January 1914
In order to get some idea of the exact fighting strength of Navarro, all the headmen were called in and told to bring with them on Monday everyone who would be willing to turn out and defend their homes and women.

26 January 1914
None of the actual people who would be required to form a defensive force turned up, although 300 elders did so. They tell me the people won't come, as they imagine I have some ulterior motive in view, conscription probably, the French having just introduced it in these parts.

27 January 1914
Chief of Sandema interviewed about the 25 recruits wanted for the constabulary. He is told to produce two from each of his ten towns.

10 February 1914
The MO detained three constables to inspect compounds in Navarro and report to him any case of sickness, which he would examine. One

constable dispatched to Paga and the boundary to inspect the traders and report if any had smallpox. A constable has been placed in charge of contagious diseases hospital, with instructions to drive off any who come near it and to see that the patients get their food and water from the allotted place where they are gathered. Another constable detailed for guard in the caravanserai to prevent all traders passing through the station until seen by the MO. The MO is of the opinion that the smallpox must have been conveyed into Navarro by traders infected with the disease who slept in, or brought food from, the infected compound six weeks ago.

(ii) Captain H. T. C. Wheeler, Ag PC, 1914

7 May 1914
Local interest is at present largely centred on the NT topographical survey. In addition to the fact that the call for carriers and labour is bringing home to the neighbourhood the fact that the resources of science are at present engaged in mapping the land of their forefathers, the erection of a beacon has been a source of wonder to the adult population, while the operation of the theodolite on the village green has provided amusement for the children.

16 May 1914
Belated parcels, mail and several mailbags came in after going to Gambaga by mistake. Good rain in the night; people are now encouraged to plant their seeds.

18 May 1914
Very busy looking after the survey. In addition to finding carriers for their present needs, one is kept quite actively engaged in listening to complaints, often desertion of carriers, often the task of endeavouring to catch and suitably punish the deserter, sympathizing with the Director of Surveys and sharing his speculations as to when he will ever get his loads up etc. Mail in and mail out.

20 May 1914
Carpenter sent out to repair canoes at the ferries in Zouaragu and Navarro districts. Two constables sent out to repair bridges and surface of Sambruno and Paga roads. The presence in our midst of a motor bicycle[33] and sidecar, with a three-foot wheel base, has brought to light details of construction of our roads not previously so noticeable.

2 June 1914
Two more runaway carriers brought in and sentenced.

4 June 1914
£50 specie arrived from Zouaragu last night. Continuous rain yesterday and today. Growth of crops should be assured now. Great change in appearance of country in a short ten days. Paid out office staff etc.

8 June 1914
A common form of complaint here is for a practically naked member of local society to complain that when purchasing a penny worth of, say groundnuts in some local market, he has been robbed of some sum, out of all proportion to what a gentleman in his station of life is likely to be in a position to go marketing with. I have felt obliged to suggest that, before risking his fortune in this way, a native should come to the DC for advice. I propose suggesting that sufficient only for the day's marketing (in most cases 2*d.*) should be taken and the remainder of the fortune left in some safe place at home.

16 July 1914
Dr Beal left the station for Churchiliga. From there he will continue his tour throughout Kanjarga country to investigate the anthrax. A constable of this detachment accompanies him as a forerunner to assemble cattle owners with their herds, for the veterinary officer to inspect the cattle and instruct the owners.

(iii) T. W. Breckenridge, Ag PC, 1914

15 December 1914
Took over charge of province from Captain Wheeler, PC, who left the station for England. Generally settling down. Interview with Navarro chief and Malam Longo.

18 December 1914
Reading up NT and provincial instructions. Visited site of old vegetable garden, where there is a permanent water supply, and decided to remake the garden at his spot.

19 December 1914
Correspondence. Gave out picks and shovels for cleaning out native water supply. General inspection of market and station. Discovered a supply of drugs in charge of a member of constabulary whose only experience is a first-aid course. As the drugs include a number of poisons, reported to MO Zouaragu.

23 December 1914
Paraded constabulary and their wives in connection with complaints re stopping of market produce on its way to market. One of the Catholic fathers reported down with blackwater.

25 December 1914
Christmas Day. Catholic father has a relapse.

26 December 1914
Criminal court and correspondence. Father much better.

11 March 1915
PC, provincial clerk and native court interpreter of the North Eastern Province arrived in this station this morning from tour. Two Tong Hills fetish priests, who are responsible for the shrine, have been brought in to stay in the town and report themselves in office every morning; also two Daraga men, who are the ringleaders of disobedience to the Nangodi chief, who are to stay in the guard-room.

22 March 1915
Interviewed Grunshi chiefs on question of cotton growing in old farms, on CC's reward to chiefs who will encourage their people to grow much cotton for 1916 cotton season, and also on the question of seniority of chiefs.

14 May 1915
Received wire instructing me to take over Zouaragu district from Dr Whyte, who is to proceed to Cameroons for service as MO. I am keeping the two stations open until further orders.[34]

(iv) A. L. Castellain, DC, 1915–16

6 August 1915
Arrived at the station today to take over the [combined] Navarro and Zouaragu districts from Breckenridge, who, by order of the CCNT and approval of HE, removed the headquarters to Gambaga.

1 September 1915
Heard complaint made by the chief butcher that his head wife bites him and burns his clothes occasionally. Warned the lady to desist from this practice.

23 September 1915
DC and clerk arrived at Navarro. The bridges over the streams at sixth and eighth mileposts were both about two feet under water, but the journey was accomplished without any mishaps. There had been very heavy rain during the night and early morning, accompanied by a strong wind, which did great damage to the buildings. The whole of the MO's bungalow had fallen down: fortunately, he had had it shored up two days previously, and so the roof did not fall in. The

DC's kitchen was level with the ground and three huts in the constabulary lines suffered similarly. English mail arrived.

23 December 1915
DC proceeded to Navarro to interview the inhabitants and inform them that if they interfered in any way with my constables or messengers they would be very severely dealt with. I then rode about the place and, when nearing the French boundary, all the people left their compounds and ran across into French territory. I then returned to Bongo having been in the saddle seven hours.

22 January 1916
Held auction sale of government cattle. Heard numerous minor complaints. Issued several gun licences (renewals) and on my asking where they got their gunpowder from, was shown some local product. It is much finer than the ordinary gunpowder and looked as if it was made of charcoal. A sergeant of French constabulary arrived with a note from the Resident at Leo, asking me to hand over the five youths who had crossed the frontier to avoid enlistment. I took them to the frontier and handed them over there.

27 January 1916
Court messenger returned and reported that the people he went to summon assaulted him, cutting open his head with a stick, and the woman who went to point out the person required was hit over the hand and had a bone broken. Proceeded at once to Pagubru and arrested three men and seized seven cattle belonging to the offender.

28 January 1916
Held auction of cattle seized yesterday and realized £16. The long delayed English mail arrived, 19 days having elapsed since the arrival of the last mail.

1 April 1916
The son of the chief of Kanjarga came in to report that one of his people has boxed his wife's ears and that the woman had not been able to eat for three days. I sent out a constable at once to bring in both the lady and her husband. When they arrived, the lady was taken to the MO who reported her jaw was dislocated on both sides and he immediately put it back in its proper place, much to the delight of the lady and surprise of others standing by. The woman denies that her husband struck her, and the MO says it could not have happened from a box on the ears. The woman says she fell, but there is no mark on her, but as she is quite all right now. I discharged the husband.

14 April 1916
Left Sandema for Churchiliga. The old chief and his followers came out to meet me, but on account of his old age, told him that in future he could meet me at the foot of the hill leading to the rest house.

15 April 1916
Arrived back at Navarro and found several criminal cases waiting investigation. These are postponed till Monday as the mail has to be attended to and the diary typed, and I have only one clerk at present.

21 April 1916
Messenger arrived from Bongo during the night and reported that two sections there had fought with bows and arrows on account of a dispute as to whom the land belonged and that ten men, including the chief, had been wounded. The detachment from Zouaragu went out and tried to stop the fighting. I sent out the corporal and three men to make arrests and to remain on the spot till I can get there. Unfortunately I cannot leave till Dr Whyte goes, as he has to be settled up with. The messenger reported all quiet when he left and considered if five more constables were at Bongo the fighting would not be resumed.[35] Busy in court all day hearing three criminal cases.

11 June 1916
A long trek through the bush to Nakong. In the evening, I rode down to inspect the ferry. There is a good canoe there. On my return, I found a constable had arrived from Navarro with my mail and also brought word that Sergeant Mania Chakosi, who is stationed at Bongo, had gone out to arrest one of the Naruga ringleaders, but had been attacked and withdrew having sent in to Zouaragu for more constables. About 11.15 p.m. a mounted orderly arrived with a message saying that there had been further trouble at Naruga and that Constable Salape Fra Fra had been killed and the sergeant wounded in the knee, and that more constables had gone from Navarro to Bongo. I sent off a mounted messenger at once, reporting the matter to Commissioner, NEP, and asking for more constables. I also sent instructions that I would proceed without delay to Bongo and that the constabulary were to avoid any further hostilities until my arrival.

5 November 1916
Got a message from the district clerk at Zouaragu to say that some people at Separi were found on their way to Aragu, carrying bows and arrows. Proceeded to Aragu and Separi and found that the Separi people were on their way to make funeral custom at Aragu for one Abiga who died in September. Told them that I did not allow bows

and arrows and spears at funeral custom, and that they must in future, comply with that order.

(v) Captain S. D. Nash, DC, 1917

1 April 1917
Left Gawa this morning and visited Yaga and Vaga. Addressed a crowd there on the subject of recruiting. The people are told that the carrying of bows and arrows when not hunting is looked upon as quite unnecessary and must cease. Visited Zoko and arranged about the renewal of the rest house. Arrived Kanjarga 10.30 a.m. and in the afternoon the people are spoken to as above. As only the chief's section of Kanjarga were present in any numbers at this palaver the people of the other two sections were told to salute me at Navarro in proper numbers. Fear of being seized as recruits is given as the reason for the absence of the youngmen of these two sections. The people are told we don't seize boys for soldiers.

Navarro, 2 April 1917
We passed through Menge this morning and the usual subjects are discussed with a very large crowd of well-dressed people. There are a number of boys in these parts wearing white drill trousers and jackets. They have been to Coomassie earning money. The chief tells me they give no trouble and obey his orders.

4 April 1917
Many trivial cases came before the court, which at Wa would not have appeared. They would have been settled by the chiefs. Here they seem to be loth to settle matters through their chiefs and headmen.

7 April 1917
The French fathers visited me this afternoon and we discussed various matters. No mission school exists now through lack of funds owing to European war.[36] I promised to assist them with some timbers etc. to renew houses.

Sunday 8 April 1917
Went for a ride this morning round the country to view the nakedness of the land and, indeed, it is at present very naked. There is not a blade of grass anywhere, not even in the valleys, and cattle seem to exist in licking up the dried grass and other vegetation in the farms. They are all in very poor condition.

8 May 1917
None of our natives are now allowed to cross the frontier by the French. The whole line is patrolled. I thought at first the idea was to

stop our people buying food in the French markets. Food is scarce up there, as a number of villages have been destroyed between Leo and Wagadugu during the disturbances last year and much food burnt. The reason, however, is due to fear of plague spreading up there. Millions of locusts have evidently visited Navarro during our absence. Fortunately, none of the crops are up yet.

12 May 1917
Long talk to Navarro chief with respect to lack of food in the market. It is peculiar that, in spite of our long residence here, there has never been a voluntary market at Navarro.

Navarro, Sunday 13 May 1917
We came here this morning. Two minor civil cases gone into. The chief has no complaints, but he is a weak man and probably likes to sit down and watch the caravans pass by.

24 July 1917
A large recruiting campaign[37] is addressed by the CC and an appeal is made to the youngmen to come forward as recruits and to parents not to throw hindrances in their way. The chief of Navarro blames the old men and fathers of the boys and says they are advising the youngmen not to enlist. The chief of Kologu offers himself as a soldier. He is told that his loyal offer will be accepted if he can get 50 of his youngmen to join him.

17 August 1917
I was busy all day issuing summons to Navarro boys to appear before the court as recruits. The system is working well and the type of boys, as far as physique is concerned, is excellent. We have now collected the quota of Navarro boys allotted, viz 30. There had been no difficulty over the matter. It has taken just a week to collect this amount, as each individual case has to be enquired into, a sort of recruiting tribunal. At this rate, it may take me at least three months to collect the 250 asked for from this Navarro district.

21 August 1917
A letter is forwarded to me (through the PC) from the PMO Tamale. The PMO complains of the stamp of recruits inspected by him. Cripples, others practically blind with dense white opacities over the eyes, lepers and men with hardly a tooth or with half a foot missing, have, he says, appeared in front of him. I think these are terminological inexactitudes and, in any case, his remarks should be addressed to his medical confrère at Gambaga, as every recruit we have sent from this district to Tamale was first inspected by the MO Gambaga.

15 September 1917
A case comes in from Doninga re supposed refusal to accept nickel coinage. Other subsidiary matters are invariably mixed up in these cases, such as the price offered. I don't think that nickel coinage is refused, but undoubtedly people get food cheaper by the cowry exchange. Sergeant Dulugu Moshi arrives to inspect the carbines of the detachment. I superintend the maxim gun team at drill. I had lunch at the mission. Monsieur Remond had sent in some excellent wine for the occasion.

21 September 1917
I hear our French neighbours are raising the tax 50 per cent. A special war tax I believe.

25 September 1917
Monsieur Remond writes to me saying that I have been misinformed and that all the people called upon to pay the tax live on the French side of the frontier. I shall, however, draw my successor's notice to this matter, as it may still be possible that the French police have made a mistake. It can be cleared up as soon as the crops are all cut. Certainly, it seems peculiar that the natives don't yet know on which side of the frontier they live.

(vi) A. W. Cardinall, DC, 1919

10 March 1919
Heard a few minor complaints. The band that met me are singing I am informed, 'The white man went away, and now he has come back.' True of this part, which has been since July [without a DC].

11 March 1919
Received an extraordinary message from Zouaragu, apparently sent by the district clerk, Nelson, and consisting of a piece of iron decorated with fowl feathers. It was wrapped in a page of a 1912 scribbling diary and there was no writing accompanying it. Shall report on this after I have seen the sergeant at Zouaragu who gave it to the bearer. Several complaints and a case of cow theft heard. Lions are troubling the people.

12 March 1919
To Kanjarga. Yesterday's cow case resulted in a maze of perjury. Except for the theft, I can so far see no daylight.

13 March 1919
Asked to kill the lions. I pointed out people must help themselves. They have not burnt the grass this year owing to general laziness,

which influenza has enhanced, and I am not hunting lions in tall grass. There must be several about as a lot of cows have been killed.

3 September 1919

Last year Lady Clifford invited everyone to write an article illustrative of 'A day in our life on the Gold Coast'.[38] I refrained because if one was to write a faithful account of an average day here one would either appear as a modern Solomon or an incompetent idiot. Not presuming yet to be the former, I had no inclination to proclaim myself the latter. Today is a good example — there were three complaints. The first left me to decide the ownership of a sacrificial place, the chief professing he was unable to reach a conclusion. In the second, a young man brought to me his two brothers-in-law. They owed him head money. They had nothing at all to offer. The youth knew this, but his own father-in-law had taken back his daughter and threatened to sell her elsewhere unless he immediately paid head money. The girl refused to disobey her father's wishes. Therefore, the youth had to find money somewhere. It was up to me to show him the way. The last case was unusual. A young man sought to recover his wife. He lived at Naja and she had been taken by a Balingo man. No chief was therefore competent to hear the palaver. The Balingo man said he had bought the girl for 25/– and hospitality from the young plaintiff; the latter said he had done no such thing; the girl said she knew nothing about sale or debt or anything else and she was a woman. I proposed she should choose her own husband from the two. She left it to me.

4 September 1919

I have noticed that my diary is becoming more and more conversational and is covering ground outside its proper area. I lay myself open to rebuke, but I attribute this prolixity to solitude. My diary resembles Captain Poole's official vapourings, as he so calls them, and maybe, like them, amuse those who peruse them.

Yesterday some wheat came for me to experiment with. As an amateur farmer, I am keen. Except for occasional shooting, it is my sole recreation and provides the only relaxation for my mind from thinking over the affairs and customs of my district. But this wheat growing is eminently unpractical to my thinking. The local native is by no means a fool in matters commercial. It was obvious that, apart from natural difficulties of the soil and climate, cotton would never be produced here willingly for the white man at three farthings a pound. Why should a man sell and carry his produce to us at a price lower than he can obtain in his own market? It is the same with strophanthus, 3*d*. a pound is offered at Tamale; and my Fra Fras sell a handful prepared for 1/– at their own house door to various French subjects in need of a little arrow poison. Now Guinea corn in the local market is 2/– the basket load (30 lbs) and millet 2/6*d.*, and these prices immediately after the harvest. How then can wheat be advocated as a substitute when its price in London is equal to the price of the local cereal in its own local market and that too when its supply is abundant? There is no inducement in this to the native commercial instincts — and that inducement would indeed have to be great to overcome the conservatism of every agricultural community, or to persuade a farmer to give up to an experimental crop. I am convinced of the wealth of this country. Had I the capital I would be inclined almost to set up in the mixed ranching business, but it does not seem good business to embark on a gamble to secure profits when established crops procure a return greater and more certain. A benevolent despotism might succeed in an agricultural metamorphosis, democracy, benevolent or otherwise, could not.

Sunday 7 September 1919
The whole day spent writing on native customs, but although I wrote 8000 words I did not finish. I wonder if they will be any use.

12 September 1919
I find that the refuse from an acetylene lamp is a success in keeping mosquitoes from frequenting stagnant pools. This is a bad place for them.

Sunday 14 September 1919
I have at last finished writing of the customs of the people, a week of much effort, but the *furor scribendi* is a powerful driver.

15 September 1919
My wheat has met with disaster. It was doing well and on Saturday only I was admiring it. Today nothing at all, not a single blade, is left. Some insect apparently amused itself gnawing the blades at the point of issue from the ground.

16 September 1919
Last night I dined with the French on the occasion of the annual mission festival. It is always most interesting to hear of their religious difficulties. I wonder how far they succeed in uprooting the hereditary superstitions of their converts?

20 September 1919
This evening a corpse was brought in, in a terrible state of decomposition. Sometimes it is not pleasant to be a DC.

26 September 1919
A man in from Chiame with a small complaint. Among other things, he told me he had been wrestling with a leopard. This is the third case of this form of sport I have heard of this year. Apparently, the idea is to enrage the beast and, when he leaps on you, you hang on. One man had his shoulder torn, but kept hold all night; but this fellow let go, the leopard, having hold of him too high up, had plenty of scope for its hind feet. Apart from a head nearly scalped, a scratched face and torn shoulder, the man was all right.

27 September 1919
Inspected a dead Moshi. He had recently come over from French territory and, at Pajai, complained of sickness. However, he came on to Navarro where he got worse and eventually died. He had 1/6*d.* on him, which I gave to the grave digger.

11 November 1919
A long morning in court, settling or endeavouring to settle domestic differences. I begin to believe that, in this small Kassina part, polyandry once existed. In no other way can I account for the excessive immorality, which obtains to nowhere like such an extent in the Fra Fra and Kanjarga parts. Often, a woman will promptly assert that a man is her seventh or even twelfth husband and, very frequently, when one asks why she moves from man to man, she will say 'such is our woman's fashion, we have always done so' – nor do the men resent this in the least.

An extraordinary state of things seems to exist north of the frontier. I cannot yet make out what is happening. To begin with, the French have disarmed the people. That was nothing, merely a fatherly piece of legislation, but now, having done that, they are preventing the annual emigration into British territory. Very few are passing. I have stopped parties and asked what was the matter, but all I can learn is that no one is allowed south, that the French are again taking the youngmen as soldiers and others are being retained for work on a large house at Wagadugu. This latter cannot require thousands of men; the former is incomprehensible. Those whom I stopped told me they had paid the French soldiers before crossing.

Yesterday, energy having been restored to me, I started to see about labour for the railway.[39] One man said he would go as headman and would find boys. Today, he arrived with 30 and said they wanted first to finish the harvest. I told them to go ahead with it. There is no doubt that if labour is recruited here voluntarily by private individuals, the response will be excellent. Through chiefs, one will have the same trouble, extortion and enforcement, as with recruits for the regiments. I do not blame so much the natural views of the chiefs, I fancy that they regard a request for labour as an order to be obeyed at once, so they just command the first at hand to go. There is no word in their language to express the difference between 'I want labour' and 'I command labour'.

Zouaragu,[40] North Eastern Province

(i) S. D. Nash, DC, 1913

6 October 1913
Various complaints from men whose wives have joined the soldiers. Such cases always occur on the arrival of a new company. In truth, these women are not the wives of complainants, but rather their 'keeps'. We have, I am afraid, made a fetish of what we call head money. A man will come in front of his commanding officer and say he has paid so many cattle to a friend and in return a friend has given him a certain woman as wife. Now, this woman is not his wife according to native custom. I am talking now of the pagan native from Fra Fra. Marriage with them appears to consist of (1) consent of parents and generally a courtship on the part of the man; (2) certain dues paid by the son-in-law, not necessarily head money, it may be farm work or some other service; (3) cohabitation for some time (indefinite). If the woman does not have children by the man she is perfectly at liberty to leave him and the contract is ended; also, if they do not get on well together they will separate and no claims to our fetish, head money, are exacted. In other words, natives and more especially the white man's followers, viz boy scouts, soldiers, clerks etc. have got this idea of head money into their brains and think that we practically sanction the buying and selling of women. Nothing could be further from native custom. The young girl, in this country, is a much freer agent than her confrères at home in the choosing of a mate.

7 October 1913
Busy taking down notes on native characteristics. No rain yet. Rumour says that a juju man at Dua is 'holding the rain' because people will not give him his proper presents so that he can intercede with the giver of all.

8 October 1913
Neither Alarri nor the chief of Yoragu can give any very satisfactory explanation of this fetish. They both appeal to custom and what their grandfathers did. Chief of Yoragu says that the fetishman of the

Durrungo section of Sheerigu has always come to his town for confirmation and Alarri has done so now. This fetish is generally consulted by women who want to be mothers. A goat, fowl or sometimes a dog is brought and sacrificed. The fetish is a cow's horn and the blood of victims is sprinkled over it. Alarri gives a similar account, but cannot explain how Yoragu got the power of appointing the fetishman. He does what his fathers did. Generally the office is hereditary and not selective. Alarri's father was fetishman before him. The other fetish in Sheerigu belongs to the chief of the town. Presents are brought to it during drought, sickness, failure of crops and also by childless women. It will generally be noticed that these fetishmen have a peculiar cunning look in their eyes, as if in communication with unseen objects. This is probably at first assumed by them and gradually becomes a habit. Small boys are often selected when quite young and reared up under the influence of these men they succeed.

English mail in a day before its time, which shows that the road must now be in good order.

10 October 1913

Some cases of family disputes and marriage questions came before the court today. Although these are sent to the chiefs to try, it is better always to get the gist of them, as many native characteristics are disclosed. Are the people seriously attached to their own blood and household? And is there any touching affection uniting wife and husband? Sometimes yes, but generally no.

11 October 1913

In continuation of the question discussed yesterday, not only is the tie between husband and wife often loose, but also that between parents and children seems equally frail. They are long-suffering with and very fond of their offspring. I have never seen a native correct his child by using the proverbial cane. As the children get older, the tie of blood seems to weaken. There is no word for family. Sometimes it is most difficult to find out who the father of a boy is, should he not be living in his father's house or countryside. The boy will call the head of the compound in which he happens to be living his 'father' and the stray bastards and natural and adopted children are all his brothers. All this points to the weakness of the blood tie and is probably either due to polygamy or else is born in the blood and due to the centuries of raiding and fighting during which the words home and family have been thoroughly effaced in the general insecurity of life and property.

13 October 1913

Out all day inspecting bridges. Practically only two trees up here have any durability and are always used by natives for roofing etc. They are, I give the native names, sheera and zumzum. The latter is a kind of mahogany. Nearly all the other trees are useless for building purposes. A good fall of rain last night, about an inch. We are still, however, seven inches below last year's rainfall.

14 October 1913
Fifteen boys arrived today from Sambruno for dispatch to Coomassie for officers' private loads. As showing how the natives up here are beginning to travel, I find that four of these boys have already been to Coomassie and, after working there on the roads and for traders, have returned to look after their farms. I have often been asked the question of what use the NT are? – no trade, no revenue in those benighted regions being constantly flung from irresponsible lips. I should like very much to know the number of NT boys now working in Ashanti and the Colony on roads, cocoa farms and other employment. I am sure the figures would astound some people.

Held a short enquiry today regarding leprosy; there are more victims in the country than I was aware of. This would probably be accounted for by the fact that the leper rarely appears at palavers. The natives do not look upon the affliction as contagious and the leper will sit down in the same compound and mix with the people without let or hindrance. The wife, however, of a leper would leave him, taking as a husband a brother or some other blood relation of her afflicted spouse. The children born of such a union would belong to the leper. With regard to the question of isolation, their reply is that whatever the white man says is good. The fact is, they look to us for a lead in everything. If we declared a tapu against the indiscriminate mixing of lepers with the people, specially if we pointed out it was a contagious disease, I think the people would quickly fall into line. As a commencement, I have ordered a compulsory registration of all lepers.

15 October 1913
A visit from the chief of Karaga this morning. Very numerous complaints from him to the effect the people do not respect him as chief. This man used to live in Karaga in Mamprussi. As nearly all the Talensi referred to him invariably as their head chief, he was brought here about two years ago to live among his people and to try to instil some cohesion into this very independent hill people. It is perhaps a little too soon yet to pass a final verdict on the matter, but, for all practical purposes, the experiment up to the present has been the reverse of a success. Karaga evidently began with some prestige. Physically, he is not a very fit person as, although fairly young, he has an affliction in both eyes rendering him practically blind. The latter

trouble, however, would not lower him in the estimation of the people, as they seem to have a peculiar affection for old and decrepit men as chiefs. For any practical end of chieftaincy, a rag doll would be equally as efficient as Karaga at the present moment. The fact is, the people will generally carry out orders for us via their own small chiefs and headmen and, as this suits our purpose very well, why waste time and energy in trying to revive an authority whose history is very doubtful? True, they always refer to Mamprussi as their father. But let Mamprussi send out one of his son's or satellites to these parts to enforce his authority. Methinks they would look upon him also as a rag doll and treat him as such.

21 October 1913
A very nice fall of rain during the night. The first we have had for a considerable time. Had a visit from six lepers this morning whose names I registered. They are all certified by the MO as suffering from nerve leprosy, which apparently is very chronic, lasts a long time, but will eventually prove fatal. One, quite a boy, from Sheerigu, had open sores all over his body and must be a source of danger to the community amongst whom he lives. In some, the fingers of both hands had been completely eaten away, while in one the disease had just started. Our best plan is at first to register all lepers. I think this is quite feasible if time is given for the work. Afterwards, when we know the numbers and their whereabouts, it will be time to discuss their compulsory isolation. If any drastic steps are taken before a fairly accurate registration is complete, we will meet a conspiracy of silence and many cases will be hidden that it will be well nigh impossible for us to discover.

24 and 25 October 1913
Inspecting bridges and laying out new roads.

Sunday 26 October 1913
A day of rest.

27 October 1913
Some marriage cases this morning. It might be expected that the people would settle these matters by means of their small chiefs and headmen. They won't do this. They would rather regard the DC as a kind of modern Peter with free powers to loose and unloose. The fact is, the chiefs have never wielded any powers except during a temporary clash of arms, or an obscure raid. The people, therefore, far from having any deification of rulers, are most individualistic in their ideas and for a very good reason too. As far as I can make out, no dominating intellect has ever risen up amongst them. An obscure raider, or a pro tem conqueror, certainly has occasionally appeared on the hori-

zon. But what did he almost always do? He certainly did not make any attempt to form even the crudest foundation of settled government. No, it was always easier for him to live by slave raiding than to foster trades and industries and promote agriculture. The people have not forgotten this and they now look with suspicion on anyone who prospers and becomes the owner of property, or on any of their so-called chiefs who, backed up by us, 'put on airs' and try to assume control over their people. The chiefs have no prestige, no historical names to quote as their predecessors, and these considerations count for more amongst an uncivilized than a civilized people. We can only go straight forward, as we are going, supporting the chiefs as much as possible in the hope that the young generation now growing up will look to them as the symbol of a settled form of government. Not much can be expected of the present generation.

28 October 1913
Had a visit from some natives from that part of the district formed by the bend of the Volta River, where the Red and White Volta join, that is southeast of Zouaragu. Four years ago I travelled through this part. It was then very sparsely inhabited. A few compounds scattered at wide intervals were seen and the people disappeared at my approach. Six weeks ago I visited these parts and find the country is becoming much more thickly peopled. These people come from all parts of the district. Zouaragu, Bolgatanga, Bongo etc. are reported to have supplied their quota of settlers. Now here we have an illustration of what happened in nearly every part of this district. A few people settle in an uninhabited part of the country. These little isolated communities will occasionally meet in the evening, like our British ancestors, and discuss local affairs. The village oracle, in the person of probably the oldest inhabitant, would be tacitly acknowledged. No chief is made and any interference on the part of the people whence the emigrants came would naturally be resented. More people will come and settle and will also form their own little communities as valley, stream or hill offer suitable places for houses or farms. So the process goes on until we get a series of communities, intensely individualistic and not recognizing any authority, even in their immediate neighbourhood. All are equally poor and all strive to get a living from Mother Earth. Here we have also an illustration of the cause of the inherent weakness of our chiefs. They are big men in their immediate neighbourhood, but as their people spread afield, they have neither the [ability] nor the energy to assert any control over them.

Some 21 lepers registered today. This brings our total up to 31 and we have already, I am afraid, only touched the fringe.

29 October 1913
Out all day on roads and bridging work. Owing to our having only four NTC men available here at present, most of the supervision naturally falls on the DC. It is hoped after a while to teach a few Fra Fras to peg out a straight line. At present, they are asymmetrical to the last degree and look with awe upon a road that happens to be straight for a few hundred yards.

31 October 1913
Dispatched 20 carriers to Tamale for medical loads. This district has been fairly heavily taxed this year in the matter of transport. Busy in the morning superintending the throwing up of an embankment over the Bolgatanga swamp. This place becomes impassable during the heavy rains. The bridging of the Bolgatanga River will tax the art of a skilled engineer.

7 November 1913
Had a visit from Nawagga, liberated from Tamale gaol a year ago. He has settled down quite nicely. In the old days he was the head fetishman of Tonzugu. He is clothed in skins and has the usual shrewd cunning of the fetishman. None of the fetishmen in these parts wear clothes, only skins and not even a loincloth. The abode of the Tonzugu fetish I visited some time ago. A grove of shady trees surrounds the Tonzugu shrine; a stream of clear water flows through and suddenly disappears under two immense rocks. Between these rocks there is a hole, hardly large enough to admit a man, which seems to communicate with the stream below. On the rocks are beads, cloth, cowries, hair shaved from men's heads etc. left there by consultants of the oracle.

Childless women were particularly prone to visit this place, and prospective mothers would also come to hear their fate and to bring good luck to their offspring. It was tapu for anyone to wear clothes on entering the hills. 'Cast off all clothes all ye that enter here' was the order. Skins, however, might be worn. The fetishman's *ipse dixit* was regarded as a kind of nostrum to cure all ills of mind and body. He can bring rain and stop it. Before we call it childish, what about the sacred grotto at Lourdes? The native is very broad minded in his outlook. He says 'different people have different gods and let each one believe in his own fetish.'

11 November 1913
Busy all day on road across Bolgatanga swamp. English mail arrived yesterday, four days before time. It must have got the assistance of a motorcar for some of the way out of Coomassie.

17 November 1913

Busy taking notes on intertribal differences of the various clans. There are really no marked differences. They all seem to have the same tapus and rites – the same houses, dress, same method of farming and outlook on life. There is no set of distinct tribal marks for any of the clans. The original Mamprussi mark survives in 99 per cent of cases. This consists of a broad cut from the nose and across the centre of the left cheek. Sometimes this is still the only mark put on, but in the large majority of cases it is supplemented by various other marks, which are added either to please the father or fetishman or to suit the whims of a lady. In every countryside there is a skilled man who carries out the work. It is evidently a lucrative business and I am informed is hereditary, the son succeeding the father.

19 November 1913

Long talk to many chiefs on the subject of reporting all cases of leprosy. On this, as on nearly all subjects, the native is misty and nebulous. He knows it is a very bad disease and I think he knows it is contagious. He calls it 'fire from good' and is, as indeed he is in most matters, a fatalist on the subject. If one should contract the disease, though contagious, it is the will of God. All calibans and other deformed people are looked upon with peculiar pity by the natives and receive the best attention. The leper is also treated in like manner.

20 November 1913

Mail from England arrived yesterday. Had an interview with many chiefs today on the subject of dispensing with their bows and poisoned arrows, at any rate on all occasions except when they are hunting. About January and February of each year, the poison is made in the bush. It is never made near houses in case small boys etc. might meddle with it. The affair is accompanied by a certain amount of ceremony, goats and fowls being slain on the occasion. Anyone is allowed to be present, but apparently only certain men know the ingredients of the mixture used. The tree, the seeds of which are used, is quite common round these parts.[41] The seeds are collected and dried for a couple of months. They are then crushed and boiled. I am creditably informed that a small fly is also caught and a number of these also form part of the poison. They are boiled with the seeds. The fly frequents grass and is said to be fatal to cattle and sheep should they eat it while grazing. The boiling is continued for three or four days, other herbs also being used. Then the mixture is ready for its lethal purpose and the points of arrows are dipped into it. If the manufacture of the poison is a secret confined to certain men in each countryside, it is probably a source of considerable profit to them and, needless to say, the disclosure of the secret would be very difficult to obtain.

Bolgatanga, 24 November 1913
Came out here on road inspection. The chief of this place is an interesting old man, tall with an interesting even handsome face. In his young days he was called by a name that seems to signify 'lady killer'. His son seems to be worthily following his father's footsteps as, even now, though quite a young man, he has a large family and a dozen robust wives. The chief has had a chequered career. He had the temerity, it seems, to act the part of a friend to the late Sir D. Stewart[42] and accompanied the latter to Gambaga. On his return, with a red fez, the symbol of chiefdom, he was chased by the people from post to pillar and seems to have had his life in his hands for many years, the people round blaming him for bringing the white man to these parts. Then, about 12 years ago, a man name Sana Moshi arrived at Bolgatanga from Gambaga armed with the credentials of a white man. He told the people he was sent there by us to teach them sense. He played off one group against another and stopped at nothing, even murdering the people. The ruins of his large castellated residence still stand. The old chief told me he frequently put him in irons for the non production of cattle etc. As this freebooter and his followers paraded the country in our name, it is small wonder that the people are only slowly beginning to realize what our methods and ideas really mean. He was eventually caught at Gambaga and atoned for his various crimes.

Sambruno, 7 November 1913
Came on here. Long talk with various chiefs on the subject of their boys going down to work in Accra and other places where labour is scarce and wages are high. The great difficulty is the distance. The population here is not very large and the majority of the boys, if they seek work away from their country, always like to return to plant crops etc. Many boys now go down and take on farm work in Ashanti, cocoa growing etc. They, however, only stay four or five months and then return. The women round these parts, unlike the Moshi women, do very little farm work. All the hard manual work is done by the boys. Women plant the seeds and harvest the crops. The result of this system is that the whole male population is engaged for about five months of the year doing farm work and for the remaining seven, although they are to a great extent idle, it would be hardly worth their while to go long distances in search of work.

26 November 1913
Another harangue to the people on the subject discussed yesterday.

The old men and chiefs generally say they would like their boys to go and earn money. Their country, however, is poor and it requires a good deal of labour and a large extent of tillage to eke a living out of it. They therefore like to be surrounded by their families, their young men to do farm work, their boys to look after their cattle and sheep and drive them to pasture by daytime, and women to look after the house. A man is a big man if he has plenty of wives, sons, daughters, cattle and sheep. One fine young man told me he was married and asked me what would become of his wife if he went away for a year or so to work in Accra? He gave me to understand that she would not await his return. This is another reason for many boys not going in search of work. Nothing would induce their womankind, except in isolated cases, to accompany them.

9 December 1913

During the last two days, 2400 loads of grass and 110 sticks have been brought in by the various chiefs for roofing the houses in the station and at least as many more will be required. The main point in this matter is to divide the work evenly, giving each countryside a just proportion. I am afraid in times gone by we were inclined to 'spur the willing horse' before we knew the country properly. The result was that the population in the vicinity of chiefs of standing did all the work, while those at a distance did nothing. With this work and also road making work, rest house building etc., all underpaid, it may justly be said that the people do pay a tax. They fully appreciate their obligations, however, situated as they are near the French frontier where the people there have to do the same work and, in addition, pay a very substantial tax.

11 December 1913

Had a talk today with some people on the subject of land tenure. With regard to land in the bush, the people assert that it all belongs to someone. What they mean by this is that the land belongs to some particular fetish. No stranger could cultivate it. People of a particular countryside who go to farm in the bush and break up new ground, always approach the fetish and elders of the countryside in a proper manner and pay certain dues to those authorities. There is no such thing as private land in our sense of the word. Shea butter and *dawa dawa* trees have all, in theory, got their owners, even when situated far away from human dwellings. The people, however, are honest enough to say that the enforcement of this particular right often depended on brute force in times gone by.

15 December 1913

The pledging of children seems to have been very common here in times gone by, and it is still practised. What generally happens is that a compound, or family, have a bad harvest and get short of food. A man, sometimes a chief sometimes a man of influence in the country, is consulted. He agrees to supply the family with food or the wherewithal to buy food, that is cattle. The family hand over their child – in 90 per cent of the cases a girl – as a pledge that the food will be repaid or the cattle returned. A case came in front of the court today in which a man had handed over a young girl to the chief of Nangodi ten years ago. The chief supplied him with cattle wherewith to buy food. The girl, in the meantime, grew up and has a child by the chief. The father of the girl now wants to redeem the pledge by paying back the cattle to the chief and regaining his daughter. The question now is as to whom the child belongs. Native opinion seems to think that it belongs to the father and that the woman can go back to her parents provided the pledge is redeemed.

16 December 1913

Busy yesterday in checking loads of grass and sticks for roofing the houses. At one time, in the heyday of my youth, I used to find this work of building interesting. When it occurs, however, every dry season at every station, the work begins to pall. Monotony is the great drawback to an outstation in the NT. The first experience cannot be repeated, the first sunrise, the first dip into the forest, the first view of miles and miles of Guinea corn. The same novelty is experienced in the first couple of years in dealing with the people. One is interested in the visits of the various chiefs. They are accompanied by their drummers – Horaces and Shakespeares singing the respective praises on Maccenas or the Earl of Southampton. The drummers used to be, and sometimes still are, interesting to me. They always accompany the chief and sing his praises in a monotonous refrain. 'The chief is a lion let everyone respect him. The white man is an elephant. Let the chief and people beware as the elephant is stronger than the lion. Unless the lion and elephant keep quiet there may be trouble. Let therefore the chief and white man treat everyone properly and give the drummers food.'

22 December 1913

My time has been practically wholly devoted to building. From 6.00 a.m. to 10 a.m. and again from 3.00 p.m. to 6.00 p.m. has been given up to this work. The very laying of each brick has got to be personally supervised in the absence of any skilled labour. With natives speaking different patois and having not the remotest idea of what the plan of the house is, the work rather assimilates to that of the Tower of Babel. I hope it will not end in a like catastrophe. After spending seven hours in the sun, with the constant annoyance of pulling down, building up, correcting etc., one is not worth much in the evening for serious brain work.

28 December 1913
Work of building goes on, varied by some court cases. The following case of paper passing as a summons from the DC was tried on Monday. Some people from Dua (Gambaga District) came in with a piece of paper. It, by a coincidence, consisted of the 'busy cupid' page of the *Tatler* with many charming photographs of English girls about to enter on the responsibilities of matrimony. The Dua people say it was given to them by some men of Pwologu who were claiming a lady, an absconding wife, evidently of a Pwologu man. On interviewing the latter people, they frankly acknowledge that they sent the paper in order to get back the girl. Any kind of paper passing as a summons from the DC was one of the most fruitful sources of annoyance and misunderstanding in the old days. It took a long time to stamp out and, according to the above case, it still fondly lingers in the memory of some of the more adventurous inhabitants.

30 December 1913
On Tuesday I enquired into a few trivial cases of debt and marriage, which really ought to have been settled by the various chiefs. In future, in all such cases, I intend to call in the chiefs and people concerned and let them try the case themselves in the precincts of the court. They really have not got the machinery or confidence to settle even small matters in their own countryside as we would wish. Very often it is due to complainant and defendant being under different chiefs ten or twelve miles apart. The idea of the chiefs or their representatives meeting and settling the case among themselves is quite a novelty to them and will take some time to establish.

16 January 1914
It is hard to impress on the people that we are not here to upset their customs, but rather to preserve order etc. Natives will often say in court that they thought our arrival had abolished such and such a custom. For instance, in a case tried today a man complains that the chief of Dusi had fined him a couple of sheep because he had not offered to the chief the usual quota of *dawa dawa* and shea butter when collecting these products. Now it is a well-established custom that, in theory, all these tribes belong to the chief. The people have, however, got the idea that on our occupying the country these customs lapsed, or the right to the trees etc. was transferred to us, as being the people now who can enforce and defend these rights.

(ii) Captain H. T. C. Wheeler, DC, 1914[43]

Sunday 22 March 1914
On fatigue all day trying to get comfortable. It is very evident what a lot of building has lately been done in the station. Unfortunately, the comfort of the DC will suffer for some time to come (in fact till he gets into the new Residency), which may be a matter of two months. There are at present, at the disposal of the DC, five round houses consisting of one sitting room, one bedroom, one storeroom, one room used as a pantry (there is no veranda to the sitting room, which could be used as such), one latrine house, assuming the necessity for a latrine house, and a place for a boy to wash plates, clean lamps etc. (a necessity which, to anyone who likes to live decently, is undeniable). The kitchen has been knocked down and not replaced, cooking having to be done in the cook's bedchamber, which he has had to vacate (cooking taking precedence) and crowd in with the other boys in the one remaining small boy's quarter. Altogether, the Residency at present is about as uncomfortable a place to live in as can be imagined.

23 March 1914
Sent £200 specie to Gambaga. Gave the gardener the following seeds – tomato, carrots, parsley, radish, cabbage, lettuce, cucumber. Found him doing nothing and he admits he had never asked for seeds.

26 March 1914
Floors of the ground floor of the new house commenced to be beaten; 60 Detekke men brought in about 2 lbs weight each of tie tie, say two loads. Rather a large expedition, as I pointed out, for so little; said they always did it that way. I believe in sending trivial complaints to the chiefs to settle. If they are too indolent or weak to do so, they have the trouble of coming in to Zouaragu to say so. I fancy that if the complainants are invariably told to take their complaint to the chief first, fewer will come on to the DC for settlement.

27 March 1914
Shiega people brought in tie tie. I trust that the new house is going according to the plans of the designer. Not having the advantage of discussing them with him, I am very much in the hands of the venerable carpenter and of the scion of the house of Zouaragu (formerly captain of the trainband in charge of the station water drums and now promoted to headman and general factotum in charge of buildings).

28 March 1914
Shiega people brought me more tie tie. Women plastered walls of new kitchen. Started the three or four men of the local detachment NTC

roofing the same, with Fra Fra labour to help them. Sent to Navarro for more bamboo for roofing the new house. Carpenter reports we have run out of nails. This last week's diary is an instructive commentary on the 'in the new house in a week'. Sent carriers to Tamale for nails. Sent out for sticks to roof new kitchen; there do not seem to be any here.

30 March 1914
Kurugu brought in more tie tie. A great deal is wanted also for the remaining WAFF quarters. Kurugu came in to see me about Winduri's application to fish in the Volta. Said Winduri wanted to fish where another man had the rights. I told Kurugu to see to the matter himself. He expressed a wish to. Sent £200 specie to Bawku. An individual came in from Navarro and said he knew all about putting grass on roof. Started putting the late A. J. Berney's grave in order.[44]

8 April 1914
English mail in. Solemnized a temporary union between a local damsel and a soldier. The soldier, with a sergeant as witness, and the bride to be with her father, or brother, as witness attend the court. The father, or brother, are asked to state their willingness to give away the lady, the soldier to state his willingness to pay as he can, the dowry (here four cows) that local custom imposes. I go into local questions somewhat fully in this diary as, by so doing, the diary becomes a useful guide to an officer taking over.

Sunday 12 April 1914
To Sekota. Addressed the assembled chiefs and villages on the subject of beeswax. Showed them roughly what one pound of wax was and explained that Miller's paid 1/– for a pound free from dust, thus a man could take a fair-sized load down and get £2 for it.

13 April 1914
To Detekke. Continued the beeswax crusade.

(iii) A. W. Cardinall, DC, 1918[45]

3 March 1918
Being Sunday, visited Moshi and Hausa *zongos*, cemetery and fort.

5 March 1918
Absent in Navarro.[46]

25 March 1918
The CC was met by a large crowd whom he addressed on the subject of voluntarily recognizing, by service, their obligations to a government that had brought them peace and freedom.

25 March 1918
In the middle of lunch, a mounted man galloped in to ask me to help kill elephants that were moving from Sambruno to Yoragu. I galloped there, but found nothing. On my return, I heard they had been surrounded near the rest house at Sambruno. I sent constables to kill them and to see no one came to harm in the division of the meat. The men returned later reporting that spears, arrows and stones had completed the work before their arrival.

28 March 1918
Shia complains his youngmen have fled to Dua on hearing about recruiting. Many small complaints and very heavy rain. The thunder, or at least one clap, was terrific. I thought the house was struck.

30 March 1918
Elephants located far in Moshi country were broken up and driven from village to village, poor beasts. The five killed here were babies.

25 May 1918
Chief of Bolgatanga came in and reported a serious outbreak of some sort of epidemic, which is having a very high rate of mortality among the children. A large number of chiefs happened to be in, so gave orders to keep the markets free from children.

26 May 1918
Rode over to Bolgatanga in the morning, where I was told that the number of deaths amounts to 188. Talked to the people. They complained about famine as well. This opened up the subject of making farms and they agreed to open up the bush. Returned to Zouaragu and planted some corn received from Gambaga. One of my Ashanti boys is ill. Hear he is unconscious and passes blood instead of water. Beyond my power to cope with, so called in local *malam*.

28 May 1918
The MO arrived in the morning.

29 May 1918
My small boy died this morning, just before the MO and myself went over to Bolgatanga, where he inspected many cases of the disease. A pitiful sight, about 200 children with it, and many in a terribly emaciated condition. For me a most trying day.

31 May 1918
In order to alleviate the shortage of food each year, have decided to plant groundnuts practically everywhere. This, together with my tree planting plans, follows the German example at Yendi.

10 September 1918
Very heavy rain accompanied by violent squalls. This weather makes me feel rotten. I trust it will soon pass.

16 September 1918
The usual numerous complaints occupied the morning. It seems a shame to keep youngmen doing government work when they are wanted, so I've started a comb out of bailiffs, messengers, scavengers, etc. They are to be replaced by old soldiers or rejected volunteers.

20 September 1918
Sometimes it seems a pity that the court reminiscences of the DCs have not been written. Today began with a complaint about farmland, followed by a goat complaint. I then heard a theft from Gauri in which one of the accused, who pleaded guilty, was amused at my request for his name. The name was Akazirti and means 'I do not steal'. Then followed a novel palaver. A small girl had wandered away from Biung, she is an orphan and no one is left to look after her. She has come to the *zongo* here and decided the butcher was a good sort of guardian. His views did not coincide with hers, so he brought her to me. After a talk, she agreed to go to the chief of Biung. I find much more work here in the court than at Tarkwa. The cases are not so numerous, it is true, but far more complicated and take longer to settle. And it is a common saying that NT commissioners can find no work!

22 September 1918
To Tongo where a fairly large attendance of people greeted me. I talked about the Red Cross, recruiting and the futility of lying.

Bongo, 11 October 1918
Down with fever.

28 October 1918
Took over district on receipt of wire from PC. [The writer is presumably Dr Moffatt who was looking after Cardinall.]

31 October 1918
Visited prison. Fresh openings in two cells have been made by my instructions to obtain better ventilation. Looked into new prison diet scale and have come to the conclusion that the scale cannot be adhered to. Mr Cardinall is improving gradually.

7 November 1918
A good deal of work is being done in the station garden. A good crop of beans gathered. These were grown by the Commissioner to give to

the various chiefs who have expressed a wish to grow them. Also a good crop of small beans, the return for the amount planted has been excellent.

1 December 1918
Went round town. Influenza everywhere.

14 December 1918
The MO left for Bawku. [Cardinall now back in charge.]

25 December 1918
Being Christmas, I spent day shooting, botanizing and collecting stone implements in the hills. There are hundreds of specimens lying about. Slept at Winduri, or rather tried to but I could get no shelter from the wind, which came seemingly from all directions and was very cold.

(iv) W. E. Gilbert, Ag DC, 1919

17 August 1919
I cannot find the [1913] letter instructing DCs to write informal diaries.[47] If I remember rightly, the diary was to be of an informal character of the writer's doings in the district. I will risk the meaning of the word informal and will record some recent thoughts of mine, which should better perhaps form the subject of correspondence. However, in diary form they can serve maybe as an introduction. Naturally, I am interested in the subject of my being relieved. As usual, however, there are many little matters partially begun by me or intended to be begun in the dry season. If I am to be relieved by a totally new man, I should like to have him staying with me some time. It is not that I feel I am so vastly capable as an Ag DC, but rather that he might understand the more fully the lines along which I have endeavoured to act and along which I had intended to travel. At present, work such as ours is intensely individualistic; the scaffolding alone is given to guide me as to dimensions of the building and as DCs are changed, so changes the building from Gothic to Byzantine with an interlarding of Norman and even Minoan. It is not to give orders that I write this, but to have time allotted so that my plans can be explained, my preparations made known, and my intentions discussed, to be adopted or not as he may deem fit. For this I intend writing a long handing over report to be submitted first to my PC before handing to my successor.

From the last mail I see that the Ford Company will shortly place on the market motorcycles at £10 and cars at £50. Should this be so, the development of this exceedingly rich country will cater for proper roads. Is it too early to formulate some scheme of co-ordination in the province? By that I mean a main trunk road[48] with its branches, a scheme, the planning of which would it seems require some trouble, forethought and survey both engineering and political. Recently, people have been running to Tamale with complaints from this district. This reflects on me and, in native parlance, tends to spoil my name. I attribute it, however, to an unfortunate piece of justice, which gave the first man who ran to Tamale his case. Such is the virtue of a paper from Tamale that now everyone who fails before me or his chief seeks refuge to Tamale and, of course, supports his going thither by some lie or other.

The shortage of money is very great here. Particularly is this so of nickel. Apparently, it is valued locally as the material for rings and bracelets. Section 301 of the Criminal Code protects gold and silver coinage, but I can find nothing about nickel. Moreover, that section makes the offence too serious for a DC to hear. Here, of course, there is no gold standard. Cows are the standard. Today it may be interesting to record the value of a cow in Bari or Doninga markets varies from £5 to £10 or even £12 is paid – and this for local-bred cattle. This is profiteering on the part of the natives, but clearly the effects of high prices will tend to create an inclination to sell the cattle and so diminish the over crowding of beasts in the pasture lands, a cause I am certain is so contributory to rinderpest. I am given to understand that traders are buying cattle here, as they experience difficulty in getting them in French territory. It is very hard to find out exactly what the French authorities are doing. In the same train of thought concerning money and the loss of nickel coinage, is the question of local blacksmiths. These are the men who melt down the coins. They too are the men who manufacture arrows. Of course, their main source of income is their supplying of hoes. I would like, however, to see them all licensed in the same way as goldsmiths in Ashanti or the Colony, that is to say, a free licence. In this way, one would know how many men are engaged in this important local industry, could check melting of coins and, if need arose, could stop the manufacture of arrows in non-hunting districts such as Zouaragu. In connection with blacksmiths, I have recently learned of a custom typical of primitive thought. Meteorites are frequently used on which to hammer the iron – their value is very great being frequently as much as five cows. It is said that if you strike the meteorite it will go right through the earth. To prevent this catastrophe a piece of wood is put under the meteorite.

19 August 1919

In the last *Accra Gazette* I see a circular letter from the Secretary of State urging utmost energy in research etc. Might I suggest that every

DC's office — up here particularly — be supplied with the *Bulletin* of the Imperial Institute? A lot of people have been dying here lately; I cannot find out any cause. They are chiefly old people. When I enquired as to the nature of the sickness I was told 'When the sickness came, the old people refused to die. There was no food. Now there is plenty. So they are dying and can have a good funeral custom.'

21 August 1919
Heard that the Treasury from Coomassie are sending me £100 in currency notes. A more imbecile performance I cannot imagine in so far as a district such as this is concerned. The notes are not even safe in my safe, for damp rot affects all paper therein. I wonder what the market women would do with them since they are all unclothed, that is the women.

23 August 1919
Peace celebrations were held. An enormous crowd attended with all the chiefs. I estimate it at over 5000. Unfortunately, rain spoilt the day, even before the people had ceased to arrive.

28 August 1919
Inspected my garden where the fruit trees seem to be flourishing. I have now pawpaws, mangoes, custard apple, limes, guavas and cape gooseberries all doing well. The cassava this year is remarkably fine. This latter is for distribution among the people and I have promised half of the roots to the Fathers in exchange for practical demonstration of how to make white bread from its flour. Their bread is excellent.

Bawku, North Eastern Province

(i) Dr Robert Whyte, Ag DC, 1913–14[49]

25 November 1913
Constable returned with mails from Navarro.

28 November 1913
Chief of Sinegara brought in five of his people accused of carrying native lethal weapons after having been warned that it was not lawful to do so. The chief fined them one £1 each, which they refused to pay, so they brought them to Bawku. They agreed to pay the fine. I don't know what the procedure would be in case they still refused.

23 January 1914
Arrived Zongoiri. Interviewed the chief of Zongoiri re his successor and disposal of his property in the event of his death. He is very old

and his demise may be expected at any time. Wrote a record of his statement for future use.

(ii) Captain H. T. C. Wheeler, DC, 1914

9 February 1914
New constabulary clothing having been issued, the old was destroyed.

11 February 1914
One gun licence issued; total 91. Sent out to towns near the German frontier for 3000 loads of grass, 1000 sticks and tie tie for the entire re-roofing of the market in Bawku. In case it is asked why the work requires doing again, since it was done 12 months ago, the answer is that for some reason the new grass was put on the old sticks, most of which were in a state of decay and useless and the work has to be done again. All sides of the market show a very good example of what, for want of a better name, I must call a dromedary style of architecture, and a couple of bad tornadoes, with their weight of water lying in the undulating folds of the roof, would probably bring about its collapse.

12 February 1914
Keeping the carpenter busy making a few necessary articles of furniture for the Residency and office. Dr Whyte had some made for the Residency shortly before my arrival, the last DC having generously presented the Residency furniture to the MO's quarters.

22 February 1914
Arranged for rest house repairs and road cleaning. Here, and to a large extent elsewhere, very little requires doing. I am convinced that the paying of the road and rest house dues is the principal agent in contributing to this satisfactory state of affairs and that the chiefs now understand the system and voluntarily do the work with the object of earning the reward.

Tanga, 26 February 1914
Chief of the Fulani came in. I enquired into the recent death of a local sportsman at one of the periodical rat and rabbit drives, which appears to have been a pure accident, but not an uncommon one. I remarked to the chief that, while sport of every description was encouraged by and took a high place in the regard of British officials, the addition of one or two members of the community to the annual bag could not but be deprecated in view of the absence of surplus population and the condition of his overgrown roads. The chief, after a little consideration, said he thought it was time to abolish these *battues* and he agreed that the bag was becoming somewhat mixed.

2 March 1914
Roofing of market complete. This is worth noting as a good piece of work on the part of the chiefs on the German frontier. Nearly 4000 loads of grass and 1000 sticks were required, as this is probably the largest marketplace in the protectorate and the material was brought in and the entire market re-roofed, whitewashed and, where required, rebuilt in 20 days. These are some of the people who, when the station was building a few years ago, ran away when ordered to work – hundreds of them – to German country, so the commissioner reported. Binduri's brother came in to report that he has got his wife back from Tamale. The lady had eloped with a constable. Binduri complains that the women of Binduri are a flighty lot and apt to run away. What is he to do? Told him to be nice to them and make it worth their while to stop, also that we would always help to get them back. Apparently, he thinks that the towns situated on a main road and the constant passing of good-looking constables has a disturbing effect.

5 March 1914
Had chief and headmen in to reward them for cleaning roads.

11 March 1914
Gave Fulani chief an order to make mats to protect the station buildings during the rains. As he came in and asked to be allowed to make them, the pleasure of giving the order was doubled.

(iii) E. O. Rake, Ag DC, 1914

24 May 1914
Heavy storm last night; good many roofs blown off; constable reporting damage.

26 May 1914
Continued taking census of town. Sent carpenter out to make canoe on Tenkedogo road.

11 June 1914
Issued 20 gun licences. Carpenter reported that the canoe on the Tenkedogo road is finished and slope to the river cut away. Have sent his assistant to start work on canoe at the White Volta Kugri–Zongoiri road. Carpenter making paddles today.

12 June 1914
One gun licence. Binduri sent in to say his people have no money for gun licences. Sent out to tell him that guns must be brought and kept here till licences are obtained. Headman of Benaba sent in to say that

he was not going to bring his guns in and would not get licences for them unless the DC went out there. Sent out a constable to arrest him. Hear that he has given trouble in this respect before and has been warned by a former DC.

18 June 1914
One of the prisoners, whose violence in prison necessitated confinement in irons, has been showing symptoms of insanity. Decided today to send him down for medical examination to Gambaga. When he got a little way out he lay down and beat his head on the ground and made it impossible for the escort to proceed. Sent out and had him brought back. A great deal of inconvenience is caused owing to the fact that we have only one cell here and consideration for the safety of the other prisoners prevents his confinement in their company.

27 June 1914
English mail came in. Sent out to try to obtain 500 Moshi hats for GCR. Chief of Bawku sent in some beeswax. An excellent sample, but too small to be of much practical value.

20 July 1914
Sent out two constables to divert native produce being taken over to French territory into Bawku market. Told the owners the Bawku market must be first supplied at fair market rates; after that they were at liberty to sell in French country, where apparently they get about 3/– for the amount of corn lately sold here for *6d*. There has been no corn in the market for some days; today a good supply was brought in under escort. Arranged a fair market price, taking into consideration the present scarcity.

21 July 1914
Navarro mail left. Sent five recruits for Colony Escort Police to be medically examined by MO Zouaragu and to proceed thence to Navarro. Interviewed chief of Bawku with reference to scarcity of food in the market. He stated that the behaviour of the constables' wives prevented people bringing in food. The sergeant, on behalf of the constabulary, made counter-accusations against the wives of the chief's sons, stating that they bought the food on the road before it came into the market and then sold it at a profit. Gave orders that no food was to be sold on the road, that a sufficient supply was to be brought in to the market and any complaints by the sellers were to be brought to court. Spoke to the chief about the cotton. He stated he was waiting for rain to plant it. Told him to get the ground prepared in anticipation of rain.

24 July 1914
Made a sanitary inspection round town. Fairly clean on the whole. The people, however, seem disinclined to use the incinerators for the purpose for which they are provided.

15 August 1914
Complaint from a Fulani at Zongoiri that his horse had been used against his will for post to post messages. Told him that he must do everything in his power to help the administration under the present circumstances and that he would receive compensation if he lost his horse when being used for post to post purposes.

Sunday 28 February 1914
Proceeded to Barrabawku (or Geru) on Togo frontier. Headman complained that the Kussassi traders in the market refused to accept the West African nickel coinage. As the market happened to be in progress, efforts were made to explain its uses and advantages over the cowry, with the result that some of the leaf-clad vendors expressed their understanding. As the result of the complaint of the headman, the undesirability of bringing weapons, particularly poisoned arrows and spears, into a crowded market was pointed out. Some confiscated by the headman were brought to me. The offenders were chiefly from Togoland, no doubt ignorant of the order against them. Two sheathed swords were returned to Hausa traders with the warning that, for the future, all weapons must be left behind on entering the market. Message sent to the recently destooled headman of Kwatia that he is to leave the village within one week, as he has made further trouble and refuses to come in to see me.

(iv) E. M. McFarland, Ag DC, 1916

4 September 1916
Official correspondence. Today a herd of 27 cattle from Putinga were granted free customs passes. They were examined by the Ag DC, as well as was reasonably possible, and all looked healthy. The chiefs of Zebilla and Benaba and some of the chiefs of Kugri, Tanga, Teshi, Winneba came into Bawku and the Ag DC explained to them the symptoms of both rinderpest and anthrax; he also explained, very fully, the seriousness of these diseases and instructed all of them. In future, if any disease among cattle, or men breaks out in their district they must immediately report to the MO at Gambaga and the DC at Bawku.

6 September 1916
Chiefs of Bawku and Binduri fined for not reporting the outbreak of

the disease they call *kugulu gumdi* as soon as the cattle became affected. Examined a herd of over 100 remarkably fine cattle. They all looked healthy. Had come from Putinga and are now on their way south. Spoke very fully to the representatives of chiefs of Tili, Timony and Sinnebaga all about rinderpest and anthrax.

14 September 1916
Dr Allan, MO for Gambaga and Bawku districts, arrived Bawku on his tour through the district for the purpose of investigating the disease among cattle. His decision is that, except at Zongoiri, he has seen no cases of anthrax. In the Binduri and Benaba subdistricts, he reported it to be pleuro pneumonia, which I am glad to say he does not consider nearly as serious as anthrax. Paid the constabulary. Accompanied Dr Allan while he examined two herds of cattle on their way from Putinga to Coomassie; he gave the owners leave to proceed via Binduri, Kugri and Zongoiri, as he says the main road is free of disease.

Yendi, Dagomba, Togoland

(i) G. A. E. Poole, DPO, 1918[50]

2 January 1918
Busy in office. Chief of Yendi called round to express his congratulations on the new courthouse, which he had been informed was built to commemorate his new rule! He said it was the finest building he had ever seen; never having been outside Dagomba, his experience is not great and German upcountry efforts are not difficult to surpass in the building line.

3 January 1918
Completed my annual report.

4 January 1918
Dispatched accounts and mail to Tamale with a GCR deserter, who came yesterday and, walking into the constable's lines, stated he would join the blue force instead of the khaki. Mohammedans called to receive printed matter, the Sherif of Mecca's proclamation amongst other things.

5 January 1918
Owing to shortage of flour, have experimented with diverse native corns to mix with English flour and find that cassava, mixed in equal quantities with wheat flour, makes excellent bread. Cattle are not coming through as should be expected at this season. The young bull

treated by the native method, that is the crushing of the testicles in lieu of castration, is going on fine and the method would appear to be effective. Legislation to limit the number of male animals would be a great benefit, not only to NT cattle owners, but to the Gold Coast meat market.

Sunday 6 January 1918
Dispatched carriers and loads to Sambul. Shod two of my horses, a difficult matter, it being a new departure for them. The interested spectators were secretly disappointed at seeing them walk off sound at completion of performance. Mail from Salaga arrived bringing English mail after an interval of a month.

11 January 1918
Letter from French commissioner at Sansanne Mango in reply to one from me asking him to return a woman and her two children kidnapped from one of our Yendi Konkomba villages. His reply was that, owing to the unsettled state of his Konkomba villages, he considered it prudent to send a constable to carry out the job. Fancy any of our villages being regarded as impossible of visiting. Sent native interpreter to Tschangbani to reassure the people as against my arrival with many constables on Monday.

12 January 1918
Feeling CD owing to very bad night due to worry about fire in Yendi plantation. Rode into Yendi and inspected plantation that the fire did harm to. Thank goodness it is not as bad as I expected. A bush fire started half a mile away was the cause of it. Sparks must have lighted on the dry doub grass and been kindled into a flame, which, owing to the absence of the boys in the market in working hours, was not attended to in time to prevent the fire running across the plantation. Afternoon spent in instructing the NCOs as to their duties on outpost.

13 January 1918
Issued 30 rounds of ammunition per man and blanks for signalling purposes and saw the detachment march off with my carriers. Spent morning compiling my mail and answering official mail from Tamale. Visited plantation and allotted work.

14 January 1918
Held a meeting at Kuntule and Tschangbani telling the people the reason for the constables and left 15 NCOs and men for this section. At Sambul, held a large meeting when was assured by the people that no one from Sambul would attempt to cross the river and any punishment their neighbours across the River Oti received would be regarded

as just retribution. In the afternoon patrolled the river, marking out the different posts allotted to the constables.

15 January 1918
At daybreak, received a letter from French commissioner from across the River Oti stating he could not meet me today. Hence, changed my plans and proceeded to Kugnau with loads, travelling along the river bank inspecting the position of different constables. There are nine crossings in the dry weather, at each of which I have a constable, although the river is not very deep and in places narrow and fordable. Owing to the thick bush on both sides, with entangled undergrowth, it is unlikely that attempts will be made to cross it except at recognized places. This thick growth is eminently suitable for concealing fugitives and quite impenetrable for horsemen. After a meeting at Kugnau explaining the force as being protective as against attack from the French Konkombas, I left with Sergeant Major for Bankundjiba.

16 January 1918
Exceptionally cold morning, even for this severe harmattan. Left at 8.00 a.m. to walk to Kutza owing to danger of tsetse at river crossing. Some delay owing to canoe not being at ford and, while the river was but chest deep, owing to cold did not feel inclined to wade or swim. Told the villagers all that was necessary re the unusual number of constables in the proximity and noting that nothing had been done in the last two months to repair their very many broken down houses, took the opportunity of keeping the constables out of mischief, as well as benefiting the Kutza people, by sending for the Kunji section to start the people off at house repairing, since the constables will not have anything to do along the frontier till the near approach of the French.

17 January 1918
At Tschangbani held a palaver and informed a crowd of women from Kanjock, who had been detained pending my arrival, that in future the river must not be crossed even by women, since women were the root of most of the trouble in these parts. They, numbering some 23, informed me they had crossed on hearing that French soldiers were travelling from Bassari over two recent murder cases at Nandutaba. It is gratifying they should run away from rumours and face British armed forces without fear, although a nuisance.

18 January 1918
Felt CD all day owing to long and tiring day yesterday in sun on river. Letter from French commissioner asking for two murderers, who are alleged to be in Kuntule. Dispatched constable for them.

21 January 1918
Dispatched carriers and loads to Kunji where, on my arrival, I visited the sentry posts. In the afternoon, three headmen of villages in French territory came in with dashes. I explained that I was unable to accept them. They were very insistent that they were British and stated they wish to be. Dispatched my water container to Yendi to have it refilled.

22 January 1918
At 8.30 a.m. a letter arrived from Major Woelffrel [French commissioner] stating he would be at Bapure tonight and expressing a wish to meet me and talk over Konkomba affairs. Replied stating should have great pleasure in meeting him in any place and hour he named, and told him of the three rest houses near the River Oti on this side, and expressing the hope that he would allow me to entertain him at one of them. At 6.00 p.m. rode into Tschangbani to give my letter to the French messenger who had rested at that place. He expressed complete ignorance of the whereabouts of Bapure and all places in its immediate neighbourhood, which I did not believe, but regarded it as fear of the people around. Sent a constable and a Konkomba with the letter. Telegram from CC arrived stating that it had been reported that one British Konkomba village is implicated in the murder of a French soldier. This is news to me and I am anxious to hear more details from the French commissioner.

24 January 1918
Late in the evening of yesterday 16 women and one man were arrested for crossing the river. They were detained in the compound of the headman of this place [Kugnau]. Today all the elders were called together and the detained persons interrogated. They were all Kugnau people. The stupidity of them disobeying orders that no one was to cross the river was pointed out. The man arrested was also a Kugnau man and was found to be with his bow and ten arrows, knives etc. After a long palaver and using my utmost efforts to dissuade these people from fraternizing with the cross river Konkombas, the accused was deprived of his bow and arrows, which were there and then burnt. As a reminder to him that orders were to be obeyed, he had 12 strokes.

At 3.30 my constable messenger returned with a letter from the French commissioner. The constable informs me that the French have burnt 11 villages and killed six men, this he gathered from talk with the troops. The whole country between the river and the present French force is full of armed Konkombas and he tells me that at Nanduka, just above the river, he saw more arrows than would fill two of my chop boxes. Major Woelffrel is coming to Sambul to meet me in, he says, two or three days' time. The French idea of bringing peace and reason to a country would appear to me humorous if not so sad. Our methods, that of a DC and a few constables (the latter but the insignia of power rather than its actuality) going round talking common sense and listening to natives' grouses, would be far more beneficial and lasting.

25 January 1918
Dispatched a letter to Major Woelffrel advising him not to bring any horses across the Oti on account of tsetse and telling him I would arrange horses for him this side if he let me know the day and hour he would be coming.

26 January 1918
Went to Kanjock ferry and supervised the cleaning of a track from there to Sambul. The country between the river and Sambul is low lying and damned every few paces for fish-catching purposes. On arrival back for breakfast at 9.30, was met by a letter from the French asking me to go over to Nanduka for lunch or dinner today. Dispatched mounted messenger telling lunch impossible. Would come over at 3.00 p.m. At 3.00 p.m. crossed the river and was met by Major Woelffrel and his Staff Officer. The cavalry, so-called, were drawn up at the approach to the village, some 50 chiefs and their followers, in fact any owner of a horse, armed with spears and dressed to taste, which I inspected. Nanduka was the scene of a very untidy would-be military camp. In the big marquee in the centre were the commissioners of Bassari and Sansanne Mango, with the doctor from the latter place. The matters concerning the Konkombas were discussed and the French seemed only too keen on doing anything in their power to assist, but told me that, as every village they had visited had been found to be abandoned, they were powerless to do anything except impress the poor savages with their might, which they did by systematically destroying the villages. They told me they had burnt and laid waste more than 12 villages, confiscating all the cattle, sheep, goats and pigs, the last if not eaten during their push, were killed and left. They also destroyed any grain and, so far as possible, the yam farms. Three of the mounted 'catch them alive ohs' had been wounded and another, the chief of Napari, killed by arrows from the bush when on their marauding excursions, for which a penalty was meted out by the deaths of 22 Konkombas. So far as I can gather, all the villages that were across the River Oti exist no more. I was told that any Konkomba seen within a bow and arrow was shot on sight. The French officers seemed very pleased with themselves and not at all upset or

even surprised at their lack of political success. They impressed me with the fact that their men, with hangers on totalling about 450, had never been so well done by in their lives, had as much meat as they could do with and any farm produce procurable. These officers have in their employment late German cooks, stewards and interpreters and have reinstated the German village policeman of old days. So much so are these men employed that a great deal of the conversation was carried on in German. What these parasites think of their new masters would be interesting to know, but, even with all the kind hospitality I was receiving, I was not enamoured with our allies in these parts. The wisest thing the Konkombas ever did was to hide, in my opinion, and they all now have my sincere sympathy. Spending the night – one of six in a marquee – in which at least two were constantly snoring and the immediate proximity being occupied by boys, soldiers, horses, sheep, goats and cattle, and the soldier guard passing the long hours in conversation and stoking up the fires, sleep and self were strangers.

27 January 1918

At dawn arose and, after bidding *au revoir* to my hosts who were continuing their triumphant march to Kanjock anticipating the destruction of at least four villages *en route*, left for Sambul via Kugnau, where I am to entertain four of my last night's hosts for dinner and the night. What strikes me is the extraordinary lack of responsibility the French appear to possess and their seeming contentment at the result of their mission. One DC with a couple of constables could have done infinitely more good and would have left no bitterness behind. Now I have the feeling of the Pharisees of old, 'Thank God I am not as other men are.'

At 3.30 met the Commandant, his Staff Officer and the MO at the river. Some half mile from Sambul the Konkombas met us, in full war paint, accompanied by their elders all dancing and singing, and escorted us into the village. The French officers expressed great pleasure at their reception, which was on a scale foreign to them in these parts. After the Guard of Honour had been inspected and dismissed, the Konkombas from silence burst out into furious drumming and wild dancing, which appeared to much interest and amuse the French. At a signal all became quiet and with the elders sitting in front, Major Woelffrel made them all a speech and, while stating that he regarded the Konkombas as the finest race in Togoland, lamented the fact that those in French territory were not as friendly, obedient and law abiding as their brothers in British territory. He told them that, owing to bad behaviour amongst themselves and also against their British brothers, he was now engaged in punishing the French Konkombas with a view to making them as friendly and desirable as those in his audience. The elders then spoke and thanked the French for coming and poured out their woes over the Kanjock affair, stating that it was only owing to the DPO Yendi they had refrained from attacking and eating up the Kanjocks. The commandant said that, if the elders liked, they can cross over tomorrow and if possible point out the men who had murdered the Sambul youths. They agreed. 'Dashes' were offered to the French, which were accepted.

28 January 1918
Accompanied the French to the river and, seeing them into their canoes, bid them goodbye. The Sergeant Major and one constable crossed with them and the elders to Sambul to hear the palaver. We parted the greatest of friends. In course of conversation, the commandant informed me that the price of strophanthus seed[51] was over 200 francs a kilo, four sovereigns a pound! It is so valuable it is sold by the gram. At 3.30 my interpreter and elders arrived back from Kanjock, the latter were very well pleased with themselves. They relate the whole of their troubles and all their statements were agreed to by the Kanjoks themselves. One of the offenders, he who shot the last Sambul victim, was present, but, before the Sambuls could inform the French commandant, he had vanished. The elders returned with a large pot full of salt and a large cloth as a present.

29 January 1918
Received a letter from the French that today Passari was to be burnt and in all probability Kanjock, after which Major Woelffrel was returning to Bassari via Nandutaba and Lieutenant Dubois was from there to proceed to Nayile and Noambach, which he would burn. I dispatched at once the Sergeant Major, two sergeants and 25 men to guard the land boundary between the River Dakpe and River Oti. The burning of the villages across the river opposite will not be at all popular on either side.

4 May 1918
Dispatched mail to Tamale and Salaga, also sent the sick wife of a constable to Tamale in a hammock for treatment, as fear she will die if left here. Last night, going through a government farm to the plantation, saw it covered with wild pigeons, never seen so many in my life before in one place. Stone throwing scarcely disconcerting them at all; had to return for a gun. The whole farm will have to be again planted. NTC clothing arrived from Tamale. Kit inspection at 3.00 p.m. and distribution of new clothing.

Sunday 5 May 1918
Interviewed the Konkombas working here. Explained the reason they

had been called in, that of cleaning the plantation on the one hand and for instruction in farming on the other. Impressed them with the wisdom of planting around their villages bananas, mangoes, etc., young plants of which will be given them from here for that purpose. Drew their attention to the fact that out of the hundreds of banana plants I distributed among them last year, not one is to be seen now.

Gushiegu, 9 May 1918
Held a large meeting in the morning. Having Mr Tamakloe[52] with me, and being sure of correct translations, am holding meetings in every village passed through on subjects of sanitation, castration of cattle, mule breeding, fruit planting, rotation of crops. One does not get much encouragement from the tedium of these discourses as these people would appear to be almost unteachable. Not feeling at all well again today, had bad headache for two days which I cannot shake off. Much afraid I shall be unable to put in another year as desired. My two long tours and short leaves have told on me.

10 May 1918
Held a two-hour meeting with the chief and people in the afternoon, varied and numerous subjects were discussed. There is a great scarcity of food here this year. So much so, that money is almost useless. I heard yams being refused at the unheard of price in the country of *6d*. Corn is also very scarce. The country here is as dry as a stick.

11 May 1918
Mail from Tamale. Had a touch of malaria the whole afternoon.

12 May 1918
Malaria giving way to quinine.

14 May 1918
My two geldings have caused quite a stir in the villages visited. I never saw natives show such a keen interest in anything before. The statement that the operation carried out on them was to demonstrate, through my own belongings, the faith I have in the teachers, has borne fruit and some 30 sheep and goats were produced for my interpreter to operate upon and teach the process. One village, after listening to the pros and cons and having their inborn distaste for new ideas somewhat dispelled stated, 'We will do a goat tomorrow, and if it dies we will chop the meat, and if it lives we will thank God,' a remark that so amused me, I roared with laughter to the surprise of everyone. No remark for years has so appealed to my sense of the ridiculous.

15 May 1918
A complaint came in that a murder had been committed at Kudza.

Sent off sergeant and three constables to investigate and bring in accused. It is apparently over a 'corpse knocking' palaver.[53]

16 May 1918
Busy listening to diverse mammie palavers and interviewing chiefs.

18 May 1918
Mail dispatched to Salaga. Allotted farmland for the new arrivals of NTC and commenced cultivation. The scarcity of hoes is the trouble; shall be glad when a fresh supply from Passari arrives. The sixpenny prewar hoe is selling in the market here for 3/6*d*. Rain is badly wanted; the new farms are looking anything but happy now.

19 May 1918
Inspected the MI and watched them being moved about under the newly-arrived sergeant for a few minutes till a drizzle commenced. Seeing the constabulary always have Friday respected as their Sunday, to give them our Sunday as a second day's laze would not appear fair to other workers, or good for them. Consequently, on Sundays they are detailed for work on their own farms.

24 May 1918
Empire Day. At 8.00 a.m. the chief, elders and subchiefs and large crowds of people assembled in courthouse. The NTC in review order, after being inspected, marched off led by the local band. Drummers, both mounted and foot, followed immediately by the DPO, the chief and a large body of mounted men to the marketplace and back to the parade ground upon which the flag was flying. The DPO immediately beneath the ensign and the chief and all his horsemen, some 30 men, just behind watched the parade (1) march past in column two deep; (2) *feu de joie*; (3) march past in column in single rank; (4) advance in review order led by the DPO, the mounted spectators following in rear. The flag was saluted and all, with hats off, gave three cheers for the King. The scene was impressive and was enthusiastically entered into by everyone. The NTC being dismissed, the drummers played beneath the flag, while the horsemen rode round and round making their horses caper and prance. This seemed to give great delight. It is only for showing-off purposes, such as this, that these people ever use their animals.

To wind up the palaver, all adjourned to the courthouse where an address was given and Empire Day explained and the sundry outside chiefs were greeted. A dash to the chief was not unappreciated. At 3.30 a large crowd assembled for horse racing and athletic sports, which went with a bang. The Konkomba labourers keenly competing in the running races and were enthusiastically cheered. The chief, seated in my buggy, gave away the prizes, which did not lessen his enjoyment. I was acting starter the whole time.

26 May 1918
Mail to and from Salaga. The runners complain that 1/– is necessary for food on the road owing to the drain on the local supplies by the numerous recruits, who are so well paid that they are able to pay anything demanded, runners on *6d.* and *3d.* per diem suffer a grave handicap. I would ask to be authorized to pay at rate of 1/– per diem.

30 May 1918
The *trindana* paid a visit and stated he was in trouble. After listening to him, during which as is usual, he related his past history from boyhood on, came to the point stating that, owing to the death of all of his sons, his wives refuse to live with him any longer unless he leaves Sambul. Three of his sons, young men of marriageable age, have all died recently. Each started with a violent headache, got very bloodshot eyes and were dead in three or four days. After most careful enquiries as to dates, it would appear that these three youths have all died since his visit to Kanjock to visit the French commissioner. I am thankful to say he does not attribute their deaths to this incident and I, of course, have been careful not to let him suspect my views as to the significance of it.

4 November 1918
The CC arrived from Tamale at 8.30 a.m. The chief and elders met him and escorted him to the courthouse. The assembly was not as large as usual owing to the numbers who are now laid up with influenza. The CC held a meeting and related at length war news and the latest armistice terms, which were received with joy. In the evening the CC visited and treated the sick — two serious cases, one a sergeant of his escort and the other the wife of my steward who, having recovered from blackwater fever, is now bad with malaria.

25 November 1918
The day was devoted to the sick and correspondence — 15 Konkombas working in Yendi are down with it as also half of the CC's carriers. At 4.00 p.m. the CC visited Sergeant Musa and Chesney's wife, giving medicines. The former was so much better in the morning, the jaundice symptoms having given way to treatment, that he was considered to be on the high road to recovery. At 9.00 p.m. I visited Musa and found him with practically no temperature, but very frightened, being surrounded by a lugubrious crowd of men and women. He was lying naked to the waist and, after covering him up, reported to the CC that fear would kill him, if anything. The CC, not being

satisfied, paid him a visit himself and, after driving away the spectators, soothed him to sleep. Half an hour afterwards, he was reported to have died. Nothing surprised me more in my life. Not crediting the tidings, we both visited and substantiated the unexpected news.

26 November 1918
The chief and elders, together with all the *malams*, attended Musa's burial. At the completion of the native ceremony, the CC and self went to the grave while three volleys were fired and the last post sounded. The flu is all through the town now, there must be hundreds of cases.

27 November 1918
The CC held a meeting of the chiefs and elders, but owing to flu the assembly was very small, when he again tried to reassure them as to the flu, which I am thankful to say appears to have arrived here in a mild form. The matter of lack of hoes was brought up. The CC said he would try and get iron workers from Dagarti country to come here and teach them smelting. My day was occupied over an enquiry as to the death of Sergeant Musa, especially in connection with the disregard of the CC's instructions as to his treatment. The evidence was appalling, especially that of the women who, though seen in Musa's room by the CC, self and all the male witnesses, stoutly declared they had not been near him!

28 November 1918
The flu is spreading. Out of 40 Konkombas, 25 are down with it and today the clerical staff of the CC, as also mine, are down with it.

29 November 1918
How are the mighty fallen. The CC is today in bed with flu. Busy all day with the available fit men thatching the *zongo* and new NTC stable. I am purposely carrying on this work now to take the people's thoughts away from disease and death. I have got so tired of the woebegone looks of the people mooning about under a chorus of coughs and I think work will act as an excellent restorative to their nerves. The CC's projected tour around Konkomba country is to be deferred. I am glad of this as, with luck, they may escape it being off the beaten track. Pneumonia rampant among an unclothed race might prove disastrous.

(ii) A. L. Castellain, DPO, 1919

Thursday 1 May 1919
From Demon to Sambul via Palbu, Tschangbani and Kuntule. At the former and latter place, the CC spoke to the people about avoiding quarrelling and also begged them to give up the stupid practice of

corpse carrying. The audience at both places listened attentively. We then passed on to Sambul where in the evening the headman, together with a representative crowd of youngmen, came to hear what the CC had to say to them. He spoke on the same subjects as at the other villages. His remarks in reference to corpse carrying, 'that it was either done to get revenge or as a means to fill the fetishman's pockets', have on each occasion brought forth smiles from the crowds.

2 May 1919
Visited Kugnau with the CC. A large crowd met us and followed us through the village, singing and dancing, to the rest house where the CC addressed them on the usual subjects. After taking a few snapshots, we returned to Sambul. Finished typing the April diary.

3 May 1919
In the evening, the usual palaver was held and after it was over a man stepped forward and said he had something to say. He said that he was a fetishman and, now that the CC had given away all his secrets, what was he to do for a living? He was told to go in for saving people's lives and not make medicine to do others harm.

7 May 1919
Said goodbye to the CC, who left for Zan and I returned to Yendi, which I reached about 6.30 a.m. Busy in office all morning. The chief of Yendi came to see me to ask permission for his people to play for and visit the chief of Bimbilla; I readily gave my consent. I then had a talk to him about his scowl of yesterday. He said that he was very pleased to see the chief of Bimbilla and, for that reason, had put on his best clothes. According to their custom, when a man puts on his best clothes he does not eat, so he was feeling the pangs of hunger. He also implied that he considered it was infra dig for a man to be smiling on an important occasion. I told him that he ought to eat a good meal before putting on his fine clothing. He then told me that when one Nasigiri was king of Dagomba he quarrelled with the chief of Kombi. He gave me the names of the kings that succeeded Nasigiri up to the present time, his father, Allassan, being thirteenth. He also informed me that when the CCNT came to Yendi in August 1914, the then chief of Bimbilla was a very old man, so he sent the chief of Nakpa as his representative to meet the CC.

12 May 1919
General inspection of station. Maize and groundnuts have now been planted in the government farm. Spent rest of morning pruning trees in constabulary lines.

15 May 1919
I am taking a load of pineapple suckers and a load of shade tree cuttings for Mr Cardinall at Navarro, and will send them off from Gushiegu to Gambaga. I find the overseer an excellent man and he has packed the cuttings splendidly. I had a talk to the chiefs of Sunson in the evening and told them that the CC regretted he could not visit more villages. I added that he urged the people to whom he had talked to live peaceably and to give up corpse carrying. I have cut down the five small cotton trees growing inside the rest house compound, as when they grow up they would have pushed the house out of the compound altogether.

17 May 1919
Started the twenty-first month of my tour today. Left for bush before dawn in the hope that I should see something to shoot. All I saw were three oribi, of which I was only able to get a shot at one and was successful. This afternoon, a tramp of four and a half hours. When I was here in March, I saw innumerable and recent spoor of bush cow, but saw none today and, on enquiry, learned that as soon as the rains started they left for Nabune. As I intend visiting Nabune shortly, I hope to meet them. I expected the mails to reach me today, both from Salaga and Tamale, but was disappointed.

19 May 1919
Up early to find a very black sky to the east, portending rain; I hoped, however, that I might get well on my way to Gushiegu before the storm broke. We made good pace to the village, about half way, when I heard that the chief of Gushiegu had come there to meet me and lead me to his town. I therefore had to slacken my pace to a walk as I couldn't expect the poor old man to canter after me. About ten minutes later the storm broke and we were soon wet through.

20 May 1919
Left at 6.30 a.m. to visit the villages in the vicinity of Gushiegu. I do not agree with Captain Poole's statement that 'The Dagomba population is decreasing to an alarming extent' (vide annual report 1918). He bases his assertion on the fact that many villages, shown on the German map, no longer exist, also that 'not a single village being now as large as then, 1907 enumerated'. Both these statements are incorrect. There are many villages now existing that are not shown on the German map. Many of the villages are hardly worth the name being, composed of from one to three compounds only. It is the custom to bring a headman from such a village to another, frequently at some distance off; and when he goes to take up his new appointment, the

remainder of the village go with him and the place is deserted. The chief came to see me in the evening and we had a talk on general matters. I showed him some of the hoes recently sent from Accra, but they are not popular and I only sold two. The headman of Niyansen, an old preventive station on the Patenga–Gambaga road, came across to salute me, which I thought very nice of him. A small English and local mail arrived from Salaga, the delay being caused by the DC Salaga instructing my postman to carry a box of specie, the escort refusing to make long marches, especially as the corporal in charge was accompanied by his wife and family.

23 May 1919
On the 20th, an escort of a corporal and two privates of the GCR arrived with £100 in sixpence and threepennies from Coomassie. This small change will be a great help to me, as about 80 per cent of the money recently sent to me, has been either one or two shilling pieces.

24 May 1919
Empire Day, general holiday. Full dress parade at 8.00 am. The chief of Yendi, his elders and a good crowd of people were present. There was a march past, the flag was saluted and three cheers were given for the King. I then addressed the crowd explaining Empire Day.

Sunday 25 May 1919
Busy entering up the records of my visit to the various villages in the information book.

26 May 1919
Had an interview with the chief about growing corn round the compound. He informed me that all the people are well aware of the order. He also said that the new canoe for the ferry on the Yendi–Sambul road was nearly ready. After visiting the new bungalow, the walls of which are about eight feet high, I proceeded down to the wells and back along the Bassari road past the chief's compound. I found some of the branches of the trees rather low over the road and the chief informed me 'that they knocked the water pots off the women's heads'. I spent the morning with a constabulary fatigue party lopping off the offending branches.

I have just interviewed the man who was in charge of the kapok ginning and baling last year with a view to commencing to pick and bale the two loads that the CC had instructed me to send to Akuse. He informs me that the ginning machine broke in the middle of the operation last year, so children were brought in to pick it, which was done very imperfectly. As it was picked, the kapok was put into a large box, which, when full, was taken to the press. Then several youths got into the press and stamped it down. No wonder, therefore, that pieces of pod, seeds and dust were found among the kapok on arrival in England. I consider that Swanzy's representative, who was here at the time, should have reported to Captain Poole.

27 May 1919
Just after 5.00 p.m. the chief came in to see me and said that Malam Iddi was troubling him, threatening to go to Tamale and make trouble if he was not made *limam*. The chief favours Malam Zakari. I told him I would go into the case tomorrow morning.

28 May 1919
I rode round the plantation before breakfast with the overseer and pointed out several things I wished done. Quite a number of young rubber trees have sprung up in promiscuous places. This is due to the sticks having been used for props etc. They are the easiest things to grow and a horrible nuisance.

30 May 1919
I had a visit from the chief. I tried to get some history of the district from him. I wanted to find out when the Germans first occupied Yendi. There must be some records at Lomé of which I would like extracts to put in the new district book that I am starting.

3 June 1919
King's birthday and general holiday. As a lot of the chiefs and headmen had come in, we had some horse and foot races in the afternoon, but in the middle of the excitement a swarm of bees descended upon the crowd and scattered it. Fortunately for me, I was at the starting point and they did not come near me. Shortly afterwards, a heavy shower of rain came so we dispersed altogether. A mail came from Tamale and also a box containing cowries from the CC.

7 June 1919
I had intended going out this morning and visiting several villages in the bush between the Demon and Gnani roads, but I cannot get my helmet on my head as I was bitten on the forehead by some insect or fly two or three days ago and there is a lump the size of a pigeon's egg, so I am more or less confined to my bungalow.

Notes

1. The diaries of Major R. A. Irvine and Captain C. A. Armitage are in GNA, Accra. Adm. 56/1/77.
2. From 16 November to 30 December 1917 the diary covers a trek through ex-German Togoland.

3. The DC in Togoland was known as the District Political Officer.
4. The Governor Sir Hugh Clifford wrote at the end of the November diary: 'I have read this diary with more than ordinary interest.'
5. Sunk by a German submarine.
6. The HQ of the NT was transferred from Gambaga to Tamale in 1907, where the PC Southern Province and the DC Western Dagomba also had their HQ.
7. The first government school in the Protectorate was opened in Tamale in 1909. The next school in the north was opened at Gambaga in 1912.
8. The cemetery exercised the minds of DCs and MOs alike. It was to discourage the various groups from burying their people haphazardly in the family compound.
9. The Yeji district diary is in a large leather-bound ledger. It is mainly handwritten, though a few pages are typed and clipped into the ledger. Between July 1915 and March 1920 Yeji was administered from Salaga. GNA Accra 64/5/4.
10. Spirits were prohibited in the NT.
11. In preparation for the visit of the Governor, Sir Hugh Clifford.
12. Sir Hugh Clifford's own diary is in CO 96/536.
13. It was not unusual for a DC to apply for more cash for sanitary and other improvements than he expected to get, knowing that his wants would be severely pruned.
14. GNA, Accra. Adm. 58/5/1. The first and only available diary for Bole Western Frontier District, NT, is handwritten in a large, hard-backed ledger, beginning in December 1913 and kept by M. G. S. Sherriff. Sherriff either resented the extra work involved or had no idea what ought go in to it, and his remarks are minimal. Captain Short took over on 31 March 1914. His entries are equally brief and uninformative. Dr Duff took over in March 1915 and was Ag DC for more than eight months, combining those duties with his own as MO. He meticulously divided his day between the two departmental responsibilities, at the expense (understandably) of the diary.
15. In late August 1916, E. O. Rake handed over the station to E. G. Dasent, who on 5 October 1916 handed it over to M. G. S. Sherriff. Sherriff's diary covers the next ten days, then there is a note in the diary by G. W. F. Wright. 'This diary was not used after October 1916, or rather this book was not kept as a diary. On taking over the station in April 1917, I made a search for the office diary, but could find only a few notes on loose foolscap, pinned together, which were handed to the Ag DC. The health of the Ag DC (who was invalided for blackwater) prevented him giving any information or from handing over the station, stores etc. So I took the station over as it stood and as I found it.' Underneath the CC, C. H. Armitage, has written, 'It would appear that Mr Sherriff kept no station diary from the date of his arrival in Bole.'
16. Early in 1917 there was an attempted rising in Bole. It was largely caused by resentment at the call by government for recruits. Because of the war in Europe, rumour was rife that the white man could no longer

rule and was leaving. The paramount chief of Yabum and the Senyon fetish priest took the opportunity to stir up trouble and fighting men were called into Bole from all the surrounding villages. If Sherriff had been respected and trusted by the chiefs and people, the revolt might not have occurred. Sherriff, perhaps due to the onset of his illness, appears to have acted in a very high-handed manner, which was greatly resented by the chiefs. Yabum complained that the DC had ordered his arrest and informed him he was no longer chief. Yabum and the fetish priest were tried and sentenced to death by the Ag CC, but were later pardoned by the Governor (see entry 6 June 1917). Sherriff was severely reprimanded by the CC for 'maladministration'.

17. Many extra troops, as well as European officers and their attendant carriers, were rushed to the district when the trouble broke out and, as always on these occasions, a huge strain was put on the food supply and local resources.
18. This was in addition to his other duties as MO.
19. Like DCs, doctors were maids of all work and were frequently called upon to act as veterinary officers (see Poole entry 3 April 1914).
20. The influenza epidemic swept across Africa, causing many deaths in the Gold Coast.
21. This proposed visit by the Governor to the NT does not seem to have taken place. Accra's apparent lack of interest in this impoverished region of the Gold Coast caused considerable resentment among the political officers in the north.
22. GNA Accra. Adm. 62/5/4. The diary is on loose sheets of paper and dilapidated.
23. The French always appeared to get outside news before the British.
24. The reference to the MO is misleading. Dr Oakley had reverted to MO for the evening. For a reversal of roles, see Walker Leigh entry of 19 November 1913.
25. This is the start of a new ledger called Tumu Wa District, Adm. 66/5/6. A. O. Rake is still Ag DC.
26. GNA Accra, Adm. 61/5/7.
27. A French station in the Ivory Coast.
28. A local creeper, the strands of which were twisted and used as rope.
29. The doctor usually took over the station when the DC was on trek.
30. Permission had to be obtained from the PC before a DC could order flogging.
31. The Colonial Secretary later wrote to the CC: 'I am to ask you to be so good as to inform ACD Johnstone, Ag DC Lorha, that HE commends him for the excellent work done by him in connection with the outbreak of smallpox in his district towards the end of last year' (GNA Adm. 56/1/177).
32. GNA Accra Adm. 03/5/3. Navarro, as it is called in the diaries, is shown on modern maps as Navrongo. The district diary is kept in a type of heavy ledger.

33. It belonged to Captain Mackey, a survey officer. Most DCs in the NT rode a pony.
34. Many political officers, doctors and part of the GCR were drafted to Togoland and the Cameroons during the war. In 1915 the two districts of Navarro and Zouaragu were combined and administered by one DC, though each district kept up its diary. The Provincial HQ were moved to Gambaga.
35. The loss of life according to the Governor (Clifford) need not have occurred if DC Castellain had acted more promptly by going himself to Bongo to investigate the trouble, instead of sending the constabulary. Nor did the CC, Captain Armitage, and the PC, Captain Wheeler, escape censure, Clifford maintaining they should have realized the seriousness of the unrest and gone immediately to the district to take charge of the situation. Clifford reported the fracas at great length to the Colonial Office, as did the CC who explained his actions (CO 96/570). A précis of Castellain's diary of 21 April 1916 to 21 May 1916 is attached to this PRO file, which may explain why it is missing from the Navarro diary in the GNA.
36. A school was opened at Navarro by the Pères Blancs in 1907. Until the government school was opened at Tamale in 1909, it was the only non-Muslim school in the NT. In a letter re the Mission Station Navarro, the Bishop of the Sudan writes on 3 September 1912, 'This station has as yet, only Fathers (Canadian). I had made arrangements to send there some of the White Sisters (Canadian) when, lo and behold, I am informed that HE the Governor of the Gold Coast, under a general order, decreed a year ago, that European ladies should no longer be permitted to stay in the northern part of the Colony. Reason: lack of creature comforts' (PRO CO 6/526).
37. In 1917 government asked all chiefs to nominate a quota of young men as recruits (see entry 17 August 1917). This work seems to have occupied much of the DC's time. His successes and failures are recorded almost daily in the diaries. The British administration claimed there was no compulsory conscription in the Gold Coast during the First World War, but it seems to have been pretty close to it. The French, who were engaged in a vigorous campaign of compulsory conscription in their West African colonies, were very anxious that Britain should do likewise.
38. Her collection, *Our Days on the Gold Coast*, was published in 1918 by John Murray in aid of the Red Cross.
39. The proposed NT railway was abandoned in 1922 due to the depression.
40. GNA, Accra. Adm. 68/5/2. By 1915 Castellain is spelling it Zuaragu, and by 1920 the modern spelling of Zuarungu has generally been adopted. The pages of the diaries are clipped together. The paper is much damaged and very brittle. Many are out of order and have been much shuffled. They are mainly typed, copies sent weekly to the CC who had made a number of pithy marginal comments. [The original hand-written diaries are in a heavy ledger in Adm. 68/5/1.]

41. Strophanthus.
42. Sir Donald Stewart led several missions to Ashanti and the NT before being appointed Resident Kumasi in 1896. According to him, the Ashantis 'had a very wholesome feeling of mingled fear and respect for Captain Stewart, whom they had known for years as a strong, but just man, who would deal with any trouble promptly and severely and stand no nonsense.'
43. GNA Accra. 56/1/184. Wheeler's diary is taken from the PC's file, Tamale.
44. A. J. Berney, DC Gambaga, died in December 1910.
45. GNA Accra. Adm. 68/5/1.
46. In May 1915 the districts of Navarro and Zouaragu had been combined and administered by one DC. He usually spent two or three weeks at each station, and kept up both diaries with the help of his clerk.
47. When G. E. Gilbert was sent up to the NT he had only been in the Gold Coast two months, having spent one month as a TC and another as Ag DC, Accra.
48. Note in margin by Ag CC: 'We are getting no trunk roads for four years. In the fifth year it will reach Tamale according to the scheme.'
49. GNA, Accra. Adm. 57/5/9. The Bawku weekly diary is written on loose sheets of paper, clipped together with rusty clips. It is partly handwritten and partly typed. Dr Robert Whyte combined his duties as MO with those of DC.
50. GNA, Accra 5F/1/229. The DC in Togoland was known as the DPO.
51. Used in making poisoned arrows.
52. E. F. Tamakloe of the Gold Coast Civil Service was from Togoland. He was interested in and extremely knowledgeable about the Dagombas, and wrote parts of A. W. Cardinall's *Tales Told in Togoland*, 1931. He also wrote *A Brief History of the Dagomba People.*
53. In a letter to Poole dated 6 August 1918, the CC writes: 'with reference to your informal diary for May, the Governor has requested to be informed what is meant by "corpse knocking palavers". I have informed him that it is the "Afunsoa custom", suppressed by order, under the native customs ordinance no. 11 of 1892.' It is usually referred to as 'carrying the corpse'. If the people believed that someone had died by witchcraft, the body was carried round the town in a cloth or mat and if it swayed or knocked against a person or house that person or the house owner was said to be a witch to have caused the death and was frequently killed or at least driven out of the village.

Appendix A
T. E. Fell's Letters from Accra, 1897/8[1]

16 October 1897
Arrived at Sierra Leone. It is absolutely lovely from the sea, looking like a sort of tropical Torquay. Lovely tropical vegetation right up to the top of the mountains and, just after the rains, everything looks so green and fresh. One could hardly realize it being called the white man's grave. We went ashore at once. The town is very quaint and amusing, tremendous variety of colours, long flowing Mohammedan robes, and some niggers and negresses dressed *à la* church parade. We went all over the native market. I bought some fresh fish for bait today and bargained with some grand old dames. By the way, the great character of this place is called Selina Macauley. She is a washer woman of very doubtful repute who always comes on board ships to get the passengers' washing. She is about 60, as black as your hat and dressed in a red gown, magenta shawl and emerald green turban. Such a sight you never saw, but the colours being so varied in her costume I rushed and of course accepted her as aunt.

23 October 1897
We anchored off Accra at 7.00 a.m. It was raining hard and looked most dismal. However, after breakfast it cleared up and Mr Hodgson, self, Williams and Bellair came on shore in a surf boat.[2] It was terrible. A ladder into the boat from the ship's side was very awkward as the boat kept rising and falling. We tossed about in it till we got near the shore where we waited patiently for a large wave to carry us in and, when it did come, by Jove it did come, we went straight on end. The canoe boys paddling like the deuce to get over the top of it and we were finally shot like lightning onto the beach. As soon as we touched we were seized by dozens of naked, more or less, natives by the legs, arms, head or anywhere they could lay hold of, lifted out of the boat and carried out of danger of the next wave. I can tell you, a first land-

ing in a surf boat is rather funking. When we were finally on shore we were met by a number of government officials to most of whom I was introduced and was seized by a man named Attrill,[3] who drove me in his cart to the Secretariat. From there, I was carried off to lunch with a Mr and Mrs Knollys, who seem to be well-connected people in England. He is a first rate sort of man, but she, although a lady, is not my style – large, bounding, slangy, colonial, and drinks cocktails. However, they were very kind and lent me their cart, blankets, lamps, soap and all manner of whatnots for the night, as I had not then got into my boxes. In fact, everyone is very hospitable. The club here too is very nice. All today I have been inundated by niggers applying for the situation of my boy. I have engaged a cook for a month named Henry Amisah, who seems a decent sort of nigger. My bungalow is very nice and cool, thoroughly tropical, although so far I have not felt the heat the least oppressive. This morning I went to the stores and bought crockery, pots and pans etc. I have a cart dragged by two Kroo boys and paid for by government, which takes me wherever I want to go.

[In a long PS written two days later:] So far the climate seems more agreeable than otherwise, always cool in the shade with a nice breeze, but of course very hot in the sun; however, a white sun hat and white umbrella give plenty of protection from it. My job, I find, is by no means an easy one. I go to the office about 7.30 till 11.30, back again at 1.30 and away at 4.30 or 5.30. Some of my work is most interesting. I have to keep a confidential register of all confidential documents and telegrams under lock and key and allow no one else to see it without an order from the Colonial Secretary.

One has to be most particular – HE the Governor, the Hon. the Colonial Secretary etc. There is a great deal of etiquette in many ways. I started learning and practising the code for deciphering official telegrams today; some of the terms are most amusing. I feel very fit and take a small dose of quinine every other day.

14 December 1897

I have gone into a bungalow with a man called Attrill, the Chief Assistant Colonial Secretary and we get on A1. He is without exception the straightest man I know; a frightful temper, but thoroughly straight and we are great pals. We are trying to make our bungalow really homely and nice with plants and ferns and planting our compound. I went out shooting last Saturday; my gun is a ripper and I bagged a bush fowl, a sort of lesser buzzard, much to my pride. Walking through the bush after game is very rough work. The grass is very thick and a certain sort of it runs into a kind of net, which catches tightly round the ankles and is the deuce to struggle through.

28 February 1898
Ag Governor Hodgson has gone on a small trip into the forest, about six hours in a hammock, to a place called Aburi,[4] where I am going to bicycle to on Saturday. Hodgson made as much fuss as if he were off to the Hinterland. Things are quickly getting to a climax in this Hinterland and Northcott, in command of our force, has telegraphed down begging permission to attack the French, who establish posts under our noses and laugh at our protests. Of course Northcott won't get leave, but things are undoubtedly getting very strained between the two forces now they are so close to each other. For years we have gone about making wretched treaties of Trade and Commerce with the Hinterland kings and chiefs while the French have supplemented them all with treaties of Protection, telling the kings that by making this second treaty with them they are in no way disloyal to us as the two treaties are different affairs. There are endless discussions going on now about French and English treaties, but the French are always the strongest and most lasting. We have undoubtedly made asses of ourselves.

16 March 1898
Nobody knows what is going on in the Hinterland. I got up a cricket match about a fortnight ago against 11 Special Service men going up the Niger. They seem a jolly good lot. They are waiting for Lugard and not one of them has the least idea what they are going to do or what they are there for. I think it is a pretty big business and Lugard seems to have it all locked up in his bosom. My clothes are shrinking horribly, but no matter.

8 May 1898
One never knows what one may have to do in this Colony but I have very nearly been sent off on a five months tour of the Hinterland with £15,000 specie and a doctor and escort, to pay off arrears of pay to the Hausas. I wish I could go, although the rains are on. The Quarter-master and Paymaster of the Hausas was detailed to go and he became ill and it is even now a question of whether he starts or not. At any rate, I have undertaken his work while he is away and move to the Hausa cantonments, four miles out, tomorrow. I shall like the life out there, there are two or three officers and a billiard table; it is cheap and in the middle of the shooting. I am awfully glad to be put onto this new job. The exigencies of the service out here are most erratic and it is very amusing to see me gazetted as a Hausa officer. Mr T. E. Fell, Chief Clerk Secretariat, to act as Inspector Gold Coast Constabulary.

10 May 1898
The Governor is getting up an entertainment for the Queen's birthday. Preserve me from their entertainment, they never leave you alone for a moment and we are all in a state of open revolt. The Hinterland sits, as usual, on different posts – French ones and English ones curiously interspersed. One day the Frenchman says to the English, 'You clear out or we'll shoot.' The Englishman says, 'Very well, shoot then we'll shoot back.' The Frenchman says, 'That would mean a Franco–English war.' And the Englishman says, 'All right you fired first and started it.' The Frenchman says, 'Well never mind it now, we'll postpone operations; by the way are you breakfasting with me today or I with you?' Imagine this in many different places in the Hinterland and you know everything that is going on.

3 July 1898
I still flourish in spite of everything and, except for an outbreak of malarial boils or 'safety valves' as the doctor calls them, I am very fit indeed. I went out for a drive yesterday with an American merchant named Yates, who has brought out the only carriage and pair the Colony has ever seen. It is a sort of trotting machine and very comfortable. Yates is a good old sort too. The surf today is very bad and, as there is a steamer in, I went down to see the boats go out to it. Two were upset in the breakers and it was most exciting.

6 August 1898
Having had three days fever, I applied for a week's change here and am quite set up again. I did the 26½ mile journey in a hammock, which is a luxurious but slow method of travelling. You are carried on the heads of four men. This place is perfectly lovely and I only wish you could have a glimpse of it. The cotton trees are now very fine and green, some of them going up to 150 feet or so without a branch. There is a large vegetable garden growing most English vegetables, which are a great treat and I revel in lettuce, spinach, radishes etc. Cocoa does splendidly here and will some day be a large export, if only the natives will take up the growing of it.

8 September 1898
There is just a chance now that I may be kept over my time. I hope not. It is a terrible business staying over one's time in this Colony and necessitates being examined by about four doctors together who report on the progress the malarial microbe has made in your system during the year. If not a hotbed of germs, you are allowed to stay. I only hope I shan't have to undergo the bother, but shall receive a minute from the Governor saying I may go on the first steamer after

2lst October. By the way, read Dr Koch on malarial and blackwater fever. He asserts that the latter is simply quinine poisoning, a theory which tends to upset all West African treatments, as blackwater fever is a terribly common and fatal thing on the Coast. The doctors here disagree entirely with him and say it is all rubbish. Certainly, quinine is the only thing for malaria.

Notes

1. His letters and diaries, 1897–1915, are in Rhodes House Library, MSS. Brit. Emp. s. 314–318.
2. F. M. Hodgson, Ag Governor; R. Williams, DC; Captain Kenny Herbert, Surveyor; Lieutenant Bellair, an officer going on the Niger expedition.
3. George Attrill, Assistant Colonial Secretary.
4. Aburi Botanical Gardens in the Akwapim hills was built in 1875 for Administrative officers in need of a rest and change of air. It was opened officially as the Botanical Gardens in 1890, but could still be used by officers wanting a change.

Appendix B

Instructions to Officers in Charge of Districts, 1899[1]

The following instructions are issued for the guidance of officers in charge of districts and subdistricts in the NT, and will be adhered to until further notice.

Officers in charge of districts will be directly responsible to the commissioner and commandant for the efficient administration of their districts, and for the discipline and training of the Gold Coast Constabulary placed under their orders. They will be given all possible freedom of action, but they must clearly understand that it is their duty to keep the commissioner constantly informed of conditions and progress of their commands. They will record for the information of the commissioner in a return to be punctually rendered on 1st of each month, a short report of anything worthy of remark. In this they will embody any similar information that has reached them from officers commanding their subdistricts and, in cases of special importance, attaching a copy of subdistrict report.

All officers will exert themselves to record information that may be of value with regard to the district in which they are serving for subsequent embodiment in an official handbook. Some progress has already been made in this direction and it is hoped that printed copies of the intelligence compiled may shortly be issued as a basis for further extension. Officers commanding districts are to study carefully the character and abilities of the officers serving under them, and to be prepared to report fully on them.

Officers commanding districts are to make themselves thoroughly well acquainted with their districts. Each subdistrict is to be visited at least once a year, and a close inspection made of the work done, particular attention being paid to the relations existing between the officer commanding the subdistrict and the garrison on one hand, and on the other the native inhabitants. It has been found that the work required from the natives can be obtained wherever our authority has been finally recognized, by the exercise of patience and firmness, and it has been noted that the necessity or frequent and heavy punishment is generally a proof of incapacity on the part of the officer inflicting them.

It is imperative that when once a promise or a threat of punishment has been made it should be scrupulously carried out. Officers must therefore exercise the greatest caution in making either, especially in making punitive menaces that, if carried out, would involve harshness or injustice and if unfulfilled would leave an impression of vacillation or weakness.

Officers commanding districts, as the command is at present constituted, are also in direct command of the constabulary in their district. They are themselves to drill and train the men.

As regards the natives, officers will act through the native chiefs as far as possible for the suppression of minor offences, and will support them in securing the execution of sentences.

In grave offences an officer, the senior on the spot, will either conduct the trial himself or be present as a referee. In the latter case, the sentence must be approved by him, before being carried into execution. In no circumstances whatever will a sentence of death be carried into effect until approved by the CC.

Officers commanding districts may fine up to £26, or its equivalent in kind, may inflict corporal punishment not exceeding 24 lashes, and may order imprisonment with or without hard labour for a period not exceeding three calendar months.

No chief or head priest is to be flogged without previous reference to the officer commanding the district, and especial care is to be taken to foster the authority of native chiefs and to avoid wounding the religious susceptibilities of the inhabitants.

Whenever the officer commanding a subdistrict considers that the behaviour of a tribe is of such a nature as to call for a punitive expedition, he will, if the circumstances admit of it, refer the matter to the officer commanding his district and the latter will refer to the commissioner and commandant if, in his opinion, the situation will not be prejudiced by delay. It is, however, to be distinctly understood that when prompt action is necessary in the public interest an officer, of whatever rank, is permitted and expected to act on his own initiative.

During expeditions no looting is to be allowed. The encouragement of trade is one of the most important of the duties falling on officers. They should explain that markets have to be established at Gambaga and Wa, with a view to providing the natives with European products suited to their needs, and they should impress on them the necessity of greater industry in order that they may obtain money to make purchases.

Every effort should be made to encourage the distribution of European goods by means of petty traders. More especially in those districts where inter-tribal feuds interfere with free movement of small parties. Robberies from native traders are to be punished with exemplary severity.

Roads are to be built so as to connect the more important towns. The main road from Kintampo to Gambaga, and thence northward to the frontier, and from Kintampo to Wa and thence to Tumu and the frontier, are to be undertaken first and are to be 14 feet wide. Subsidiary roads are to be eight feet. In both cases good ditches are to be made and the earth excavated to be used to raise the roadway. Culverts are to be made of stone where possible, at all points where small streams cross the road. In making the roads, care is to be taken to grub up the roots of felled trees.

The policing of these roads is to be a subject of special attention. Caravans and individuals must be enabled to proceed along them without molestation or extortion, and arrangements must be made to throw upon the chiefs of the principal halting places, the responsibility for providing good markets of supplies at reasonable rates.

Instructions to MOs

The MO of a station is responsible for measures being taken to keep uncontaminated the water supply of the town or village where he is quartered, as well as that of the troops. He will see that sanitary measures are taken in the town, such as the provision of latrines, the periodic removal and destruction of rubbish. Destruction of all growing vegetable matter within a reasonable distance of the huts.

He will cause a slaughterhouse to be erected, and will inspect every animal intended for slaughter, rejecting such as are unfit for food. He will collect the tax on slaughtered animals, and supervise the dairy arrangements connected with the supply of milk for Europeans.

MOs are encouraged to treat serious cases of sickness among the natives and for this purpose government drugs etc. may be employed. Such attendance will be gratuitous, but there is no objection to officers receiving voluntary 'dashes' from grateful patients. They must, however, carefully watch that their subordinates do not make this the occasion for obtaining presents for themselves from the natives.

C. J. Fortescue
Gambaga
9 March 1899

Note

1. Both sets of instructions are to be found in GNA, Adm. 56/1/35.

Appendix C
Establishment of Navarro Station, 1905[1]

To Lieutenant P. J. Partridge, OC 'A' Company *from* CCNT, Gambaga.

On Friday and Saturday next 20th and 21st you will proceed with your company to Navarro, in the Fra Fra district, with the object of opening up a station in that neighbourhood.

The reason for this move is the enormous populated region that exists in this part which, up to date, has only been brought into touch with our administration by somewhat hurried raids to punish either single acts of murder or refusal on the part of the chiefs to come into the headquarters of the Protectorate when ordered to.

The tribes in these parts settle all disputes by immediate recourse to poisoned bows and arrows, and only within the last few weeks one village has fought among themselves over a trivial dispute, resulting in the loss of several lives.

Constant complaints of cattle stealing from merchants are heard in this court from that district, pointing to a trade, which may or may not reach Salaga, or may be exchanged at Daboya for salt, the caravans returning direct to Leo and Wagadugu. As you are aware, in many of these towns, where part are friendly a part has been found hostile, professing no allegiance to the titular chief. These indulge in looting and murder whenever lucrative opportunity occurs. When troops have been sent these people have usually been found to have left their compounds and taken away their cattle and it has generally been found impossible to punish them, though a certain amount of destruction of property has been done and, at the same time, considerable harm has been caused by the looting by followers (as often as not) in the friendly part of the town, causing more mischief than good towards any possible friendly relations with these people as a whole.

In opening this station, therefore, I have great hopes of getting into touch with these people, and at the same time making a revenue out of untouched caravans and it will be most necessary to impress on the men under your command two things in particular: (a) there must be no looting of any sort by them, their wives nor their boys. (b) All food must be obtained by payment at a rate which shall be laid down. You will deal severely with any offences under these heads.

With a view to attracting people to the market, a trade goods store will be opened at a time each day, to be fixed later, and the goods, now on their way from the Coast, will be sold to natives only and not to the soldiers.

Dr Le Fanu, who will accompany you as MO, has undertaken to look after this. The store will not be opened more than three hours a day, and probably only three times a week.

Any serious cases brought to your notice will be forwarded to Gambaga, but in dealing with minor offences I rely on your tact and discretion to do all you can to get the confidence of these people, and at the same time be extremely lenient in punishments inflicted. You will have the power of a DC and may inflict fines of 100 sheep or 50 cattle.

In going out to this station you will go by Zongoiri and take the greatest care to give no encounters with any hostile village *en route*. It is most important that the opening of this station should not be accompanied by anything approaching a raid or a fight, and towns like Yaraga and Nangodi should be left, to be dealt with later, after confidence has been restored in the surrounding districts. It is more than probable the hostile parts of these towns will come in to you.

You will therefore, in going to Navarro, avoid, as far as your knowledge allows, all the hostile parts of villages you pass through, and unless directly attacked, take no notice of war drums and shouting. See that the friendly parts of towns you stay in are well treated, and a present given to the chief. For this purpose, I authorize you to draw a £5 chargeable against the Gambaga presents for chiefs' vote.

Dr Le Fanu, who will undertake the collection of the caravan taxes, has orders until further notice to accept French money from traders going south.

Details and general instructions forwarded herewith [see below].

General Instructions

(a) Soldiers

The men will take their wives and be allowed one carrier to eight men. No Moshis are to accompany them in any capacity. They will be paid subsistence till they are in quarters, which they will start to build as soon as you have, in conjunction with the MO, selected a suitable site.

Two months' supplies for yourself and MO should be drawn and paid for.

(b) Stores
Table and chairs for office should be taken out. Supply of carpenter tools drawn viz crosscut saw, 6 pickaxes, 6 shovels, 2 saws (hand), 2 chisels, 2 crowbars, 2 sledge hammers, 20 machetes, 4 water drums, 2 Union Jacks, frame work for target, supplies of dynamite.

(c) Ammunition
The Maxim gun will be taken out and 20,000 rounds ammunition (26 loads).

(d) Tents
You are authorized to draw besides one tent complete, a spare fly which should be returned to MO later when your swish house is completed.

(e) Buildings
The following buildings will be put in hand as soon as possible.
1 guardroom with prisoners' cell and small prison enclosure.
1 store close to guardroom.
1 small hospital and hospital store.
Till these buildings are ready a compound had better be used for which payment may be made.

(f) The country
Being so thickly populated, the towns round should be called on for labour, and a good house for two white men should be put in hand at once, near the guardroom.

(g) Water supply
The stream running south from Paha will probably be your water supply, and should be examined by the MO up to Paha on arrival and a fencing put round the part where the supply is taken from. Part of Paha town is in a turbulent condition at the moment, though the chief is quite friendly.

(h) Specie
Two boxes of money will be taken out and the monthly indent sent for further supplies.

(i) Mails
Should be sent under escort weekly to arrive at Gambaga on Sunday. They will return with the English mail on its arrival.

(j) Maps
You will take any opportunity that occurs to fill in information on the unfinished map of the district.

(k) Returns
The usual monthly returns will be forwarded:
State of troops.
Arms and ammunition.
Return of punishments awarded.
Diary of parade occurrences.
Return of changes in companies.
Return of all government property in store.
Copy of district accounts.
District report.
List of criminal cases disposed of.
Livestock returns.
Caravan tax returns.
Return of all wild animals killed.
Return of alien children.
Return of maps in possession of DC.
Flogging returns of Hausas and carriers.
General report of district.

To Dr Le Fanu from CCNT
On Friday or Saturday 20th or 21st a company under Lieutenant. Partridge will proceed to Navarro for the remainder of the dry season. You will accompany it as MO.

I understand that the Ag SMO has detailed dresser B. R. Tokonu to accompany you.

On arrival you will with Lieutenant Partridge select the best site for a permanent camp taking into account the following considerations.

(a) Proximity of a good water supply.
(b) Good ground for building on.
(c) Proximity of trade route.
(d) Position with a view to defence if attacked.
(e) Proximity of existing market if one exists.

The collection of caravan tax will be in your hands. A trade route from Moshi south of some importance has been reported as passing through this country. A local headman should be selected to help round up the passing caravans and the OCT has been told to help you in giving you men to watch the side roads. Caravan Tax forms and books will be drawn by you from the Treasury.

Some trade goods have been ordered from the Coast. A store should be built in the market. The OC 'A' Company has been instructed to give you the service of the Co. Pay Clerk, to assist you in this for a few months. I should think three hours three times a week would be sufficient to have the store open.

A cash book will be kept showing all receipts from this store. The sale prices will be fixed by the CC and the debits against the amount received will be the original cost, the pay of the carriers from Coomassie and 3 per cent commission for the clerk and contingent allowance for the station.

You will keep a general supervision over the market and collect slaughter fees as in Gambaga.

For yourself draw two months' supply from the quartermaster's store before going out.

The price of food in the market should at a start be fixed at about 33 per cent less than the existing prices in Gambaga.

A. E. Watherston, CCNT
Gambaga
16 October 1905

Note

1. Both sets of instructions are in GNA, Adm. 56/1/38.

Appendix D

Instructions to Touring Officer, Sunyani, 1911[1]

Mr Ross, Ag DC

Please proceed to Tanosu on Thursday and on via Nkwanta and Tekimentia to Dema. Dr Wade will accompany you as far as Tekimentia. You will be provided with a lance corporal and two men of the GCR in case arrests are to be made. [The next paragraph is quite unreadable, eaten by termites.] In Techimentia deal with any matters requiring attention and inspect the town with Dr Wade. Owing to reports of its dirty condition an Inspector of Nuisance has been sent there to have latrines built and the town generally cleaned. From what I hear I should gather that there has already been a great improvement in its condition.

Generally, you will find the chiefs anxious to improve their towns, and demonstrations and advice is more wanted at present, in outlying villages, than coercion.

At Dema, representatives of Bechem should meet you. I wish you there to ascertain what the true position of affairs as to Offinso is. Bechem accuses Offinso of still sending tribute collectors over the boundary fixed by the CC. If this is true I want sufficient details to enable a summons for damages for trespass to be taken against the actual offenders viz names, position and name of rubber camp etc. At the same time you should satisfy yourself that Dema or Bechem are not offending in a similar way.

You should read up the palaver in my record book before starting.

From Dema go to Sabranu, a fetish village full of fetish priests and a village seldom visited and is subordinate to Bechem. Tell them that fetish priests are not exempt from working on a road, and any fetishman refusing to do so will be fined by Bechem. Tell them, as an example, that Yao Jemfi, head fetishman of Susansu, has worked hard and well and laughs at Sabranu.

From Sabranu proceed to Bechem and read the attached letter re refund of Coronation fines. At the same time deal with any cases that may arise.

Mr Nomo will accompany you, and you should take a court book, receipt book and summons book. All the country you pass through is subject to government licences, and you should try to obtain information as to illicit selling. Your soldiers should be provided with handcuffs by the gaoler. It is advisable when travelling to send on one man a day ahead of you.

[Signed] T. E. Fell, PC
Sunyani
25 July 1911

Note

1. Sunyani Letter Book, GNA 54/1/3.

Appendix E

Estimate for Station at Sefwi, 1914[1]

Item	£	s.	d.
Three-roomed bungalow and office combined for the DC, with kitchen, boy's room and latrine shed	£16.	0.	0
Two-roomed bungalow for MO with kitchen, boy's room and latrine	£12.	0.	0
Dispensary (2 rooms)	£5.	0.	0
Quarters for ten escort police, wives and children	£15.	0.	0
Police guardroom with two cells	£5.	0.	0
School house	£8.	0.	0
Carpentry for above buildings viz			
16 doors and posts	£8.	8.	0
26 windows and frames at 4/6 each	£5.	17.	0
hinges and bolts for doors and windows	£4.	7.	0
10 drums of lime wash	£5.	0.	0
6 drums of tar	£4.	10.	0
school furniture, 4 benches at 4/6 each		18.	0
4 desks at 10/– each	£2.	0.	0
1 table at 8/6, one chair at 4/6		13.	0
1 padlock for door		10.	0
TOTAL	£93.	3.	0

The cost of clearing the site is included in the cost of building. All the buildings to be single-storeyed and of swish with walls one foot thick and thatched roofs. All to have verandas 12 feet round them, all except the school, police quarters, guardroom and cells where verandas would be six-foot wide. The verandas are necessary not only for coolness, but also to protect the swish walls from the weather.

I have endeavoured to keep the estimates as low as possible but at the same time to cover everything. It is comparatively high, I know, but the fact that the position of the new station at Sefwi will probably be unpopular, with the consequence that there may be difficulty in getting the work done by the *omanhene*'s people, has to be taken into consideration. If the *omanhene* will contract to do the work for a lump sum, less than the amount I have estimated, it will of course save expense to accept his offer.

Note

1. Submitted to CWPA, Colony, by W. Johnstone, DC, 31 January 1914.

Appendix F

Hints on Outfits and the Preservation of Health[1]

Clothing
Europeans wear on the West Coast the same clothing as in England in the height of summer, but the waistcoat is generally discarded in favour of a cummerbund. Flannel trousers and suits of dark-blue serge or the thin tweeds, which are specially made for the tropics, are much used. Undyed merino socks are recommended. Flannel shirts are required, and woollen pyjamas should be worn at night. Three cholera belts and a flannel dressing gown should be taken out.

Strong tin boxes are best for officers who are not resident at HQ, or who may be required to travel, e.g. DCs and Supervisors of Customs.

Helmet
Light pith, well over temples and back of neck.

Umbrella
Either white linen with green lining or an ordinary black one with a white cover.

General Advice Towards the Preservation of Health
Wear woollen material for vests and drawers. Sleep in soft flannel. Wear a light flannel cholera belt.

Drink
All drinking water should be boiled and stored in clean and corked vessels. If the water is muddy it should be strained or filtered first and boiled afterwards. Brandy ought never to be touched, unless ordered. Claret, hock or German lager beer may be drunk with the evening meal, of course in moderation. Stimulants should be avoided before sundown.

Of spirits – brandy, gin, rum, absinthe should be regarded as poisonous. Old Scotch whisky, in great moderation, well diluted is perhaps the least deleterious of spirituous liquor and the slowest poison. A little good champagne, occasionally, when one is exhausted is a useful and safe stimulant.

Coffee, tea and cocoa are excellent restoratives for the fatigued body or wearied brain and are far better in the performance of hard work than alcohol.

Avoid notoriously malarial spots for recreation. Sleep as far off the ground as possible, and always use a mosquito net. Light fires round a tent or hut at night, when camping in the bush.

Morals

Cultivate an impassive and philosophic temperament, as irritability, a very frequent product of the climate, makes a man uncomfortable and has, undoubtedly, a bad influence on general health. Moderation in all things should be the rule of the tropics.

Medical and other Preventive Measures

Prickly heat. After washing with soap it is a good plan to rub the body over with fresh limes.

Chills. The least feeling of chill, shivering or repugnance to the bath, generally means mischief. It is an indication that the bath must be abstained from, or taken warm, or postponed for the day.

A good helmet ought always to be worn out of doors and an umbrella should be used. Remember, once sunstruck, always sunstruck.

Note

1. Colonial Office pamphlet, first published 1897 for the Nigerian Service. Copy in PRO CO/96/424.

Appendix G
Practical Advice for Colonial Administrators[1]

Officials at most stations on the coast are supplied with furnished quarters; bedroom, dining room, latrine room, pantry, kitchen and boy's room. The bedroom has bed, press for clothes, table and washstand with toilet set, towel horse, a few chairs and sometimes a mirror. Dining room has table, chairs and cupboard. The veranda has wicker work sofa chairs and tables. The pantry has a filter and stand, meat safe. There is always a wooden bath, a bucket and a water drum, and often a bathroom.

In travelling in the bush eight men are allowed for carrying the hammock and a variable number of carriers for bedding, food, cooking utensils, clothes etc. All articles are carried in wooden boxes. The carriage of loads is expensive, about 1/3*d.* a day per load for long distances, and at a fixed price for short journeys. The government will send goods free for officials in the NT.

Clothes
As for the Coast, except that evening dress is not needed, nor white linen shirts. Strong boots for marching.

Sundries
Water bottle, enamel iron, covered with felt, revolver, camera, cap to wear in hammock, literature to read at night, patience cards, dressing case, housewife.

Food to take into the Bush
Flour, rice, sago, biscuits, milk, sugar, chocolates, butter, bacon, ham, tongue, kippers, salmon, sausages, soup, Maconochie rations, vegetables, oatmeal, tea, coffee, sauces, curry powder, pepper, salt, mustard, vinegar, lard, potted meat, pickles. (Most of these can be got in tins.) Florida water is refreshing in the bath; sparklet bottle, two gross of sparklets.

Matches, cigars, cigarettes (American only) and tobacco can be bought on the coast.

Medicines must be taken into the bush.

Camp furniture
Camp bed, fitted with mosquito curtain rods, folding table and chairs, folding bath and washstand and valise. A Lord's lamp and candles.

Simple Rules for Health
Avoid chills, don't expose yourself to the sun without proper headgear. From 7.30 a.m. to late afternoon wear a helmet.

Venereal disease is very common in West Africa and should be carefully avoided.

A Kroo boy's teeth are apt to inflict a most serious poisoned wound.

When going out at night use a lantern, as dangerous snakes abound in many places.

Good servants are essential. A cook at about £2 a month and a boy at about £1, are generally enough.

With good food and a little stimulant it is surprising what an amount of hard work can be done daily.

Riding, shooting, tennis, croquet, billiards, cards (games of patience will while away many an hour at night, when alone in the interior). Music, dinner parties etc. can be got up in many places, and help the general wellbeing of the community.

Five grains of quinine should be taken about twice a week during the rainy season.

The following instruments should be carried:

Artery forceps to seize a bleeding point which is then tied with silk.

A lancet to prick a boil or cut round a snake bite.

Needles to stitch a large wound. One stitch is often enough.

Small syringe, to syringe deep wounds with lotion. Useful for arrow wounds and snake bites.

Note

1. By A. J. Chalmers, Assistant Colonial Surgeon, Gold Coast, 1903.

Biographies (Based on the *Gold Coast Civil Service Lists*)

ARMITAGE Cecil Hamilton, DSO, CMG, KBE (1869–1933). *Career*: 1889 Commissioned into South Wales Borderers.

1894 Assistant Inspector Gold Coast Constabulary.
1895 Ashanti expedition.
1900 Promoted TC.
1900 Ashanti Campaign. Ag Resident siege of Kumasi.
1901 Ag CC Ashanti (also 1906, 1908,1909).
1902 DC Ashanti.
1910 CCNT.
1914 Attached to Togoland Field Force.
1921 Governor, The Gambia.

Publication: *The Ashanti Campaign of 1900*, 1901 (with A. F. Montanaro). [Captain Armitage boasted that he was the adopted son of Florence Nightingale – T.W.]

ATTERBURY John Lucas. Born 1877. Education Christ's Hospital. Solicitor 1899. *Career*: 1900 Served with Imperial Yeomanry Royal Bucks Hussars in South Africa.

1908 Appointed DC Gold Coast.
1912–14 DC Tarquah, Colony.
1917–18 PC Western Province Colony.
1919 DC, Cape Coast, Central Province, Colony.
1923 Ag Secretary of Native Affairs.
1924 PC, Central Province, Colony.

BERKELEY, Harold Maurice. Born 1878. Education Chigwell School, Essex. Magdalen College Cambridge. *Career*: 1900 Appointed 2nd class Supervisor Preventive Service.

1905 Ag Commissioner NE District, Ashanti.
1906 Inspector Preventive Service.

1907 Transfer to Political Service, ADC, NT.
1910 DC Navarro.
1919 PC, Wa.

BOYLE David Hugh Montgomerie. Born 1883. Education Wellington and New College Oxford. *Career*: 1904 Customs Department Peking.
1906 Tea plantation, Ceylon.
1907 Bombay Burma Timber Corporation.
1912 Appointed ADC Gold Coast. PS to CC Ashanti.
1913 Ag DC new Juaso District, Ashanti.
1914 DC Wenchi, NW Ashanti.
1917 DC Ejura, Ashanti.
1919 Ministry of Pensions.
1921 Foreign Office, Far Eastern affairs.
1922 Far East tour of enquiry.

Publication: *With Ardours Manifold*, 1959.

BRECKENRIDGE Thomas William. Born 1871. *Career*: 1900–1 Served in South African War.
1902 Appointed temporary Supervisor Customs, Gold Coast.
1902 Ag DC Asafo, Colony.
1905 DC Sefwi, WP, Colony.
1907 TC.
1909 Ag PC Ashanti.
1913 DC Kintampo, Ashanti.
1917 PC NT.
1917 Died yellow fever on way home.

CARDINALL Allan Wolsey. Born 1887. Education Winchester College; Melle, Belgium; Heidelberg. *Career*: 1914 ADC Sunyani, WP Ashanti.
1915 Ag DC Ahafo, Ashanti.
1916 Seconded for service Yendi, Togoland.
1918 Ag DC Navarro and Zouaragu, NT.
1924 DC Kratchi and TC Attabubu and Ashanti Akim.
1928 Ag Commissioner SP, NT.
1932 Representative for Great Britain at League of Nations (Togoland Mandate).
1934 Commissioner and Judge of Grand Court, Cayman Islands.
1940 Colonial Secretary, Falkland Islands.
1941 Governor, Falkland Islands.

Publications: *Natives of the Northern Territories of the Gold Coast*, 1920; *A Gold Coast Library*, 1924; *In Ashanti and Beyond*, 1927; *Tales Told in Togoland*, 1931; *A Bibliography of the Gold Coast*, 1933.

CASTELLAIN Alfred Louis. Born 1870. Education Eton. *Career*: 1890 Lieutenant 3rd Suffolk Regiment.

1893 Constable RNW Mounted Police, Canada.
1900 Served in Lord Strathcona's Horse, South African War.
1901 Lieutenant and Sub-inspector South African Constabulary.
1909 Appointed DC, Tamale, NT.
1911 DC Salaga, NT.
1915 DC Navarro, NT.
1918 Seconded for Service in Togoland as DPO.
1921 Promoted PC.
1924 Ag CC, NT.

CLARIDGE William Walton, MRCS (1874–1923). Education Norwich Grammar School; Norfolk and Norwich Hospital; Middlesex Hospital; Moorfields Eye Hospital; London School of Tropical Medicine. *Career*: 1900–1 Served in South African War.

1903 January. Appointed MO Gold Coast.
1903 August–February 1904 Ag Commissioner Sefwi, Colony.
1905 Ag DC and Deputy Sheriff, Elmina.
1910 Authorized to act as TC.
1911 Anum, working on sleeping sickness investigation.
1913 PMO, Kumasi.
1914 Attached to Togoland Field Force.
1914 Seconded for service in Cameroons.
1915 Resumed duty at Seccondee.
1917 Transferred from Tamale to Lomé, Togoland.
1918 SMO Lomé, Togoland.
1919 Retired on grounds of ill health.

Publication: *A History of the Gold Coast and Ashanti*, 1915

CLIFFORD Sir Hugh, CMG, KCMG, GBE (1866–1941). Educated privately at Woburn Park. *Career*: 1883 Joined Malay States Civil Service as Cadet.

1887 Special mission to Sultan of Pahang.
1889 Superintendent Ulu Pahang.
1890 Ag Resident, Pahang.
1894 Commissioner to Cocos-Keeling Islands.
1896 British Resident, Pahang.
1903 Colonial Secretary, Trinidad and Tobago.
1907 Colonial Secretary, Ceylon.
1912 Governor, Gold Coast.
1919 Governor, Nigeria.
1925 Governor, Ceylon.
1927 Governor, Straits Settlements.

Publications: *Studies in Brown Humanity*; *In a Corner of Asia*; *The German Colonies*.

COVEY Arthur. *Career*: 1900 Appointed 3rd class DC.

1902 DC Quitta.
1902 Ag Colonial Secretary.

CUTFIELD Arthur John. Born 1885. Education Epsom College. *Career*: 1904 Cadet, Sarawak Service.

1907 Assistant Resident Sarawak.
1910 ADC Gold Coast.
1910 Ag DC Elmina.
1910 Ag DC Cape Coast.
1913 Ag Assistant Colonial Secretary.
1914 Ag DC Central Province, Ashanti.
1915 Promoted DC, Ashanti (at Ejura).
1918 DC Bawku, NT.
1922 Ag DC Navarro and Zouaragu.
1927 Promoted PC.

DASENT, Edward Guy. Born 1892. Education Weymouth College. *Career*: 1915 Appointed ADC, Ag DC Obuasi, Ashanti.

1915 Ag DC Salaga, NT.
1916 Ag DC Yeji, NT.
1918 Ag DC Tumu, NWP.
1920 Ag DC Salaga and Yeji District, NT.
1921 Seconded for duty NT railway and mines labour.
1922 Ag DC Lorha, NT.

DOWDALL Dr Arthur Merville, MRCS, LRCP London; DTM Liverpool. Born 1880. *Career*: 1908 Sunyani, WP, Ashanti.

1910 Ag DC Saltpond.
1911 British Kratchi as MO.
1912 Togoland, sleeping sickness investigation.
1914 In temporary charge of Volta River District in addition to normal duties.
1918 MO Bole and Wa, also Ag DC Bole.
1920 Transfer from Seccondee to Cape Coast as SMO Cape Coast.
1920 December. Transfer to Quitta.

DUFF Dr David, BA, MD, BAO, DPH. Born 1883. Education Trinity College Dublin. *Career*: 1910 Assumed duties at Seccondee.

1913 Ag DC Ada in addition to normal duties.
1915 Ag DC Bole, NT.
1925 Ag SMO.

DUNCAN-JOHNSTONE Angus Colin. Born 1889. Education Glenalmond and Sandhurst. *Career*: 1908 Passed army entrance examination, RAMC.

1912 Served with British Red Cross expedition Turkey.
1913 Assumed duties in Southern Province, Ashanti.
1914 DC Sunyani, Western Province, Ashanti.
1915 Seconded for service with British Forces, Togoland.
1917 Ag DC Lorha, North Western Province, NT.
1922 DC Ashanti Akim.
1924 To Seychelles in charge of ex-King Prempeh's repatriation to Ashanti.
1925 Ag CC Ashanti.
1925 Staff officer, Ashanti, for visit of HRH Prince of Wales.
1928 PC, Central Province, NT.
1936 Ag CC, NT.

[The career and reputation of Duncan-Johnstone are said to have advanced considerably during the 1920s when he became engaged to a niece of Lady Guggisberg – T.W.]

FELL Thomas Edward. Education Royal Grammar School, Lancaster; Owen College, Manchester; Pembroke College Cambridge. *Career*: 1897 Chief Clerk Colonial Secretary's office Gold Coast.

1899 Ag Assistant Colonial Secretary.
1899 December. Inspector of Customs, Preventive Service.
1902 TC.
1903 Ag Secretary of Native Affairs.
1905 DC Ashanti.
1907 PC Western Province Ashanti. HQ Sunyani.
1916 Colonial Secretary Barbados.
1916 St Kitts.
1922 Fiji. Died at sea while returning to Fiji.

FREEMAN George Bovet. Born 1886. Educated Winchester. *Career*: 1914 Appointed ADC, Saltpond, later Seccondee.

1920 Ag DC Bawku, North Eastern Province, NT.
1920 April. Ag PC North Eastern Province, NT.
1920 July. DC Navarro and Zouaragu, North East Province, NT.
1922–25 DC Southern Mamprussi.

FULLER Sir Francis Charles, KBE. Born 1865. Education St Charles' College, London. *Career*: 1884 Cadet, Fiji.

1892 Lagos, Nigeria.
1897 Resident Ibadan, Nigeria.
1902 Assistant Secretary to Government of Malta.
1905 CCA.
1920 Retired.
Publication: *A Vanished Dynasty: Ashanti*, 1921.

GILBERT William Eric, MC. Born 1885. Education Lutterworth Grammar School and privately. *Career*: 1908 Rhodesian Civil Service.

1914 Joined lst King Edward's Horse.
1915 Served in France. Commissioned 1917.
1918 Served in Italy. Awarded MC.
1919 Appointed ADC Gold Coast.
1919 Ag DC Navarro and Zouaragu, NT.
1921 Ag DPO Yendi, Togoland.
1922 DC Eastern Dagomba.

HARPER Sir Charles Henry, CMG, OBE. Born 1876. Education Blundell's School Devon; Exeter College Oxford. *Career*: 1900 Gold Coast Cadet. Attached Ashanti Field Force.

1901 Ag Chief Clerk Colonial Secretary's Office.
1902 ADC Winneba.
1905 Ag PC Eastern Province, Colony.
1908 Cantonment Magistrate, Coomassie.
1909 Called to Bar.
1915 Chief Assistant Colonial Secretary.
1920–23 CCA.
1925 Governor St Helena.

HEATHCOTE Gilbert Cockshott, Lieutenant-Commander. Born 1883. Education Lieutenant Royal Navy. *Career*: 1913 Appointed ADC Saltpond, Gold Coast.

1914 Seconded for service with military operations Togoland and Cameroons, as Commander SS *Marina*.
1914 November. Left for England on escort duty with POWs.
1915 Ag DC Saltpond, Colony.
1917 Ag DC Ashanti, Juaso District.
1918 Ag DC Obuasi.
1919 DC Ashanti at Coomassie.

HOBART Edward Herbert. Education St Marks, Windsor and Repton School. *Career*: Captain 9th Battalion Kings Royal Rifles.

1897 Served in operations in hinterland of Gold Coast.
1898 Appointed Assistant Inspector Gold Coast Constabulary.
1900 Ashanti Campaign.
1900 Commissioner Western Frontier.
1902 Captain of Infantry GCR.
1906 Ag DC North Eastern District, Ashanti.
1910 Ag PC Ashanti.
1912 Ag PC Tamale, NT.
1918 PC Tamale.

HOLLIDAY Arthur Robert. Born 1884. Education St John's College, Johannesburg. Articled to various firms of solicitors Pietermaritzburg. *Career*: 1901 Attorney and Notary of Supreme Court Transvaal.

1915 Appointed ADC Ancobra, Gold Coast.
1916 ADC Seccondee.
1917 Transferred to Lomé, Togoland.
1918 Ag DC Bole, Southern Province, NT.

HULL Henry Mitchell, CMG. Born 1861. Education Charterhouse. *Career*: 1888 Clerk to Legislative and Executive Council.

1891 TC Ashanti to bring it under British protection.
1892 British Commission for Boundary Commission between the Colony and German Protectorate of Togoland.
1894 British Commissioner to delimit the Western Frontier with the French.
1899 Assistant Colonial Secretary.
1900 Raised and armed 3500 local levies during Ashanti rising.
1902 Secretary of Native Affairs.
1906 Assistant Colonial Secretary.

IRVINE Richard Abercombie, Major, CMG, DSO. *Career*: 3rd Battalion Lancashire Fusiliers.

1892 Assistant Inspector GC Constabulary.
1900 Served Ashanti Field Force.
1901 TC.
1905 Ag DC NT.
1915–18 Served European war, after retiring from GC.

KORTRIGHT Hugh Albert, Captain. Born 1870. *Career*: 1894 Inspector British Guiana Police.

1900 Assistant Inspector Gold Coast Constabulary.
1905 Ag Cantonments Magistrate.
1907 Transfer to Political Service as ADC Ashanti.
1908 TC, NT.
1913 DC Wenchi, Western Province Ashanti.
1915 Ag PC Ashanti.
1918 DC Volta River District.

LAMOND Claude Henry Pitt. Born 1878. Education Brasenose College Oxford. Called to the Bar, Middle Temple 1903. *Career*: 1909 DC Seccondee.

1911 Ag PC Central Province, Colony.
1912 DC Axim.
1913 DC Winneba.

MAXWELL Sir John. Born 1875. Education Dumfries Academy; Glasgow University studied law. *Career*: 1902 ADC Gold Coast.

1903 Ag DC Wassaw District, Colony.
1906 Ag Solicitor General.
1908 Ag Attorney General, Secretary Native Affairs.
1909 Commissioner, Eastern Province, Colony.
1912–18 CWPA, Colony.
1919 Governor's Deputy.
1924 CCA.

Publication: *Gold Coast Handbook*, 1st edition.

MIGEOD Frederick William Hugh. Born 1872. *Career*: 1889–98 Entered Royal Navy as Assistant Clerk.

1898 Ag Transport Officer WAFF.
1899 2nd class Supervisor Customs, Gold Coast.
1903 Appointed DC.
1909 Transport Officer, Gold Coast.
1925 Leader, British Museum East Africa Expedition.
1927 Expedition to Cameroons.

Publications: *Mende Language*; *Hausa Grammar*; *Languages of West Africa*; *Earliest Man*; *Across Equatorial Africa*.

NASH Sidney Dawson. Born 1874. Education Fermay College and Trinity College Dublin. Served in South African War. Mentioned in dispatches. *Career*: 1903 Lieutenant of Infantry, GC Regiment, WAFF.

1906 ADC, NT.
1907 Transferred to Political Service as ADC, NT.
1908 DC Gambaga.
1910 DC Zouaragu.
1913 Ag PC Southern Province, NT.
1915 Seconded to GCR as Recruiting Officer.
1917 DC Navarro and Zouaragu.
1920 Promoted PC.

NORRIS Alexander Woodburn. Born 1879. *Career*: Lieutenant 1st Battalion Royal Berkshire Regiment.

1901 Lieutenant, GCR WAFF.
1911 ADC Central Province, Ashanti.
1912 Special duty road construction and boundaries.
1913 Ag DC Western Province, Ashanti.
1916 Ag DC Ejura.
1920 Transfer to Togoland, DPO Kete Kratchi.
1921 DC Kratchi.
1927 Special duty, Ashanti, Eastern and Western Province Boundary Commission.

NORTHCOTT Lieutenant-Colonel Henry P.

1897 Commissioner and Commandant of NT.
1899 Died in South Africa.

OAKLEY Dr Phillip Douglas, CRE, MRCS, LRCP, DTM. Born 1883. Education Shrewsbury School; Leeds University. *Career*: 1911 MO Gold Coast, Seccondee.

1911 Ag TC in addition to medical duties.
1912 Transferred to NT.
1914 Ag DC Lorha in addition to medical duties.
1915 Coomassie.
1916 Lomé, Togoland.
1917 MO Sunyani and Wenchi, Ashanti.
1926 SMO.
1933 Director of Medical Services, Sierra Leone.
1939 Medical Transport Officer, Casualty Evacuation Trains, EMS Ministry of Health.

PHILBRICK Arthur James. Born 1866. Education Rugby; Trinity College Cambridge, RA, LLB Cambridge, Called to the Bar (Middle Temple) 1889. *Career*: 1901 ADC Gold Coast.

1902 Ag DC Seccondee. Promoted 1st Class DC.
1910 PC Ashanti.
1912 Ag CC Ashanti (also 1916, 1917, 1919).
1915 Temporarily employed in UK with War Office.
1916 PC Southern Province Ashanti.
1921 CC NT.
1923 Ag Governor.

POOLE G. Arthur Evered, MBE. Born 1873. *Career*: 1899 Cadet, Ag Chief Clerk, Colonial Secretary's Office.

1901 Ag Clerk of Councils.
1903 Lieutenant GCR.
1907 Ag DC North West District, NT.
1910 Transfer to Political Service as ADC.
1910 Ag DC Volta River District.
1915 Seconded to Cameroon Field Force.
1917 Seconded for service in Togoland as DPO Yendi.
1920 Ag PC, North Western Province, NT.
1921 PC NT.

POTT Phillip Alfred Holiday. *Career*: 1901 ATO.

1907 Promoted DC as ADC Ashanti.
1909 Ag Cantonments Magistrate.
1912 Ag PC Sunyani, Western Province, Ashanti.

1913 DC Central Province, Ashanti.
1916 PC Sunyani.
1918 Commissioner, Southern Province, Ashanti.
1920 DC Kintampo.

RAKE Eustice Olpherts. Born 1886. Education Bradfield College; Pembroke College, Cambridge. *Career*: 1914 ADC Tamale, NT.

1914 Ag DC Gambaga, NT.
1914 Ag DC Bawku, NT.
1915 ADC Bole.
1918 Ag DC Bawku.
1922 Seconded as Headmaster Trade School, Tamale.
1923–25 DC Western Dagomba District.
1932–37 Ag CCNT.

RATTRAY Robert Sutherland. Born 1881. Education Stirling High School; Exeter College Oxford. Barrister-at-Law; Diploma Anthropology, Oxford. *Career*: 1901 Trooper in Imperial Yeomanry, South African War.

1902 African Lakes Corporation, British Central Africa.
1907 Appointed 2nd Class Supervisor of Customs, Accra.
1908 Transfer to Yeji, VRPS.
1909 Ag DC Yeji, NT in addition to ordinary duties.
1911 ADC Ashanti.
1914 Attached Togoland Field Force.
1914 DPO Misahohe, Togoland.
1918 DPO Kratchi, Togoland.
1920 Ag Senior Assistant Colonial Secretary.
1921 Seconded for anthropological research, Ashanti.
1929 Pioneer solo flight England to Gold Coast in a Tiger Moth.
1929 NT, on anthropological research.

Publications: *Hausa Folklore and Customs*; *An Elementary Mole Grammar*; *Ashanti*; *Religion and Art in Ashanti*; *Ashanti Law and Constitution*; *Tribes of the Ashanti Hinterland*.

READ B. Mountray. Born 1874. *Career*: Captain Cheshire Regiment. Assistant Inspector Lagos Constabulary.

1900 Served in Ashanti War.
1902 Commander Lagos Coronation Contingent.
1903 Appointed Captain of Infantry GCR, WAFF, on transfer from Lagos.
1907 Promoted PC North West Province, NT, Gold Coast.
1913 Transfer to Wa as PC, North West Province, NT.
1915 Ag CCNT.

ROSS Alexander Howard (1881–1964). Education Epsom College; HMS *Worcester*. Joined Merchant Navy. *Career*: 1905 2nd Class Supervisor of Customs, Volta River.

1908 Supervisor, VRPS, British Kratchi.
1908 Exercising powers of DC Gonja District, NT.
1911 Ag DC Western Province, Ashanti.
1914 Sunyani. Promoted DC.
1914 DC Western Frontier District, Wioso, Sefwi.
1916 Ag PC, WP Ashanti.
1918 DC Ancobra District, WP, Colony and Deputy Sheriff.
1919 Ag Commissioner EP at Koforidua and Ag Secretary of Native Affairs.
1920 Transfer to Sierra Leone, PC Southern Province.

RYAN Dr William Arthur. Born 1878. Education LRCP, LM, Dublin. Certificate of London STM. *Career*: 1911 Appointed MO Seccondee.

1912 Ag DC Zouaragu in addition to medical duties.
1913 Ag DC Tumu in additional to medical duties.
1915 Seconded for service in Cameroons.
1917 Ag DC Salaga and Yeji in addition to medical duties.
1920 Cape Coast.

SHERRIFF Morris George Sutherland. Born 1881. *Career*: 1900 Served in South African War.

1904 Transvaal Civil Service.
1911 Appointed ADC Bole, NT, Gold Coast.
1913 Ag DC Zouaragu, NT.
1915 Seconded for service with GCR as recruiting officer.
1916 Ag DC Bole.
1917 Invalided.

SKENE Charles Edward. Born 1889. Education St Paul's and Wrens School. *Career*: 2nd Lieutenant Gold Coast Volunteers.

1912 ADC attached to Secretariat.
1914 PS to Ag Governor.
1916 Ag DC Ashanti, Akim District, Central Province.
1919 DC Ashanti, Juaso.
1922 Ag Police Magistrate, Coomassie.
1931–2 Ag PC Central Province, Colony.

STEWART, Sir Donald. Captain.

1894 Sent to Kumasi with Mr Vroom to make treaty.
1895 Political Officer on march to Kumasi.
1896 First (and only) Resident Kumasi.
1902 First CCA.

1904 Commissioner and Commander in Chief, East African Protectorate.

TAYLOR Bertie Harry Waters, Colonel. *Career*: 1893–1902 Served Cape Mounted Rifles, annexation of Pondoland; Griqua rebellion; South African War Commission in Royal Berkshire Regiment.

1905 Officer in charge of detachment WAFF, and Bole District NT, Gold Coast.
1906 Ag DC Black Volta District, NT.
1907 TC.
1909 Transfer to South Staffordshire Regiment, Nigeria.
1915 European War, Australian and New Zealand Forces.
1916 Staff duty, Egypt; acted as Military Governor Jerusalem and Military Governor Galilee.

WALKER LEIGH Arthur Henry Chamberlain. Born 1871. Education Cheltenham and Jersey. *Career*: 1888 2nd Lieutenant Royal Munster Fusiliers.

1898 Assistant Inspector Gold Coast Constabulary.
1898 Served in Fra Fra expedition with Colonel H. P. Northcott.
1900 Resigned with approval of Secretary of State to South African War.
1901 Reappointed Inspector GC Constabulary. Served Talansi expedition.
1907 Appointed ADC Lorha, NT.
1909 Ag PC North West Province, NT.
1915 Cameroons on active service. Wounded.
1916 Seconded O in C Training Camp, Lomé.
1921 Ag CCNT.
1924 CCNT.

WATHERSTON A. E. G. *Career*: 1901 Director of Surveys, Gold Coast.

1900 Chief British Commissioner Anglo-French Boundary Commission.
1905 CCNT.
1910 Died of blackwater fever at Gambaga, NT.

WHEATLEY Leonard Havelock. Education Blundells School. *Career*: 1903 Junior Assistant Treasurer, Gold Coast.

1906 Ag DC Winneba.
1908 DC Ashanti.
1910 DC Southern Province, Ashanti.
1911 Ag PC Southern Province, Ashanti.
1914 Attached to Togoland Field Force.
1916 Ag PC Western Province, Ashanti.
1917 Ag PC Southern Province, Ashanti.
1921 PC Eastern Province, Ashanti.

WHEELER Henry Thompson Camden. *Career*: 1902 Lieutenant GCR.

1906 TC, NT.
1907 Transfer to Political Service, ADC Salaga.
1908 Ag PC Western Province, NT.
1909 DC Navarro, NT.
1910 DC Bawku, NT.
1912 DC Zouaragu, NT.
1916 Died of yellow fever at Gambaga.

WHITTALL Percival Frederick, Lieutenant-Colonel. Born 1877. Education Felsted School. *Career*: 1895 Joined Royal Engineers, in ranks.

1899 Served in South African War.
1907 Lieutenant of Infantry, GCR, WAFF.
1909 Ag Superintendent of Roads, Ashanti and NT.
1909 Lincolnshire Regiment.
1912 Reappointed ADC Tumu, NT.
1915–19 Seconded for military service in Europe.
1919 Reverted to civil appointment DC Tumu, NT.
1919 Additionally DC Lorha.
1920 Promoted Chief Transport Officer.
1922 DC Wa, NT.
1928 PC NT.

WHYTE Dr Robert F. *Career*: 1908 MO Western Province Colony, Gold Coast.

1913 MO, NT.
1915 Ag DC Zouaragu in addition to medical duties.
1916 MO for Bole in addition to Wa.
1918 Transferred from Elmina to NT.

WOOD Leslie William. Born 1890. Education Merchant Taylors; Queens' College Cambridge. *Career*: 1914 Appointed ADC Southern Province, Ashanti.

1916 Ag DC Wenchi.
1917 ADC Sunyani.
1918 ADC Coomassie, Ashanti.
1920 Ag DC Ashanti Akim, Central Province.
1921 Ag Colonial Secretary.

WRIGHT George William Fosdike *Career*: 2nd Lieutenant 6th Battalion Liverpool Regiment.

1901 Assistant Inspector Gold Coast Constabulary.
1907 ADC, NT as Lieutenant of Infantry GC Regiment.
1907 Transferred to Political Service.
1908 ADC Tumu, NT.

1910	DC Lorha.
1911	Ag PC Southern Province, NT.
1914	Attached to Togoland Field Force.
1917	DC Bole, NT.
1920	DC Bawku.

Select Bibliography

Adler, P. and N. Barnard, *Asafo: African Flags of the Fante*, 1991
Agbodeka, F., *African Policy and British Politics in the Gold Coast*, 1971
Arhin, K., *Traditional Rule in Ghana*, 1985
West African Traders in Ghana in the 19th and 20th Centuries, 1979
Armitage, C. H. and A. F. Montanaro, *The Ashanti Campaign of 1900*, 1901
Baden-Powell, R. S. S., *The Downfall of Prempeh*, 1896
Biss, H. C. J., *The Relief of Kumasi*, 1901
Bowditch, T. E., *Mission from Cape Coast to Ashanti*, 1819
Boyle, D., *With Ardours Manifold*, 1959
Boyle, F., *Through Fanteland to Coomassie: A Narrative of the Ashanti Expedition*, 1874
Boyle, Laura, *Diary of a Colonial Officer's Wife*, 1968
Brackenbury, H., *The Ashanti War*, 1874
Cardinall, A. W., *The Natives of the Northern Territories of the Gold Coast*, 1920
Tales Told in Togoland, 1921
In Ashanti and Beyond, 1927
Claridge, W. W., *A History of the Gold Coast and Ashanti*, 1915
Clifford, Lady, *Our Days on the Gold Coast*, 1919
Ellis, A. B., *The Land of Fetish*, 1883
Fage, J. D., *Ghana: A Historical Interpretation*, 1966
A History of West Africa, 1969 (1955)
Fortes, M., *The Dynamics of Clanship among the Tallensi*, 1945
Fuller, Sir Francis, *A Vanished Dynasty: Ashanti*, 1921
Gailey, H. A., *Clifford: Imperial Proconsul*, 1982
Hodgson, Lady, *The Siege of Kumasi*, 1901
Kimble, D., *A Political History of Ghana*, 1963

Kuklick, H., *The Imperial Bureaucrat: The Colonial Administrative Service in the Gold Coast, 1920–1939*, 1979
Lewin, T., *Asante before the British*, 1978
Lucas, C. E., *The Gold Coast and the War*, 1920
McCaskie, T. C, 'R. S. Rattray and the Construction of Asante History', *History in Africa*, 10 (1983), 187–206
State and Society in Pre-Colonial Asante, 1995
Machin, N., 'Government Anthropologist': A Life of R. S. Rattray, unpublished manuscript, *c.*1979
McLeod, M. D., *The Asante*, 1981
Metcalfe, G. E., *Great Britain and Ghana: Documents, 1807–1957*, 1962
Northcott, H. P., *Report on the Northern Territories of the Gold Coast*, 1899
Pennie, M., *Friday's Rain Takes a Long Time to Stop*, 1994
Rathbone, R., *Murder and Politics in Colonial Ghana*, 1993
Rattray, R. S., *Ashanti Proverbs*, 1916
Ashanti, 1923
A Short Manual of the Gold Coast, 1924
Religion and Art in Ashanti, 1927
Ashanti Law and Constitution, 1929
Tribes of the Ashanti Hinterland, 1932
Reade, R., *The Story of the Ashantee Campaign*, 1874
Sarpong, P. K., *The Sacred Stools of the Akan*, 1971
Schildkrout, E., *People of the Zongo*, 1978
The Golden Stool, 1987
Smith, E. W., *The Golden Stool*, 1923
Staniland, M., *The Lions of Dagbon*, 1975
Swithenbank, M., *Ashanti Fetish Houses*, 1969
Tamakloe, E. F, *A Brief History of the Dagomba People*, 1931
Tordoff, W., *Ashanti under the Prempehs: 1888–1935*, 1965
Turner, G. W. E., (ed.), *A Short History of the Ashanti Gold Fields 1897–1947*, n.d.
Ward, W. E. F., *A History of the Gold Coast*, 1948
Watherston, A. E. G., 'The Northern Territories of the Gold Coast', *Journal of the African Society*, 7 (1908), 344–73
Wilks, I., *The Northern Factor in Ashanti History*, 1961
Asante in the 19th Century, 1975
One Nation Many Histories: Ghana Past and Present, 1996

Index